Jacket illustration:
Enchanting, cosy atmosphere of the interiors of Samode Haveli in Jaipur. In turning the eigteenth-century family mansion into a hotel, two brothers of the aristocracy, Yadavendra Singh and Raghavendra Singh, preserved its charm and the patina of time.

Delhi (in the north), Agra (in the northeast) and Rajasthan form a magic triangle where Indo-Muslim art achieved its highest expression. Bordered by Pakistan (to the west), encroached upon by the Desert of Thar (to the west, the yellow part), Rajasthan, the surface of which amounts to a little less than two-thirds that of France, unveils its Rajput fortresses and lofty cities: Jaisalmer (to the far west), Bikaner (to the north), Jodhpur (in the centre), Udaipur (to the south) and Jaipur (to the west).

Artistic and technical director:
Ahmed-Chaouki Rafif
Editorial and iconographic coordination:
Marie-Pierre Kerbrat
Texts and photographs:
Philippe Bénet and Renata Holzbachová
Cartography:
Yves Korbendau
Editing:
Ellen Krabbe

Translated from the French by
Susan Wise

© 2005, ACR Édition Internationale, Courbevoie (Paris)
(Art - Création - Réalisation)
www.acr-edition.com
© 2005, DR
ISBN 2-86770-176-7
Publisher reference 1177
Copyright registration: November 2005

All rights reserved for all countries

Printed in France by Mame in Tours

City mentioned in the text
Other city
Main road
Secondary road
Summit
Marshland
River
Large artificial river
Plain
Desert
Mountain
Scale in kms.
0 25 50 75 100
PAKISTAN
HARYANA
DELHI
UTTAR PRADESH
GUJARAT
MADHYA PRADESH
Thar desert
Indira Gandhi Nahar
Bikaner
Desnok
Jhunhunu
Mandawa
Shekhawati
Nawalgarh
Alwar
Mewat
Deeg
Sikandra
Agra
Fatehpur Sikri
Yamuna
Ganges
Samode
Amber
Nahargarh
Jaipur
Banganga
Ramdevra
Jaisalmer
Marwar
Osiyan
Jodhpur
Pushkar
Ajmer
Luni
Morel
Tonk
Banas
Ranthambore
Khari
Bundi
Aravalli Range
Ranakpur
Mewar
Banas
Rana Pratap Sagar
Hadoti
Sukri
Luni
Mount ABU
1722m.
Berach
Udaipur
Delwara
Devi Garh
Gandhi Sagar
Khali Sindh
Parwan
Bambora
Karni Fort
Dungarpur
West Banas
Chambal
Dehli
RAJASTHAN

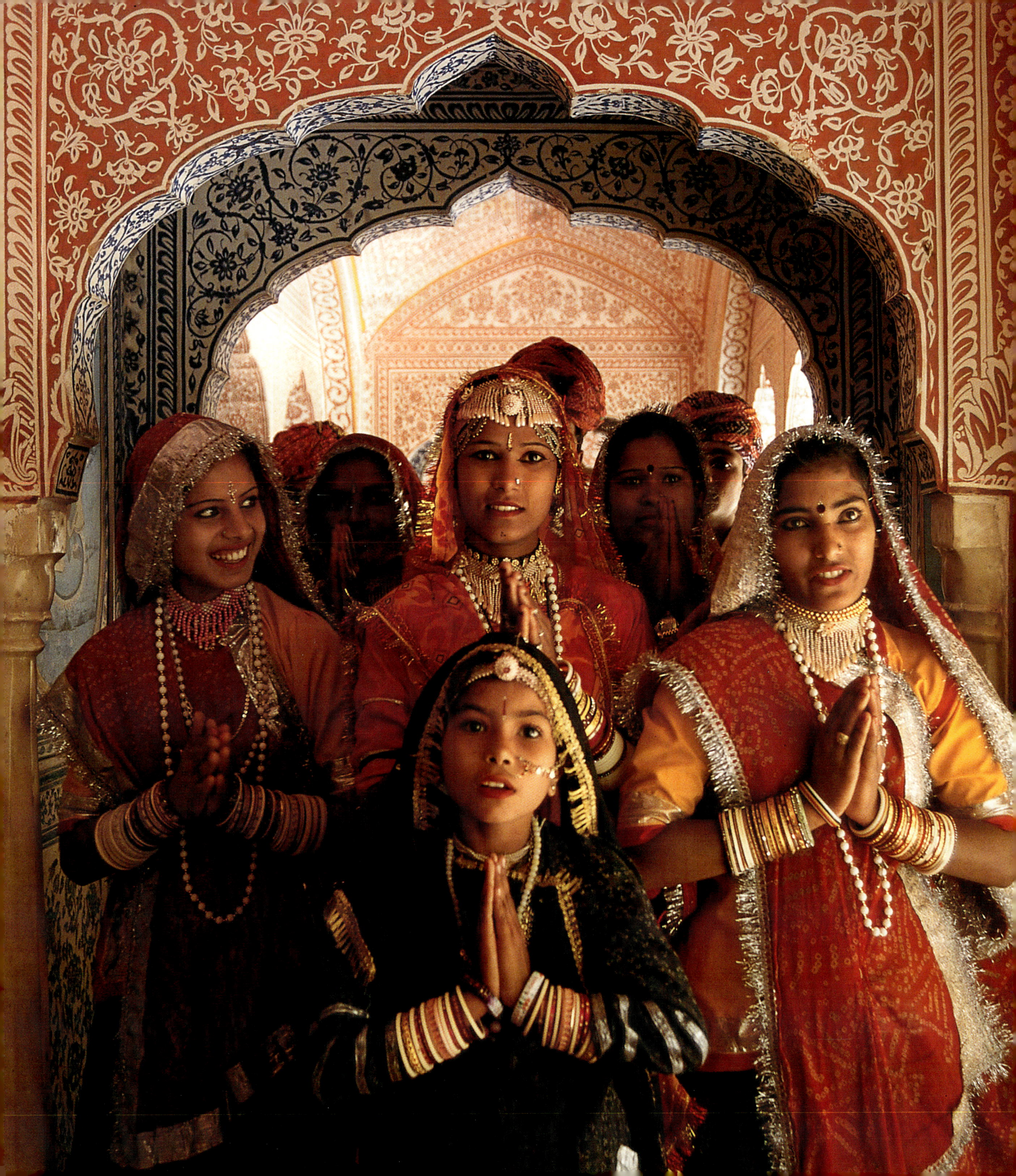

Philippe Bénet
Renata Holzbachová

Rajasthan
Delhi - Agra

An Indo-Muslim Lifestyle

ACR Edition
Bookwise Edition

Contents

	8	*Extracts from the Authors' Travel Diaries*
	10	*"The Largest Private Palace in the World"*
	14	*Introduction*
History	20	*The First Inhabitants – The Ones Called Aryans – Islam and Architecture – The Moghul Emperors and the Persian Influence – Akbar, the "Great Moghul" (1556-1605) – Akbar and Unity – Akbar, the Tolerant – Akbar's Successors – The Moghul Influence on the Rajputs – Assessment of the Colonial Period – Toward Independence*
Delhi	46	*New Delhi – The City of Seven Cities – Old Delhi – The Red Fort – The Qutab Minar – The Old Fort, Purana Qila – The Mausoleum of Humayun – Following the "Lodi Road"*
Agra	74	*The Mausoleum of the Itimad ud-Daula – The Mausoleum of Akbar at Sikandra – The Taj Mahal – A Sublime Mausoleum – The Fort of Agra – Life in Akbar's Time*
Fatehpur Sikri	106	*A Moghul Ghost Town – Akbar's Ideal City*
Rajasthan	116	*Land of Contrasts – Cities Encroached upon by the Desert – Nature Presently Preserved – The Indian Countryside – Traditional Arts in Rajasthan – The States of Rajputana – British Promises – Independence – The Maharajahs' Automobiles – More about the Maharajahs! – The Palace-hotels of the Maharajahs*
The Kingdoms of Alwar, Deeg and Tonk	136	

The Fortress-hotels of Neemrana, Karni Fort, Devi Garh and Samode	144	
Jaipur	168	*Mysterious Women of the Zenana – The Survivors – The Chandra Mahal – Alliance with the Moghuls – The City of Jai – A Glamorous History – The City Palace – The Bazaars of Jaipur*
The Fortresses of Amber, Jaigarh and Nahargarh	202	
Bikaner	210	*The Haveli of Bhanwar Niwas – The Fort of Junagarh – The Lalgarh Palace History*
Jodhpur	234	*History – The Fortress of Mehrangarh – Guided Tour of the Largest Private Palace in the World*
Ranakpur	252	*Beautiful and Mysterious Jain Temples of Ranakpur*
Shekhawati	258	*The Rich Merchants – Discovering the Haveli*
Hindu Pushkar	298	
Muslim Ajmer	304	
Jaisalmer, the Honey-coloured Citadel	310	*History – The Citadel – The Haveli in the Lower Town*
Udaipur, "the City of Dawn"	322	*"His Highness" is up in the Air! – History – The Royal Palace – The Magic of Lake Pichola – The Most Beautiful Palace-hotel in the World!*

EXTRACTS FROM THE AUTHORS' TRAVEL DIARIES

"March 10th: arrival in Jodhpur…"

"…The maharajah of Jodhpur, Gaj Singh II, is expecting us. His palace (one of his palaces), the 'Umaid Bhawan', which we fly over late in the evening, is an extravagant festival of stone domes, towers and columns, lit by the setting sun. Surrounded by 250 servants, the maharajah, his wife the maharani Hemlata Rajya, their two children and a great-aunt who speaks fluent French live very comfortably in this elegant ensemble raved about by those who look back with nostalgia to the Roaring Twenties. And it is supposedly the biggest private palace in the world: 394 rooms each as vast as an apartment, lobbies as tall as cathedrals, halls as long as New Delhi avenues. Leaving the Thar desert and flying over the city of Jodhpur, the second in Rajasthan, is sheer magic. The bluish houses of the lower town, caressed by a friendly sun, look like such a restful oasis!

"Perched on a rock looming over the city, the fort of Mehrangarh, that Rudyard Kipling called a 'construction of giants', stands aloft against the sky like an imaginary citadel. From the top of its 120 meters-high walls, for years the maharajah's ancestors resisted the Moghul invaders before becoming their allies. Built in the middle of the fifteenth century, chronicles of the time report it took 500 elephants and 10.000 slaves to erect the fortress that survived the onslaught of time.

"Across from it, almost challenging it, on a promontory of the other side of the city, proudly stands the 'Umaid Bhawan', the residence of His Highness, as everyone here calls him. The 38th maharajah of the Rathor Rajput warriors, proud descendent of Rama (hero of the famous Ramayana epic), member of the lineage of the 'Race of the Sun', had just completed his 50-year reign, a reign without power. He was only four when he ascended to the throne in 1952. After the Independence in 1947, when all the princes' privileges were cancelled in the name of democracy, the old royal families had to find some way to afford their 'luxurious lifestyle' and maintain their patrimony. Some never adjusted, and let their fortresses and palaces fall into neglect. Others, successfully, had the daring to try the hotel business. Today the Umaid Bhawan is one of the most prestigious addresses in Rajasthan. Its fascinating art deco suites have been praised in every interior decoration magazine in the world. The maharajah's family kept a wing of the palace as their private residence. We are to meet him there."

The fortress of Mehrangarh, at Jodhpur: "A construction of giants", Rudyard Kipling wrote.

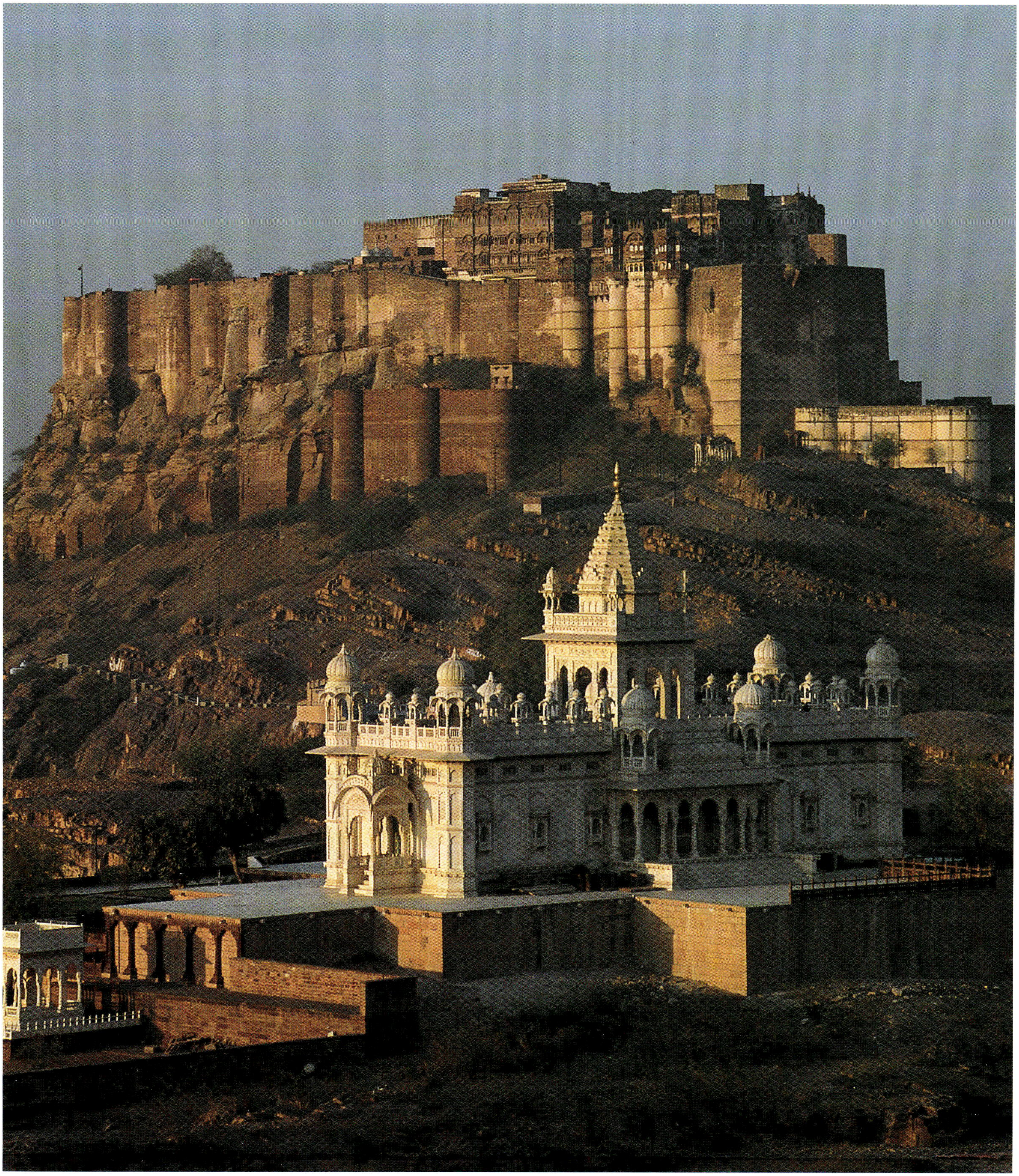

"THE LARGEST PRIVATE PALACE IN THE WORLD"

"The evening turns to blue. The palace lights shine in the dark. From the windows of our aircraft it looks the size of a town. Umaid Bhuwan means the palace of Umaid, the name of the present maharajah's grandfather. Umaid Singh commissioned English architects of genius to build the palace in the 1920s. It arose from a generous idea: to give work to the population driven to despair because of the rampant famine. So 3.000 of them, inhabitants of the city and the state of Jodhpur, were employed for years. A record at the time!

"The airport where we gently land was also designed by Umaid. An aviation enthusiast, he owned a fleet of twelve airplanes. Ours comes to a halt. A wave of heat: the desert is not far.

"The welcoming committee, a mile-long 1947 cream-coloured 8-cylinder Buick convertible, is waiting for us with a driver. The hotel clients and VIP guests can choose from among the cars of the family collection that can come to fetch them at the airport: a 1941 and a 1947 Cadillac; two 1942 Phantom Rolls II; a 1947 Packard. There is also the 1934 Morris Minor and several others, more up-to-date. We chose the 1947 Buick, a gift to the son of the maharajah, Prince Yuvraj, from his grandmother for his eighteenth birthday. The palace is a stone's throw from the airport. Leather interior, powerful engine, the long Buick rides without a sound. Every day, not less than eight chauffeurs run the engines, polish and pamper the old vehicles.

Tea-time for Gaj Singh II, 38th maharajah of Jodhpur, in the gardens of the Umaid Bhawan, the biggest private palace in the world: 394 rooms, 8 dining-rooms and an Art Deco swimming-pool.

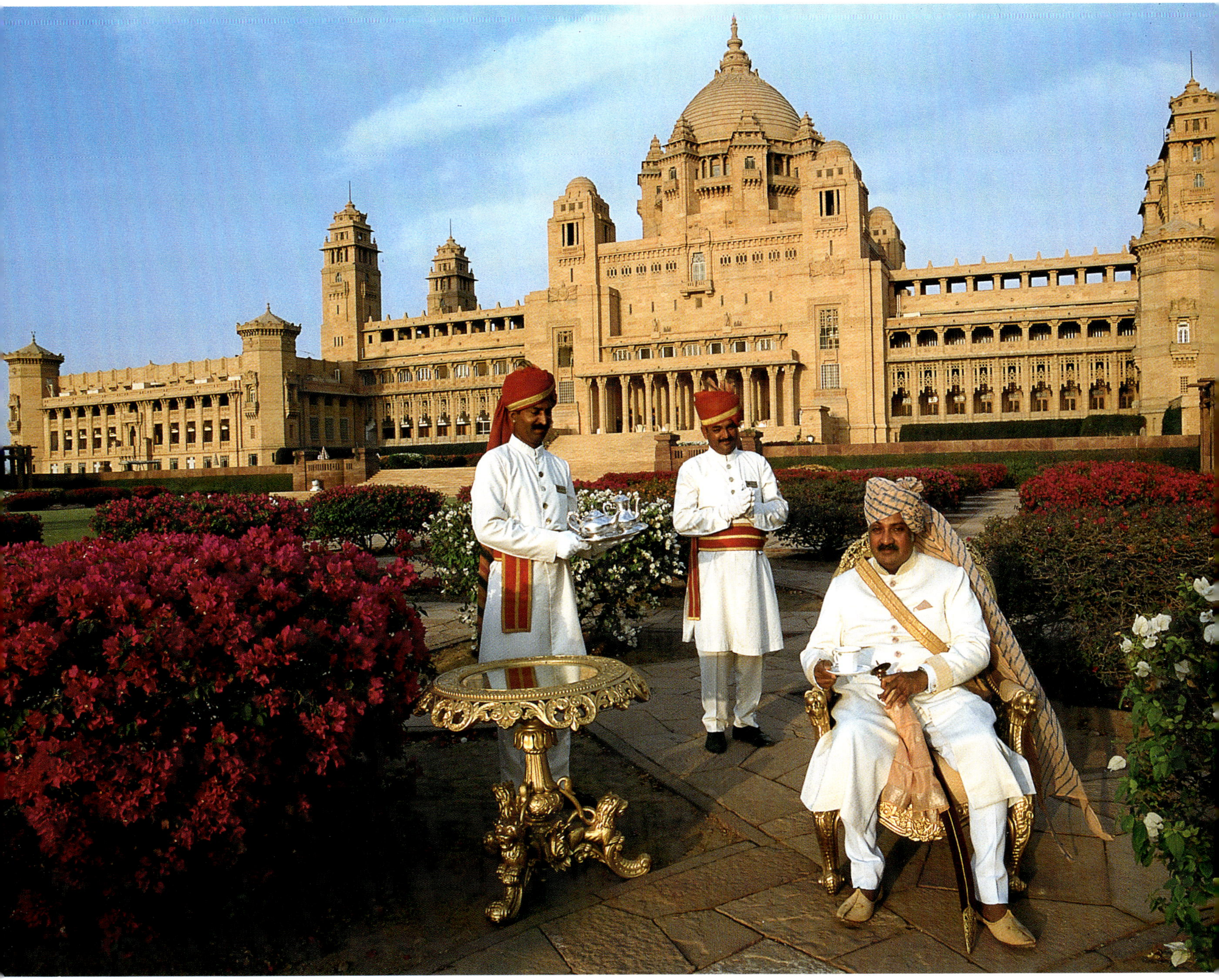

The Rajputs have kept all their elegance and their panache. Prince Yuvraj Shivraj Singh, son of the maharajah of Jodhpur, in front of his 1947 8-cylinder Buick, a gift from his very sweet grandmother for his eighteenth birthday.

"Kipling was right. In his 1887 travel memoirs *From Sea to Sea*, the English writer already mentioned in 1887 that 'Jodhpur is different from the other states of Rajputana (the former name of Rajasthan, before the Independence), because the royal family was particularly hospitable toward visitors seeking information…'

"We spend a blissful week in the enchanting Umaid Bhuwan as guests of His Highness. 'Tell me, Your Highness, have the maharajahs become businessmen?' 'We are merely the custodians of our history', Gaj Singh II explains. At twenty-five, his son, Prince Yuvraj Shivraj Singh, embodies the appealing aspect of modern India: brilliant studies at Oxford, polo champion, internet fan, involved in charity work, travelling all over Europe (he adores the French), he manages the family hotel with the same panache as his father. He is a true Rajput…"

After studying at Oxford, prince Yuvraj Shivraj Singh has taken over the management of the family patrimony. Excellent polo player, fond of horses and involved in charity work, he represents modern India.

INTRODUCTION

All year long the psychiatrist of the French Embassy in Delhi has to try to reassure French travellers who go into a state of shock on discovering this upsetting and fascinating India. In the "stay and die" hotels in Benares (now called Varanasi) did they run into the visionary eyes of the men or women who are hoping for death, wishing their ashes to be cast into the sacred Ganges to attain Nirvana even sooner? In Calcutta or Bombay were they approached by the flocks of beggars that looked so poor and yet so rich within (but how do they manage it?). Did they spend too much time listening to those odd "wise men" for whom everything is futile? Did they tell them the present life was nothing and that the next will be better? Or were they bewitched by those unbelievable tales of maharajahs' wives who became sati by self-immolation on a pyre to follow their hero into eternity?

Going to Rajasthan means exposing yourself to the temptation of beauty and the fantastic. It's a defiant temptation for lovers of Romance and the spirit of chivalry. What remains of these some twenty states, which before the Independence formed Rajputana? Looming in the blue sky, superbly rising up out of the desert, the once impregnable Rajput fortresses of Amber, Jodhpur, Jaisalmer, Bikaner, Chittaugarh, sublime parentheses of silence in the midst of the roar of cities that grew up too fast, still speak to us of a glorious past. The exquisite palaces of Samode, Lalgar and Devi Garh are jewels that have adorned Rajasthan over the centuries, despite wars, invasions and historic compromises. The colourful haveli (in Persian, closed houses) of the former Shekkhawati or Jaisalmer merchants recall the days of the rich caravans that crossed the Thar desert.

Drums and dances in the Durbar Hall (reception room) of the palace of Samode, a sublime example of Rajput-Moghul architecture built in the early nineteenth century.

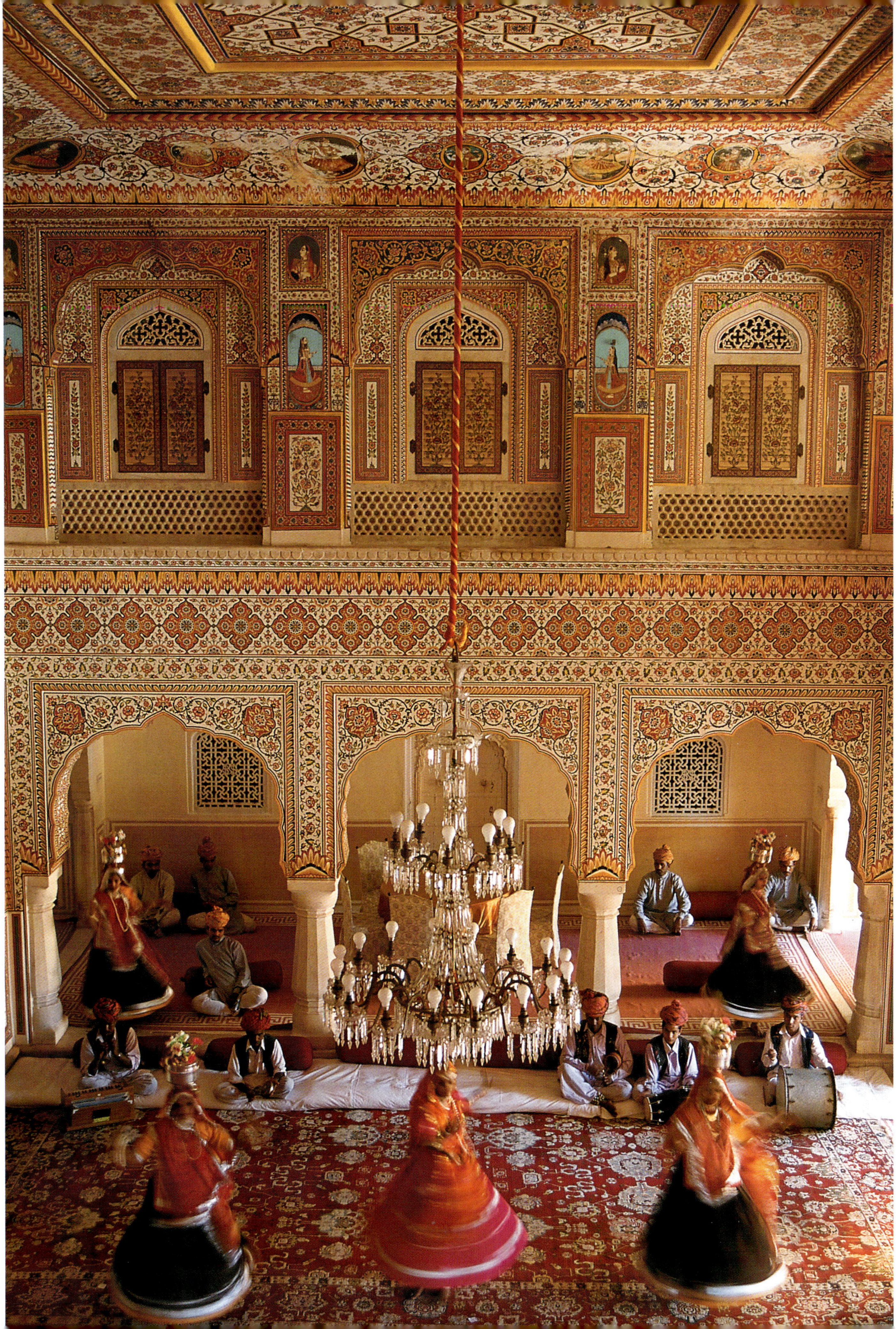

Detail of precious stones inlaid in marble using the Italian pietra dura technique. Motif of the diwan-i khas (private audiences hall) of the Red Fort in Delhi.

*Opposite:
Not the ghost of a rich, capricious maharajah in sight! Rajput princes, who today run their palace surfing on the net and travelling in private jets, left these luxury trains of old to tourists some time ago. Visiting Rajasthan on board the "Palace-on-Wheels", inspired by the maharajahs' trains, is still a must. "Would you like tea or coffee?"*

Lending itself to every mirage and every mystery, Rajasthan, this "land of kings", deserves its name. We discovered the panache of these last kings, today deprived of their power, these maharajahs and aristocrats with their princely airs and dazzling outfits: maharajahs of Jaipur and Jodhpur; maharana of Udaipur, princess of Bikaner; rawals (aristocrats) of Samode; thakurs of Karni Fort and Alsisar; nawab (Muslim prince) of Tonk.

These heirs of living legends, these descendents of Rajput warriors or Muslim nobles, opened up for us their palaces, their private mansions and sometimes their hearts. As a new century begins, we must admit their panache is still intact! Everything has already been said about their ancestors during their rule: their lavishness, their prodigality, their wealth and their extravagant expenditures. The great storyteller of British India, Rudyard Kipling said of them: "They were created by Providence to provide the world with picturesque decors, stories about tigers and grandiose spectacles." That was not so bad! Everything remains to be discovered about the twenty-first century maharajahs: their generous sponsorship to protect or boost craftsmanship, their involvement in charity works, their sense of hospitality, their talent in managing a patrimony by creating thousands of jobs for the local population. As for their palace-hotels, worthy of the tales of A Thousand and One Nights, they were often fashioned by the marvellous encounter of Hinduism and Islam which strongly marked the local culture.

With its countless fortresses inundating the desert, Rajasthan is like a bare musical score. Moghul art and its exquisiteness added the counterpoint and phrasing.

Delhi, featuring gorgeous Muslim vestiges; Agra, proud of its Taj Mahal and several other incomparable mausoleums, and Rajasthan form a magic triangle onto which Turks and Moghuls cast the silk and brocade mantle of Arab-Persian culture and where the Indo-Muslim art blossomed into beauty.

17

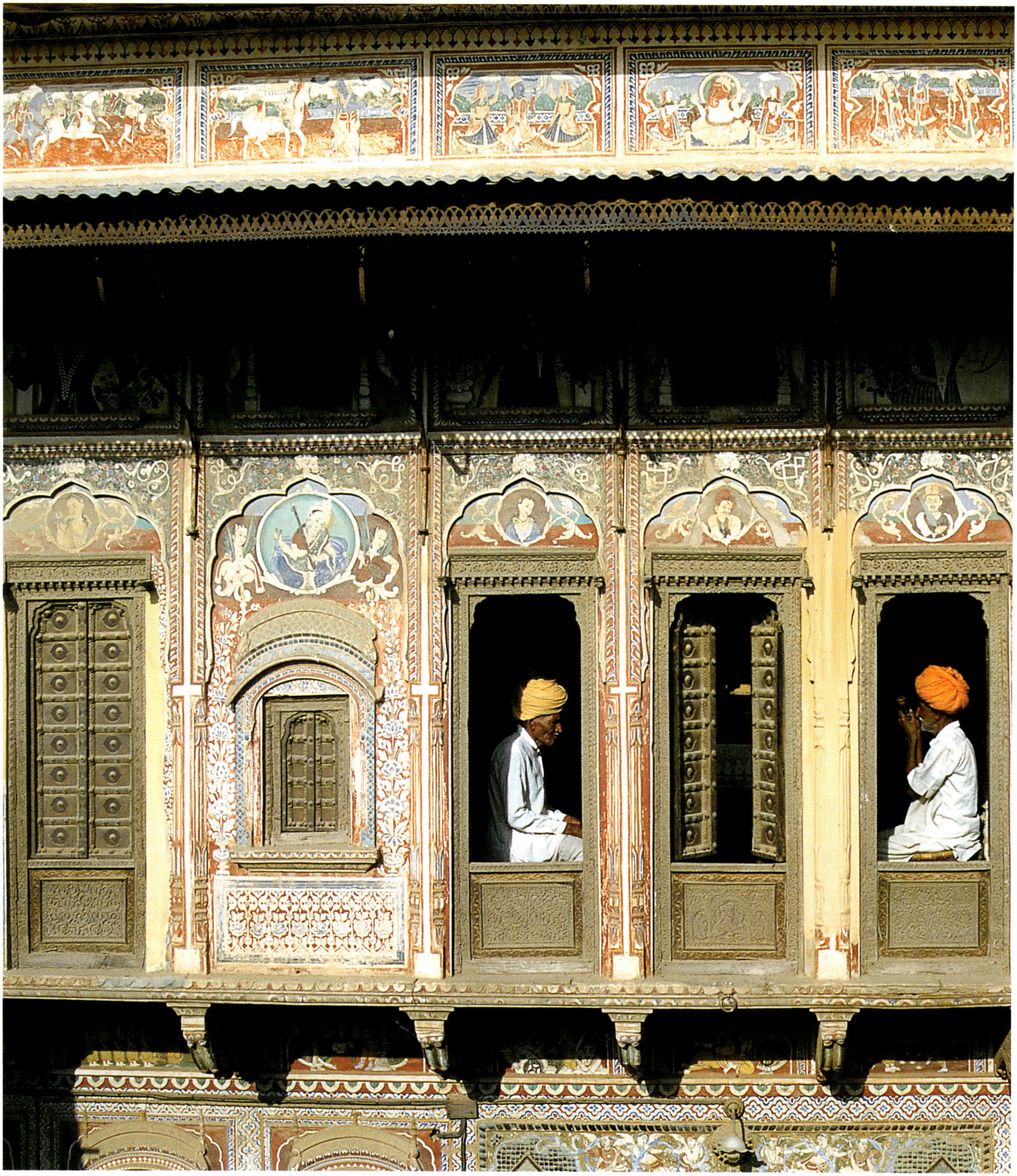

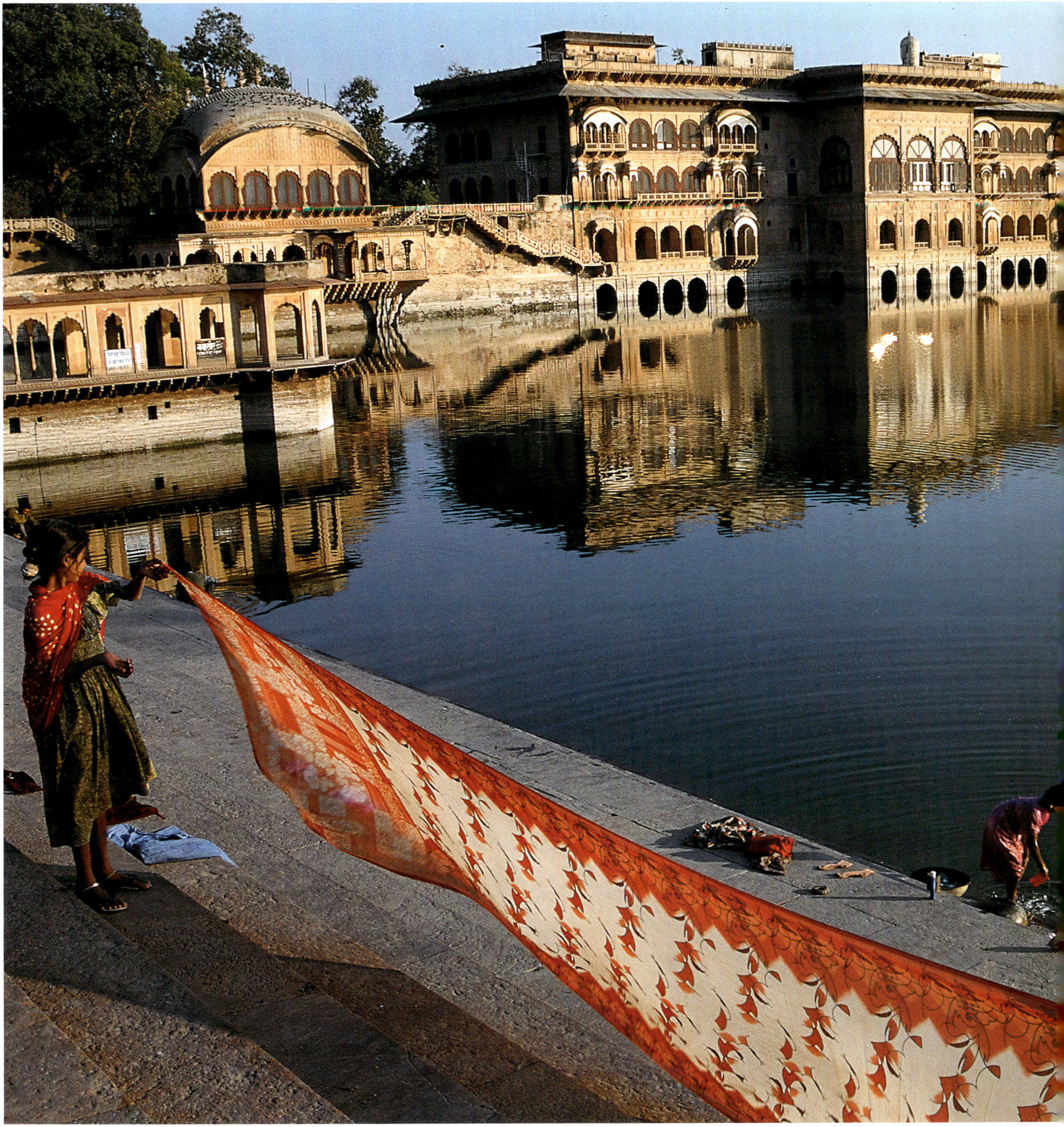

HISTORY

The First Inhabitants

Red, blue or green uniforms, long carefully braided hair, impeccable socks, … in good weather flocks of well-behaved schoolgirls throng the Lodi gardens, in Delhi, chattering gaily around the mausoleums of the sultans Mohammed Shah (1450) and Sikander Lodi (1517). "The Muslim presence is an intrinsic part of our country", their teachers repeat all together. The same speech is echoed in front of the minaret tower Qutab Minar that signals the crushing victory of the Muslim Mohammed of Ghor over a little Hindu king.

A quick poll with the man in the street concerning the influence of the Moghul emperor Akbar proves the Indian population's respect for that exceptional sovereign, born in India, married to a Rajput princess, unifier of the country and protector of the arts, who practiced tolerance in matters of religion.

Unquestionably Islam left a profound mark on the architecture and the history of this land the British called a sub-continent. This block, comprised of India, Pakistan and Bangladesh, has a 6.000 kilometres-long coastline, is occupied by immense plains like that of the Ganges (twice the size of France) and is shielded by the highest mountains in the world. Three thousand kilometres long, they form an almost insurmountable barrier. A few gaps like the famous Khyber Pass, between India and upper Asia, on the present-day Afghanistan border, were used by the waves of invaders hungering to reach the fertile plains of Hindustan (former name of Northern India). The list is long: the Aryans as of 1500 B.C., followed by the Persians with Cyrus and Darius, the Greeks of Alexander, Scythians, Parthians, Huns, Turks, Arabs and Mongols…

The first immigrants, the Aryans, discovered in India a brilliant civilisation called the Indus, of which the National Museum in Delhi preserves outstanding relics (jewellery, pottery, statuettes, engraved seals) attesting to its great evolution. At the height of its glory between 2500 and 1800 B.C. it spawned remarkable cities such as Harappa and Mohenjo-Daro (in present-day Pakistan).

Page 18:
With their naïve, bright-coloured frescoes, the haveli (patrician houses) of the region of Shekhawati have preserved the poignant charm and the nostalgia of the olden days (Bhagton ki Haveli at Nawalgarh).

Page 19:
Brightened up by a lush Moghul garden, built in the middle of the eighteenth century and inhabited up to the 1970s, the palace of Deeg tells the story of the mighty Jat sovereigns.

The Ones Called Aryans

Who are these first immigrants we call Aryans? They were nomadic tribes, the Arya (nobles, in Sanskrit) who, hailing from the Caspian Sea, followed the route of the Iranian high plateaux around 1500 B.C. Progressing toward the plain of the Ganges, absorbing the existing culture, the Aryans introduced their language (Sanskrit), their religion (Vedaism) and built cities such as Indraprashta (Delhi).

The first unification of India was accomplished by Ashoka of the Maurya dynasty who ruled from 264 to 226 B.C. Converted, he spread Buddhism throughout his empire that included, aside from Afghanistan, almost all of India. Among the various barbarian incursions, the invasions by Parthians, Scythians, Huns and the Gurjaras would be the ones to give rise to the Rajputs, founding small kingdoms between the sixth and the tenth centuries.

Construction of the oldest mosque in India, Quwwat ul-Islam (the Might of Islam), began in Delhi in 1193.

Islam and Architecture

"We are of Persian birth, we are restoring the paintings executed by our ancestors hired by the Rajput princes in the sixteenth century." The chance meeting in the fort of Junagarh, at Bikaner, of two young artists fervently and patiently working on restoring the antique paintings of the wonderful Palace of the Flowers (Phul Mahal) and the Palace of the Moon (Chandra Mahal) is meaningful. The influence of Persia, a model of refinement in the Middle Ages, deeply influenced Muslim art in India.

After the death of the prophet Mohammed (570-632), the first caliphs dominated Syria, Egypt, Persia and North Africa. In the tenth century, the eastward Muslim progression reached present-day Afghanistan. A Turkish dynasty settled at Ghazni whence Soubouk Tegin (977-997) made incursions into India. In the early eleventh century came the turn of Mahmud of Ghazni to rush over the northern plains of India where he founded the city of Lahore (today in Pakistan). At the end of the twelfth century the occupation of Delhi by the Afghan sultan Mohammed of Ghor, conqueror of the Rajput armies, marked the real beginning of the history of Islamic art in India. If the Turkish sultans first called upon craftsmen from Iraq, Iran and Afghanistan to spread their talent in building mosques, later they turned to local Hindu sculptors who had to learn the Persian style. Despising vacuums, they delighted in carving every square inch of their temples crossed by dark passageways leading to the "cella", the venerated holy image. Only a very few Hindu vestiges prior to the eighteenth century have survived in the north of India, because the conquering Muslims strived to eradicate every single trace of Hinduism. They had every mark of idolatry erased by hammering the images of the gods, animals and humans, replacing them with Koranic inscriptions, intricate interlacing and arrangements of rippling stems. Mosques were built, liberally open onto the outdoors, and resting upon a profusion of Tudor arches and domes on squinches. They display lovely polychrome facades in red sandstone embellished with white marble.

After Mohammed of Ghor, one of his officers, Qutab ud-Din Aibak, an emancipated former Turkish slave, proclaimed himself sultan of Delhi and set up his capital around a soaring minaret-tower, symbol of the victory of Islam. It is the Qutab Minar, a sort of twin tower of the Giralda that rises in Seville at the other end of the Muslim world. It took thirty years to complete. In the capital of the sultanate, Iranian art and its simplicity became very "trendy". Like everywhere else they used the old to make the new. The columns of the Jain and Hindu sanctuaries became building materials. Openings were made in the facade of the prayer room in the Iranian (Persian) style, which was considered of utmost refinement.

But in 1398 the Turkish-Mongol Tamerlane marched on Northern India and seized Delhi, asserting the Sayyid dynasty, supplanted in 1450 by that of the Lodis. In the shelter of their impregnable fortresses, the Rajput kingdoms of Rajputana were quite able to resist this first Muslim wave.

The Koranic inscriptions covering the facade of the prayer-room of the Adhai-din ka Jhonpra mosque, built in the thirteenth century at Ajmer (p. 23), are some of the loveliest masterpieces of Muslim art.

*Pages 24 and 25:
The Persian influence is entirely expressed in the elegant arabesques and stone inlays in the Palaces of the Flowers and of the Moon nestled in the Fort of Junagarh, at Bikaner.*

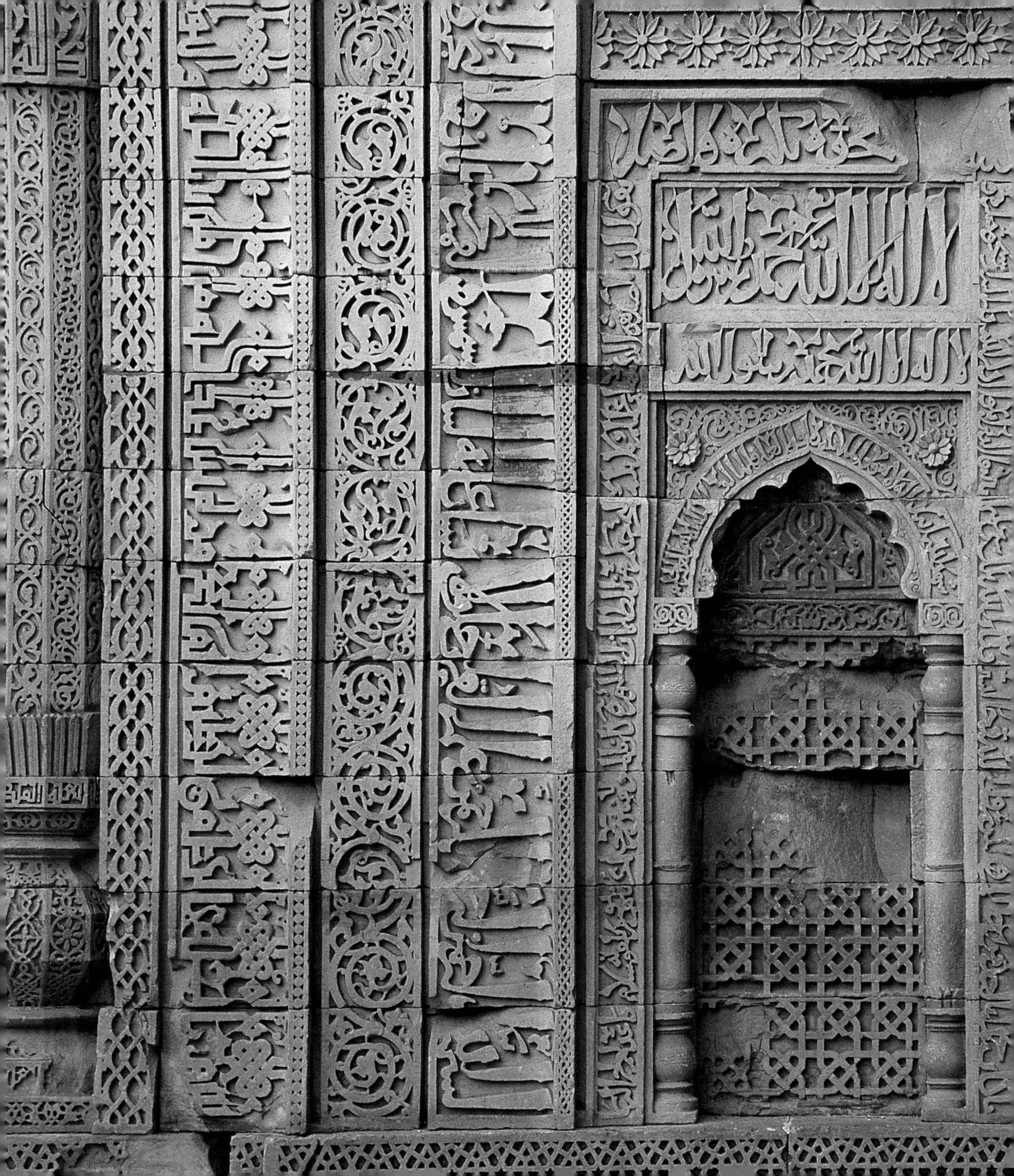

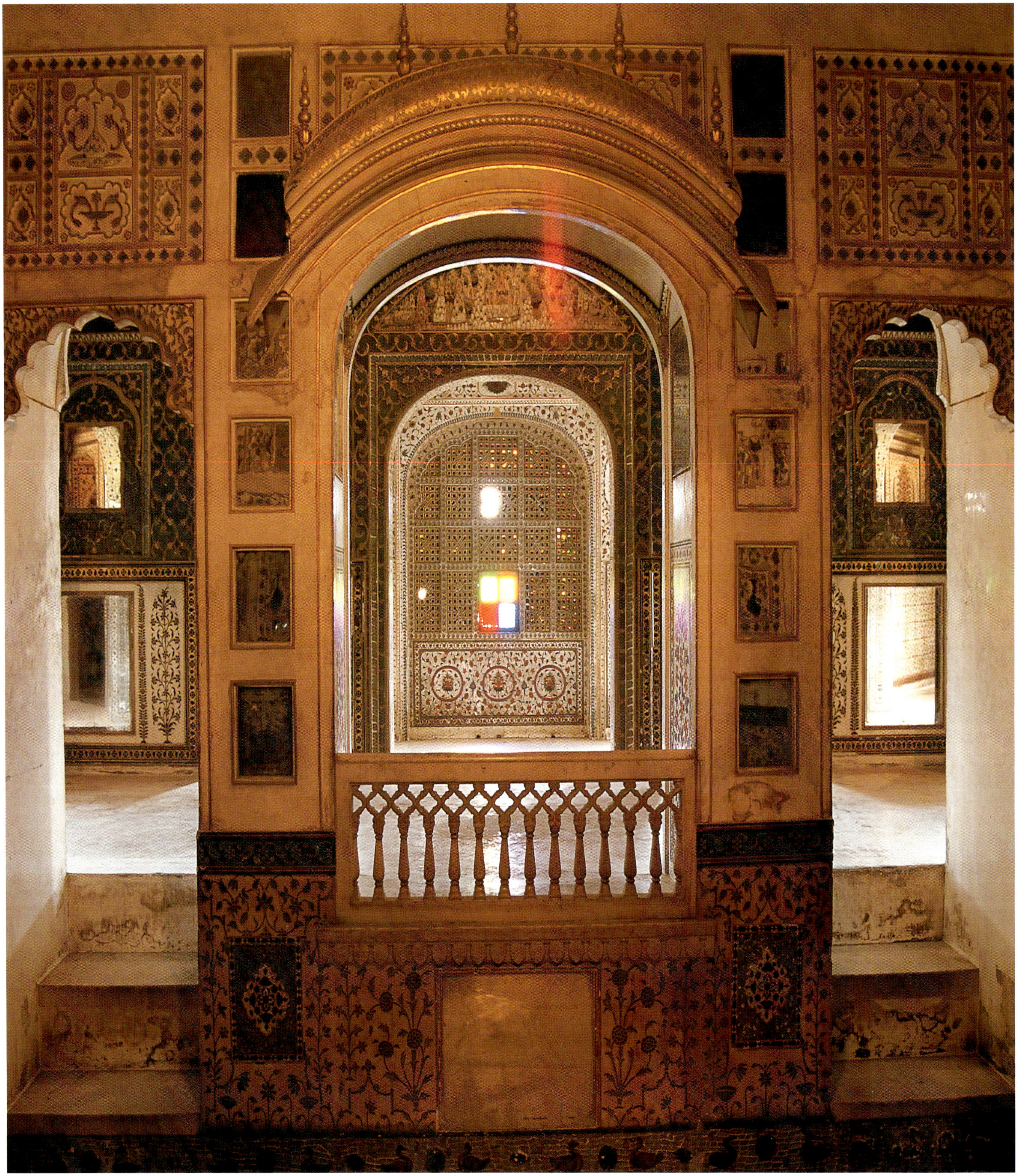

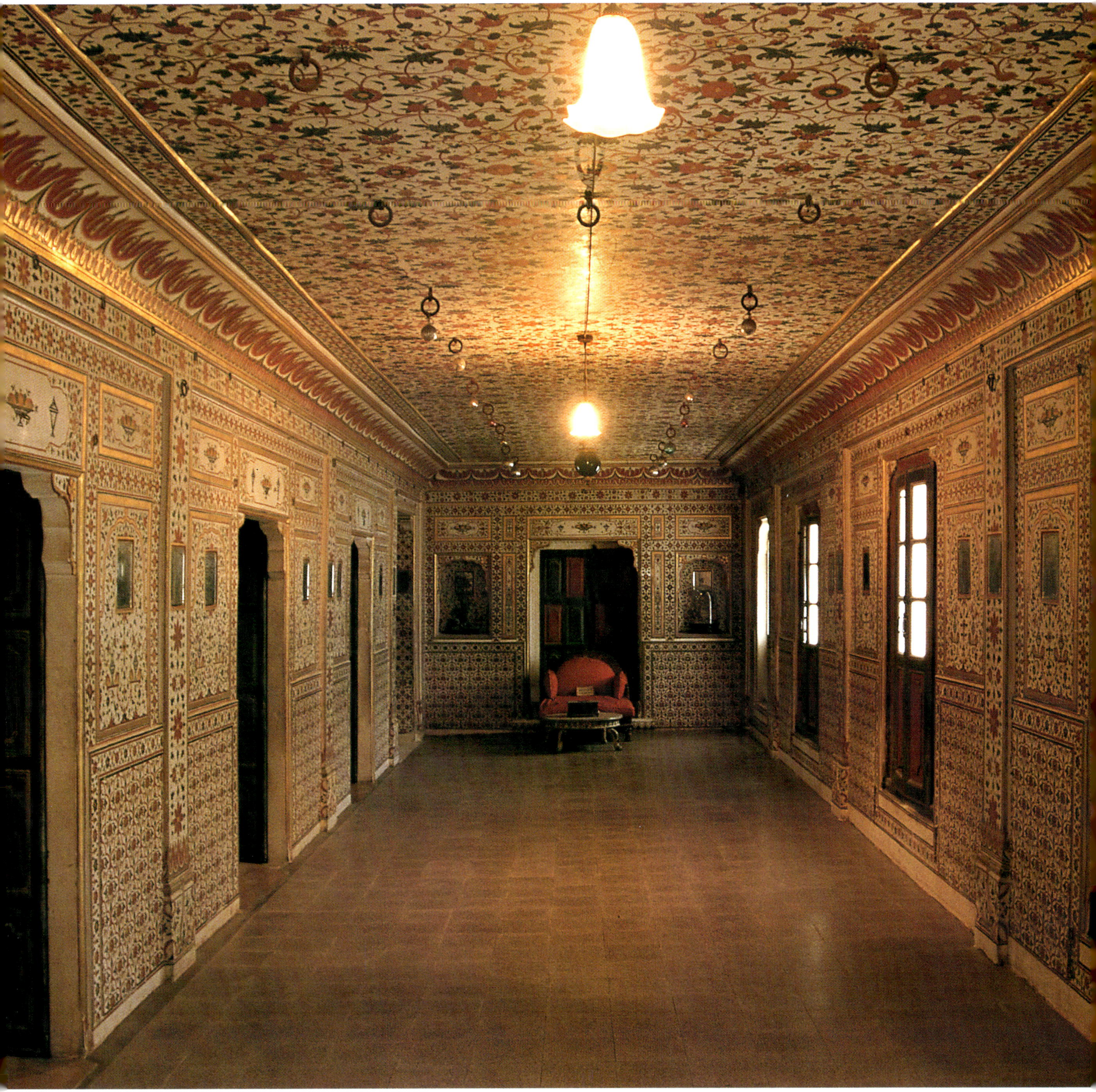

The Moghul Emperors and the Persian Influence

The magic of the shish mahal (Room of Mirrors) in the Samode Palace.

Commissioned by the Moghul emperor Shah Jahan, Akbar's grandson, in memory of his favourite wife who died in childbirth, the Taj Mahal no longer hears the praise: "A solitary tear on the cheek of time".

A descendent of the Mongol Tamerlane by his father and of Genghis Khan by his mother, Babur, who ruled from 1526 to 1530, seized the city of Lahore from the Afghans, yet it was from Kabul that he launched his hordes toward Northern India in 1526. He wiped out the troops of the sultan Ibrahim Lodi and took Delhi where he had himself proclaimed emperor. In so doing he inaugurated the dynasty of the Moghuls (Moghul is the Persian translation of Mongol). Recollecting the shaded parks enhancing Kabul, he introduced the vogue of Moghul gardens with which he adorned his palaces in Agra. The Moghul garden or chahar bagh, supposed to symbolise Paradise, is divided into four equal parts, separated by two very shallow canals enlivened by fountains. Flowerbeds were planted. Too busy warring to consolidate his power, Babur, who did not foster important constructions, nonetheless signalled the beginning of a new lease on life for Muslim art in Northern India between the sixteenth and the eighteenth century. The first Moghul died in Agra in 1530, leaving his son Humayun (1530-1556) an immense but shaky kingdom that covered all of Northern India. His armies, composed of Turks, Afghans, Persians, Uzbeks and Indians, lacked discipline.

In 1540 Humayun was forced to abandon his empire to the Afghan governor of the region of Bihar, Sher Khan, although he had been appointed by Babur. Sher Khan became emperor under the name of Sher Shah Sur. Hamayun, who withdrew to Kabul, lived for fifteen years in exile at the Persian Court. In 1555, mightily armed, he undertook to win back his land, regaining his throne in Delhi, just a year before his demise in 1556.

Persian artists and architects, who accompanied the Moghul, were engaged by his widow, Haji Begum, to design a grandiose mausoleum in Delhi for the deceased. The Persian influence is obvious. Set in the midst of gardens – a great novelty –, the edifice is enhanced with ogival arches, marble and red sandstone facades and topped with a double shell crowned by a dome.

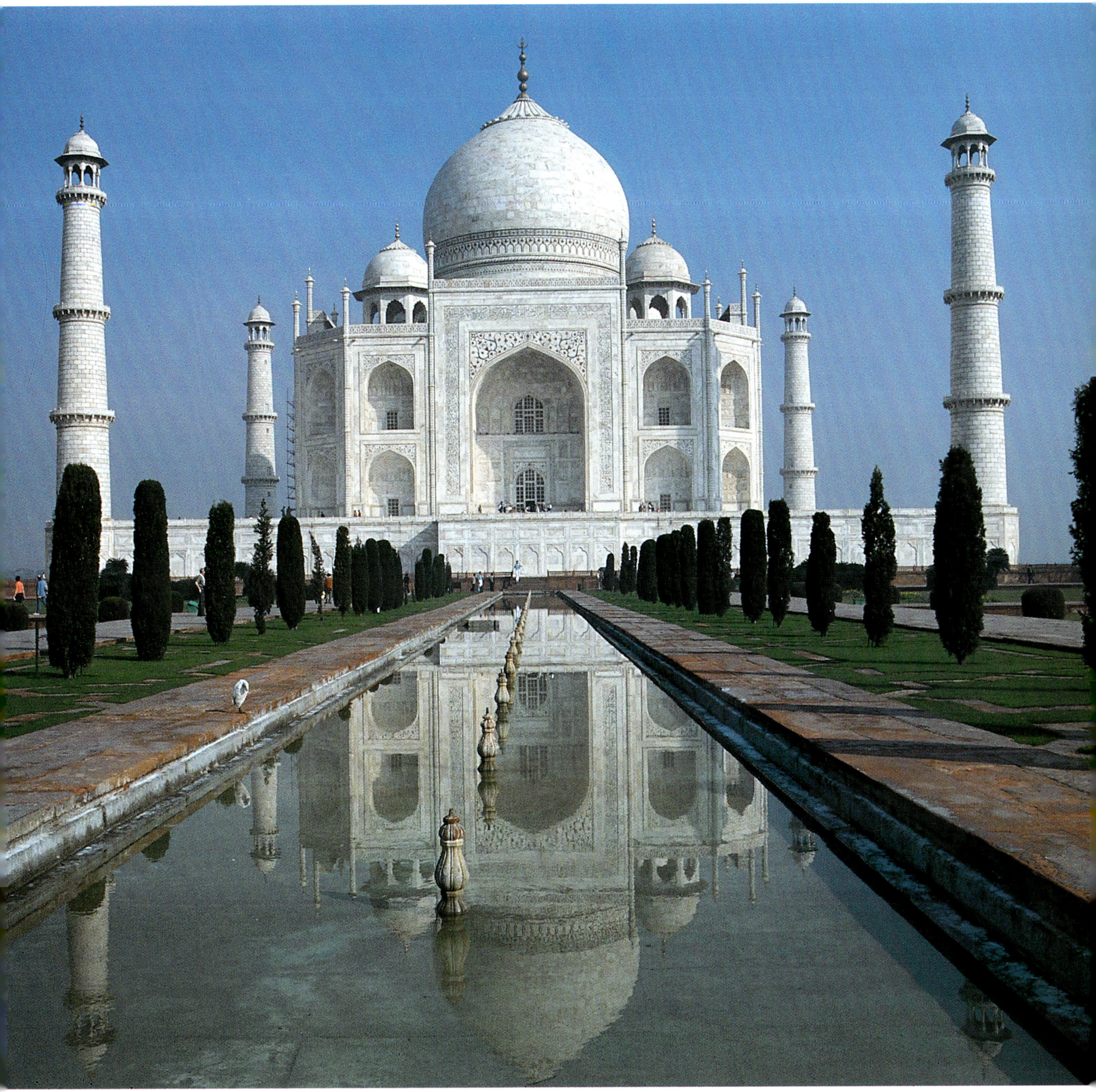

Framed by Moghul gardens, the mosque of the emperor Humayun (1530-1556) is a haven of peace in bustling Delhi. Red sandstone, white marble, double-shell dome, the Persian influence is clearly visible.

The shish mahal, or Room of Mirrors in the Samode Palace. Brought from Persia, the art of mirrors embellished many palaces in Rajasthan, where the walls and the ceilings are dotted with bits of mirrors. Sometimes, blown-glass balls, silvered inside, were broken and the fragments inlaid in the plaster of the ceilings and the walls. Candles or oil lamps placed on the floor made the place enchanting.

29

Akbar, the "Great Moghul" (1556-1605)

Born in India, succeeding his father Humayun, this contemporary of Henry IV of France would leave a deep mark on the history of India. For the Indians of the twenty-first century, Hindus and Muslims alike, Akbar's name forever symbolises prosperity, peace, justice and unity. Whereas since the twelfth century the Muslim sovereigns had ruled this Northern India broken up into small states governed by Afghans, Turks and Hindu rajahs by force, Akbar became the forerunner of the Indian nation. Of course he first ruled with arms, relentlessly waging war from his bases of Kabul, Lahore, Delhi, Agra, Fatehpur Sikri. His kingdom, as vast as Europe, finally stretched from Afghanistan to Bengal, from the Himalaya to the Dekkan plateau. Yet he had nobler ambitions and would make India politically and spiritually one.

He aspired to be a great builder as well, using red sandstone all over his huge empire, at Lahore and Agra, with ensembles featuring official buildings, private palaces and mosques. He called upon the greatest master craftsmen from Iran, had them work with the local painters, developing miniatures to depict the Indian culture he loved. His short-lived capital, Fatehpur Sikri, expresses wonderfully the syncretism of the one who strived to unite the peoples of his empire, their religions and cultures. Rather like his taste for combining in architecture Persian elements such as the arch and the iwan (vaulted space) with Indian ones (red sandstone, columns, porch roofs, entablatures…).

A contemporary of Henri IV of France, the Moghul emperor Akbar strived during his reign to unite India politically and spiritually (left).

Among the Rajput princes, the maharanas of Udaipur always put up fierce resistance to the Moghuls. Eighteenth-century miniature of the Udaipur School depicting the departure for the hunt. We recognize the solar emblems worn by the soldiers and the white marble Lake Palace.

31

Akbar and Unity

By publishing a series of edicts Akbar democratised a society that certainly needed it. He abolished slavery, asked the governors of the towns to respect individual rights. He also attacked polygamy. In 1587, he forbade Hindus as well as Muslims to have more than one wife, unless she were sterile or could no longer give birth. Even if during his reign a well-provided harem always accompanied him on all his campaigns and journeys, he confessed at the end of his reign: "Had I been wise earlier in my life, I never would have taken a woman of my kingdom into my harem, because my subjects are to me as children."

A great pacifier of human relations, he allowed widows to remarry (which went against Hindu customs) and decided marriages would henceforth be performed by mutual consent yet with the parents' agreement. Another striking revolution: the spouses' legal age. Before Akbar, unions were often arranged by the parents for their very young children, sometimes before the age of five (which is still true for some very remote regions of Rajasthan). The Moghul emperor decided boys could marry after the age of sixteen and girls at fourteen.

He wished to eradicate begging, considering it backward. "Sloth is the cause of every evil", he claimed. "Those who seek happiness have to learn a craft and practice it." He also determined to control prostitution, permitted only outside the town walls. On the level of economy, thanks to a better policy of taxation and land distribution, Akbar's India grew rich, producing more than it could consume so it could export.

The Moghul emperor Akbar gave Hindus the same rights as Muslims (page 32). Forced to accept an alliance with the Moghuls at the end of the sixteenth century after resisting them at length, the Rajput princes surrounded themselves with a lavish Court, following the example set by the invaders (page 33).

33

Akbar, the Tolerant

His thoughts, his laws are known to us thanks to his faithful confident, the poet and historian Abul Fadl. Akbar sought to fight religious fanaticism by granting total freedom to believe and to build places of worship for every religion. Each could be preached as long as the public peace was insured. He even had the Gospels translated in Persian as well as the epic poem of the Mahabharata. A devout Muslim, he was passionately interested in other faiths, summoned Jain and Parsee thinkers and in 1594 sent a letter to Goa to invite some Jesuit fathers. Three of them arrived a year later at Lahore where the Court was assembled. The Great Moghul gave them a site on which to build a church and confessed his desire for learning: "I know all the religions in the world except that of Jesus Christ which is the belief in a God recognised by many faithful. Since I feel deeply inclined to prove my friendship to the fathers, I wish them to teach me their religion…"

But his behaviour began to annoy some members of the Court, who saw him holding paintings of the life of Christ and of the Apostles brought by the priests or even attending their ceremonies on his knees.

The poem signed by the historian Abul Fadl that Akbar had engraved on the pediment of a temple says a great deal about the spiritual search and tolerance of the Great Moghul:

"O God, in every temple I see humans
Seeking Thee and in every tongue
I hear those who praise Thee.
Hinduism and Islam approach Thee.
Each religion says: 'Thou art the incomparable One'.
In a mosque, the holy prayer is murmured.
In a church, bells are made to ring
For the love of Thee.
Sometimes I enter a cloister,
A Hindu temple,
And sometimes a mosque.
But it is always Thee I seek
From one temple to another."

Henna makeup for the women of the zenana. Miniature of the Kishangarh School.

Miniatures of the Mewar School (Udaipur) are very colourful and expressive. We can recognise the Lake Palace in the middle of Lake Pichola and the royal palace in the foreground.

Akbar's Successors

Although they did not inherit Akbar's aspiration for a tolerant society, his descendents still wished to be enlightened in matters of architecture. Akbar's son, Jahangir (1605-1627), who let his wife rule, chose white marble which became the favourite material of the next Moghul, Shah Jahan (1627-1658), who had a wild obsession to build. He was the one to add the gorgeous palatial parts to the forts of Agra and Lahore. He also had the Red Fort built in Delhi and raised the seventh historic town of Delhi, gracing it with the largest mosque in India, the Juma Masjid. But his greatest glory remains the Taj Mahal, the mausoleum dedicated to his wife. The finest craftsmen of the empire spent twenty years perfecting this "white marble poem". Because of his fanaticism, Aurangzeb (1658-1707) endured the uprisings of the Rajputs, the Sikhs and the Jats. After him the empire swiftly declined.

The hero of one of the most glamorous stories of all, the Moghul emperor Shah Jahan (1627-1658), Akbar's grandson, in the company of his favourite wife Mumtaz i Mahal who died giving birth to their fourteenth child. Torn with grief, Shah Jahan had a mausoleum built for her as great as his sorrow: the Taj Mahal.

Shah Jahan is often depicted with a luminous halo around his head, to express his superhuman nature.

The Moghul Influence on the Rajputs

Entrenched inside their fortresses, the Rajputs often had to yield before the Moghul assailants to whom they were forced to pay huge tributes. In the sixteenth century, the rajah of Amber, Bhar Mal, chose to become the ally of the Moghul Humayun, even giving his daughter's hand to the emperor's son and future Akbar. As a reward the rajah became governor of the provinces. After that many other Rajputs were tempted to treat with the Moghuls to obtain certain advantages such as peace and prosperity for the kingdom. The local arts and crafts benefited from this fruitful exchange. His ancestor having come to terms with the Moghuls, the maharajah Sawai Jai Singh created the new capital Jaipur in 1727, and to embellish it sought out the best artisans from Agra and Delhi who were working for the Moghul Court at the time.

At the end of the sixteenth century, the Rajput princes began to borrow Moghul architectural features and lavishness to enhance their fortresses.

What did a Moghul palace look like at that time? Within walls surrounded by ramparts, it comprised several official buildings as well as the public court room (diwan-i am) for receptions. The private apartments were divided into the mardana reserved for men, whereas the women (wives and favourites) were secluded in the zenana where only the emperor and the eunuchs were admitted (from the Persian word zan meaning woman). Fretted stone screens called jali allowed the recluses to see without being seen. There were hot and cold hammams for the leisure of the emperor and the concubines. Ministers and intimates were allowed in the private court room, the diwan-i khas. The shish-mahal, a room decorated with chips of mirror, was reserved for receptions and ceremonies.

Somewhat like the Moghuls, the Rajputs built lavish palaces inside their fortresses. They, too, secluded the women in the zenana, apartments arrayed around inner courtyards, and played with Persian-style multifoil arches and floral motifs. Constructions were scattered with flat-roofed pavilions, always Moghul-style. Jharokha were built, sorts of balconies crowned with Bengali roofs hanging down on each side. The palaces were adorned with chhatri, little domed pavilions. Another indispensable feature: the Durbar Hall where the Rajput gathered his durbar, assembly of nobles.

The art of the mirror, also originally Persian, is a striking example of Indo-Muslim exchange. Almost all the fortresses dispersed throughout the mountains of Rajasthan have these tiny rooms whose ceilings are dotted with bits of mirror. It was a whole industry. Craftsmen developed workshops producing blown glass spheres lined with silver. The balls were broken and their many pieces inlaid with plaster in the ceilings. This kind of "mirror room" was called shish mahal. There, seated on rugs from Iran or Afghanistan, the Rajput kings celebrated great events such as weddings, births and victories. Some candles, a few oil lamps placed on the floor were all that was needed to create an enchanted atmosphere, the dots of light being reflected from the ceiling onto the walls as many times as there were curved balls. This enchanting decor was invented to remind the Rajputs of their nomadic origins, recreating the overwhelming starry skies they used to observe from their bivouacs.

Either Moghul or Rajput in style, the miniatures illustrate scenes of everyday life: hunting, courting, marriage… The peacock, the emblem of Rajasthan and of the Indian Union, appears frequently.

Assessment of the Colonial Period

In 1498 the Portuguese Vasco de Gama landed in Kerala and opened to Europe the route to India. Trade competition was launched. The Portuguese chose Goa as their capital; the English settled in Bombay (1534-1660), then in Calcutta (1690); the French and the Compagnie Française des Indes Orientales adopted Pondichéry (1674). In 1613 the emperor Jahanghir had already authorised the East India Company to found a trading post at Surat. The managers earned fortunes with Indian silver that flooded England. Unlike the other Europeans, the English did not seek to buy spices, calico or land. Instead they sought markets to sell their woollens and their manufactured items, thus stifling the prosperous Indian crafts. Locally the two civilisations remained quite separate. Yet a few positive points should be mentioned: a more highly organised lifestyle, the most developed railway network in all of Asia, roads crossing deserts and jungles, irrigation on a vast scale and the advantage of European medicine increasing life expectancy. A paradoxical story! It was the British education and the contact with European ideas that would spawn the most inflamed nationalists.

Often enhanced with wavy arabesques, accurate in the facial expressions, Moghul painting influenced the Schools of Jaipur, Bikaner, Bundi, Jodhpur and Alwar. The Mewar School (page 41), with its warring themes, is very typical. This early nineteenth-century miniature illustrates the handing over of the credentials of lieutenant-colonel James Tod, the famous topographer, to the maharajah Bhim Singh II (1778-1828) in the midst of his durbar (assembly) of nobles.

Toward Independence

The Moghul empire had become a mere shadow of itself after the death of Aurangzeb in 1707. His successors gave up their authority. Delhi was ransacked; the Rajput sovereigns could no longer resist the invasion of the Marathas from Central Asia and asked the British for help. Adroitly acknowledging the privileges of the maharajahs and signing defence treaties with them, by the middle of the nineteenth century the English had ended up ruling over the region, controlling all of Northern India from the Afghan border all the way to Burma.

The uprising known as the Sepoys began in 1857 during a distribution of cartridges to the Sepoys, a name given the native Indian troops of the British army. The cartridge cases were coated with grease and the soldiers had to open the wrappings with their teeth. The rumour spread that the grease was fat from pigs or cows, scandalising both Muslims and Hindus. The revolt did not last long. Some Europeans were massacred. Even Delhi was seized by the mutineers who sought to consolidate the Moghul empire. The mutiny was finally put down.

Queen Victoria became "Empress of the Indies" in 1877. The Empire of the Indies, the Raj, unified the territory that at the time comprised 550 princely states. In the meantime, a middle class arose in India and the demand for democracy increased. The Indian National Congress was founded in 1885. However, the maharajahs remained faithful to the British. A barrister, Mohandas Karamchand Gandhi, who would soon be a legendary figure better known as Mahatma, meaning "great soul", became the leader of the passive resistance, non-violent movement. The party of the Congress, under the control of Jawaharlal Nehru, officially demanded independence.

In 1947 the English announced their decision to withdraw permanently from the Indian sub-continent. Lord Mountbatten was the last viceroy of the Indies. The Congress voted for a secular nation. But the Muslim League demanded the creation of two states: India, with a Hindu majority and Pakistan, with a Muslim majority. On 15 August 1947 India and Pakistan were born. Ten million Hindus and Sikhs left Pakistan for India while eight million Muslims withdrew from India to populate Pakistan.

Photo taken on the occasion of the reunion of the Chamber of Princes in Delhi in 1924 (to the right of the Viceroy Owen, the maharajah of "Kasmir").
Below: Madhho Singh II (1880-1927), maharajah of Jaipur, was one of the most powerful Rajput princes.

Page 42:
The maharajah Ram Singh II (1835-1880) is responsible for the "old pink" colour of the city of Jaipur.

43

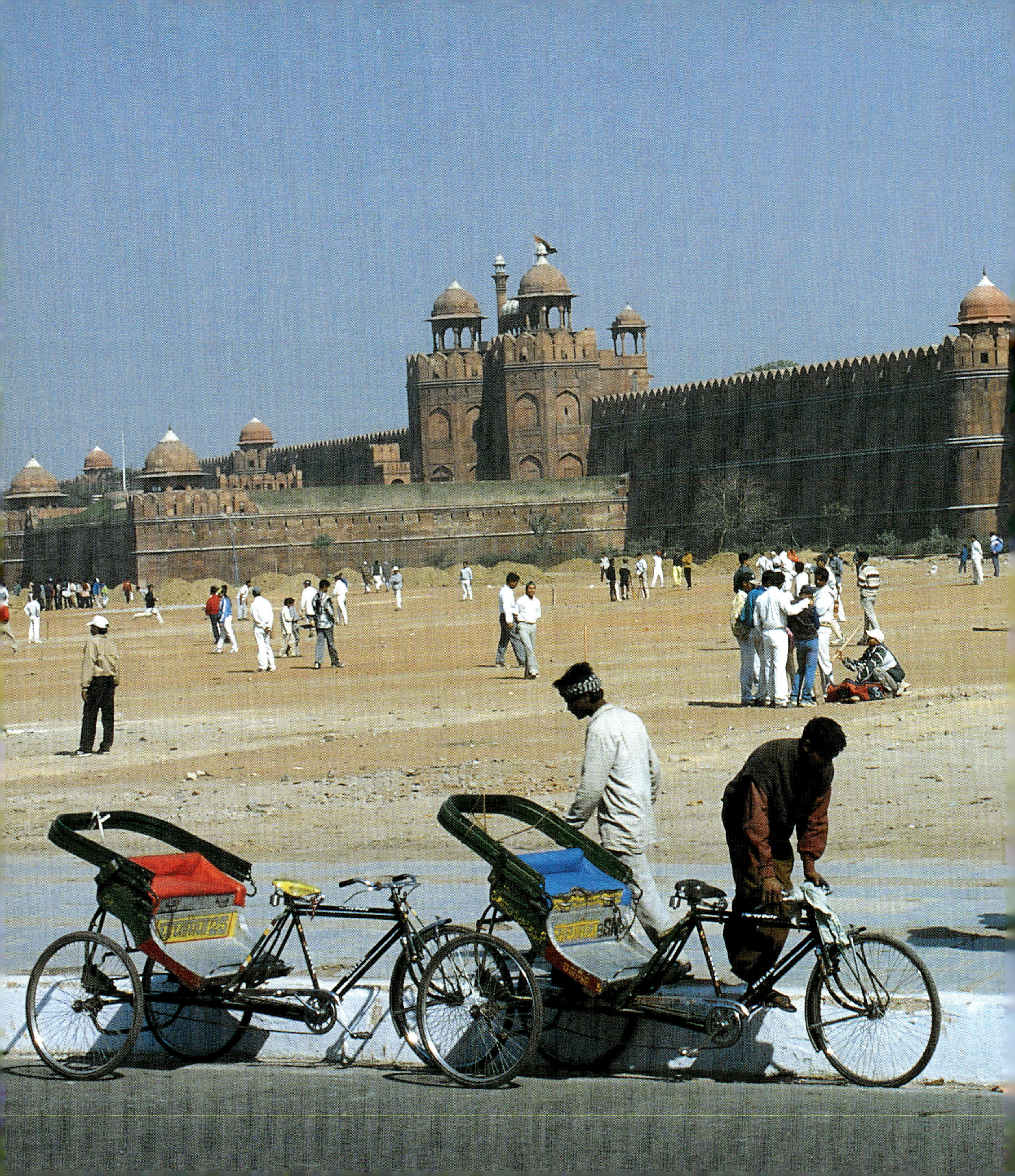

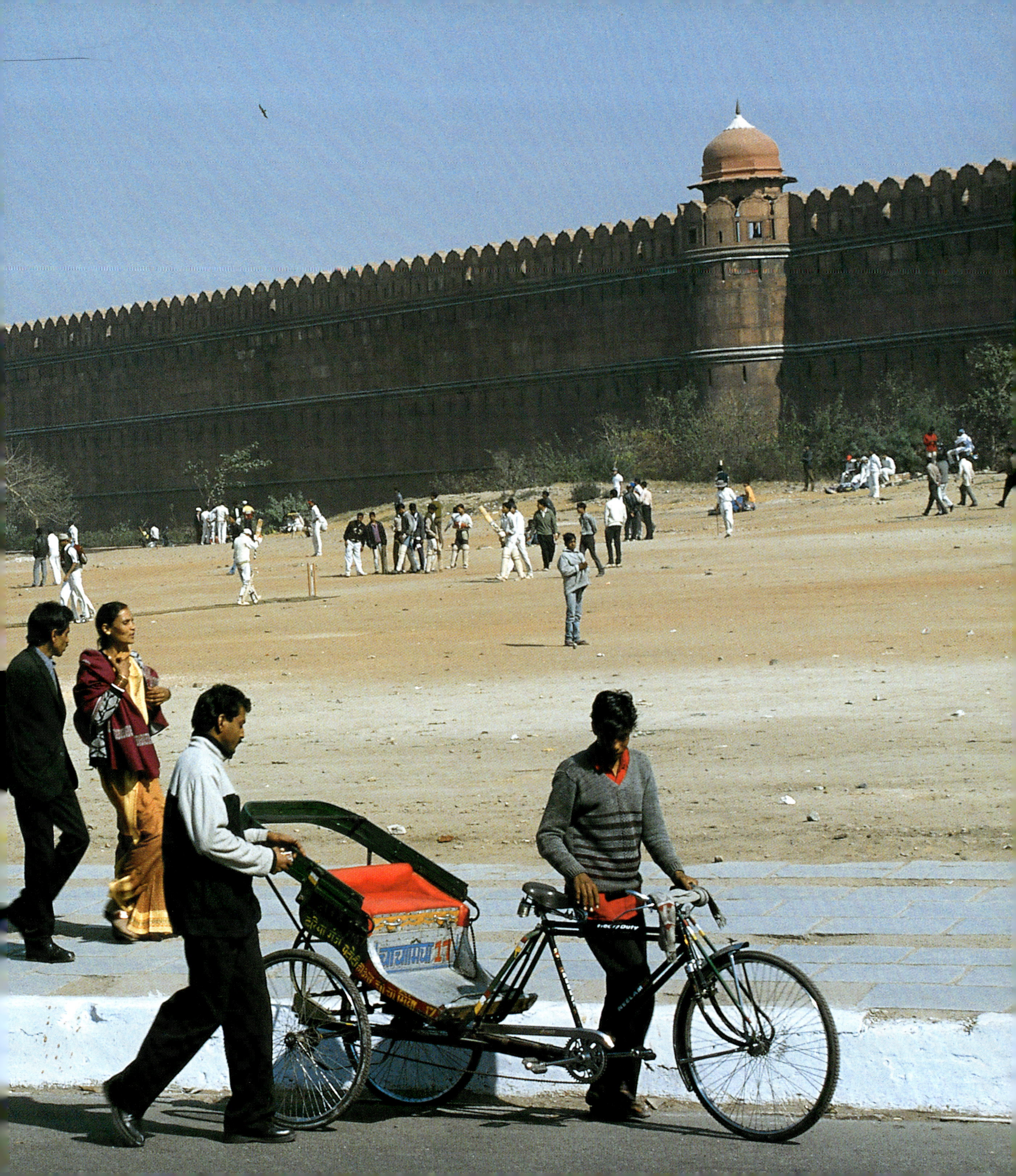

DELHI

No, New Delhi is not at all a museum-city stifled by the echoes of past splendour, even if, inaugurated in 1931, it came straight out of the portfolios of the British architect Sir Edwin Lutyens. Facing, the presidential palace, Rashtrapati Bhawan, completed in 1929.

Traffic jams are nightmarish, even on the wide Raj Path avenue leading to the presidential palace. The elephant is the most efficient means for making your way.

New Delhi

Every morning and every day the same ceremony takes place at the gates of the luxurious presidential palace, the Rashtrapati Bhawan. Through the sweet-smelling gardens filled with bougainvillea and jasmine, surrounded by the screeching of the green parrots, a white-gloved servant solemnly brings to the palace the two loveliest roses of the day, delicately resting on a silver tray. One of them will end the day in the buttonhole of the President of the Indian Union.

Completed in 1929 the Rashtrapati Bhawan, the presidential palace and its gardens, surrounded by ministries, the Parliament and parks crossed by wide avenues, offers a well-deserved pause after the turmoil of Old Delhi.

It was in 1911, on the occasion of the last great gathering of the Indian princes, that King George V solemnly proclaimed the transfer of government from Calcutta to Delhi. The architects Sir Edwin Luytens and Herbert Baker were engaged to design this new capital, "neither neo-Classic nor Moghul, simply imperial", inaugurated in 1931. They chose the site of Raisina Hill and designed wide avenues, of which King's Way (today Raj Path) was the main artery. Perched on the heights of the city, the new palace, enhanced with sublime neo-Moghul gardens, was the residence of the viceroy of the Indies. After the English left in 1947 it became the residence of the president of the Indian Republic.

Somewhat in disarray, the unconditional champions of "British style" settled down in the vintage lounges of the Hotel Imperial inaugurated in 1931 by Lord Willingdon himself. Sitting comfortably in the deep rattan armchairs on the veranda which used to be called the "Garden Party", it is time to relax and muse over the good old days of the Raj, while sipping "a very English afternoon high tea" under the delighted eye of the waiters in their impeccable red liveries.

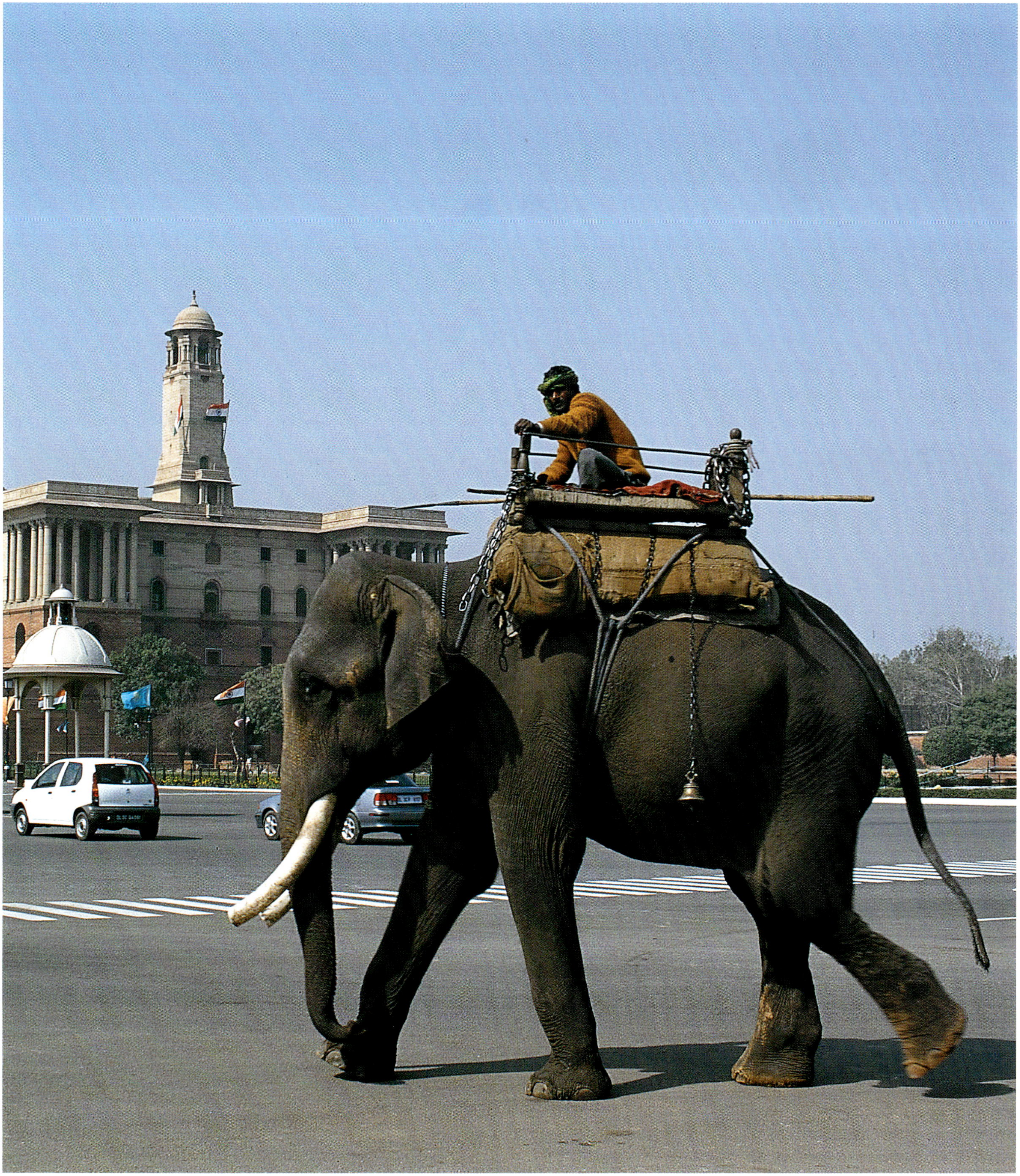

The City of Seven Cities

With a population of almost 7 million, Delhi is the third largest Indian metropolis after Mumbai (Bombay) and Calcutta. The capital of the Indian Union has the status of Union Territory. Located on the right bank of the sacred river Yamuna, a tributary of the Ganges, it appears to be turning its back on it. That is more than a symbol, since Delhi is not by tradition a Hindu city.

When we speak of the city of seven cities, it is to evoke the same number of capitals designed by the Turkish or Afghan invaders who followed one after another. Just where is the soul of this Janus-like two-headed city? Perhaps in the popular districts and the Chandri Chowk bazaar in the heart of effervescent Old Delhi. Indian history textbooks claim that potteries dating to at least 1000 B.C. were found in the bowels of the city, that the emperor Ashoka had an edict carved into the rock seven centuries later and that the Rajputs of the Tomar clan erected the fortress of Dilli toward the eighth century.

In 1192 the sultan Mohammed of Ghor and his troops hailing from Afghanistan seized Delhi from the Hindu king Prithviraja III. Feeling homesick, the conqueror left the city to his general Qutab ud-Din Aibak, a former Turkish slave who proclaimed himself sultan and built his capital in the complex of Qutab Minar. Delhi was Muslim. Two Turkish dynasties followed, that of the Khiljis and the Tughluqs who inaugurated four new Delhi cities. But in 1398 Tamerlane ransacked it. One of his Afghan lieutenants founded the Sayyid dynasty in the middle of the fifteenth century, followed by that of the Lodis (1550-1526) who ran things from Agra. But they did not measure up to Babur, descendent of Genghis Khan and of Tamerlane, who founded the dynasty of the Moghuls and occupied Agra. His son Humayun fell in love with Delhi instead. The next Moghuls, Akbar and Jahangir, governed from Agra and Lahore (today in Pakistan). The emperor Shah Jahan (1627-1658), the one who created the Taj Mahal, came back to Delhi and designed the ninth city, "Shahjehanabad", present-day "Old Delhi", embellishing it with emblematic edifices such as the Red Fort and the Juma Masjid mosque.

After the death of Aurangzeb, Delhi was successively destroyed by the Persian king Nadir Shah in 1739, the Afghan chief Ahmed Shah in 1756 and lastly by the Jat Rajah of Bharatpur in 1764. The English, who appeared in the peninsula, governed from Calcutta but detached a Resident to run the capital alongside a Moghul emperor who was a mere onlooker. But the Indians became angry. When the uprising of the Sepoys broke out in 1857 and the emperor Bahadur Shah II took sides with the insurgents, the British seized the opportunity to evince the emperor, deporting him to Burma. In 1911 King George V proudly announced the construction of the tenth Delhi. Designed by Sir Edwin Luytens and Herbert Baker, New Delhi arose in 1918 and was inaugurated in 1931.

When Independence was proclaimed and Pakistan was formed, thousands of Muslims left the capital to go to Lahore, while the Sikhs and the Hindus fled Pakistani Punjab. Delhi almost became a Punjab city. Since 1956 the city has the status of Territory of the Union.

Astonishing, because so incongruous in the midst of the buildings of New Delhi, the astronomical observatory Jantar Mantar, designed in the eighteenth century by the maharajah who founded Jaipur, Jai Singh II.

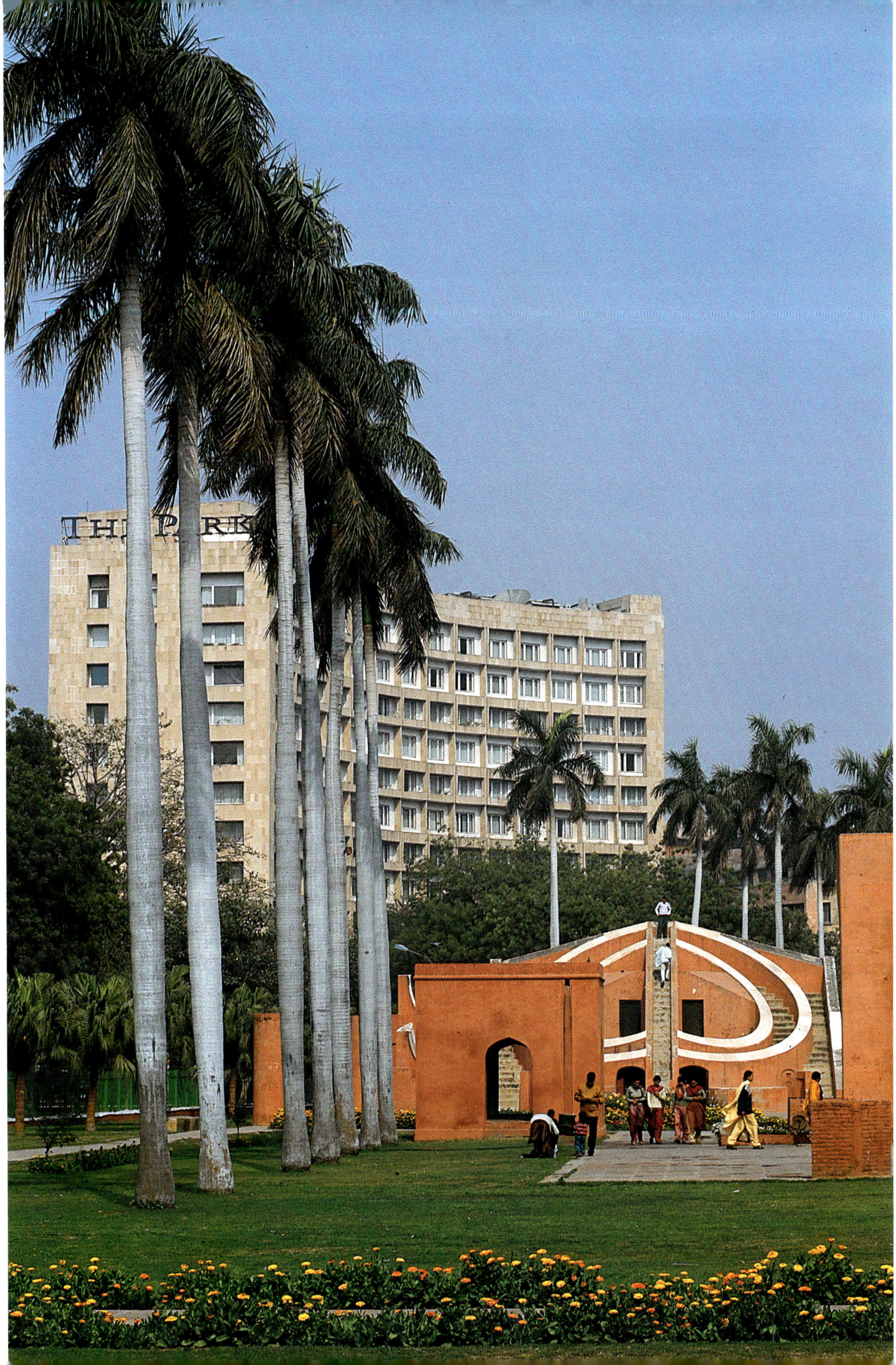

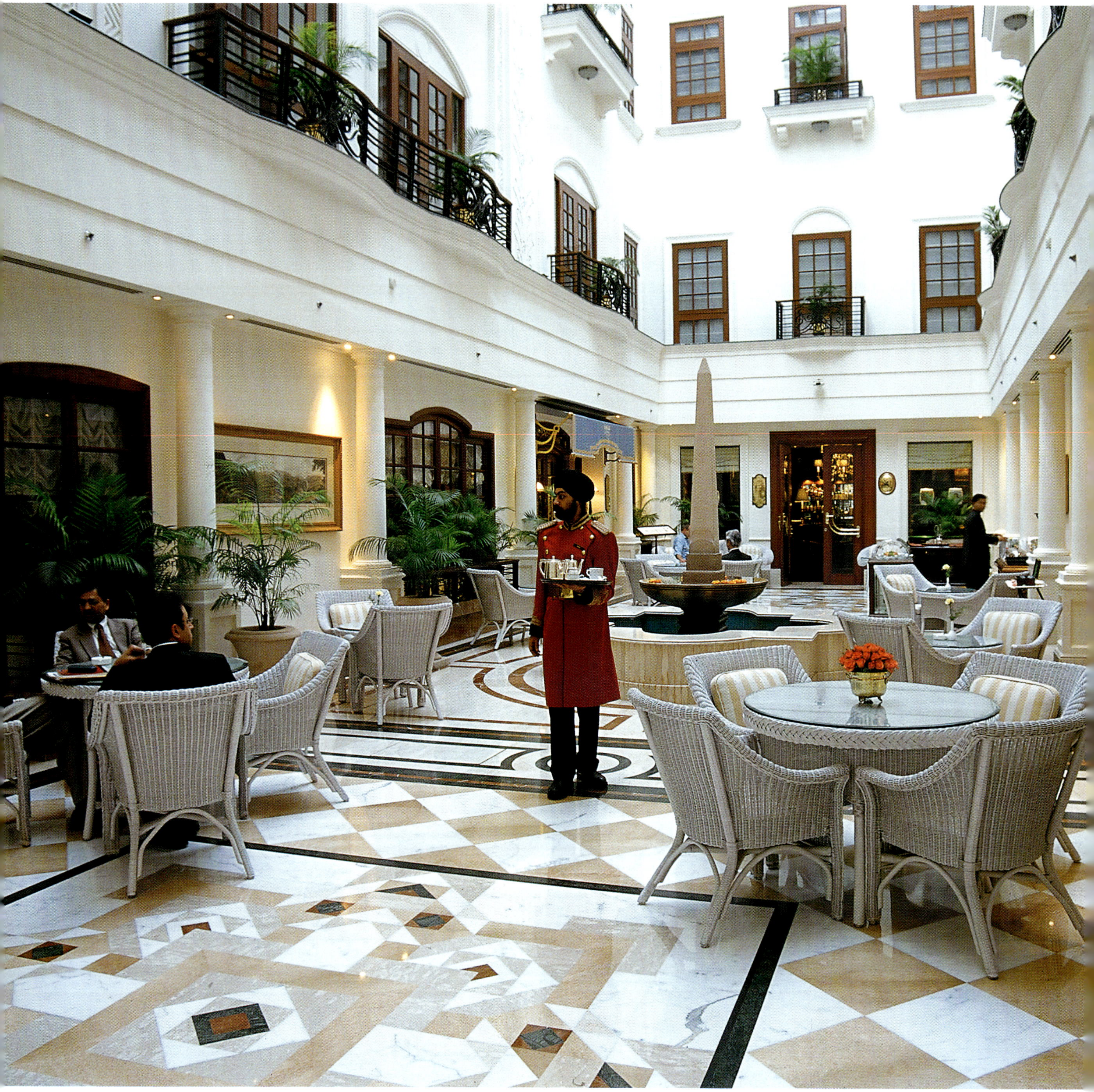

The post-modern home of the Poddar family. Mrs Lekha Poddar, her husband Ranjan and their children live in the fashionable district of Rajokri, in the suburbs of Delhi. To build the house of their ultra-modern dreams, they gave an opportunity to a pair of young, highly talented architects: Inni Chatterjee and the decorator Samir Wheaton. A sort of wavy flying roof made of wood and copper rests on concrete pillars. Polished wood floors, granite pavements, cement and teak ceilings. Light flows everywhere. The first floor is laid out around a glass sculpture by the American Danny Lane. The furniture reflects what caught Lekka's eye (her signature is on the minimalist decoration of the Devi Garh Palace Hotel, near Udaipur) during her travels: rattan armchairs from London, articles in teak from Assam and Kerala, jars from Burma…

Page 50: The comfortable lounges of "The Imperial" hotel, a sublime relic of the colonial era. To get your fill of nostalgia.

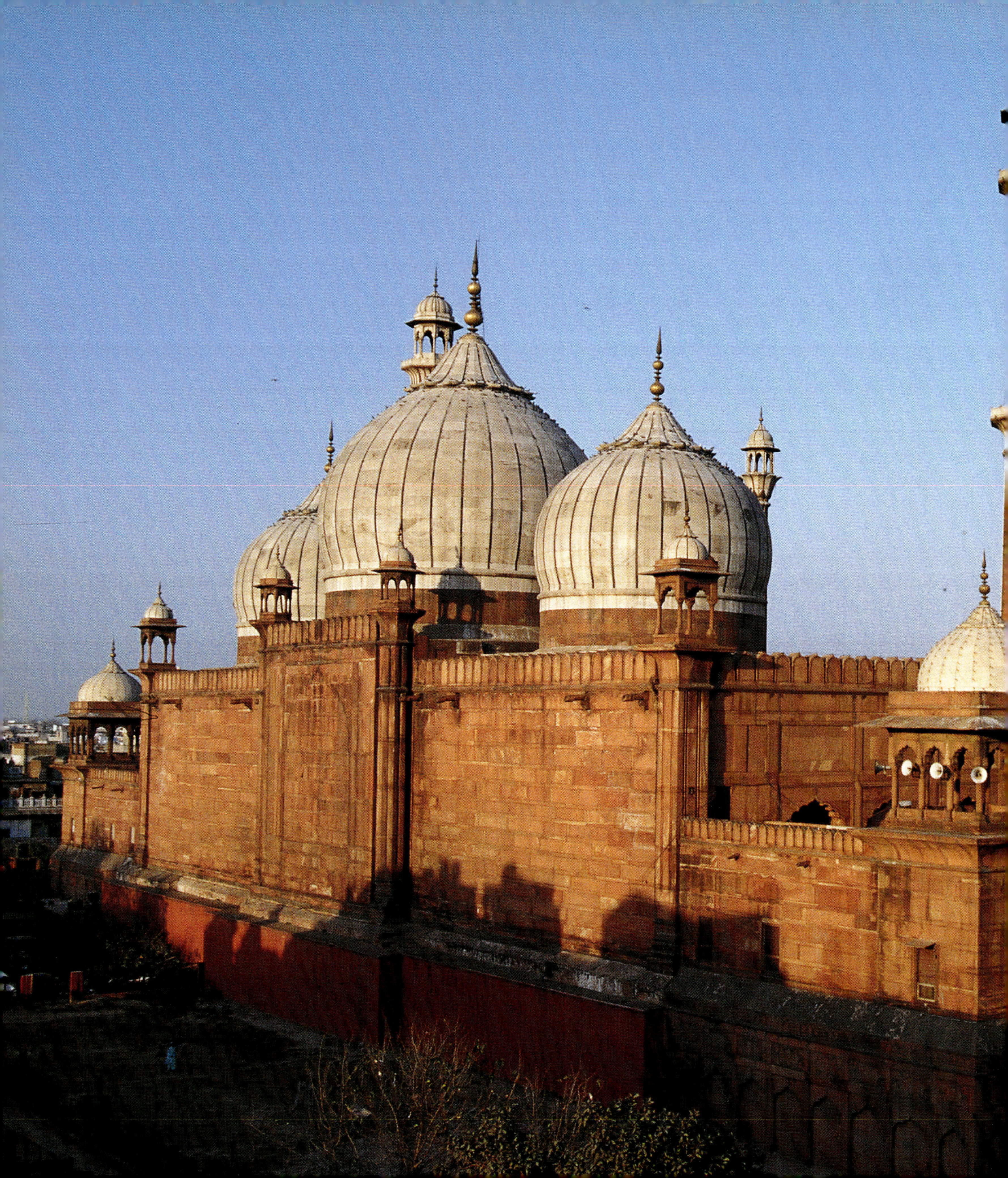

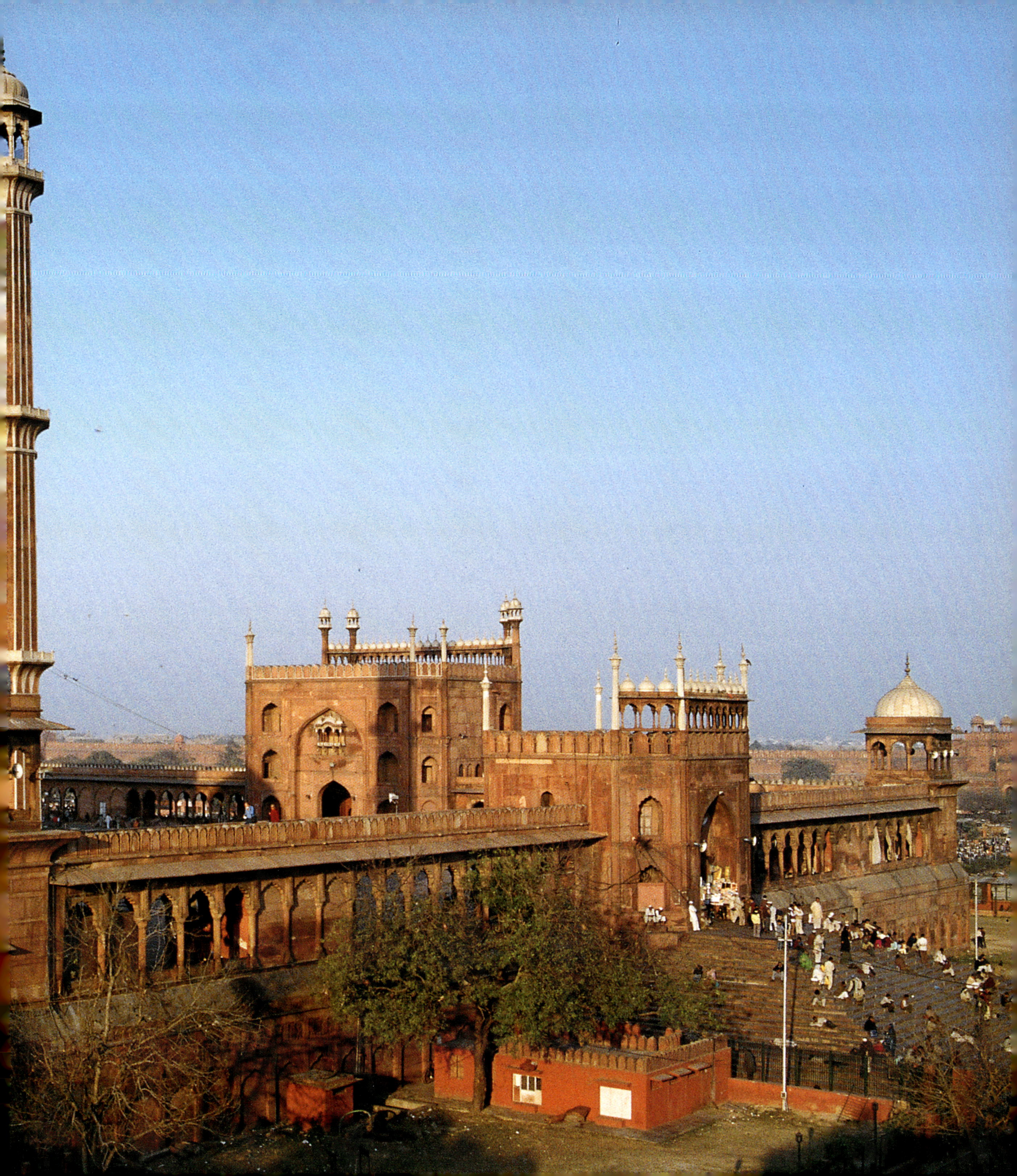

Preceding double page, facing and next double page: Completed in 1658, the Juma Masjid mosque in Delhi is the largest in India. The last great mosque to be built by the Moghul emperors, a symphony of red sandstone and white marble, every Friday it welcomes 30.000 faithful assembled for the great prayer.

Old Delhi

To capture the mood of this very old capital founded in the seventeenth century by Shah Jahan, the thing to do is take a stroll on a Friday morning, the great prayer day, around the Juma Masjid, the largest mosque in India, built in the mid-seventeenth century. In the narrow surrounding streets, you have to make your way in the midst of a thick, colourful crowd continually passing in front of the displays of the shopkeepers of the Meena Bazaar. People are calling, meeting, and inviting one another. The hotels are full up with pilgrims. Sitting cross-legged at the entrance, restaurant owners extend their welcoming smile to the foreign passer-by and offer delicious tea with milk. Gradually the biggest mosque in India will be thronged with its 30.000 faithful, who first climb the steps of the impressive stairway, going under the high gate enhanced with a stunning iwan (vaulted space). At the centre of a large courtyard there is a pool for ablutions. People ready themselves, purify themselves, and greet one another.

The dimensions of this last huge Moghul mosque are very imposing, with its main facade framed with two minarets and crowned with three huge white onion-shaped Moorish domes. Surrounded by elegant arcades with three gates, the faithful take their places. Adorned with a multifoil arch, the central gate (pishtaq) opens onto the prayer room where the imam prepares his homily. Taking a narrow inner stairway, you reach the top of the south minaret offering a magnificent view of Old Delhi and the Red Fort opposite it which looks like it is standing guard. The great Friday prayer can begin.

55

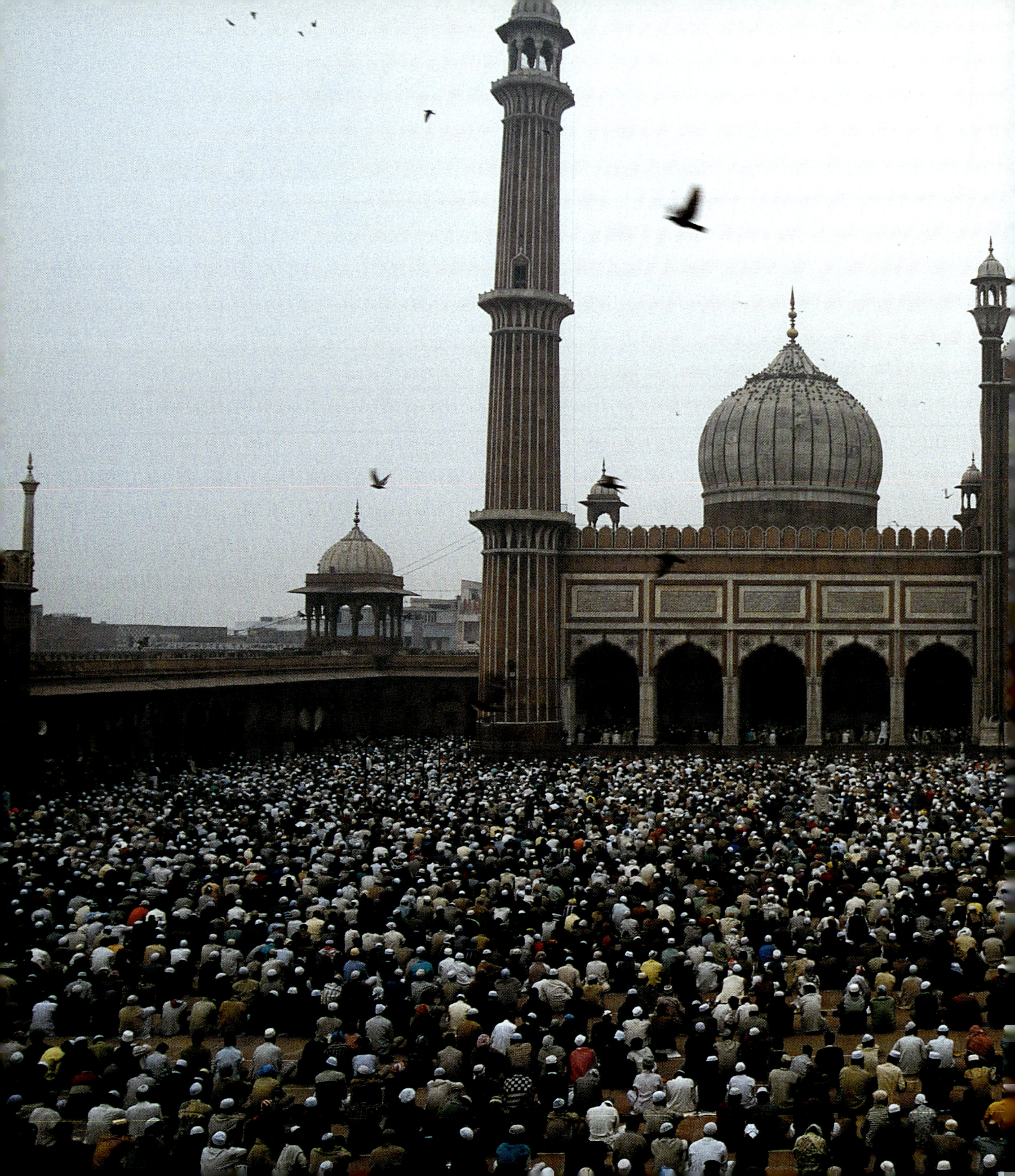

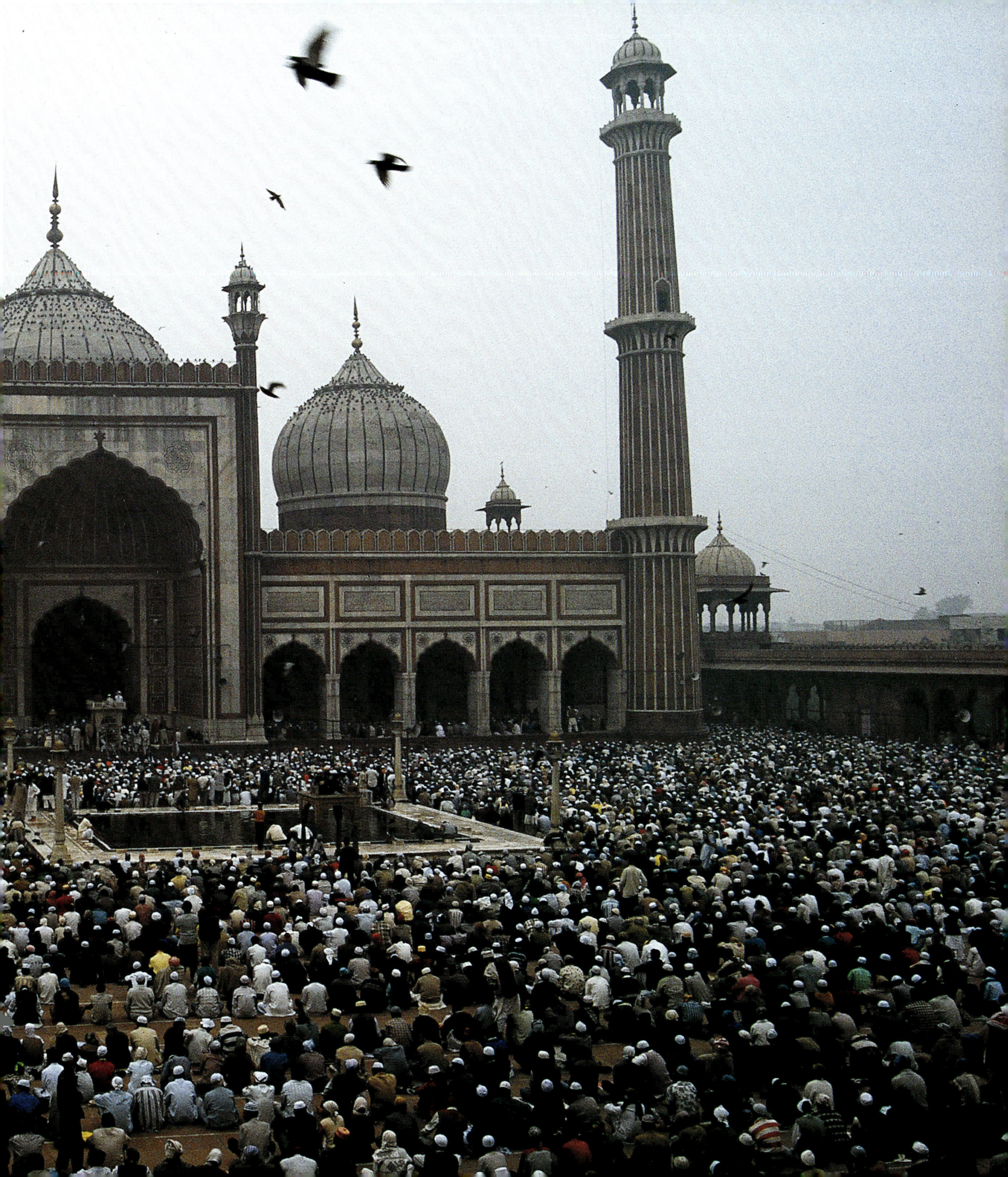

The Red Fort

The ample esplanade, which is the setting for the Red Fort, has now become the favourite playground for young Indians practicing polo right below the over two kilometres-long red sandstone ramparts. This impressive ensemble was designed by the emperor Shah Jahan who left Agra for Delhi in 1638. To build it he razed a fortress erected in the eleventh century by the Rajputs.

The Lahore Gate is the entrance to this "forbidden city" which contained residences, the government palace and official buildings. A long lane leads to the diwan-i am (hall for public audiences) where the emperor cut a brilliant figure receiving his guests, seated majestically on his marble throne crowned with inlaid semi-precious stones. Laid out in Persian style and enhanced with canals and pavilions, the gardens called Hayat Baksh Bagh (life-giving gardens) invite the visitor to a sweet reverie on the theme of the lavishness of the empire, between the Rang Mahal, the palace reserved for the emperor's first wife, and the Khas Mahal, the palace carved with jali (fretted screens) where the emperor lived. Every morning he appeared on his balcony like "the shadow of God over the world" before going to the white marble-walled diwan-i khas (hall for private audiences) and to the hammams.

Behind the austere red sandstone ramparts of the Fort of Delhi (above), the Court of the Moghul emperors was lavish and rich as shown in the delicate pavilion of the fountain (page 59) named Shah Burj (1725) that provided water to the palace.

59

The Qutab Minar

Erected in Delhi in 1192, the minaret-tower of the Qutab Minar symbolises the overwhelming victory of Islam. 73 m high, featuring five sections separated by extremely elegant stalactite galleries, it was used as a minaret for the first Indian mosque named Quwwat ul-Islam (Might of Islam).

All the schoolchildren in Delhi are familiar with the interminable Qutab Minar minaret their teachers call "the tallest building in all of India". It is the Eiffel Tower in Paris, the Pyramid of Cheops in Gizeh. Historically it represents the victory of Mohammed of Ghor over the Hindu king Prithviraja III in 1192. Symbolically it is the stunning victory of Islam. It is named after Qutab ud-Din Aibak, general in chief of the victorious armies. To reward this valiant warrior, he was given the title of governor and proclaimed himself sultan of Delhi. This former Turkish slave took the opportunity to found his capital on the site of the Qutab Minar and the "dynasty of slaves".

Seventy-three metres high, the Qutab Minar consists of five superimposed layers, separated by stalactites (muqarna). Bands of Cufic writing run around the building. Next to it the cubic construction of the Ala-ì Darwaza displays exquisite Koranic inscriptions carved by highly talented Hindu artists.

After the Qutab Minar, the schoolchildren, who are out for a good time, holding hands, cross a courtyard with strangely carved columns… "This is the oldest mosque in India", their teachers repeat. And they are not mistaken. This mosque named Quwwat ul-Islam (Strength of Islam) was started in 1193. Columns taken from seventeen Hindu and Jain temples were brought to hold up the edifice. We easily recognise the cube-shaped columns of the eighth-century Hindu style. In the middle of the courtyard stands an iron stake, a singular testimony of the Hindu period, that supposedly was dedicated to Vishnu in the fourth century.

The wall surrounding the Qutab Minar contains other handsome relics of the Muslim era, such as the ruins of the tomb of Ala ud-Din Khilji, who was sultan in the early fourteenth century, or those of a Koranic school rather typical of the Seljuk period (Turkish origins of the first Muslim conquerors of India). To complete your visit of the famous Qutab Minar, go by the tomb of Illtutmish, successor of Qutab ud-Din. Raised in 1236 it displays a richly carved decoration. Linger on and let your gaze wander over this extravagant work. Hindu sculptors could not bear an empty space!

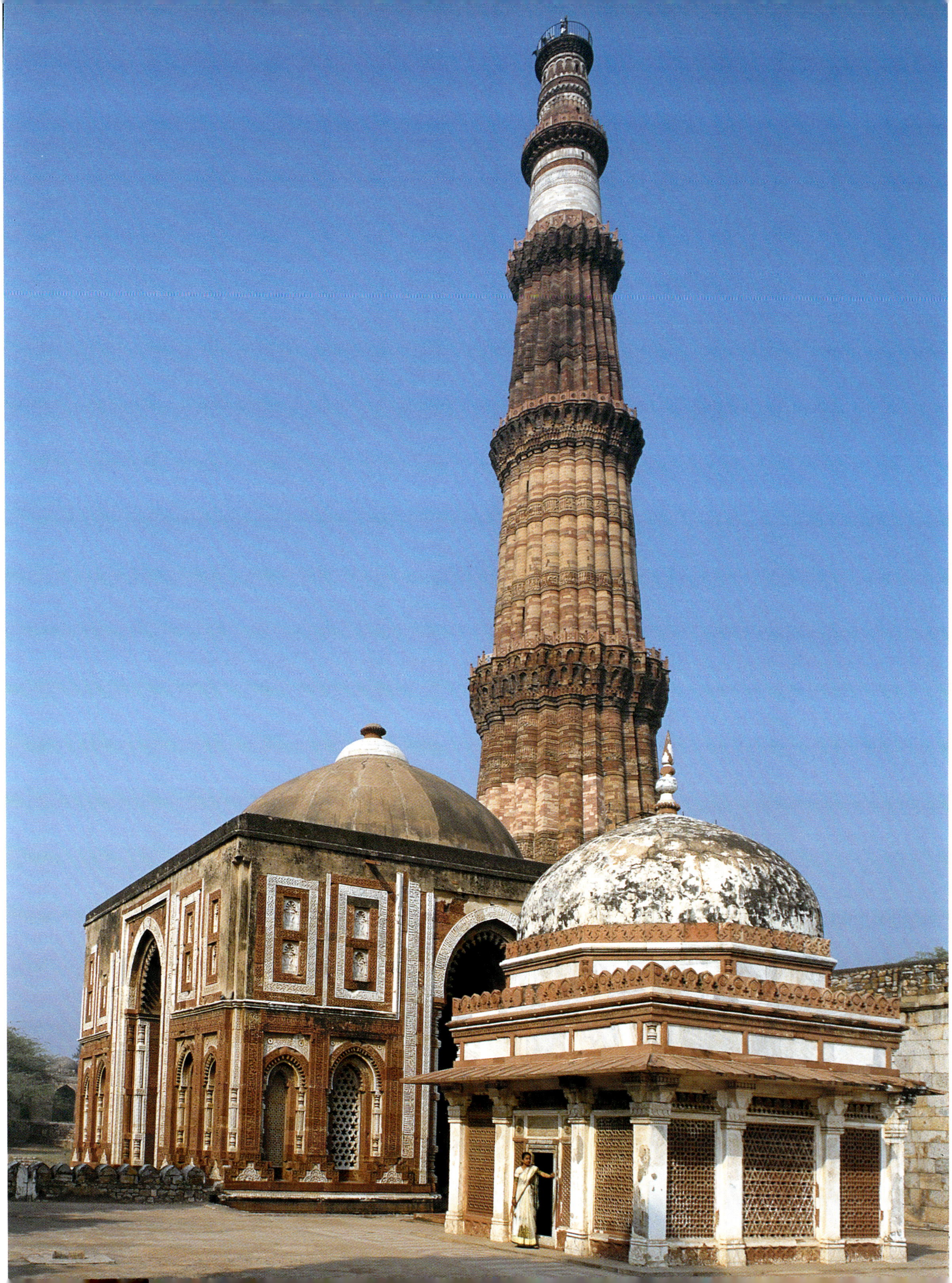

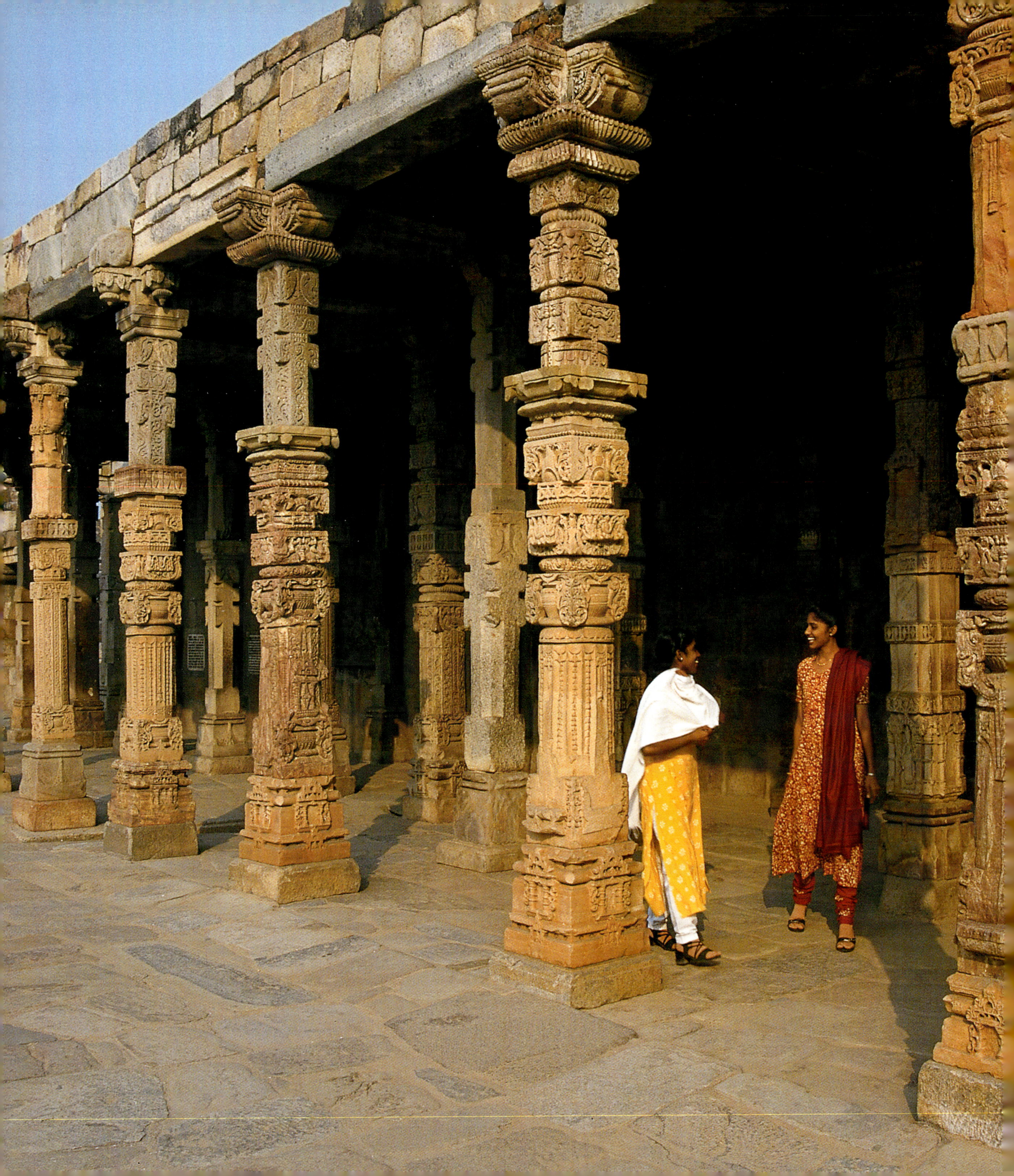

The pillars of the mosque were taken from Hindu and Jain temples (page 62). The delicacy of the stonework of the buildings of the Qutab Minar, with its decor of geometric motifs, floral arabesques and Koranic inscriptions covering the arcades, expresses the genius of the Indian sculptors of the period.

Banishing the Moghul emperor Humayun, an Afghan chief, Sher Shah, proclaimed himself sovereign of Northern India in 1540 and had a new citadel built, Purana Qila, in Delhi.

The Old Fort, Purana Qila

The best time to discover the Old Fort, the Purana Qila, is in the early morning mist. The place is so peaceful, filled with gardens inhabited by squirrels and planted on a hill where the legendary Indraprashta mentioned in the Mahabharata, the first Delhi, used to lie. You enter through one of the four doors opened in the wall. At the beginning of his reign, after succeeding his father Babur in 1530, the Moghul emperor Humayun had this fort built, naming it Dinpanah, "refuge of faith". In 1540 the Afghan chief Sher Shah Sur evinced the Moghul and took over the site. Shining golden in the sunlight, the Sher Shah mosque is extremely elegant. Experts will recognise a transition monument between the Hindu style and the Persian influence. The central arch of the façade, with its epigraphical bands, forms a pishtaq, a sort of monumental gate. The interior mosaic decorations are exquisite. A few steps from there, overlooking the low hill of the Old Fort, a tower perforated with niches and topped with chhatri is known as Sher Mandal. It recalls Humayun's tragic death. After spending fifteen years in exile, the Moghul emperor recovered his empire and returned to Delhi. To meditate on the inconsistency of power, he was fond of retiring to this tower, which he also used as a library and where he met his death from a fall in the stairway. What a tragic fate!

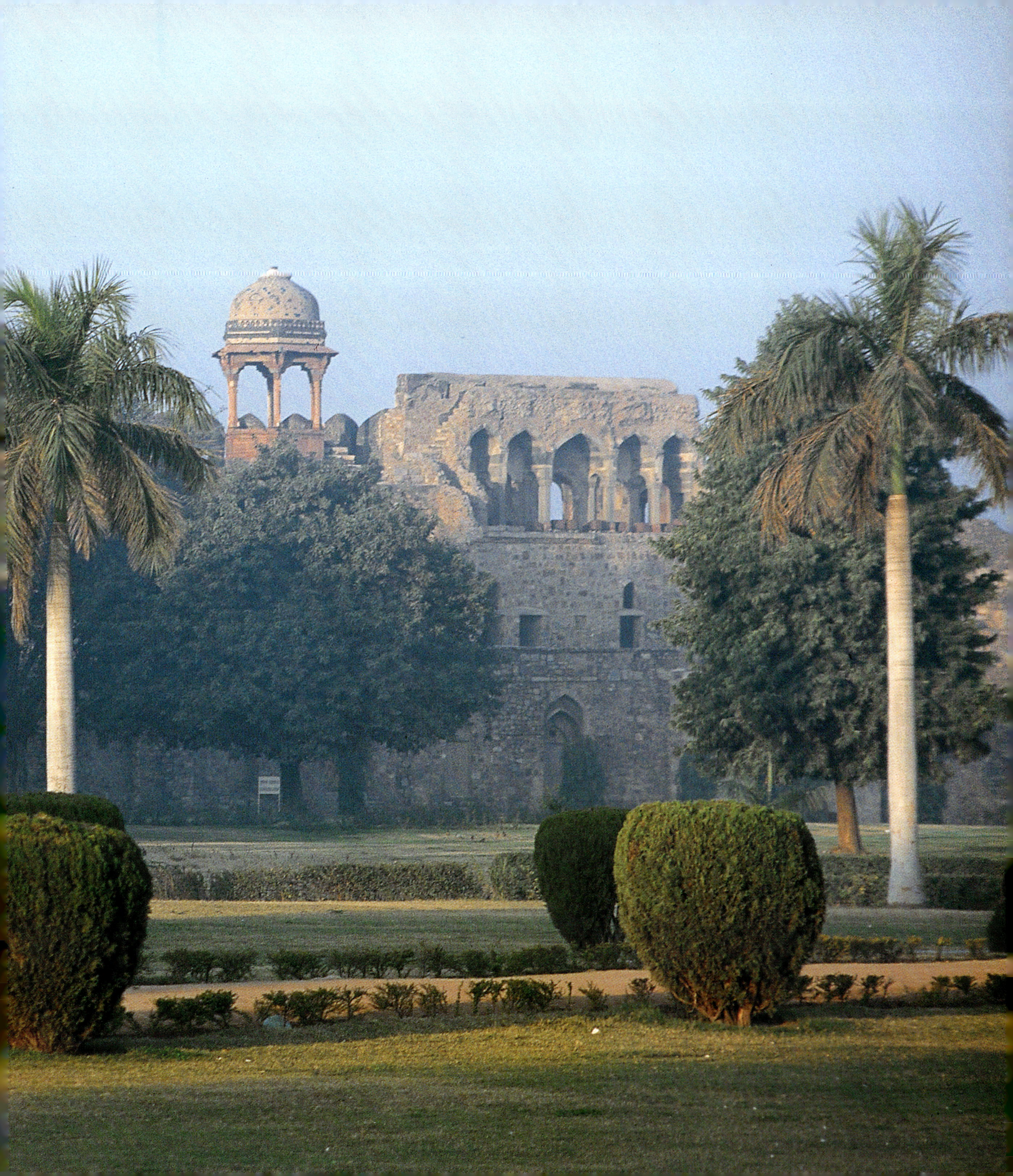

66

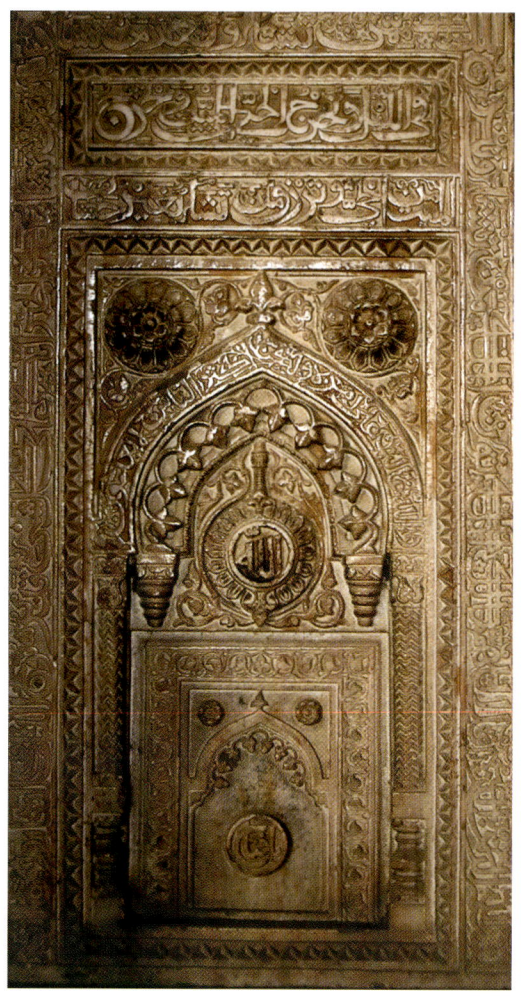

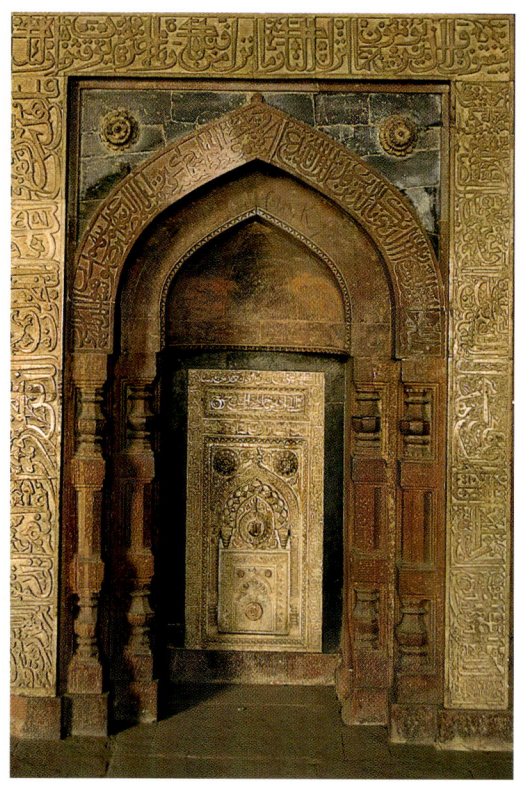

This elegant mosque, Qila-i-Kuhna (Mosque of Sher Shah), built in 1541 inside the Old Fort (Purana Qila) of Delhi, features five arches on a courtyard with remarkable epigraphic strips that stand out around the central balcony of the main arch. Details of the decor of mosaics and polychrome earthenware tiles of the mosque.

Red sandstone, white marble Moorish dome, impression of lightness, beauty of forms and materials: the mausoleum of Humayun is the first great Moghul masterpiece, built between 1557 and 1565.

*Page 69:
Not far from the mausoleum, pilgrims purchase rose and jasmine petals to strew them over the dargah of Hazrat Nizam ud-Din, a Muslim saint.*

The Mausoleum of Humayun

And what if this mausoleum were the most beautiful monument in Delhi? Anyone weary of the bustle of the capital (we can easily see why) will appreciate this quiet isle. Humayun can rest in peace. Exiled for years to the Persian court, the Moghul emperor recovered his empire in 1555. He brought Persian artisans back with him. When he died, his widow commissioned the erection of a mausoleum from the Persian architect Mirak Mirza Ghiyas who aspired to be a forerunner in India: Moghul gardens, red sandstone and white marble, double shell domes… An authentic revolution!

Surrounded by a remarkable garden, the mausoleum appears at the end of a long tree-lined path. The dimensions are very pleasing to the eye, the materials utilised – a masterly combination of red sandstone and white marble – give the edifice an impression of both lightness and strength. The tomb is set on a raised platform, a central iwan (vaulted space) graces each facade, four chhatri (domed umbrella-shaped cenotaphs) surround the dome. It again has Tudor arches and iwan niches. This tomb became a model for all the Indo-Muslim mausoleums to come, concerned about the Persian style.

KAMRAN TRAVEL
DARGAH HAZRAT NIZAMUDDIN
NEW DELHI - 110013
RES. 4626434 OFF. 4631691

When the early morning mist offers a glimpse of the majestic silhouette of the mausoleum of Safdar Jang, the vision is striking and serenity all-encompassing. The last Moghul masterpiece, built in 1754 almost a hundred years after the Taj Mahal, it rises in the midst of typical gardens, divided into four parts by canals. A square podium, corner towers with chhatri, white marble decorations.

Following the "Lodi Road"

*I*n the midst of sloping gardens (the Lodi Gardens) that run along Lodi Road, Indo-Muslim architecture between the fifteenth and the eighteenth centuries is spelled out in the various mausoleums, resting-places of several important figures. Raised in 1754 the one of Safdar Jang was used as a last refuge for one of the emperor's Prime Ministers. Placed in the middle of a Moghul walled garden divided into four parts by canals, the mausoleum, rising on a podium, is decorated with gorgeous stucco stalactite ceilings. A bit further on, we easily recognise the tomb of the sultan Mohammed Shah (1450) by its octagonal shape, its central room with eight sides, a spherical dome and eight typically Hindu chhatri. Other tombs invite us to meditation, like the Bara Gumbad (1494) with its characteristic window-recesses, the Shish Gumbad and the octagonal tomb of the sultan Sikander Lodi (1517).

*Next double page:
One of the three domes of the Great Mosque of Agra completed in 1648.*

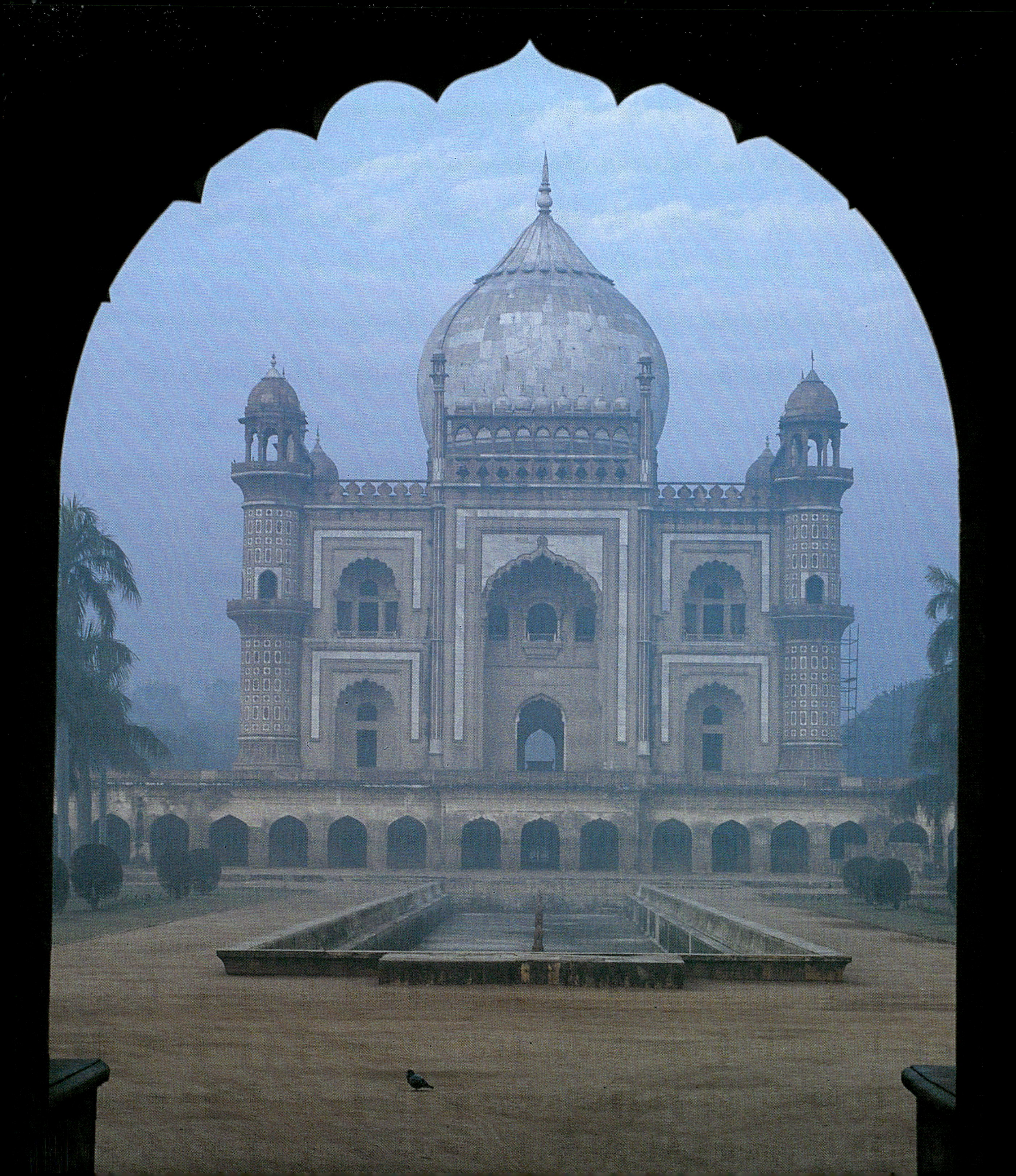

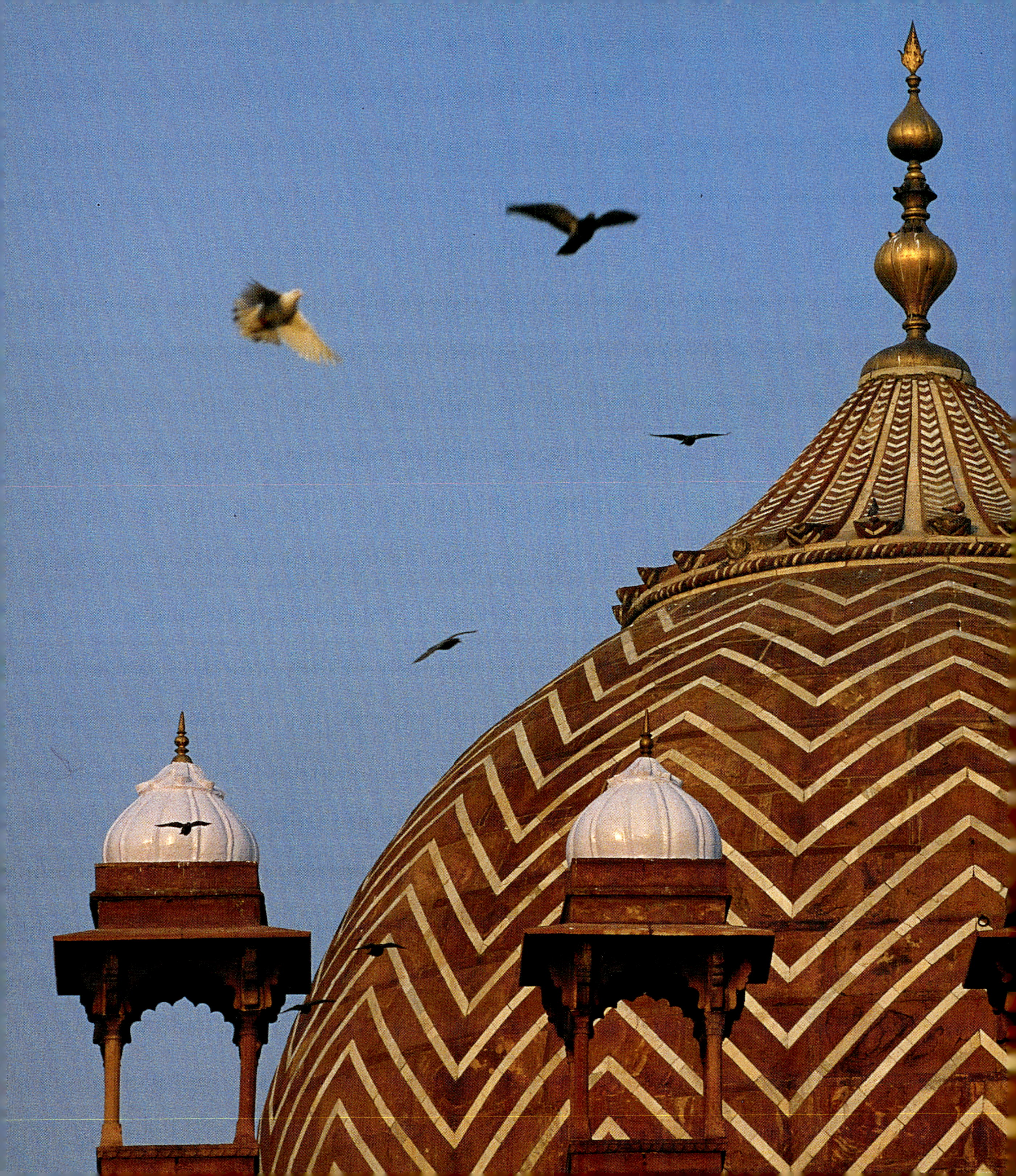

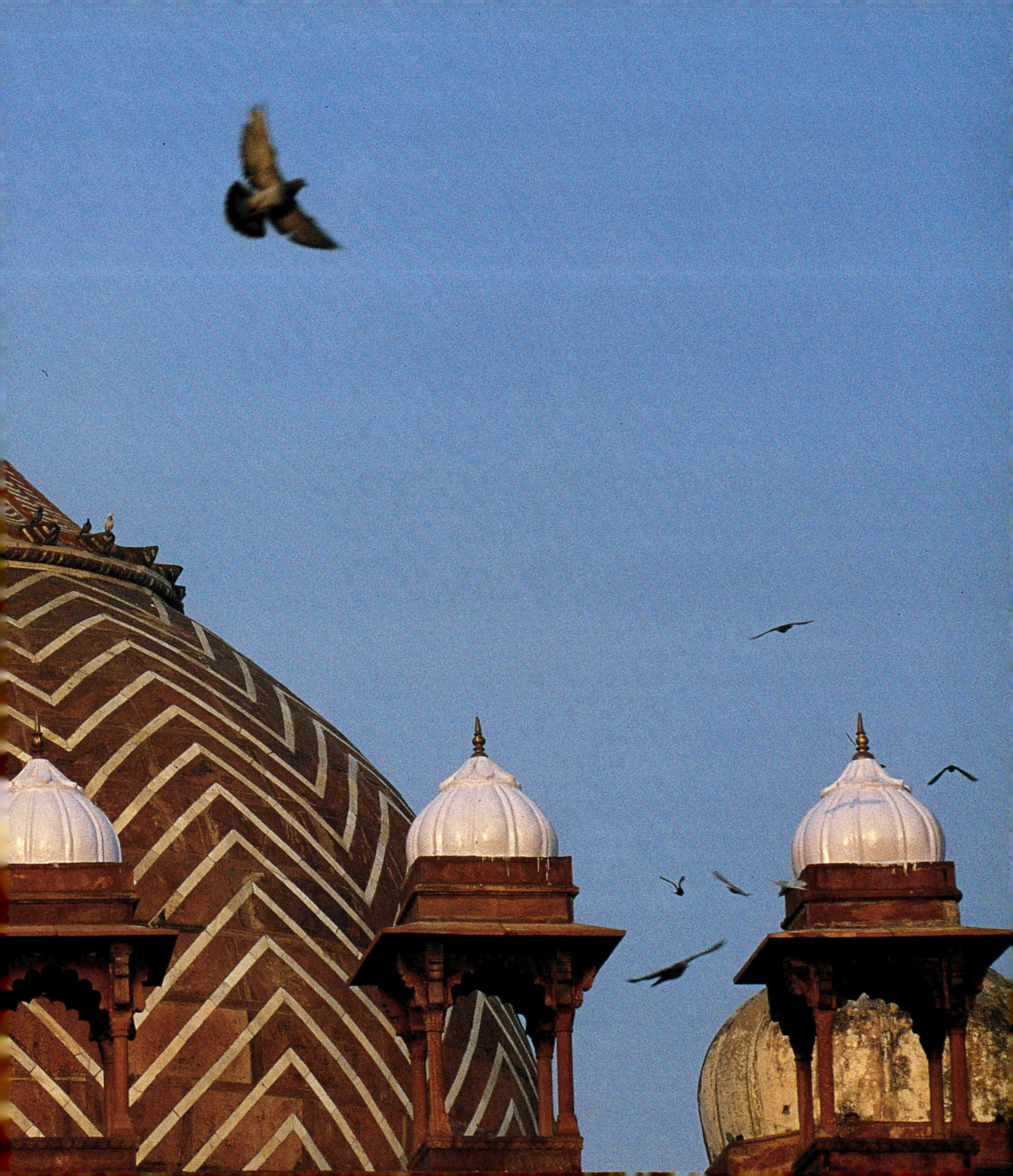

AGRA

Mohammed K.K. is a happy man, almost overwhelmingly so. This Muslim, an archaeologist with a passion for architecture, bears the envied title of Superintendent of the Archaeological Survey of India for Agra. From his offices, in the former colonial quarter consisting of low houses with verandas, he ensures the protection of the Taj Mahal. Like a ritual, every morning he rediscovers "his Taj" during the inspection visit hours before the tourists. And he never wearies of it. "In 2001 the chemical industries began leaving the area to preserve the mausoleum, which is cleaned every six or seven years with natural products", Mohammed K.K. explains. Proud and knowledgeable, he adds: "Although the Taj Mahal is the most visited monument in the world, it does not represent a revolution. A better word would be an achievement, a synthesis. Here we can recognise the minarets of Sikandra, the wonderful pietra dura craftsmanship of the mausoleum dedicated to the Itimad ud-Daula and the dome of the mausoleum of Humayun in Delhi."

Although the city grew up in a disorderly fashion, encroaching upon the Taj Mahal with cheap hotels and souvenir shops, it displays several wonders of Moghul art in the curve of the river. The enchanting mausoleum of the Itimad ud-Daula, the glorious mausoleum of Akbar at Sikandra; the Taj Mahal commissioned by the emperor Shah Jahan and the Red Fort where Akbar's Court, that of his son Jahangir and of his grandson Shah Jahan lavishly followed one after another.

Behind the tall red sandstone portals, beautifully inlaid with white marble, the Taj Mahal appears very lightweight despite its dimensions: the onion-shaped dome supported on a drum peaks at 72 m. It is said that sketches of its gardens and pools, drawn in 1632, brought back to Europe by travellers, might have been used for the designs of the parks and gardens of Versailles.

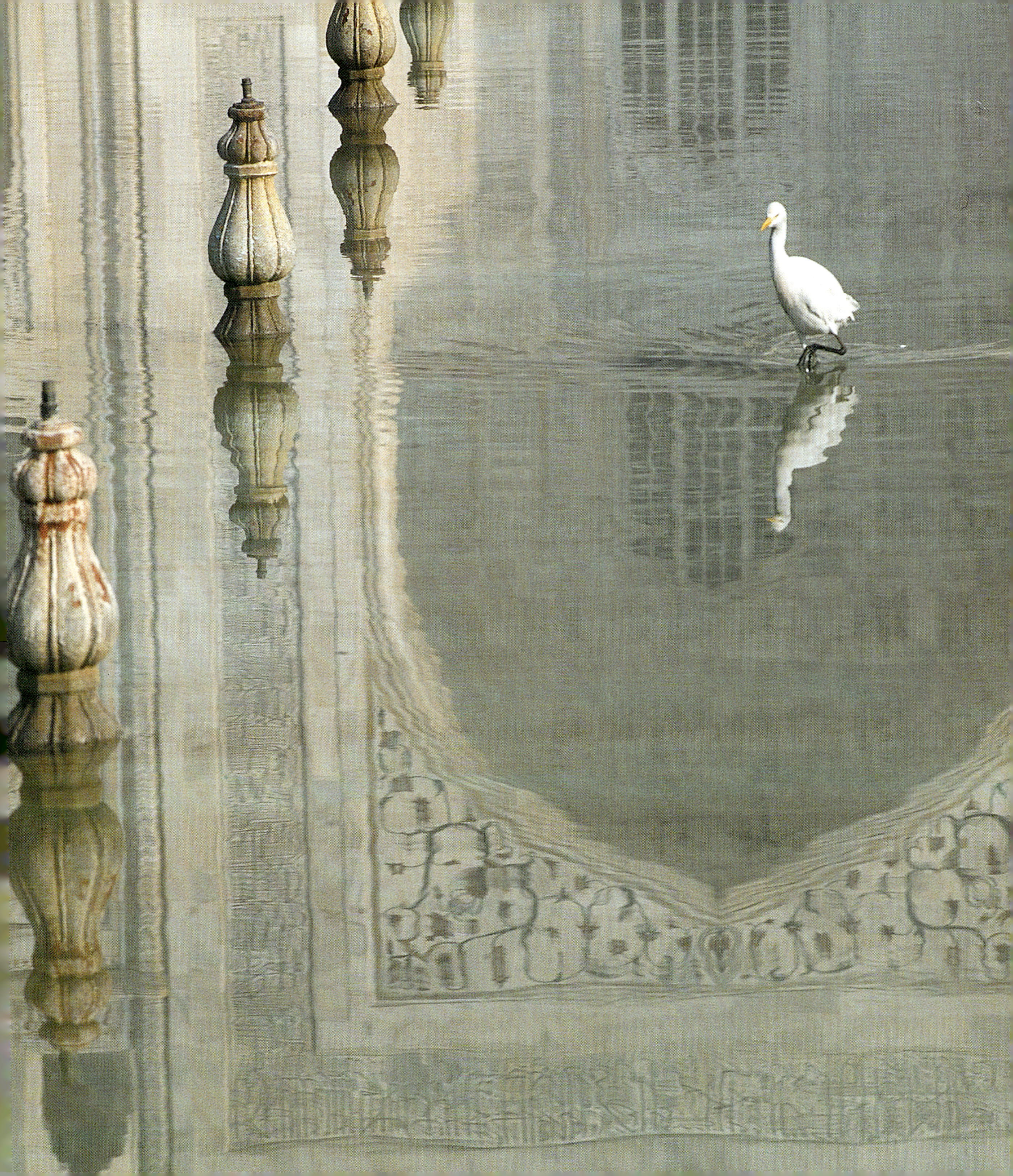

The Mausoleum of the Itimad ud-Daula

Lovers like to meet in the romantic Moghul gardens surrounding the mausoleum of the Itimad ud-Daula. Rising above the morning mists, this architectural jewel quietly emerging amidst palm trees is appropriate for all kinds of vows and promises. To resist its charm is simply out the question. Some purists (and many visitors) claim it is the most refined building in all of Northern India.

The work of a woman to the memory of her father… While the Moghul emperor Jahangir was engrossed in poetry and opium, his hard-working wife Nour Mahal ran the empire with her father Mirza Ghiyas Beg. Treasurer and grand vizier of the emperor, he was allowed to bear the title Itimad ud-Daula, meaning "Pillar of the Empire". At his death in 1628 (four years before the Taj Mahal was inaugurated), his daughter had a mausoleum built for him in Persian style, with perfect dimensions: a square plan bordered by four low minarets. Chronicles of the period reveal that Jahangir doubtlessly paid for its construction to be forgiven for having Nour Mahal's first husband assassinated. In the middle of a square garden inspired by charbagh Persian gardens, the mausoleum looks as though it had been designed as a home, perhaps the very one where the grand vizier lived, with nine small rooms on the ground floor. Inside niches carved in the walls we discover motifs recalling some of the delights of the promised paradise: cypress trees, pomegranates, bottles of perfume… But its great originality is its amazing inlaid marble facades, an extravagant revelry of delicate precious stones inlaid in the pietra dura technique and admirable file work creating geometric motifs in arabesques performed by the greatest Indian stone carvers of the time.

A forerunner of the Taj Mahal, the mausoleum of the Itimad ud-Daula is a small jewel, or better said, a jewel case. Its dimensions are indeed modest (Ghiyas Beg was just grand vizier of the emperor Jahanghir, and was granted the title of "Pillar of the State", Itimad ud-Daula). Its architecture: a square terrace in the middle of a garden, square as well, Persian style; low minarets topped by chhatri, framing a central pavilion. Its decoration: a real festival! Since the facades of the mausoleum are entirely covered with marble inlaid with colourful precious stones using the pietra dura technique.

*Next double page:
As soon as you enter the splendid red sandstone gate, inlaid with white marble, you can see the mausoleum. But you must draw nearer to appreciate the multicoloured puzzle adorning the funerary monument: geometric motifs matching the most elaborate Persian rugs, inlays forming long-necked bottles to contain an elixir of immortality, cypresses and pomegranate trees, bouquets… Heavenly!*

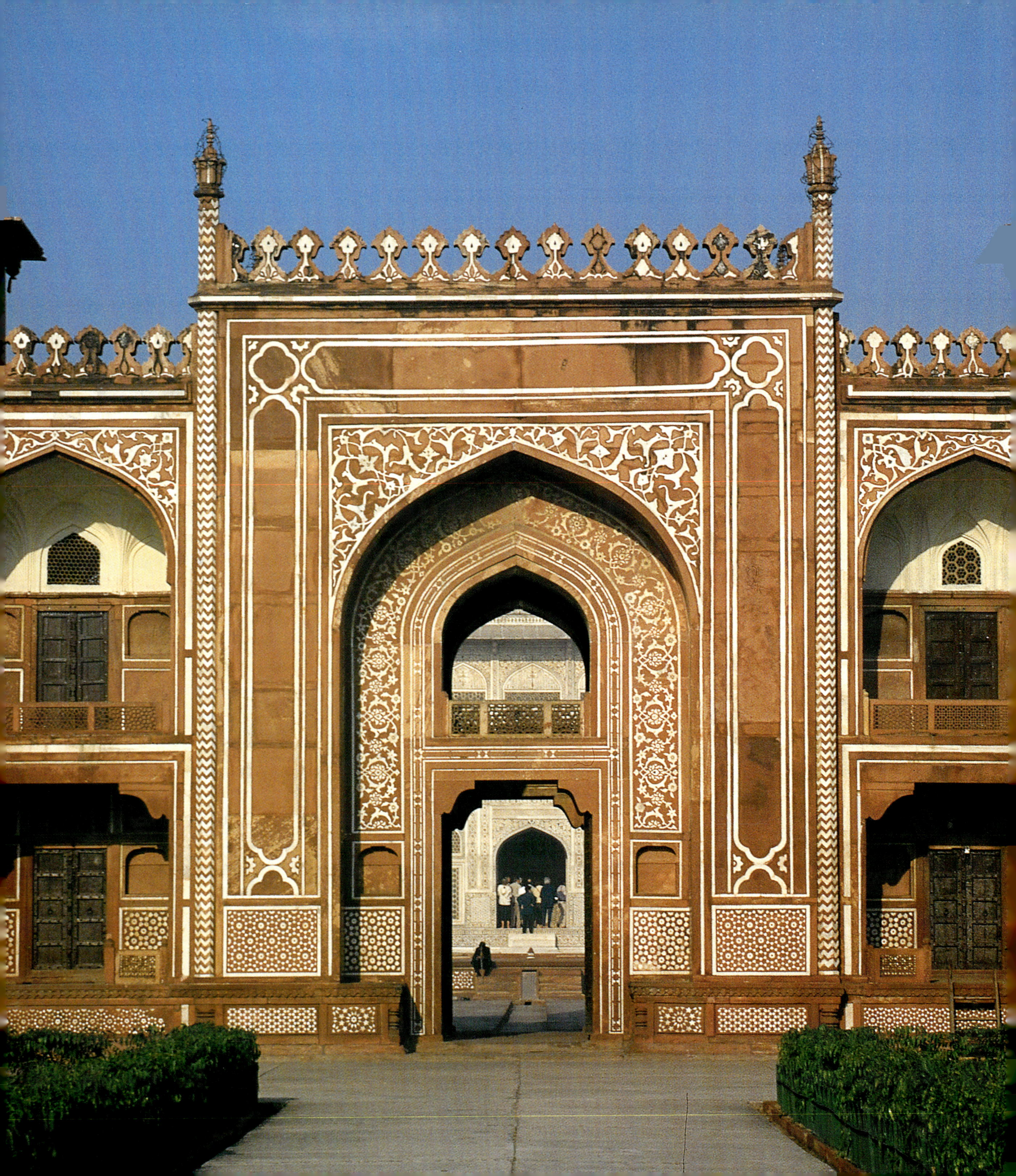

79

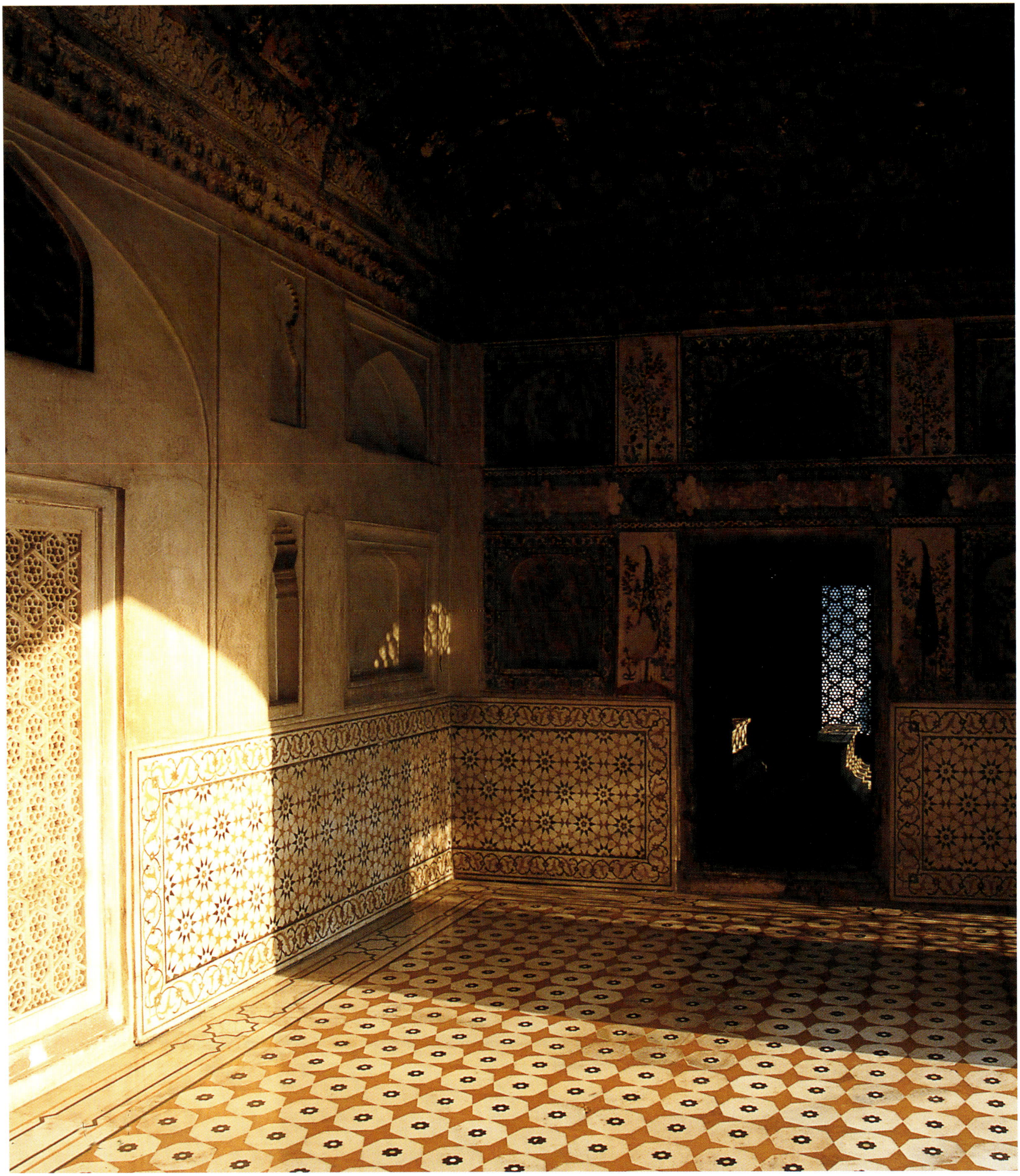

At the request of Nour Mahal, to pay tribute to her father, the Hindu artists used only bright-coloured (semi-?) precious stones they inlaid in marble to create mosaics, gracefully alternating with fretwork executed with a file. Great Moghul art!

The Moghul emperor Akbar himself drew up the plans for his mausoleum begun in 1602. Surrounded by parks embellished by fountains, it was meant to be a sublime link between heaven and earth.

The Mausoleum of Akbar at Sikandra

Akbar consulted the most qualified astrologists of the empire. They designated the site of Sikander, some ten kilometres from Agra, to shelter his mausoleum. The first excavation work began in 1602. Akbar, who was familiar with the style of the mausoleum dedicated to his father Humayun built by Persian architects, wanted a more "Indian" style for his own resting place. He chose a terraced pyramid with a sarcophagus deposited at its centre, in keeping with the Hindu symbolism: "the mountain and the cave".

The final form of the tomb was not completed until 1613 by his son Jahangir. Old chronicles describe Akbar's death in the Fort of Agra, on his seventy-third birthday: it was on 27 October 1605, after an absolute reign that had lasted 49 years, 8 months and three days. He passed away after having the Muslim act of faith recited to him and having chosen his son as his successor. The day after, an opening was made in the walls of the Fort because according to some customs the living and the dead should not use the same passages. Preceded by drums, a solemn procession in which converged Jesuit priests, women of the harem and barefoot, bareheaded nobles reached Sikandra. The coffin was lowered into the grave and the white marble top sealed. The remains were covered with an immaculate cloth and roses placed on it in keeping with the Hindu custom. His son Salim, the future Jahangir, placed a turban and a Koran at the head of the tomb, with Akbar's sabre and shield. The Moghul empire would never be the same again …

The site has preserved its rather unusual dimensions. A monumental entrance door covered with polychrome marble mosaics inlaid with red sandstone opens onto a spacious park shared peacefully by several herds of deer. The last mausoleum of the Moghul period to have been built in red sandstone has the appearance of a pyramid with four steps, galleries and chhatri. You enter the edifice through a first room adorned with wall paintings. Then a dark corridor, formerly graced with paintings illustrating all the religions in the world, leads to the tomb proper, which is empty. The bones of the Great Moghul were brutally scattered by the Jats, a caste of warrior peasants. This happened in 1761.

You enter the enclosure through a grandiose gate crowned by four marble minarets adorned with polychrome stone inlaid in the red sandstone. Here again, a profusion of geometric mosaics and floral motifs. Sublime, of course!

Next double page: The funerary monument is a four-storied pyramid, flanked by two colossal gates (pishtaq) (page 84), also richly ornamented. The actual tomb was inside a dark crypt you reached through a room faced with gildings and Koranic inscriptions (page 85). At the end of a hall loomed the white marble sarcophagus adorned with a single word, "Akbar", in black.

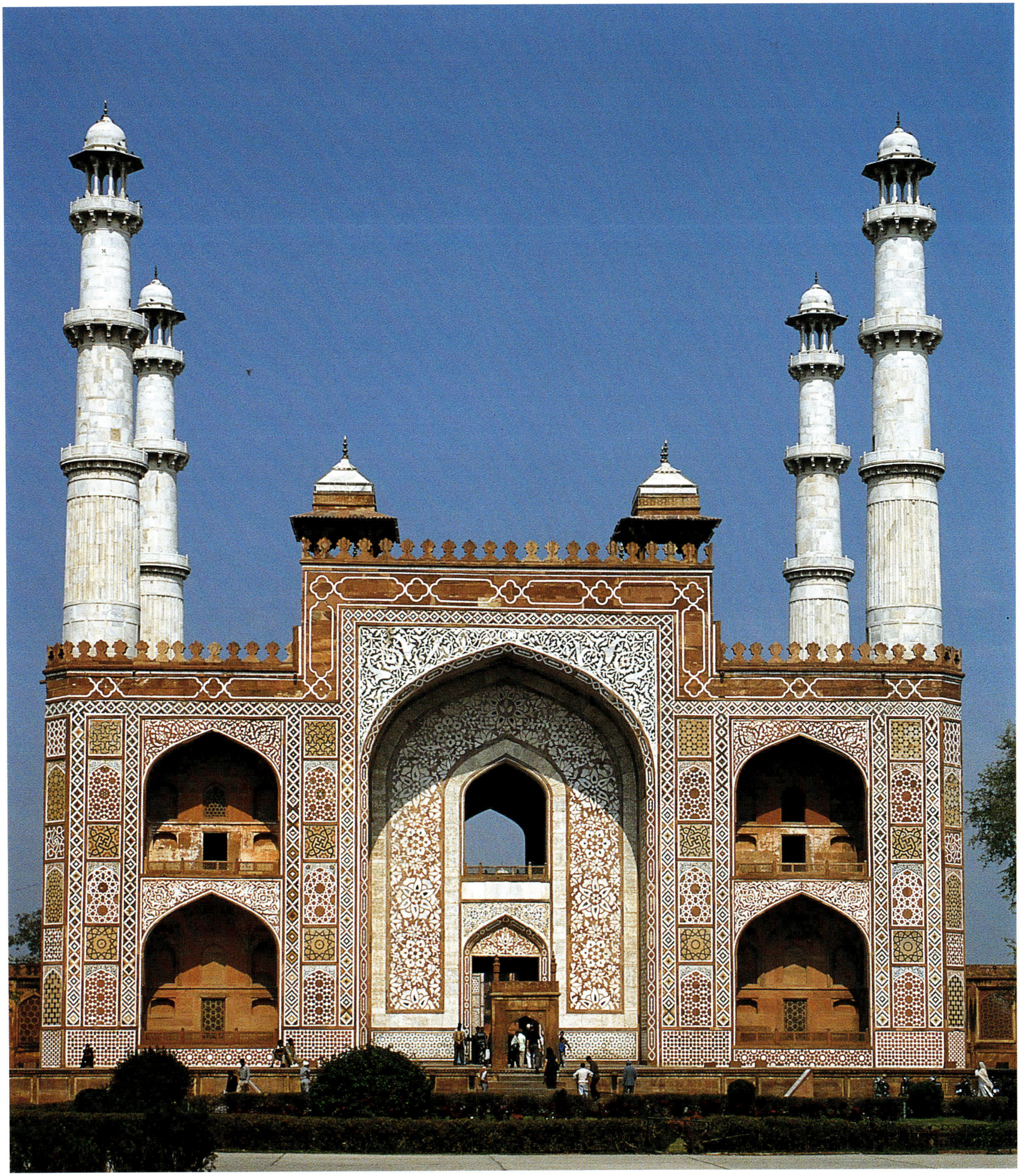

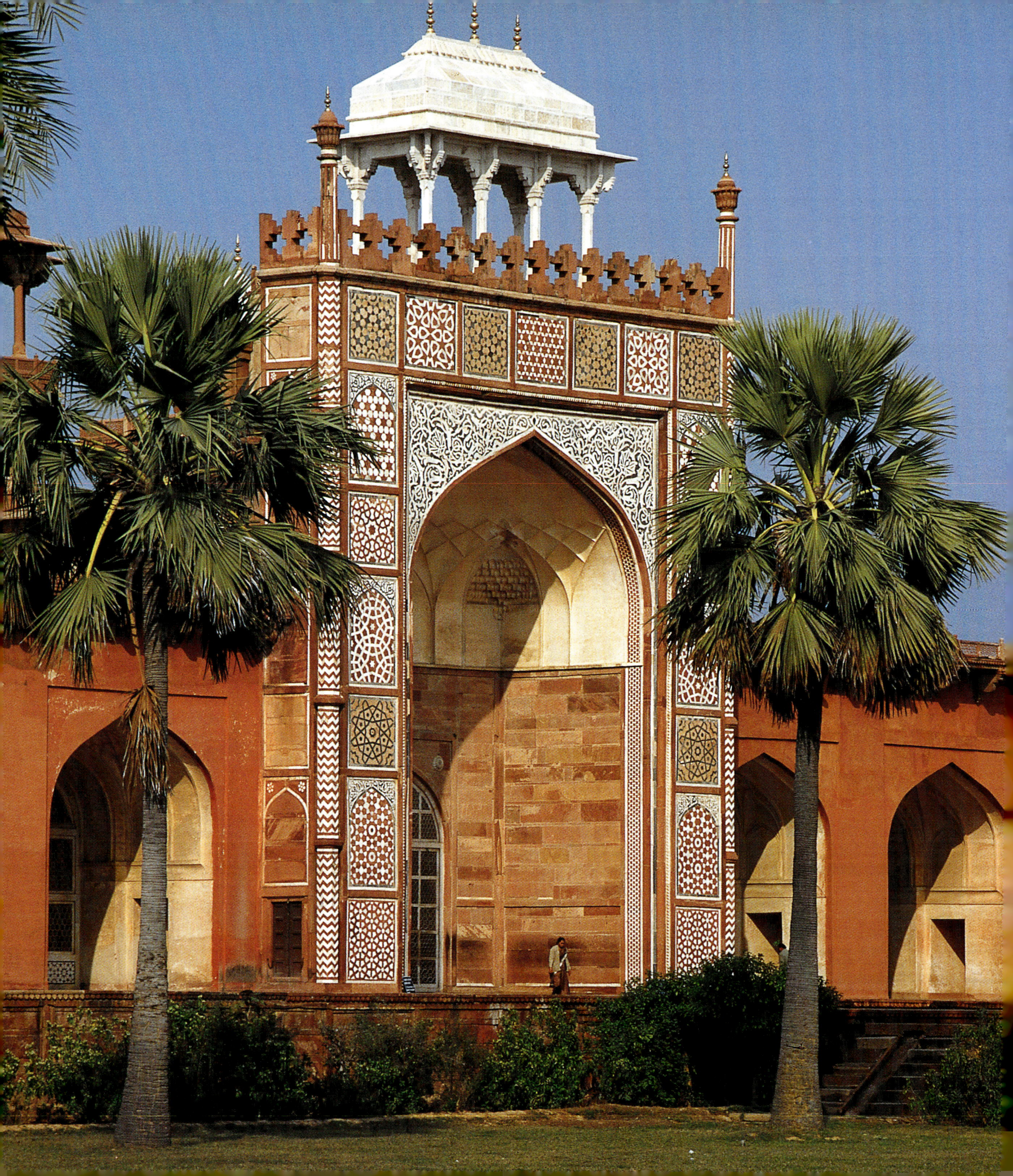

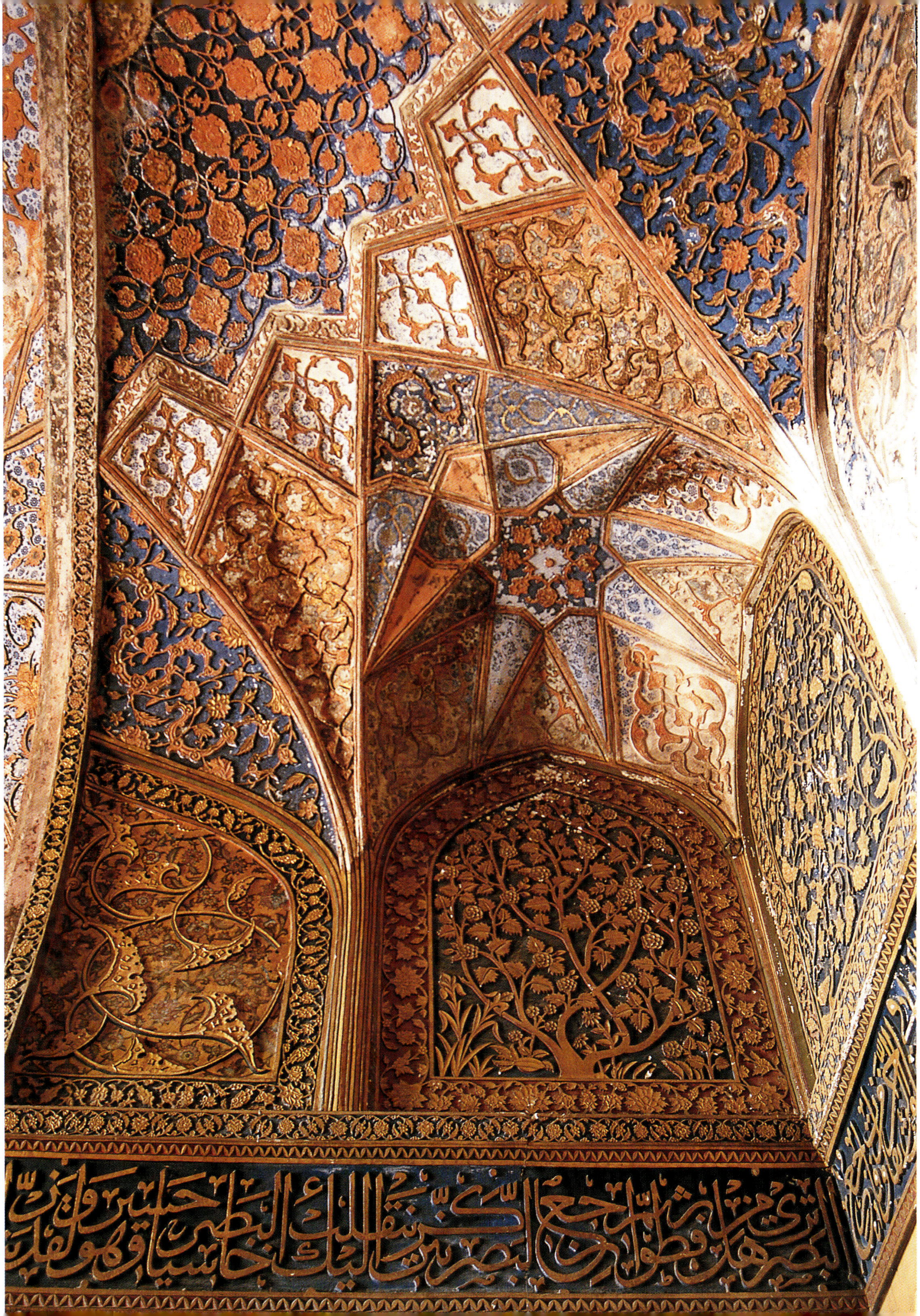

The Taj Mahal

Backed up to an over-grown city, the Taj Mahal perfectly matches the comparison by Rabindranath Tagore: "A solitary tear on the cheek of time". You do not "visit" the Taj Mahal like some other monument. It has to do with contemplation and meditation. It is like a little inner journey as well. Because this magnificent mausoleum contains several of man's greatest mysteries: the image of beauty and of love, the memory of the beloved and death. Everyone can see himself in it, everyone seeks to take possession of a small piece of this paradise on Earth. Palace of Beatitude, the Taj Mahal wonderfully tells a love story that has thrilled the world for centuries. That of the emperor Shah Jahan, Akbar's grandson, for his favourite wife Mumtaz-j Mahal, to whom, as a proof of his great trust, he delegated part of the affairs of State (an extremely rare thing to do at the time). She even regularly accompanied him on his campaigns. In 1631, during a long journey in the south of the empire, she died in a camp while giving birth to their fourteenth child. Despairing, Shah Jahan refused to eat for an entire week, decreed two years of mourning at the Court, forbade festivities as well as the use of jewellery and perfumes. Inconsolable, he then imagined a mausoleum as great as his grief. It would be Mumtaz Mahal, the "Palace of the Favourite" which by deformation became the Taj Mahal, "Palace of the Crown". Its architect is still unknown. He worked on it for twenty-two years, from 1632 to 1654, with the best artisans of the kingdom. It took 20.000 labourers to build. If, as some experts claim, Shah Jahan wanted a matching construction in black marble on the other side of the river for his own mausoleum, this hypothesis has never been verified and seems somewhat unrealistic.

The proportions of the Taj Mahal are perfect and the decoration is as discreet as it is refined, often simple floral motifs delicately carved in the marble. No, honestly, this mausoleum does not make you feel sad. Far from grieving, the emperor Shah Jahan used to give lavish parties here, with fireworks, musicians and poets, in memory of his beloved wife.

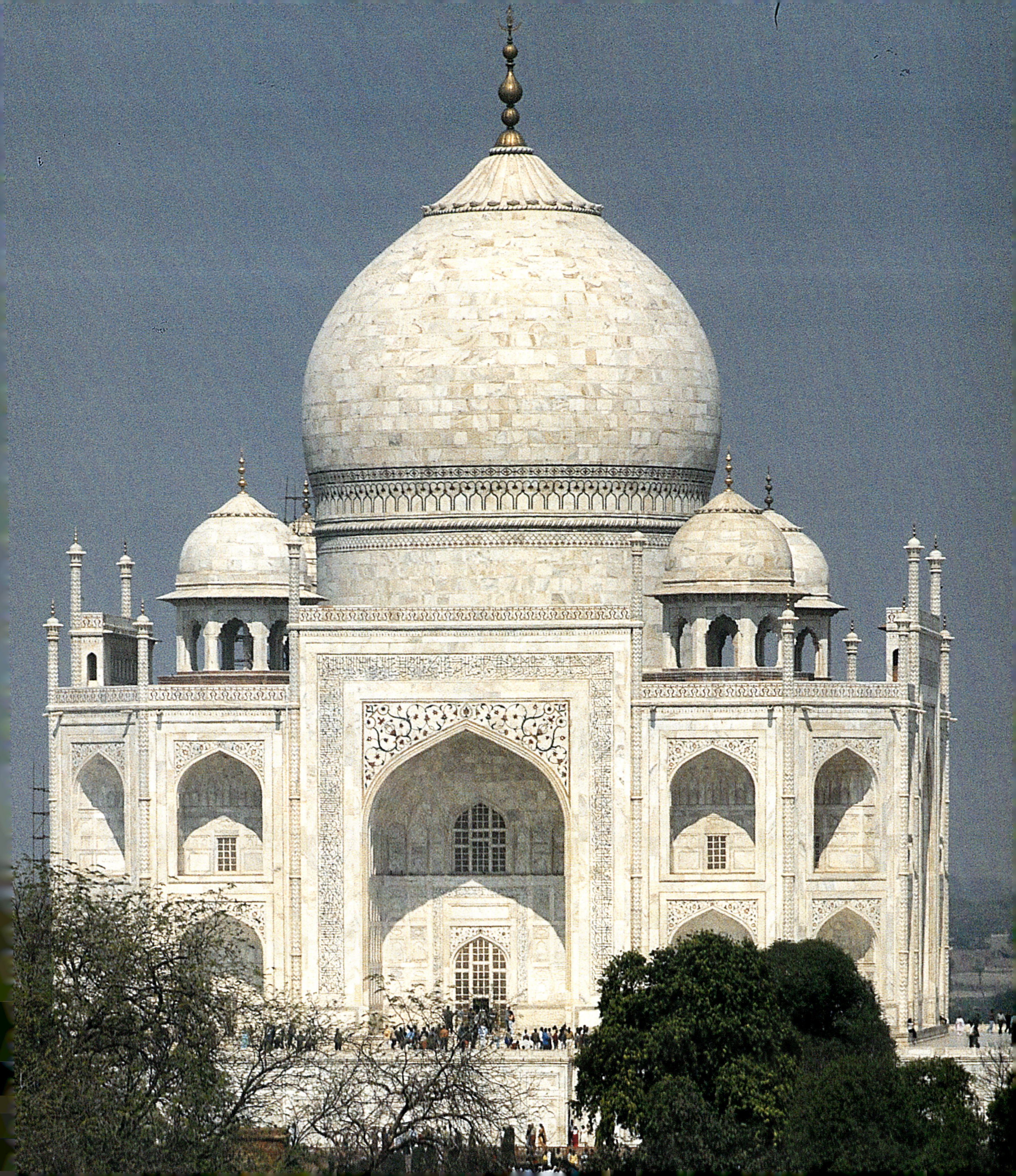

A Sublime Mausoleum

First of all we discover the profusion of luxuriant gardens. After going through a first door, a path leads to the West Portal in red sandstone graced with white marble. From afar looms the Taj Mahal. A dream! A model! We recognise in it, sublimated, the park and terrace of Humayun's tomb in Delhi; the minarets of Jahangir's tomb in Lahore; the double dome of Tamerlane's tomb in Samarkand.

Everything seems to have been designed to impress and surprise the visitor, to create a sense of wonderment; certainly not to sadden him. In fact the palace was the setting for brilliant festivities with fireworks given by Shah Jahal who yielded to these mundane pleasures after considering possible abdication. To its soaring forms it owes its elegance; to its materials, its harmony; to a boundless message of love, its spirit. First the eye follows a long canal lined with cypresses leading to the marble edifice, set on a vast base. Four minarets 47 metres high frame the tomb crowned by an onion-shaped dome supported on a drum. The dome is surrounded by four chhatri. The building is a square with cut angles each side of which is hollowed out to make a central iwan (vaulted space) framed by a portal (pishtaq) and two rows of niches.

Following the middle canal, the enraptured visitor lingers by the central pool. The Taj is entirely reflected in it. It is like a whole world contained in an image and we have a hard time tearing ourselves away. Beyond, on the podium of the mausoleum, there is marble everywhere. Immaculate, it was brought from the quarries of Makrana, not far from Ajmer. We are wide-eyed with admiration. The decoration is generous and refined, consisting of floral motifs, scrolls

The Taj Mahal, flanked by its "hostelry" for pilgrims and a red sandstone mosque, overlooks with supreme elegance the banks of the Yamuna River. Shah Jahan was only thirty-nine years old when he decided to build the most fabulous monument in Moghul India. Because she died in childbirth, his wife had the status of a martyr and her mausoleum could be designated as a pilgrimage site.

89

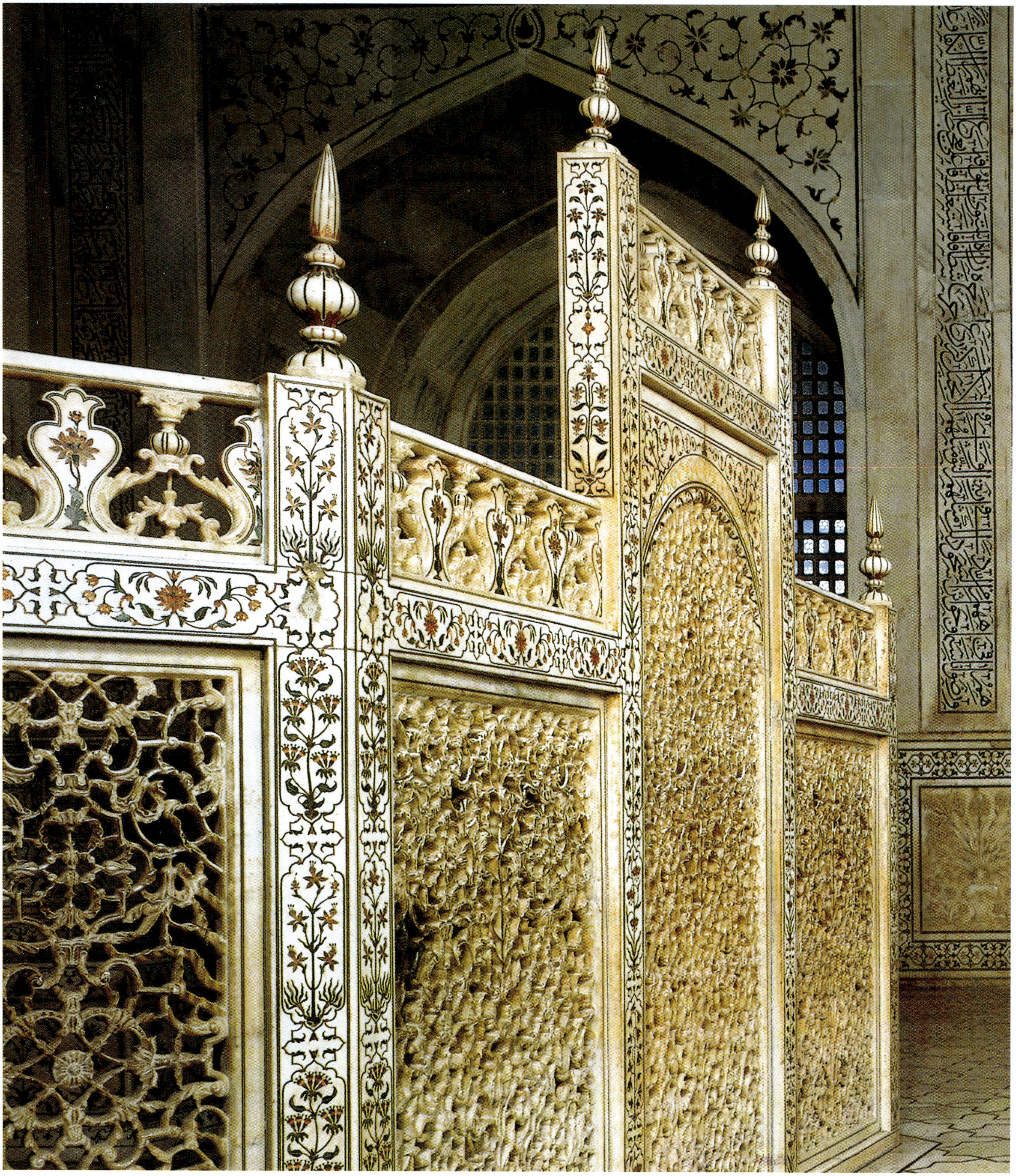

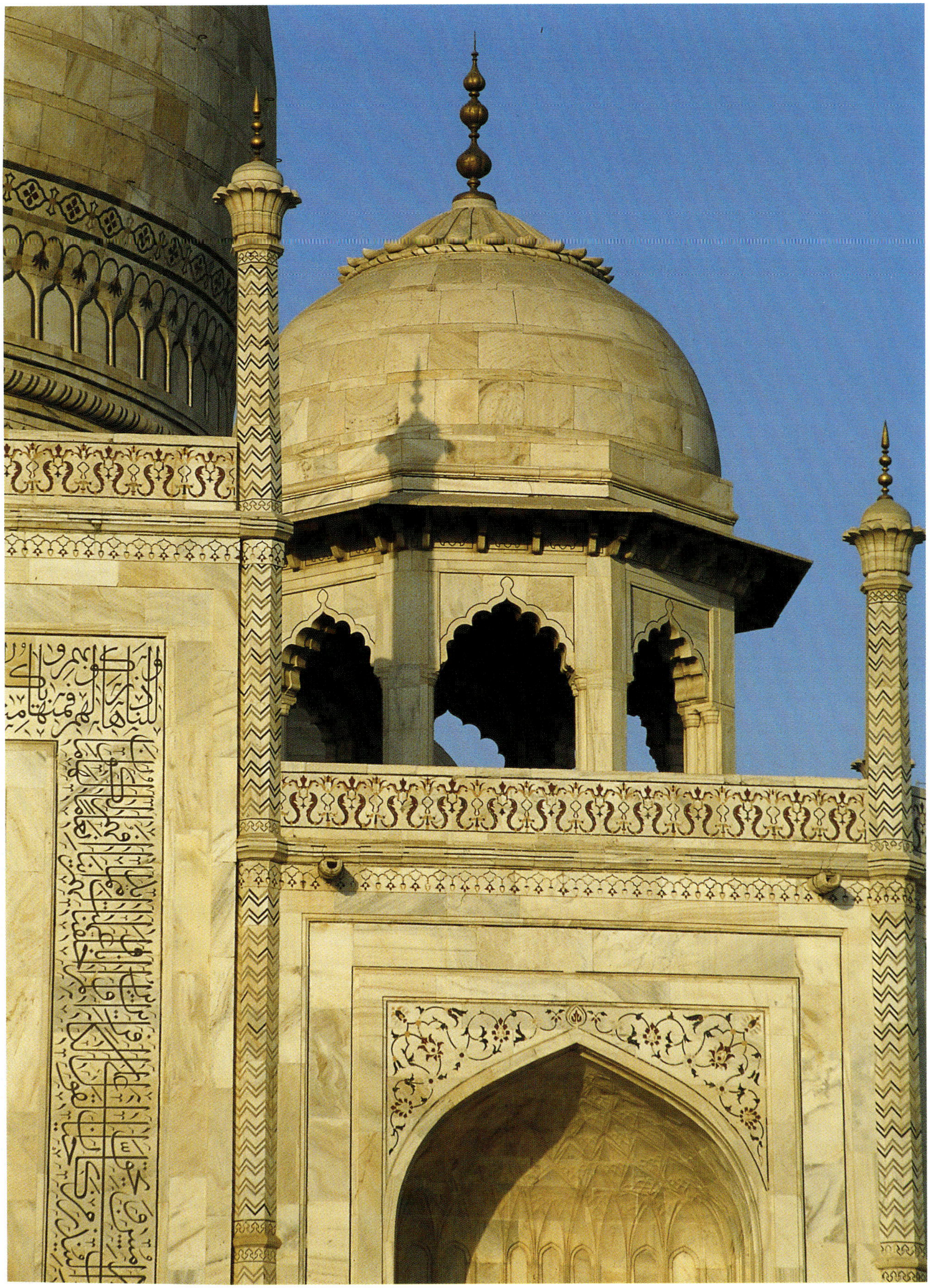

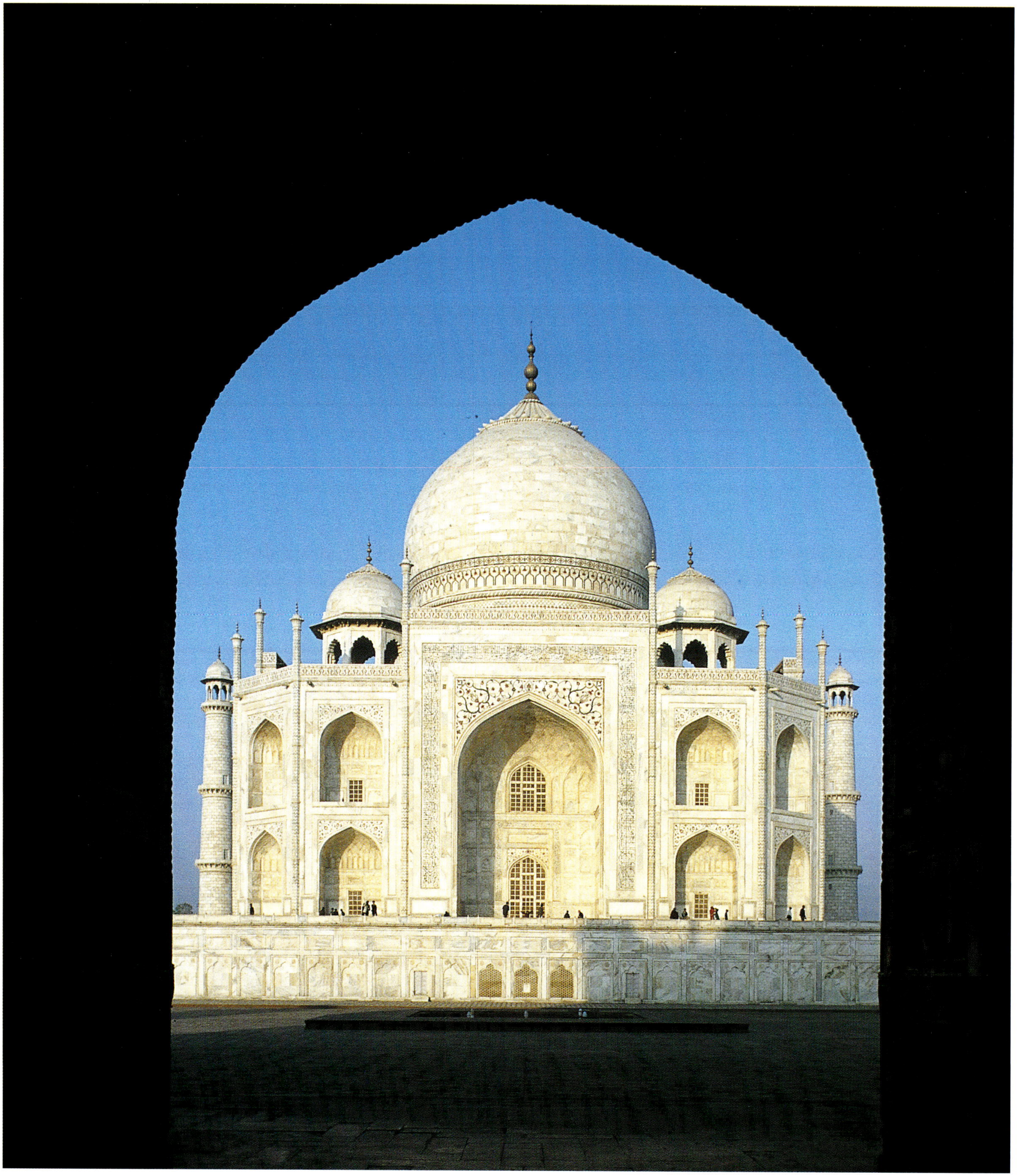

and Koranic inscriptions adorned with semi-precious stones in the pietra dura technique. Then, with deep emotion, we enter the octagonal death chamber in which are placed the couple's imitation tombs, the real ones being in the crypt. We are carried away by all this refinement. But we hasten to come out and explore the surroundings… On each side of the mausoleum, two almost identical red sandstone edifices are worth visiting. The one to the west is a mosque where the Muslim worship is still held. Its twin, which no longer has its mihrab (the niche showing the direction of Mecca), formerly sheltered the pilgrims who had come to pay tribute. An entire day is not enough. The different shades of the marble appear at different times: a tender blue at dawn, pink in the sunrise, then the colour of honey. Its immaculate white dazzles at noon. The Taj Mahal is not for someone in a hurry.

The best decorators from Persia and all over Northern India were hired. 20.000 workmen worked for twenty-two years to execute the exquisite ornamentation: epigraphic bands reproducing verses from the Koran, marble from Makrana (not far from Ajmer) inlaid with jasper from Punjab, amethysts from Persia, sapphires from Sri Lanka.

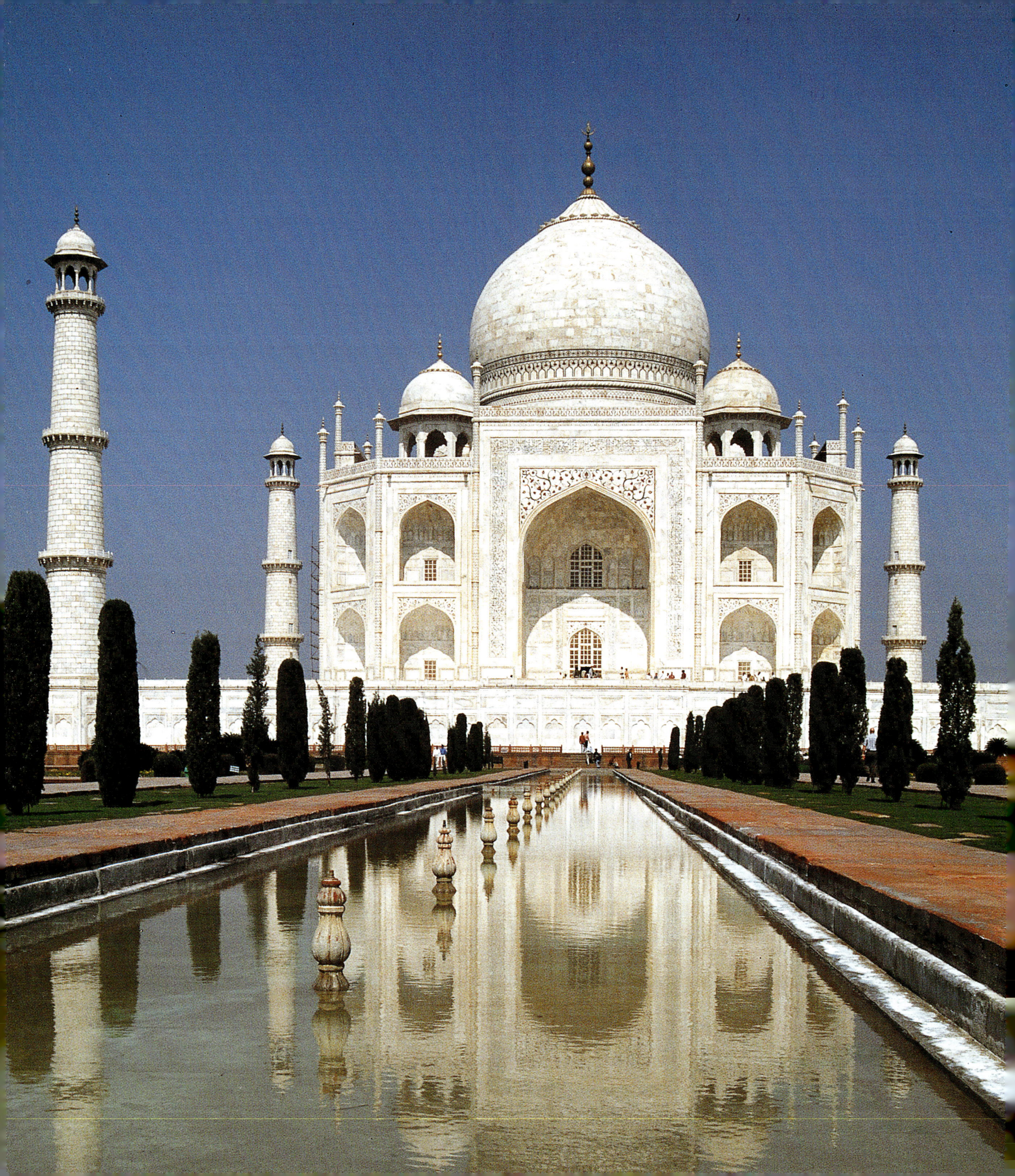

95

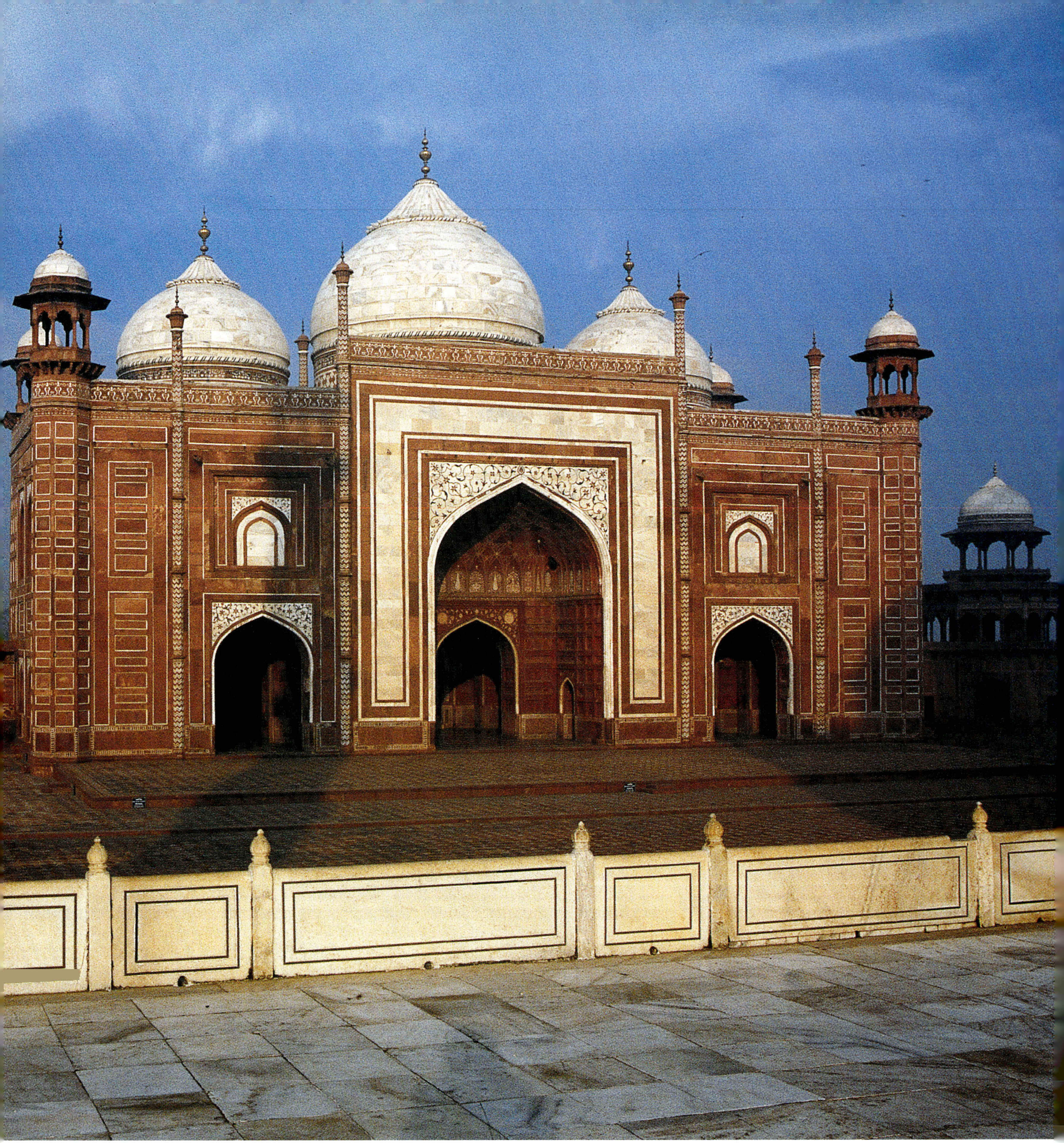

Preceding double page:
You will miss the purity of the Taj Mahal if you are in a hurry. From dawn to twilight, the reflections of the sun caress its silhouette with shadow or light, might or mystery. But noon is when the "pearl of India" sparkles with a thousand glimmers. Nothing was left up to chance to delight the visitor; neither the four elegant minarets slightly tilted at the top to give the building an impression of stability, nor the width of the central pool, which entirely reflects the Taj Mahal. What a sublime gift to mankind!

Devotees of the Taj Mahal tend to forget the two red sandstone almost twin buildings framing the mausoleum, on an east-west axis. Too bad! Because they are wonderful islands of peace far from the crowd thronging to the mausoleum. The ornamentation of their bas-reliefs, with scrolls, wavy arabesques and geometric motifs, are truly worth seeing (pages 98 and 99). The edifice, facing west, is a mosque where the tomb of the defunct was placed until her mausoleum was completed. The other twin building, without a mihrab (niche showing the direction of Mecca), was reserved for guests.

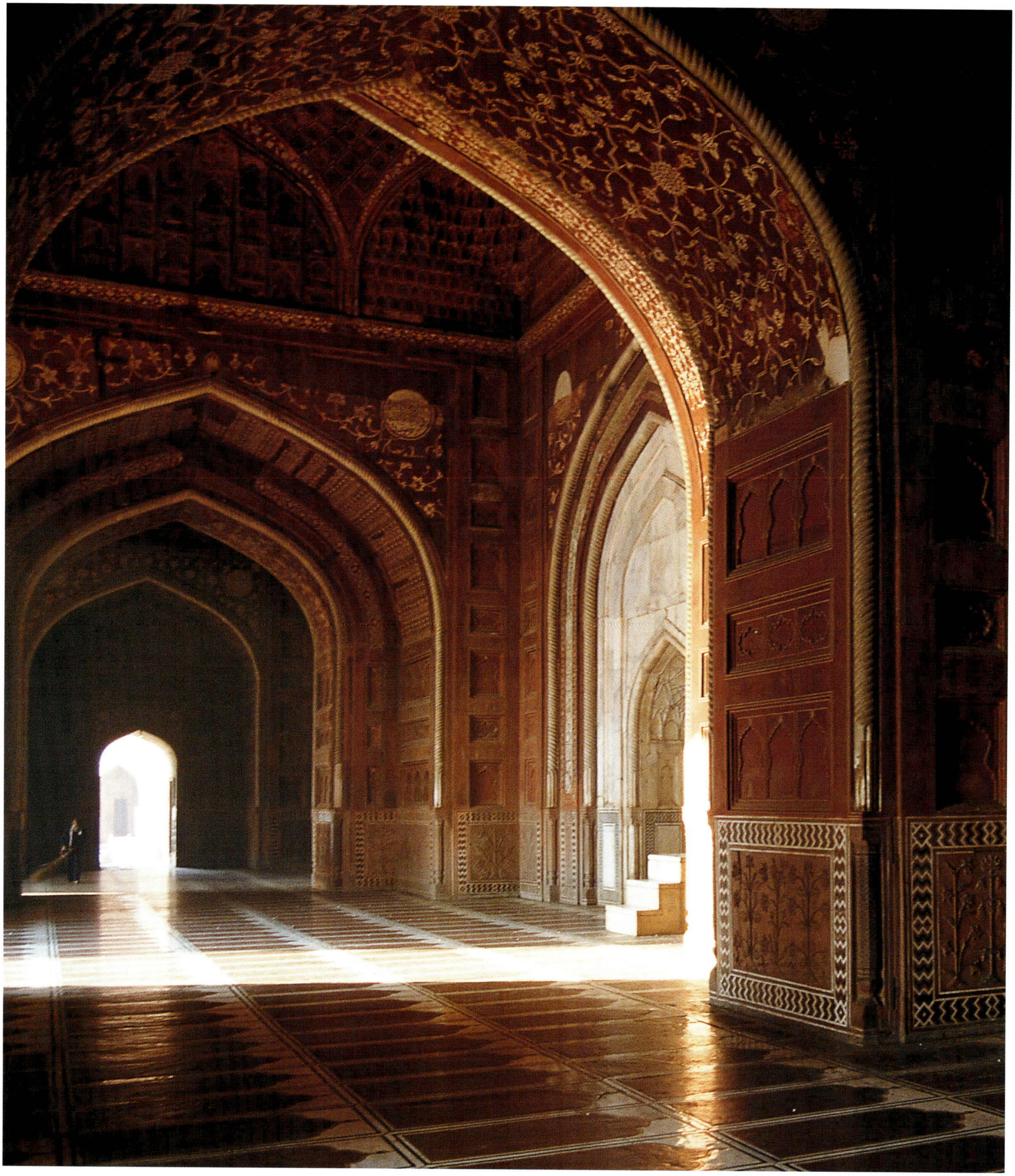

99

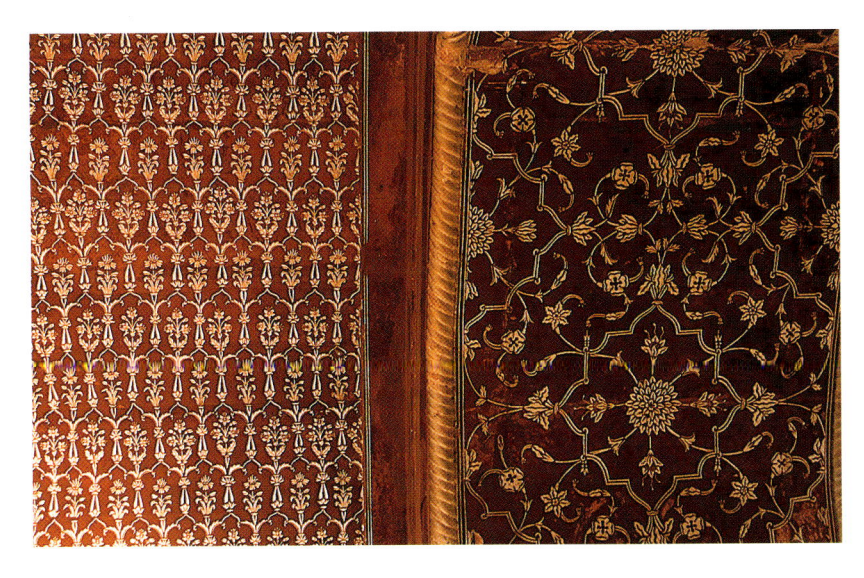

The Fort of Agra

With its moat and double red sandstone walls, the Red Fort gives a good idea of the cyclopean might of the Moghul empire. Although its looks impregnable, it was besieged and ransacked quite a few times during its history. At the beginning of his reign, in 1565 (it took nine years to build), Akbar had it erected for his Court, in the stead of a Rajput fortress. To overlook his immense empire, the "Great Moghul" had to be mobile. With his harem and elephants, he would prefer his new capital Fatehpur Sikri between 1574 and 1585, and then Lahore. He returned to Agra in 1598 from whence he managed the empire until 1605. His grandson Shah Jahan would embellish the fort with graceful white marble palaces and mosques that mark out a pleasant stroll inside.

You enter through the Amar Singh Darwaza south gate that opens onto a ramp leading to a vast courtyard framed by the palace where Akbar's son, Jahangir, lived. An impression of great refinement prevails in a second garden-courtyard flanked by a remarkable diwan-i am (hall for public audiences), a hypostyle room in red sandstone where Akbar received visitors. Inside these time-mellowed fortified walls, the private apartments are surprisingly refined. You wander off to the right into an admirable patio with arcades: its name, Anguri Bagh meaning Garden of Grapes, suggests quietude and sweetness. The oldest books claim that some 300 bunches of grapes made of emeralds, gold and rubies graced the small courtyard flanked by the Khas Mahal, Akbar's entirely white marble private palace. This dreamlike world is irresistible.

Beyond, overlooking the river and the plain, we imagine ourselves delighting in the Shish Mahal (Palace of Mirrors), again astonishing by its delicacy, or relaxing in the two hammams, one for hot baths and the other for cold baths. The octagonal tower that comes next, the Musamman Burj, recalls some rather grim memories. It was first the residence of the deceased heroine of the Taj Mahal, Mumtaz Mahall. Before becoming a "luxury" prison for her husband the emperor Shah Jahan at the end of his life. Poor man! Deposed by his son Aurangzeb in 1658, he died at the Fort in 1666. His only solace was to be able to contemplate his Taj Mahal from the tower as often as he wished. The diwan-i khas (hall of private audiences) is here to remind us as well that Shah Jahan was a brilliant builder. If the Mosque of the Pearl (Moti Masjid) is closed to the public, you can linger in the little Nagina Masjid mosque reserved for women. It boasts ravishing decorations.

*The red sandstone Akbar so fancied makes the over 2.5 kilometres-
long double walls of the Red Fort of Agra look absolutely invulnerable.*

Life in Akbar's Time

Akbar was sixteen years old with a tutor and an empire to conquer when he decided to leave Delhi for Agra from where he would rule during the first fifteen years of his reign. Its climate is pleasanter and its location enabled him to keep an eye on the very troublesome Afghans in the Bihar and on the Rajputs perpetually up in arms. The journey to Agra took 21 days, interrupted by memorable hunting and fishing parties. When he arrived he found a worn-out fort, rather unsafe since built of brick. It hardly mattered: it would be rebuilt in stone. There were plenty of quarries in the area and soon 4.000 workers were hacking away. The blocks travelled by sailboat to the foot of the fortress of Agra. Akbar, who was fond of the style of the palaces of the Gujarat and Bengal, had the interiors adorned in the same fashion. Today nothing is left.

Just what was Akbar's life at Agra like? When he was not at the hunt with his cheetahs and his harem, he organised elephant fights, his favourite entertainment. He also hosted ambassadors such as those of the Shah of Persia who showered him with presents: Arabian horses, precious fabrics and delicate rugs. Akbar was an early riser. After prayers, he would appear to his people at his jharokha, Window of the Apparition. Then he received petitions and his courtiers, went to the harem to deal with household matters, discussed affairs with his ministers and visited the stables. In the evening, colourful festivities were held to entertain the Court. Hindu and Muslim artists and musicians performed together.

Inside the fort of Agra there remain but a few vestiges of Akbar's red sandstone palaces. For his Court, his grandson, the Moghul emperor Shah Jahan, preferred to replace them with white marble palaces that mark out an elegant promenade to the Musammam.

Burj (facing), also called the Prisoner's Tower. Shah Jahan was held there for eight years by his third son, Aurangzeb. His one solace: he could look out and see the Taj Mahal, the resting-place of his wife, whom he would rejoin in 1666.

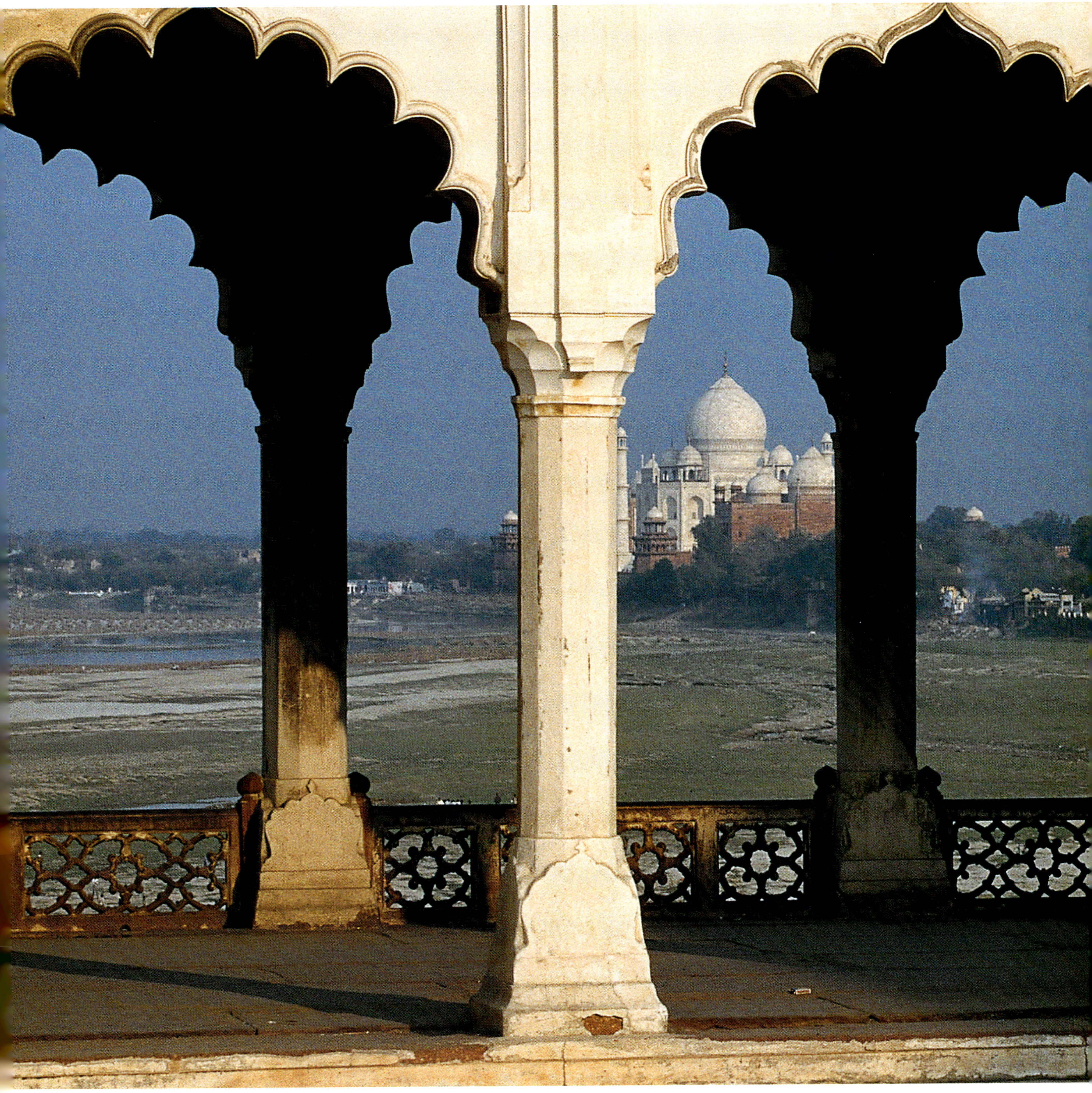

Behind its ramparts, the Fort of Agra leads a double life with delightful palaces recalling the lavish court of Shah Jahan, with the diwan-i khas (private audiences hall) and the diwan-i am (public audiences hall). That is where the Moghul emperor received ambassadors and princes in great pomp.

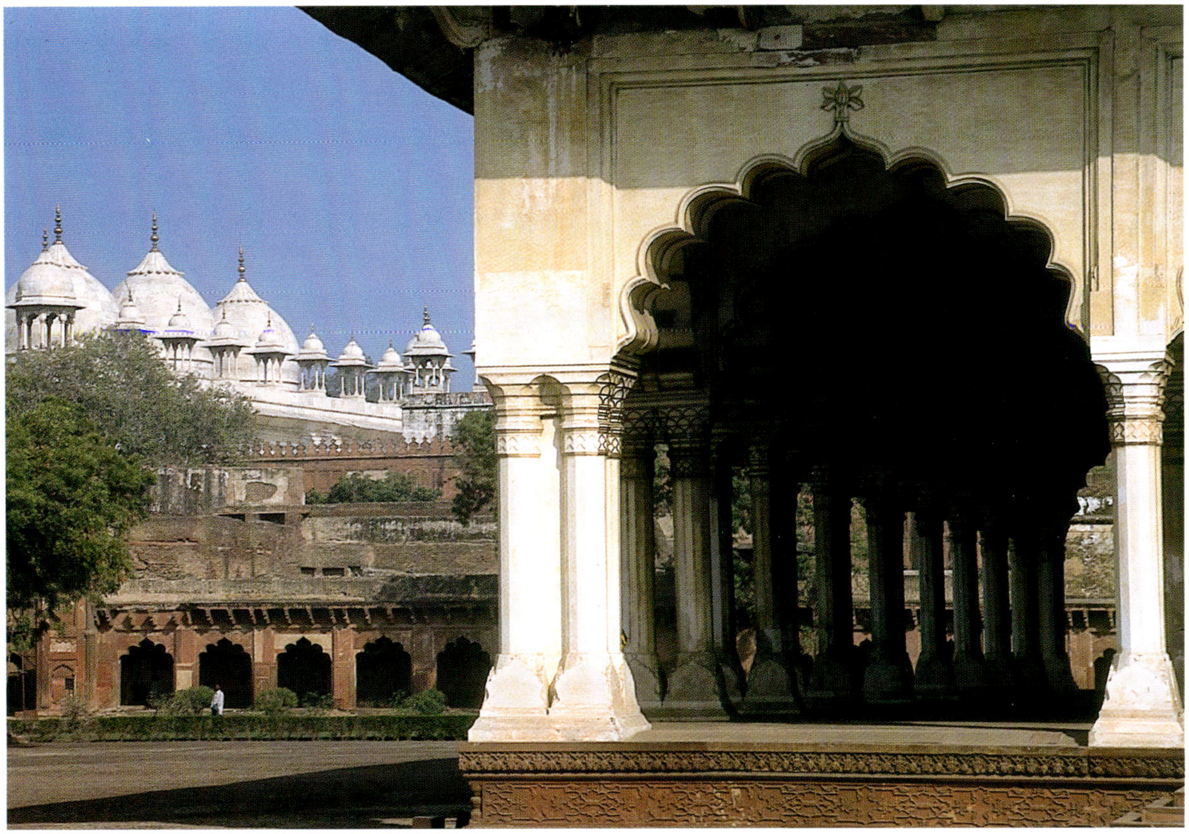

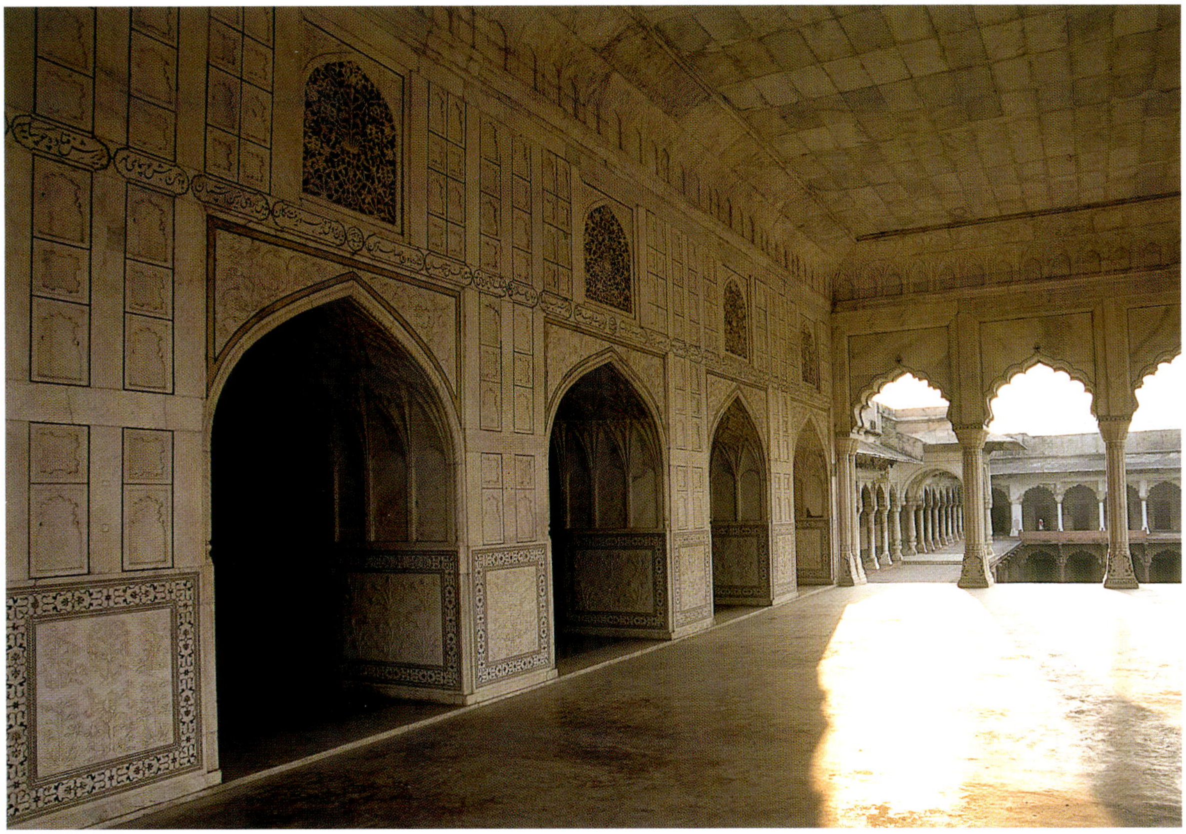

FATEHPUR SIKRI

A Moghul Ghost Town

Overlooking a drab plain some forty kilometres west of Agra the red walls of Fatehpur can be seen from afar. It is best to arrive in one of those horse carriages awaiting the visitor at the entrance of the town, with a swarm of gesticulating youngsters to welcome you. The atmosphere is like a quiet village. In any case it is a far cry from the description by Ralf Finch, the English traveller who in 1585 came "to this city where the king holds Court". Listen to what he wrote: "If the streets are not as lovely as those of Agra, this city is nonetheless bigger and its very large population includes Moors and Indians. In any case, Agra and Fatehpur are far larger and more populated than London. All along the road there is a market selling food and various items. Buildings are so close to one another that you have the impression you are in a city, and the crowd is as great as in an authentic market."

Those who are fond of Moghul art and have "delicate palates" will be more than satisfied by the "City of the Victory". The buildings of Akbar's former capital are wonderfully well preserved and the local culinary specialty, khataies, a kind of butter biscuit, is an utter delight. The ornate narrow streets of the mostly Hindu lower city have a number of bakeries where in the evening the pastries are put in the oven in the midst of the overwhelming smell of fresh cream. It would be sacrilegious to refuse the temptation for just a few rupees. Simply irresistible!

In the upper town, around the Juma Masjid (Friday Mosque), lies the Muslim district where a few families live in houses with steep stairways and terraces left to the "family" ewe. What do the two communities share, aside from respect and friendship? They all are mad about khataies and all worship Akbar, the great unifier of religions, styles and architectures. Because the ancestors of these quiet inhabitants were no doubt called upon to make Fatehpur Sikra an ideal Moghul city with palace, mosque, caravanserais…

At the height of his glory, weary of Agra, the Moghul emperor Akbar decided to build his new capital on this site in 1570. Renaissance France was already graced with several of its loveliest jewels at Blois, Chambord and Chenonceau. Having lost infant twins, Akbar, who was twenty-six

One of the niches, or mihrab, of the prayer room of the Fatehpur Sikri mosque, showing the direction of Mecca.

Akbar loved red sandstone. His capital, now fallen, is full of it. A few steps from his palace, he had raised the Great Friday Mosque built in the sixteenth century. Its prayer room features an impressive central door, or pishtaq.

The cordial imam of the Fatehpur mosque certainly would not have minded living in the days of Akbar, when the "Great Moghul", surrounded by his Court, would appear at the Badshahi Darwaza, the Royal Door (on the right).

years old, confided his grief to a holy Sufi, sheikh Salim Chishti, who lived in seclusion on a hilltop. The pious man advised him to settle his wife here, predicting the birth of three sons to the emperor who was anxious about his heir. The following year a son was born, who was named Salim, the future emperor Jahangir. His wishes come true and filled with joy, Akbar then chose to set up a kingdom which would be very ephemeral, since it was too secluded and difficult to provide with water. In 1585 he would leave it for Lahore.

109

Akbar's Ideal City

The arrival at Juma Masjid by its south side is something of a shock because the triumphal Buland Darwaza Gate appears so enormous. It was built in 1575 to celebrate Akbar's victory over the sultan of the Gujarat and on its inside wall it features a moving inscription in Persian: "The world is a bridge. Cross it but do not build on it." It leads to a very tranquil courtyard, surrounded by arcades topped by chhatri. There is red sandstone everywhere. On the west side, the prayer room with its monumental central gate draws the faithful and visiting foreigners whom the old imam greets with equal benevolence. Almost in the middle of the courtyard, a small, amazingly elegant marble pavilion is visited by Hindu and Muslim pilgrims. It is the mausoleum of Sheikh Salim Chishti. In 1606 the emperor Jahangir enclosed the original tomb in the pavilion featuring a gallery closed by jali.

As the emperors did, we enter through the Royal Door, Badshahi Darwaza, to reach the residential palace behind its walls. We feel a slight tremor on entering the vast ensemble of large or intimate courtyards, palaces and pavilions where in its day the rich Court of Akbar used to strut about. The place is steeped in a sort of indolence that inspires us to reverie. Ruins have far more to say than guides. We easily discover the vestiges of the rooms for the Archives, the Mint and the Astrologer. There was even a hospital, a library, as well as stables for the horses and camels. Akbar's scribes described his conception of the perfect city. Eliminating the notion of streets or plazas, he opted for open space and rejected the monumental. He preferred pillars and lintels to vaults and domes. Hindu columns are Islamised with geometric motifs; again Akbar's syncretism. And anyone who thinks this stone decoration is lacking in warmth should think again! Akbar's court was of the utmost opulence, but we do miss the colourful tents set here and there, multicoloured cloths hanging on hooks and dividing spaces to make them more intimate.

All these relics have their secret, like the Panch Mahal, the elegant palace with its five hypostyle storeys in decreasing

The children of Fatehpur, Hindus and Muslims, love to play in the courtyard of the Great Mosque in front of the mausoleum of Sheikh Salim Chishti. They feel perfectly at home! Their ancestors, stone carvers, were the ones who built Akbar's city.

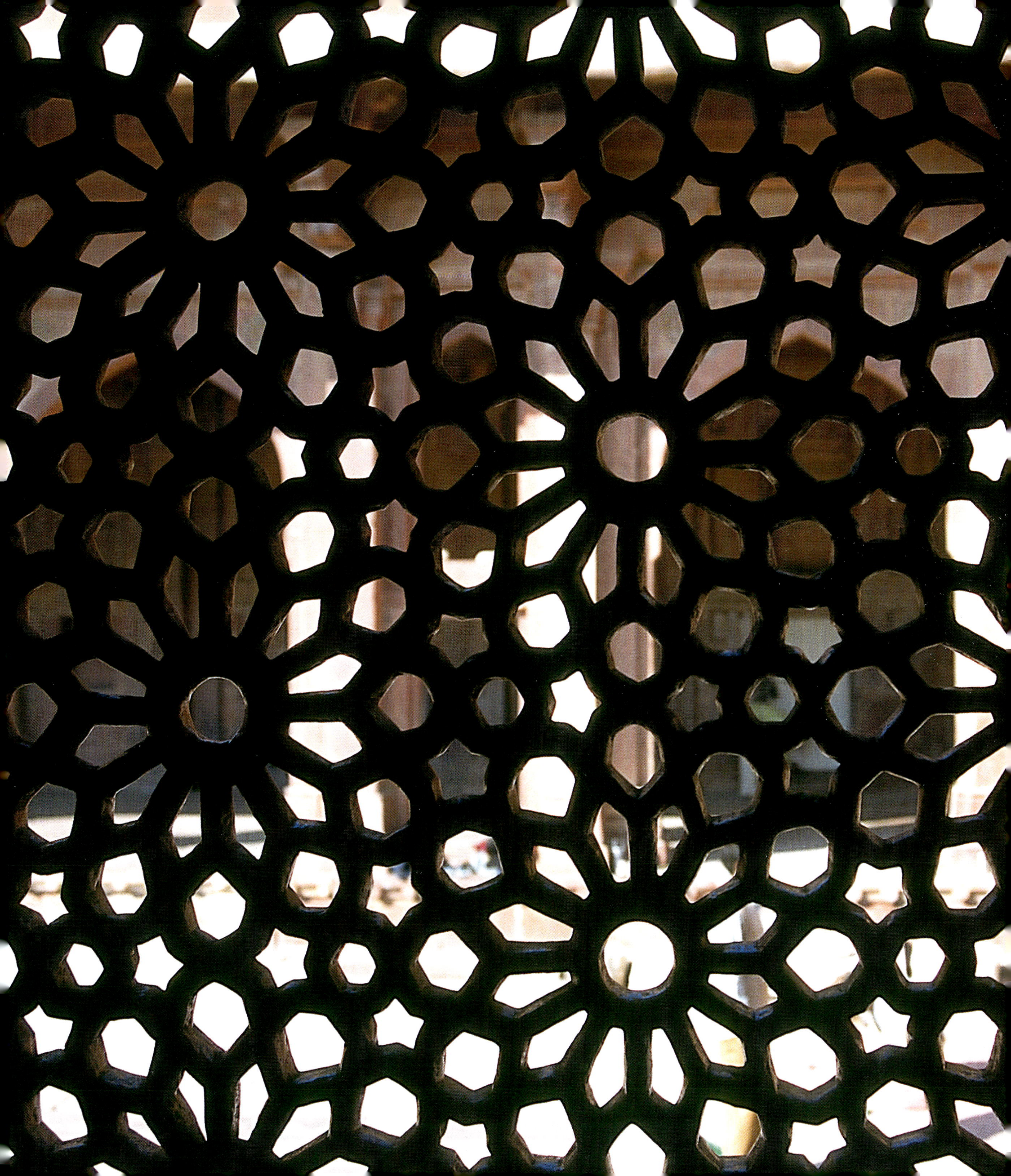

dimensions with its 176 carved columns. Even more unusual was the Haramsara, the women's quarters where hundreds of concubines and wives lived, guarded by eunuchs. Some of them were more fortunate! Akbar's first wife resided in the house known as Maryam's, while her daughter pranced about in the fabulous Birbal house with its facades graced with beautiful arabesques.

For a full immersion in the Moghul Empire, we should go into the diwan-i khas (hall for private audiences). Akbar, like a truth-seeker, seated on a throne under a canopy, attended all the philosophical and religious debates he enjoyed organising. Open in all four directions, this small two-story building is highly original. At the centre, a monolithic column supports a platform on which the throne of the "master of the Universe" was placed. The diagonal walkways crossing the space are there to recall the Hindu cosmogony. At Fatehpur Sikri, each house, each tiny plaza has a story to tell. After meditating, the emperor dispensed justice in the vast diwan-i am (hall for public audiences) and received his counsellors in the diwan-i khas (hall for private audiences). Then weary of the affairs of the world, he could at last enjoy the performance of the dancers and musicians who enlivened the evenings around the square pool, the Anup Talab. And on with the show!

All around the mausoleum of a Muslim saint, Sheikh Salim Chishti, this delicately chiselled white marble hall, early sixteenth-century, is one of the loveliest treasures of Moghul art. The marble was cut out with a file to create geometric structures arranged in delicate, continuous fretwork. The hall permits the pilgrims to accomplish the circumambulation rite around the tomb.

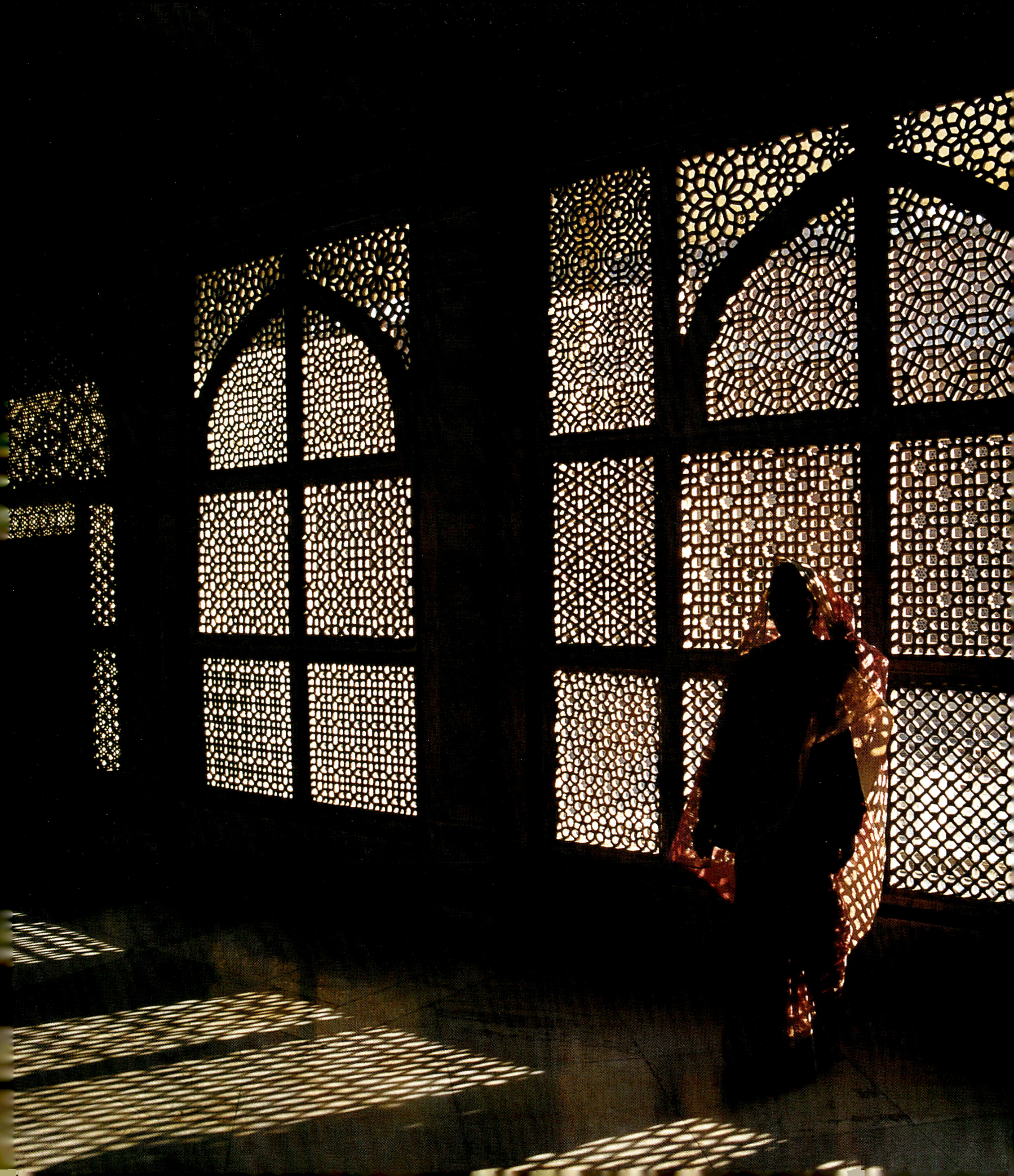

Fatehpur Sikri, the City of the Victory, which was only inhabited by Akbar's Court for some fifteen years, until 1585, offers an authentic testimony of the life of the Great Moghul. The diwan-i khas, or private audiences hall (above), is the most phantasmagorical room. Seated under a canopy, at the top of this strange column, like the master of the Universe, Akbar partook in philosophical discussions in the midst of his prestigious guests. Another red sandstone architectural jewel: the house of Birbal, Akbar's minister (page 115), covered with a delicate network of tracery and arabesques evoking woodwork.

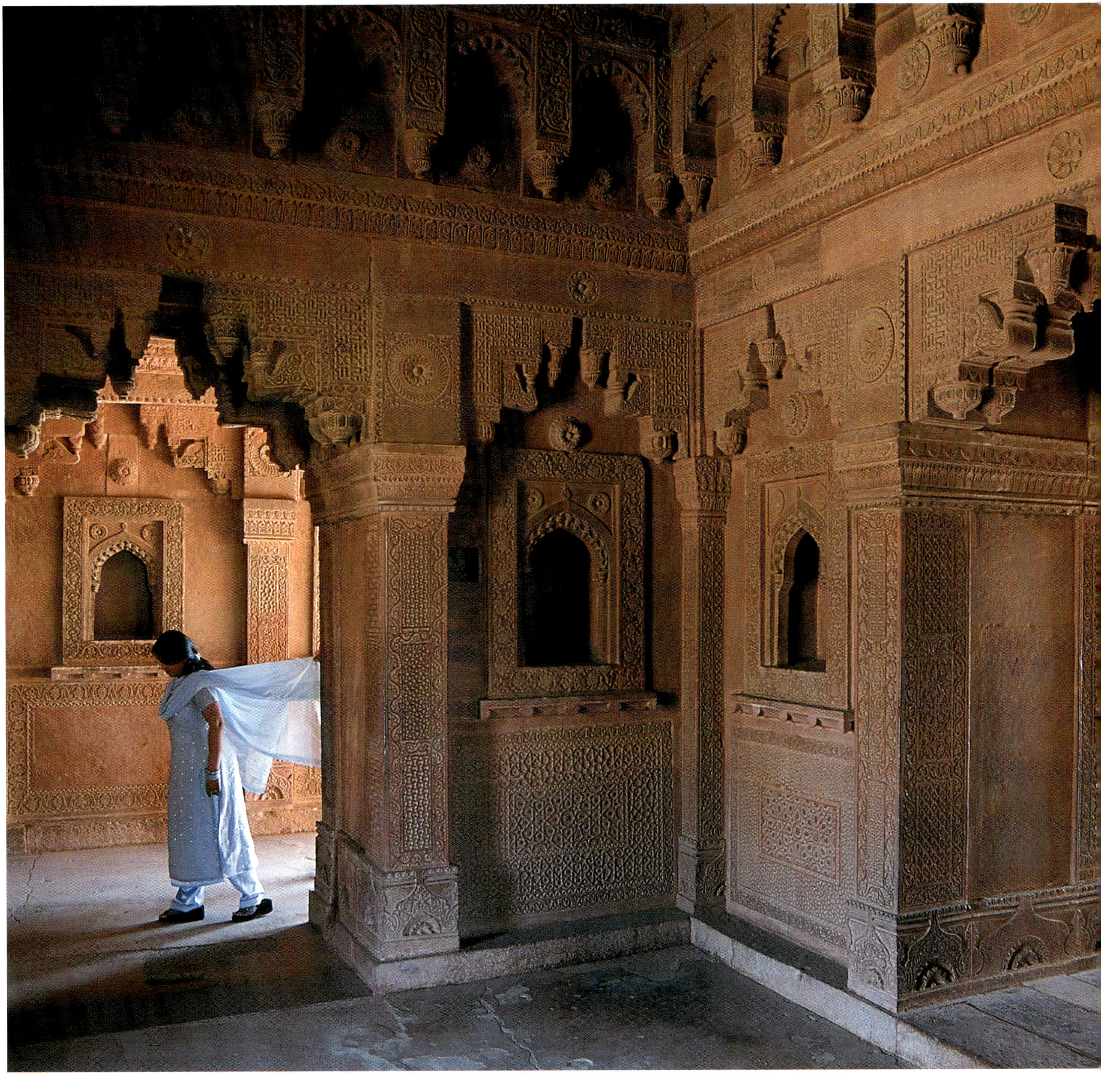

RAJASTHAN

Land of Contrasts

Rajasthan, with its lofty, overwhelming fortresses, its tranquil villages where life is governed by the rhythm of harvests and its sparkling deserts, is a land of strong contrasts. Second in size of the 25 states forming the Indian Union (that also has seven Territories, including Delhi), it extends toward the northwest over a surface of 342.000 square kilometres, that is, approximately two-thirds the size of France, forming a sort of rounded star, the extreme tips of which are 700 kilometres apart. Bordered by Pakistan to the west, it is surrounded by several other Indian states: Punjab, Haryana, Uttar Pradesh, the Territory of Delhi, Madhya Pradesh and Gujarat. Today Rajasthan consists of thirty or so districts, each named after their capital.

Geographically, the chain of the Aravalli mountains, peaking at 1.722 metres, cuts this area in two by a northeast-southwest diagonal, delimiting three large natural regions: an almost barren zone of steppes to the west petering out in the dunes of the Thar desert; a mountainous relief in the centre; fertile plains and basaltic plateaus to the southeast where corn, barley, millet and maize are grown.

A semi-desert region, Rajasthan has three distinct seasons: the hot season (from mid-March to June) with peaks of 45°C; the rainy season from July to September; the cold season, from October to February, when temperatures can go below 0°C. The monsoon, which comes from the south, is essential for crops, bringing 90% of the yearly precipitation. Covering but 10% of the surface of the state and located mainly in the south and the east, the forests are rich in teak. There are mango trees, bougainvillea and deep-rooted banyans as well.

The simple, peaceful life in the villages inhabited by the Bishnois is marked by almost commonplace, but infinitely authentic everyday scenes: the men prepare the opium, the women the hearth. The women are the ones who enliven with rustic scenes the walls of their homes made of clay mixed with cow dung.

Cities Encroached upon by the Desert

Rajasthan is irresistible, with its scattering of ostensibly different cities. The capital and showcase of the state, Jaipur, "the pink city", is a crossing of roads and landscapes. In the north the region of Shekhawati is dotted with large sand-swept towns and houses called haveli decorated with gorgeous frescoes. In the west the barren Marwar stretches all the way to the Pakistan border. On the edge of the Thar desert cities that grew rich with the transit of caravans offer the visitor their share of legends: Bikaner, Jodhpur and Jaisalmer. In the south the slopes of Mewar add a gentle note to the journey in the vicinity of the romantic city of Udaipur, the pride of Rajasthan.

There is colour everywhere in Rajasthan: on the cottons, on the walls, on the men's turbans and on the veils of the women who walk kilometres to fetch water from the wells, graced with jewellery from head to toe.

Tireless workers, Indian women in their gestures and costumes have preserved true distinction.

Nature Presently Preserved

*I*n matters of ecology, Gaj Singh is not easily taken in. His ancestor bore the highly respectable title of "Minister of the forest and wild animals" under the reign of the colossal maharajah Madho Singh II who ruled Jaipur in the middle of the eighteenth century. Owner of the elegant Alsisar Haveli palace-hotel which is the highlight of Jaipur, Gaj Singh is proud of his Rajput roots and aristocratic title. He is thakur like others are count or duke, and his sense of hospitality is unsurpassed. But when a guest criticises the maharajahs, like accusing them of having massacred thousands of animals in the course of memorable hunting parties, usually in the company of British guests, his warrior roots flare up. He runs to get the photograph of his Minister ancestor whom he ardently defends: "Until the Independence it was forbidden to cut down a tree without the maharajah's authorisation," he explains. "And animals were protected as well. The ones killed during the hunts were scrupulously counted."

Times have changed. The former estates of the maharajahs have been turned into reserves for the protection of various species, protected areas and national parks. As part of the UNESCO World Heritage list, the park of Keoladeo Ghana, between Agra and Jaipur, shelters over 350 species of rare birds including cranes, marabous, herons and teals that come and reproduce in complete security. Tigers, panthers, hyenas, jackals, are also under the protection of man. Cervidae like the sambar stag and elegant antelopes lead a blissful life here and there as in the park surrounding Akbar's mausoleum at Sikandra. The peacock, symbol of the Indian Union, can fan its tail in complete safety: men have decided to assist nature. As for the Indian city, it is a huge circus where cows, dogs, pigs and monkeys wander about freely, along with squirrels that will eat out of your hand and geckos, those inoffensive lizards whose mysterious cawing resonates in the evening air.

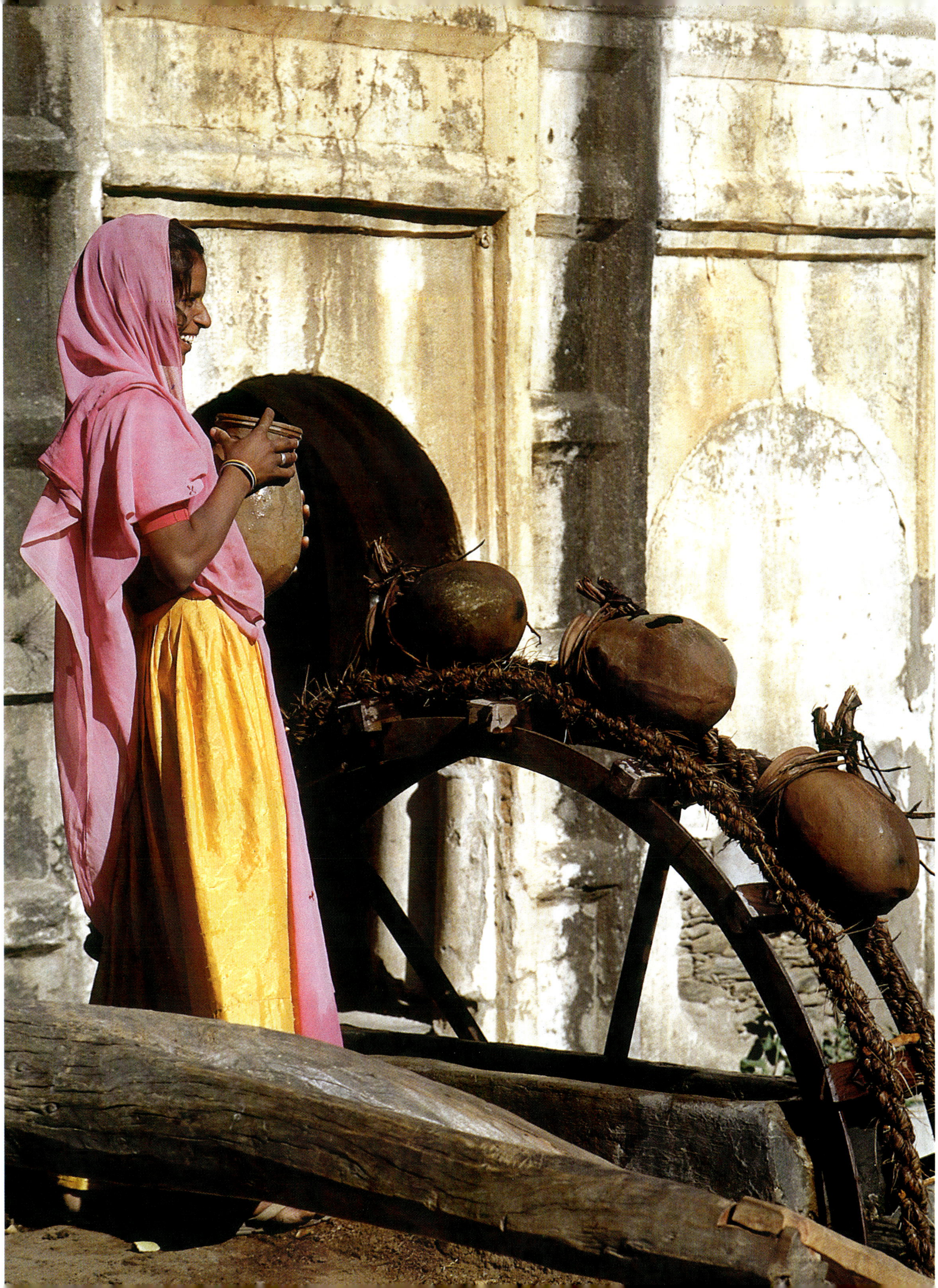

This year's harvest will be good on the land of Delwara, in the Udaipur region.

Next double page: Gold work, painting, weaving, textile, pottery, sculpture… The traditional arts of Rajasthan inherited the fruitful encounter between Hinduism and Islam, the Moghuls and the maharajahs, and are still very much alive.

Page 124: Production of Jaipur blue pottery.

Page 125: Shield and swords from Bhanwar Niwas.

The Indian Countryside

"India is in the country", Gandhi used to say. 80% of the population of Rajasthan makes a living from agriculture. A great many irrigation canals have been dug since the Independence, enabling to irrigate 30% of the land, but it is never enough.

Life is simple and peaceful in these villages where the same almost timeless customs persist: turbaned men sitting together and drinking tea with milk and women readying the fire. In the country, houses are built low, the roofs often made of straw. Smells of incense, patchouli and sandalwood are omnipresent and there is colour wherever you go. The adobe walls are decorated with frescoes of gods and animals or adorned with geometric motifs drawn in the clay. The well is a place for getting together and having a nice chat. Women come or go, on the road or the track, carrying their jar on their head. These women are so elegant, with their ghagra, a long bright red, purple or acid-green gathered skirt; their short bolero (kanchli), their tight blouse (kurti) and the veil covering their shoulders (orhni). The hems with their gold thread sparkle, steeped in sunlight; the bracelets on their arms and ankles tinkle with the same rhythm as the bells of the animals ploughing the field nearby. Fatality helps make life so much easier. If the crop is lost or if the buffalo dies, the small landowner will put the blame only on himself, believing it is the price to pay for sins committed during a former life; written in the book of fate.

123

Traditional Arts in Rajasthan

In the course of history, invasions and influences, Rajput and Moghul artisans combined their skills. In peacetime, the arts often blossomed, encouraged by the maharajahs. In wartime, the winners took in their service the losers' artists, who then provided their experience. The example of the art of blue pottery, still crafted in Jaipur, is a good illustration. Arisen in Persia or China, this art was first introduced in India by the sultans of Delhi, then encouraged by the maharajah of Jaipur, Man Singh (1590-1615), in his city. The tradition is still alive in "the pink city". Made of earth and gum, without clay, handcrafted and fired only once, the pottery is decorated with Persian motifs and arabesques blended with the turquoise blue obtained from copper sulphate.

What fascinates us most when we arrive in Rajasthan is the sheer beauty of the costumes. The fabrics and their colours are like a display of fireworks. But this is not really so surprising. The sight of small flocks scattered in the desert is as common as that of women spinning wool in the village or that of the weaver, the julaha, at his loom. The dyer is at the end of the chain. The colours chosen and the shapes of the costumes are inherited from tradition. It all has a meaning, such as red, the symbol of love that is a must for wedding costumes. As for the shape of turbans, which can be ten metres long, it indicates the caste and the birth of the wearer.

Another surprise is the quantity of jewellery (often silver) gracing the women. A whole collection: bracelets, necklaces, armlets or anklets, bhanvatiyo (nasal ring linked to the earring), a pendant on the forehead called tikka... It goes way beyond mere vanity. It is almost a feature of society. For ages these jewels were the only legal possession granted Indian women, whose right to inherit was not recognised until 1955. If silver prevails, it is because it could always be converted into cash by the saraf, the village jeweller. The jewels are rarely antique since usually old jewellery was melted down to fashion new forms.

In many of its aspects craftsmanship in Rajasthan was boosted by the wealth of its ores of granite, marble and red sandstone which inspired the sculptors to create impressive lace facades and jali (fretted stone screens) to adorn the haveli. Copper and zinc deposits (the alloy of the two metals produces artistic bronze) also enabled the skilled Hindu and Muslim ironworkers, the lohar, to express their talent on blades, daggers, doors...

The Moghul emperors and the maharajahs fought each other before joining forces, but they shared the same taste for beauty and refinement. The emperor Akbar had the master weavers of Persia brought to India. In the seventeenth

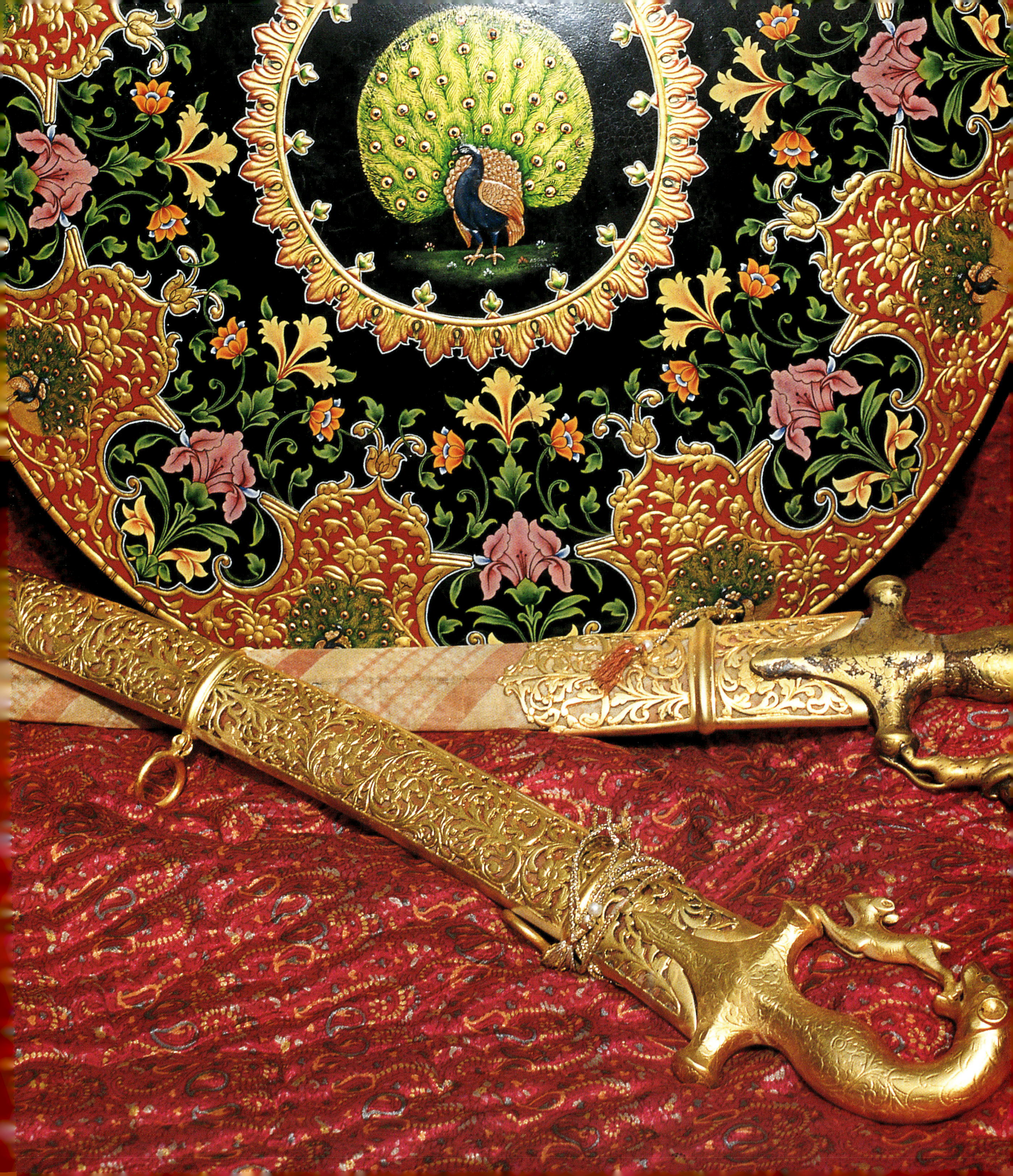

In the seventeenth century, after years of fruitless fighting, the Rajputs finally sought an alliance with the Moghuls and at last could begin to display their wealth and develop workshops in their kingdoms. The maharajahs became patrons of the arts (jewellery and fabrics worn at weddings in the Jaipur region).

century, the maharajah Man Singh invited five families of enamellers from Lahore to come to Punjab to develop the art of enamel, minakari, which is still practiced in Jaipur. The eighteenth century was less involved in warfare. The maharajahs put it to advantage. They flaunted their fortune and opened royal workshops at Jaipur, Jodhpur and Bikaner where the best craftsmen were hired. The art of embroidery blossomed as well and tailors designed magnificent Court garb adorned with gold thread embroidery.

The Moghul emperor Jahangir had a passion for miniatures. To immortalize pomp and ceremonies, weddings, kings' hunts, the painting schools of Mewar, Bikaner, Jaipur, Marwar and Bundi-Kota were founded, each with its own style. The artists from Mewar preferred very bright colours, concentrated on faces and almond-shaped eyes, brought to perfection the beauty of animals; we recognize the Bundi-Kota school by the representation of graceful women, the straight line of their nose. The painters from Bikaner often featured Moghul scenes, whereas those from Jodhpur specialized in epic frescoes showing mighty Rajputs mounting high-stepping coursers. In 1864 the maharajah Sawai Ram Singh II (1835-1880) founded a weaving workshop specialized in the manufacturing of fabrics, rugs and kilims. For a long time now Rajasthan's expression of art and culture has looked to the future.

127

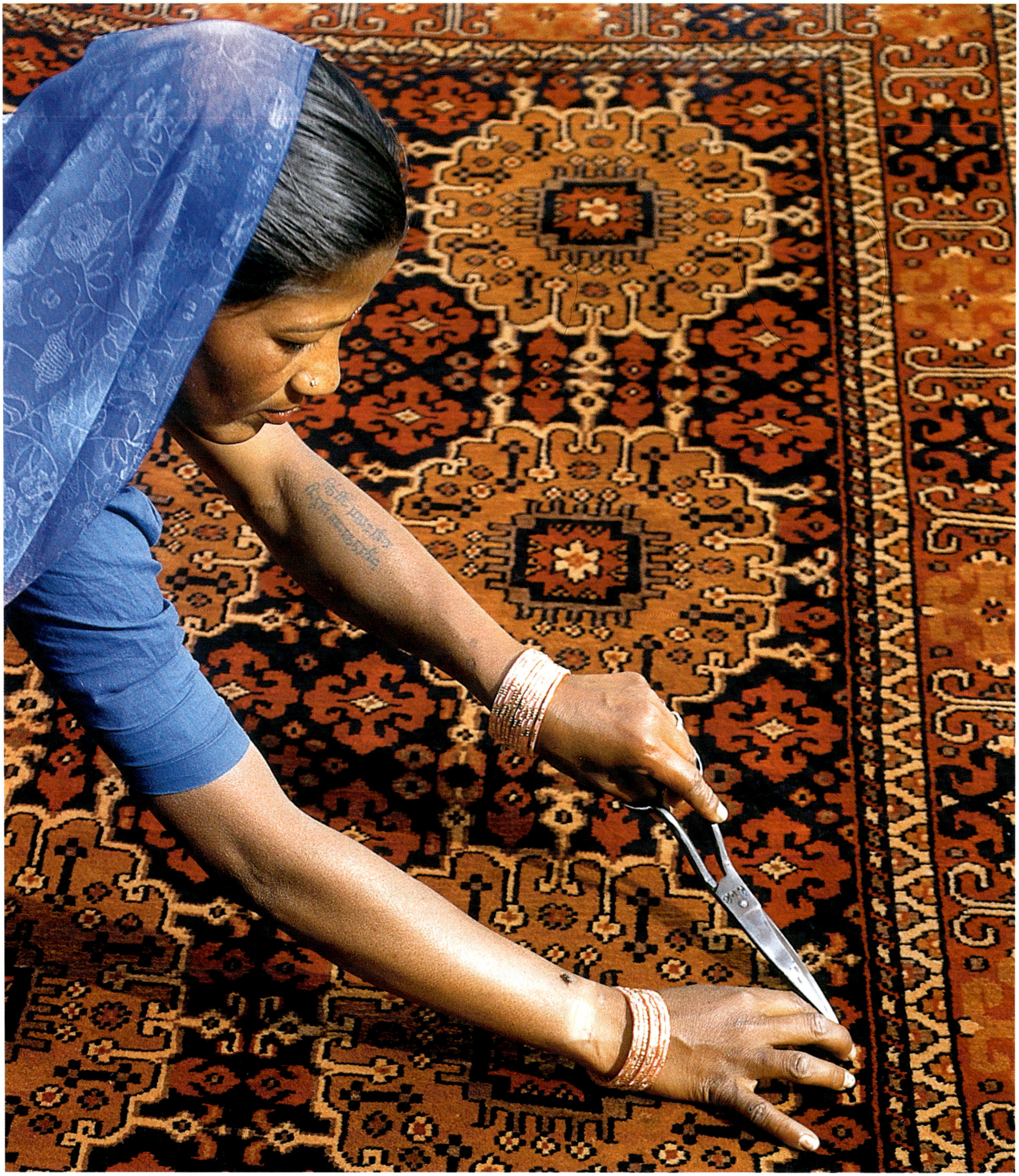

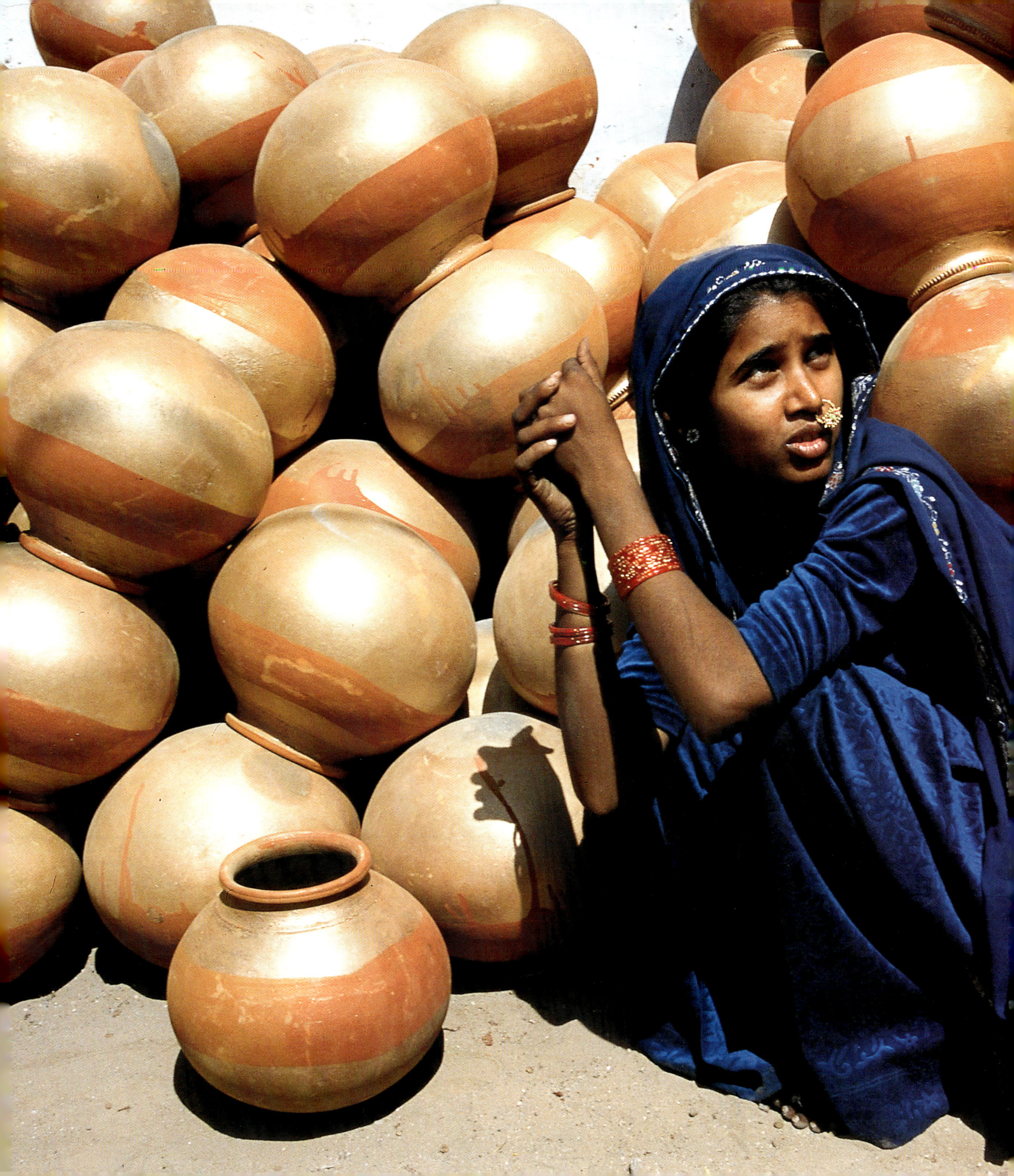

Rudyard Kipling wrote that the maharajahs "were created by Providence to provide the world with picturesque settings, stories about tigers and grandiose spectacles". Ruling supreme over their kingdom and their subjects, many were ardent champions of the arts and courageous entrepreneurs. The maharajahs of Jaipur: Man Singh II, the last ruling maharajah, and Madho Sing II, below.

The States of Rajputana

*I*n his book *The Rulers of India and the Chiefs of Rajputana between 1550 and 1897*, lieutenant-colonel Thomas Holbein Hendley counted 21 states forming Rajputana, which at the time of the Independence would become Rajasthan. Seventeen of them were Rajput by tradition: Bundi, Kotah, Jhalawar, Sirohi, Jaisalmer, Karauli, Jaipur, Alwar, Jodhpur, Bikaner, Kishangarh, Udaipur, Dungarpur, Banswara, Partagarh, Khetri and Shahpura. The states of Bhartpur and Dholpur were in majority Jat (peasant warriors) and that of Tonk was Muslim. At their head, were nawabs (Muslim princes) and Rajput clans from the warring caste whose origins are often associated with longstanding legends, some claiming they descend from the sun; others from the moon. Their sole duty was to protect their kingdom. To do so they spent centuries in internal struggles and wars against the Moghuls before becoming their allies.

Of all the Rajput clans, that of the Sisodya of Mewar (Udaipur), whose origins are said to go back to the seventh century, is reputed the most heroic. Having always resisted invaders, it often rivalled with the Marwar clan (Jodhpur). Toward the sixteenth century, the Kachwaha (from Amber and Jaipur) offered a princess to the Moghul emperor Akbar and became the rising power. Peace brought prosperity to the kingdom of Jaipur. We would have to wait until the nineteenth and early twentieth centuries to see the rise of the maharajah of Bikaner, Ganga Singh, who stole the show from the other clans by offering his army to the British in 1914. He embodied the image of the most progressive maharajah, representing India at the post-war peace conference and signing the Versailles Treaty. In 1913 he even gave his state a Legislative Council and in 1935 attempted to persuade the other princes to join a sort of federation with British India.

*Preceding double page:
Invited by Akbar, master weavers from Persia had a profound influence on the art of rug making, especially at Jaipur, the first city to create royal textile workshops. The maharajah Ram Singh II even decided to use prisoners to make the rugs that still adorn the royal palace museums (inside a family workshop and a pottery workshop in Jaipur).*

British Promises

The princes took sides with the British, who promised them almost everything. In 1858 Queen Victoria proclaimed the British would respect the rights, the dignity and the honour of the autochthonous princes as if they were their own. The maharajahs were allowed to keep their interior sovereignty and the right to choose their heir. The borders of their state were even recognised by a treaty, and they could have their own currency and postage stamps. But declaring war and having diplomatic representatives was out of the question. Furthermore the princes of India had to come to the rescue of England should it be threatened. In exchange, there was glory! In 1861 Queen Victoria had written up a list of the honours to be rendered to the maharajahs by the English troops. There were two kinds of gun-salutes: the first in recognition of the state and the second to honour the maharajah himself. The number of salutes ranged from 9 to 21. A premium for the princes of over 11-gun salutes was the title "His Highness". But misdemeanours were punished. One of the viceroys, haughty Lord Curzon, exasperated by the lavish expenditures of several maharajahs during their trips to Europe, even went so far as to depose them in 1900, imposing on them resident administrators.

Royal hunting parties and honours abounded… One of the most impressive receptions took place in Delhi on 29 December 1902 on the occasion of the lavish assembly of maharajahs. 430 armoured elephants paraded during this great durbar. Dozens of European guests, more than 400 kings figured in the procession in the honour of Edward VII who succeeded Queen Victoria and had himself proclaimed emperor of the Indies. A somewhat short-lived glory.

Assembly of maharajahs in great pomp, before the Independence.

Independence

Mahatma Gandhi, who was preparing the Independence, in a way despised the maharajahs. "They are puppets created or tolerated for the survival and the prestige of English power", he claimed in 1947. And he added: "The absolute power they exert over their peoples is certainly the worst abuse of the British Crown".

Out of the 629 princely states India counted at the outset of the twentieth century, only 554 were taken into consideration at the time of the unification of India. What were the maharajahs promised this time in exchange for their giving up their sovereignty? Almost everything: the full enjoyment of their personal possessions, the respect of their dynastic prerogatives along with the allocation of "privy purses" equal to a tenth of their former income. This allowed them to cover their personal expenses, those of their families and pay their servants. They were to enjoy this sum up to their death but their heirs would receive a great deal less. All things considered, they lost everything!

The Maharajahs' Automobiles

Nostalgic visitors usually perform their devotions in the small museum of the Lalgarh palace in Bikaner, built by the maharajah Ganga Singh in the early twentieth century. A world in itself, an impressive collection of items and photos of the glorious days gone by. You must admit the maharajahs had taste; they were fond of precious stones and jewellery, palaces, pretty women and automobiles. And what automobiles! Bhupinder Singh, the maharajah of Patiala, owned not less than 27 models of Rolls-Royces and three times more cars of other makes. As for the nizam of Hyderabad, he owned over 200 limousines. The maharajah of Alwar specialised in Hispano-Suizas, bought in sets of three,

Bikaner is proud of three generations of outstanding maharajahs: Ganga Singh (seated left) who modernised his state and fought in World War I; Karni Singh (elected member of Parliament after Independence) and Sadul Singh (standing right).

with blue upholstery. He also owned a Lanchester specially made for him in 1924, because he had it gold-plated. And there is more to come: the back section was the replica of the British Coronation carriage and there was a seat for two lackeys and an ivory steering wheel. He died of apoplexy in Paris in 1937, so his remains were returned to India. His faithful Lanchester awaited him with its chauffeur at the border of his state, to comply with his last wishes. The "gilt hearse" carried the dead sovereign to the pyre: sitting straight up, gorgeously dressed and wearing white gloves and sunglasses. A man of fashion to the very end…

More about the Maharajahs!

The extravagant tales about the lives and whims of the maharajahs are countless and sometimes touching. Travelling through Europe in 1900, Jagad Jit Singh, maharajah of Karpourtala, fell in love at first sight with France, the French, the chateau of Versailles and the Sun-King Louis XIV. He was worse than in love, he was out of his mind! He wanted to be the reincarnation of the Sun-King. So once he was back in his kingdom, he commissioned French architects to build a real palace in the style of Versailles, with gardens à la française. He ordered his entire Court to wear Louis XV costumes with white wigs and learn to speak French. The "made-in-India Versailles" was inaugurated in 1909 after spending seven years building it. Nothing was left up to chance. Each of the 100 apartments was named after a French city or personality. The decoration featured wooden panelling, drapes, Sèvres vases, Gobelins tapestries. He even created a National Assembly, a palace of justice and a hospice-town for elders. But to share his future life, he had to attract a true French woman… whom he never found. He made the best of it with a Spanish woman, whom he married in 1906. She held out for ten years, but finally enough was enough!

The gäekwar of Baroda preferred the British style. "No problem!" Major Charles Mant, architect and officer of Her Gracious Majesty, concocted a residence matching his taste and his fortune: three times the size of Buckingham Palace. Completed in 1890 after a yard that lasted twelve years, the Lakshmi Vilas palace housed 1.000 servants. It was so vast the gäekwar used a scooter to go from the dining room to his bedroom. As regards decoration, a dozen Venetians worked 8 months to lay down the mosaic floor of Durbar Hall. Nothing could be too beautiful. The marble was from Carrara, the chandeliers from Venice. You might call it living in style!

The Palace-hotels of the Maharajahs

Gandhi had advised the British: "Quit India as masters". They come back as tourists with everyone else, greeted with open arms in these palaces and fortresses converted to luxury hotels in which Indians take great pride. After the Independence, some aristocrats had the bright idea of transforming their residences into luxury hotels to preserve their heritage.

The very glamorous maharajah of Jaipur, Sawai Man Singh II, was the first. The Rambagh Palace opened its doors to nascent tourism in 1957. Although these days the atmosphere is slightly lacking in warmth, the suites are truly irresistible. The authors took a fancy to the Prince's Suite, with its marble pool at the foot of the bed and its terrace overlooking the gardens…

The royal family of Bikaner followed with the Lalgarh Palace and the Laxmi Niwas Palace, today two impeccable hotels. The maharajah of Jaipur did the same with his immense Umaid Bhawan palace, one of the choicest hotels in Rajasthan. The suites of the Shiv Niwas Palace and the Fateh Prakash Palace, which are a part of the Udaipur Palace, are not bad either. But for a truly memorable honeymoon, the most romantic will agree on the Lake Palace: it appears to be floating upon Lake Pichola. A jewel among palaces!

If you are in a romantic mood you can perform your devotions at the Lake Palace: it appears to be floating upon the quiet waters of Lake Pichola at Udaipur. Even if it has lost a bit of its soul, a few suites, like the Khush Mahal Suite and the Danshya Suite, will introduce you to a special world.

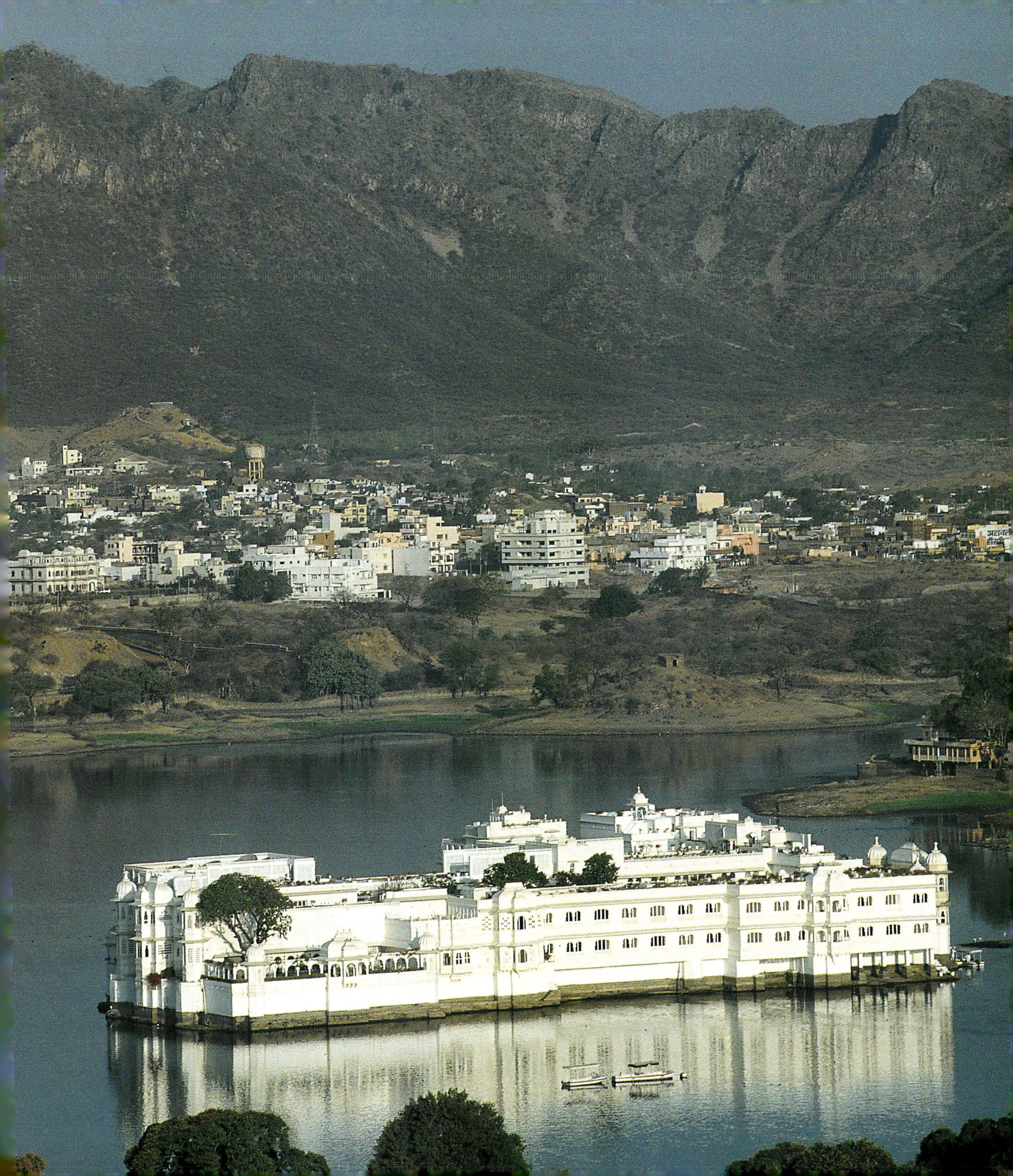

THE KINGDOMS OF ALWAR, DEEG AND TONK

Tired of the bustle of Delhi and curious to explore Rajasthan, on the way to Jaipur the visitor comes upon the ancient kingdom of Alwar, surrounded by the first foothills of the Aravalli mountains. While the village is quiet and offers little of interest, the palace known as the Vinay Vilas is quite a surprise. Enclosed in mountains dotted with ramparts and turrets, it is a symphony of pavilions, porticoes, stucco facades gracefully reflected in a pool that overflows during the rainy season. Moghul and Rajput styles are blended with the curved Bangaldar roofs.

While the origin of the town is unknown, the kingdom was founded by the Rajput Pratap Singh (1740-1791). Built in 1793 by the rajah Bakhtawar, today the palace is occupied by an army of civil servants and partitioned into dusty offices crowded with prehistoric typewriters and heaps of files. Time-worn and even dilapidated in some places, it is still evidence of the wealth of the princes of Alwar who flaunted their might, won through their submission to those who were mightiest: Moghuls, Jats, Marathas, British… and now civil servants!

A great fan of tiger hunting parties he organised in his region, Jai Singh was perhaps the most extravagant hunter of them all. He had himself called "Sawai", which means a quarter more than a mere human being, and had a weakness for blue Bugattis (blue is the emblematic colour of Alwar). He ordered them in sets of three and had them buried when he grew tired of them. The British were finally annoyed by his little foibles (such as having his horse burned alive) and dismissed him without further ado. The maharajah died in Paris in 1937.

The fortress of Alwar (125 kilometres northeast of Jaipur) is a choice stopover for dreamers and solitary strollers. Not a lot of tourists, but a lot of style! If part of the royal palace is now occupied by an army of civil servants, democracy's heroes, in the mountains you can discover admirable palaces and temples.

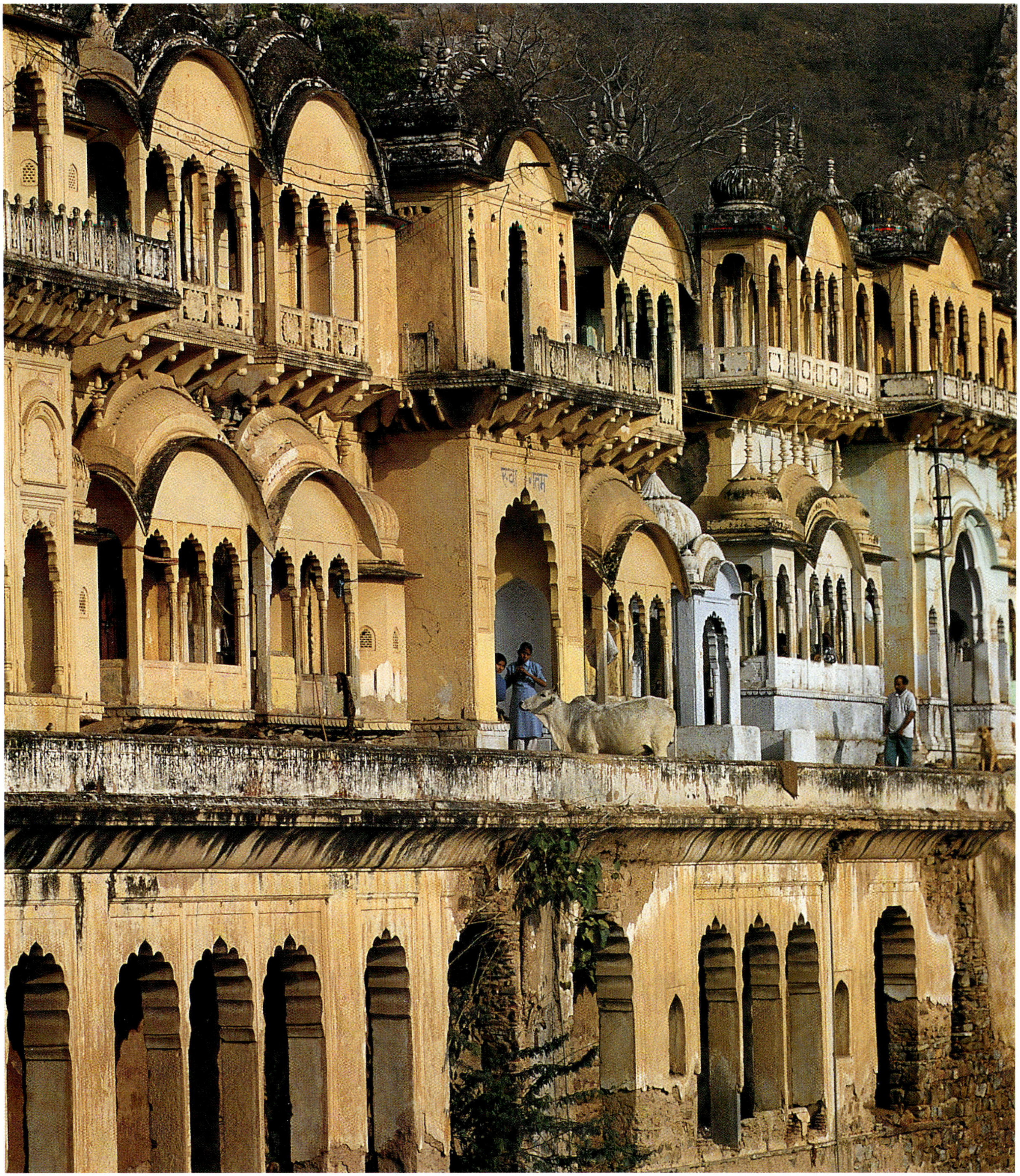

Behind the royal palace of Alwar, the elegant cenotaph of the maharajah Bakhawar Singh is venerated by all. History tells that his wife became sati by sacrificing herself in the funeral pyre. The red sandstone lower floor is enhanced with pavilions while the white marble first floor has Bengali roofs and is crowned with a beautiful ribbed dome.

Various articles, costumes and documents evoking Court life are assembled in the museum on the top floor of the palace. You can ferret out some true wonders: eighteenth-century copies of the Ramayana, a fine set of miniatures of the Alwar School and arms having belonged to Akbar.

Outside, the terrace offers a fine view onto the central courtyard, framed by lovely marble palaces and by the durbar, the hall for public audiences, adorned with frescoes and arabesques. But there are more treasures in store! Behind the facades, the cenotaph of the maharajah Bakhtawar Singh built in 1815 is quite moving. It commemorates the sacrifice of his deceased wife who became sati by leaping into his funeral pyre. This small pavilion is very striking with its soaring columns, its display of red sandstone and white marble, its carvings, its painted interiors. The entire place gives an impression of serenity with its wealth of temples and old houses surrounding the pool, formerly the palace reservoir.

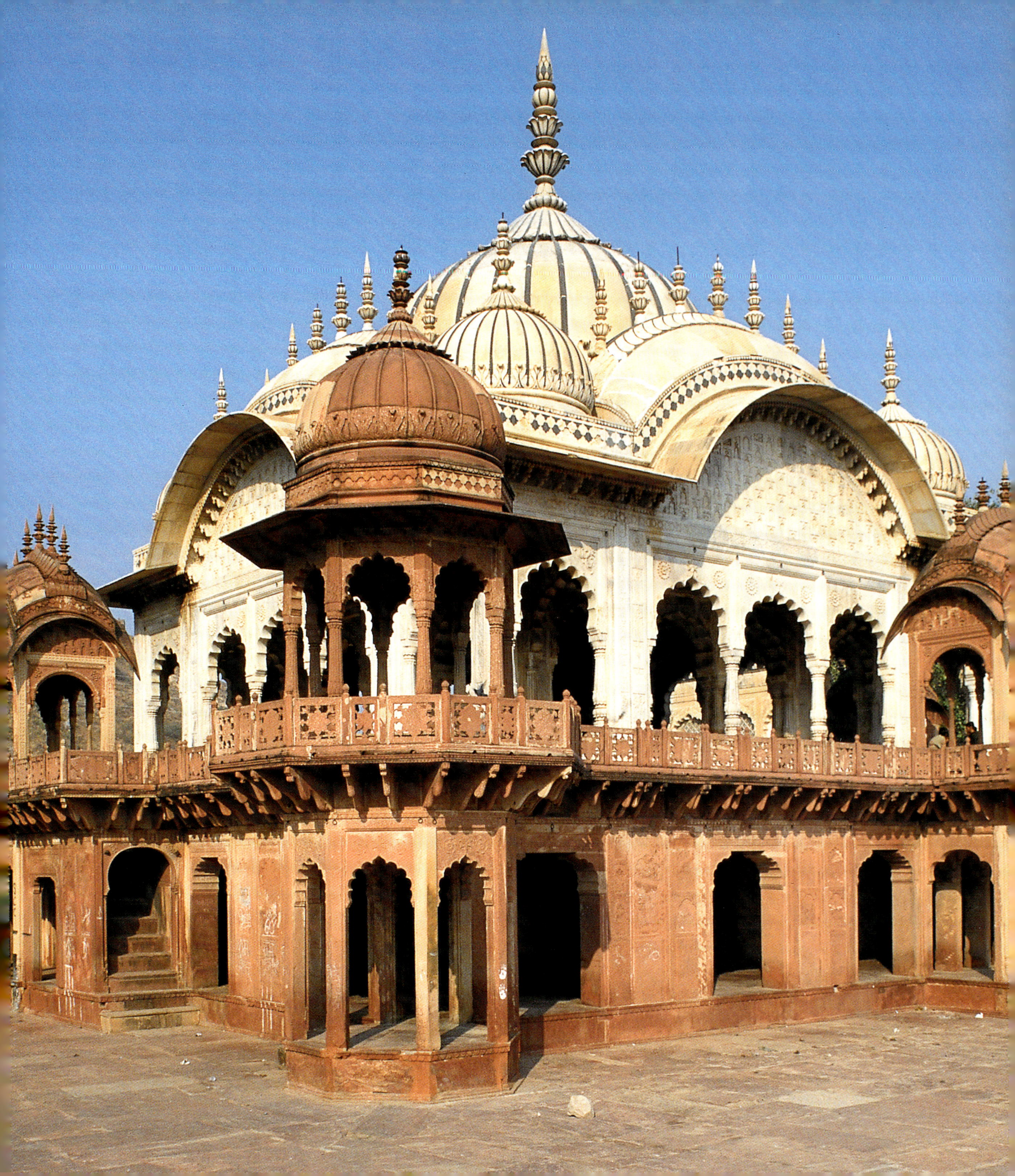

The palace of Deeg is steeped in a sort of indolence that goes with the old-fashioned decor of "old pink" facades and Bengali roofs overhanging the water... Behind the multifoil arches of the palace erected in 1763 according to a Moghul design, worn sofas, moth-bitten rugs and voiceless gramophones display the last splendours of the royal family of Bharatpur who left the palace in 1951.

Ninety kilometres east of Alwar, you cross the former kingdom of Bharatpur where the fortresses of Lohagarh and Ranthambhor, as well as the palace of Deeg, again attest to the power of the Jats, those fighting peasants who ruled with their might and their looting in the eighteenth century. Forced to sign the peace treaty with the British in 1818, the maharajahs of Bharatpur had the custom of inviting all the generals and lords in India at the time to extravagant duck hunting parties. VIPs were driven to the battlefield in Rolls-Royces. The most impressive of these hunting parties took place in November 1938. Organised in honour of the Viceroy of the Indies, Lord Linlithgow, it brought about the death of over 4.000 ducks and other birds. Presently, the Keoladeo Ghana Reserve is prized by nature lovers around the world. Over 350 species of birds, including Siberian cranes, live there in peace.

If the Jats were considered fearsome but rather coarse warriors, the palace of Deeg belies that reputation. The summer residence the maharajah Badan Singh had built around 1730 is extremely refined. You can visit the main building, the Gopal Bhawan, where it looks as if almost nothing has changed since the departure of the royal family of Bharatpur in 1951. The furniture is still there. The couches are just a trifle moth-bitten! On your way out, the Moghul gardens graced with pools and 500 slightly worn-out fountains recall the bygone days when the fountains played amidst their rainbow reflections during royal receptions.

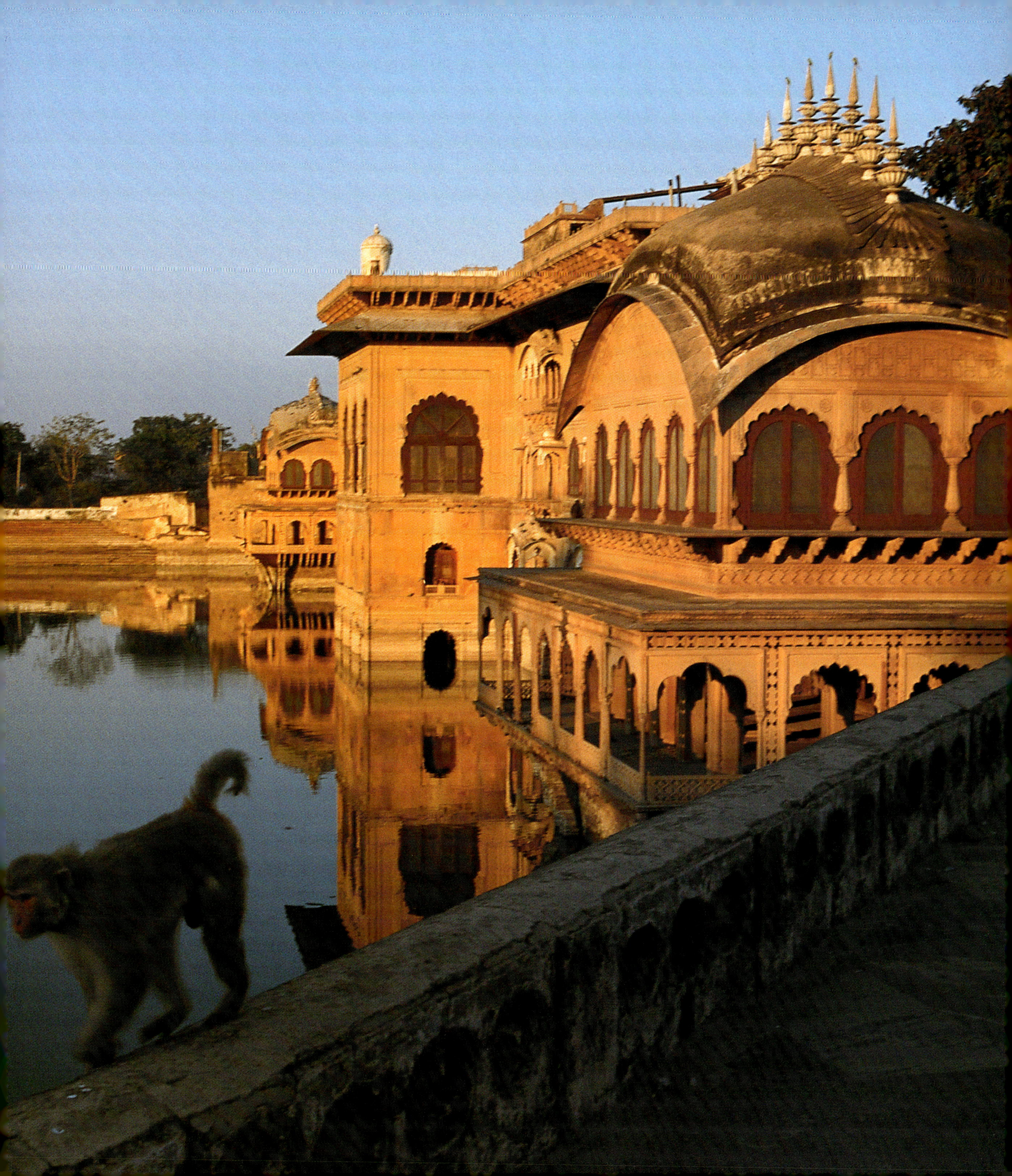

Restoration is under way on what used to be the royal residence of Tonk, the only Muslim kingdom of the former Rajputana. It is like a heaven-sent gift: on the first floor, the Sunehri Kothi (Golden House) displays walls and ceilings covered with remarkable mosaics made of mirror and fragments of painted glass.

On the way to Tonk, 95 kilometres southeast of Jaipur, the local bus usually stops in front of the mosque. Surrounded by children, the imam is accustomed to warmly greeting foreigners and for a few minutes becomes an inexhaustible guide. History claims that Tonk was a Muslim state of which Ibrahim Khan, born in the tribe of the Pathans, was the first nawab (Muslim lord).

If scholars flock from afar to consult precious Arabian and Persian manuscripts adorned with gold and rubies in the city library, lovers of old buildings usually undertake the trip for the former royal residence, the Sunehri Kothi (Golden House) in the process of being restored. An authentic jewel on two levels. The walls and ceilings of the first floor are lit with bits of mirror and lovely painted glass. But the soul of Tonk is elsewhere. At the bend of a narrow street you discover the simple but authentic residence of the family of the last nawab who ruled until 1948, Ibrahim Khan. They are all there, young and old with so many recollections to tell.

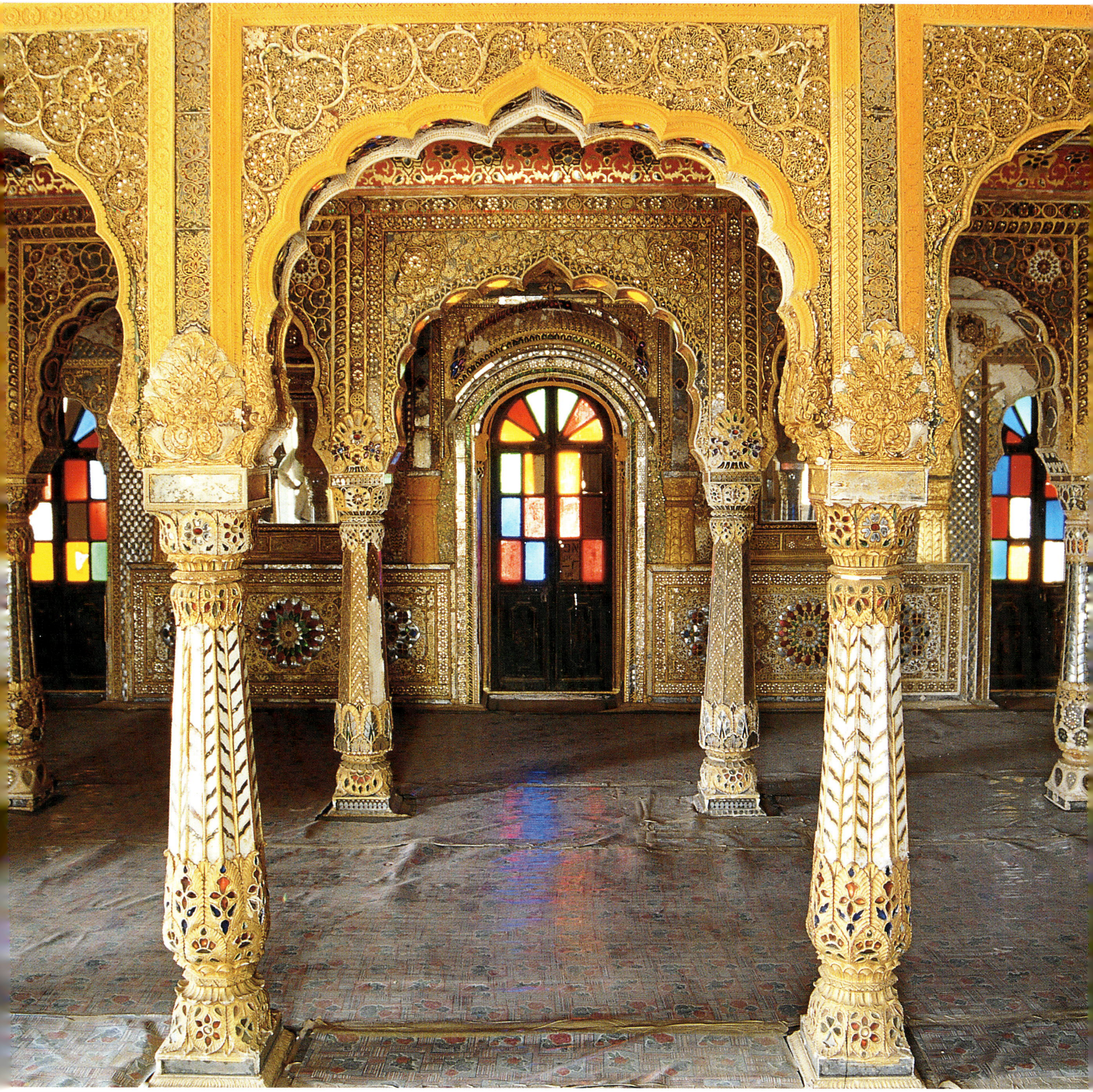

THE FORTRESS-HOTELS OF NEEMRANA, KARNI FORT, DEVI GARH AND SAMODE

Welcome to Neemrana

Let the celebration begin! Gone are the combat elephants, horses and dromedaries. The entrance of this impressive Rajput fifteenth-century fortress is open only to visitors seeking peace and quiet. Restored, consolidated, fitted out, inhabited, Neemrana has recovered its past magnificence with its eight storeys of carved balconies and Bengali roofs.

Exhausted after so many battles and their heroic resistance against the enemy, often Moghul or Maratha, some fortresses are ending their lives agreeably, thanks to patrons heedful of the heritage. Built along the rather tricky road connecting Delhi to Jaipur, the impressive construction of Neemrana, on the mountainside, caught the eye of the French writer Francis Wacziarg who was passing by. Feeling sorry for this melancholy yet lofty mid-fifteenth-century ruin, he finally succeeded in buying it in 1986 after having lived for years in India. He and an Indian friend, Aman Nath, spent years remodelling bastions, turrets and walls that clambered ten storeys down the rocks, to convert it into an ideal weekend haven with truly delightful suites, furnished with the finest Indian antiques. Ambassadors appreciate it!

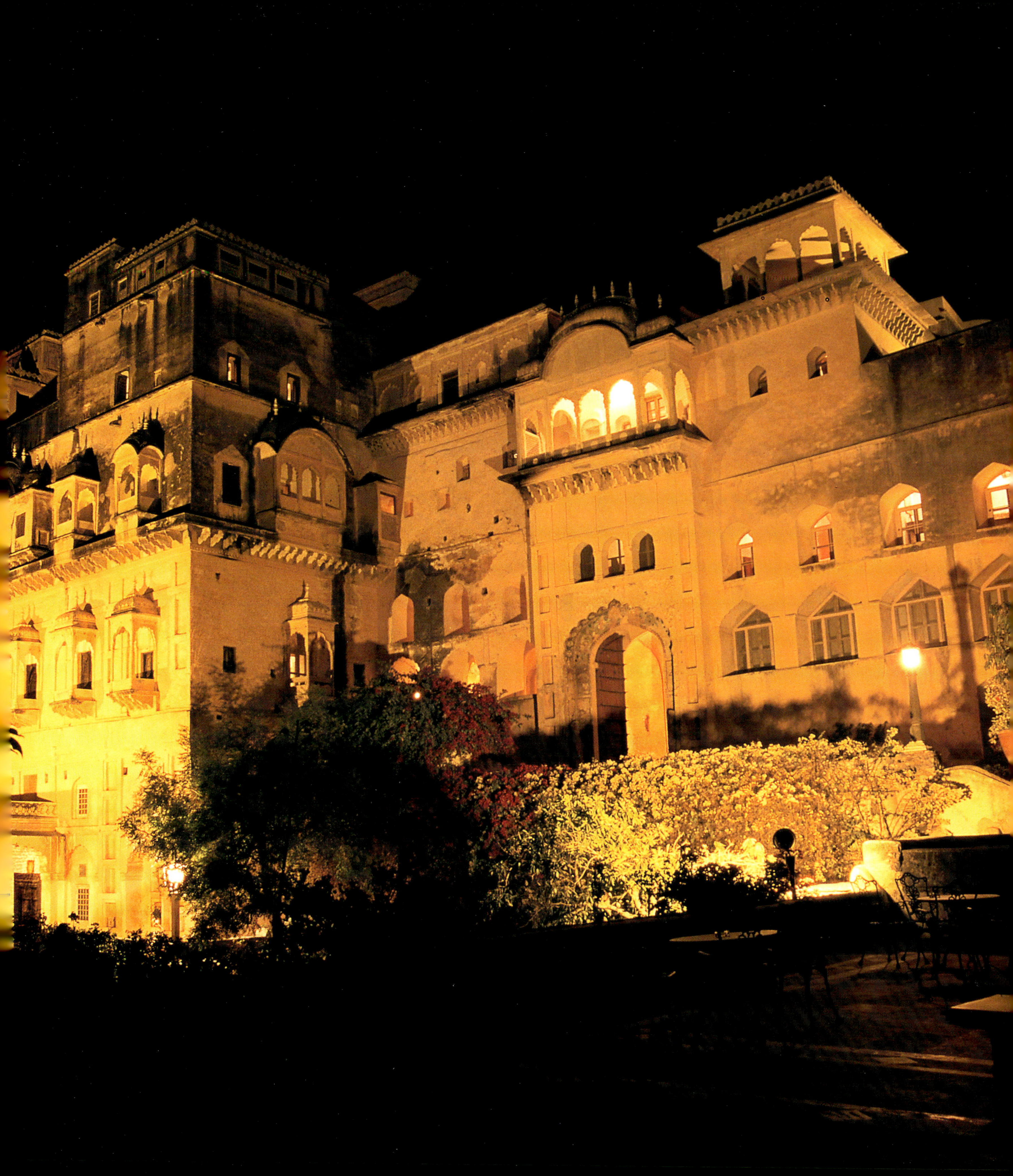

Both art patrons and designers, Aman Nath and Francis Wacziarg entirely renovated this Rajput fortress that was practically in ruins and located in a rather uninspiring region. A small miracle! Today all Neemrana hears is compliments for its swimming pool, its Ayurvedic cures, its comfortable suites with their multifoil arches and rustic Indian furniture. Bravo!

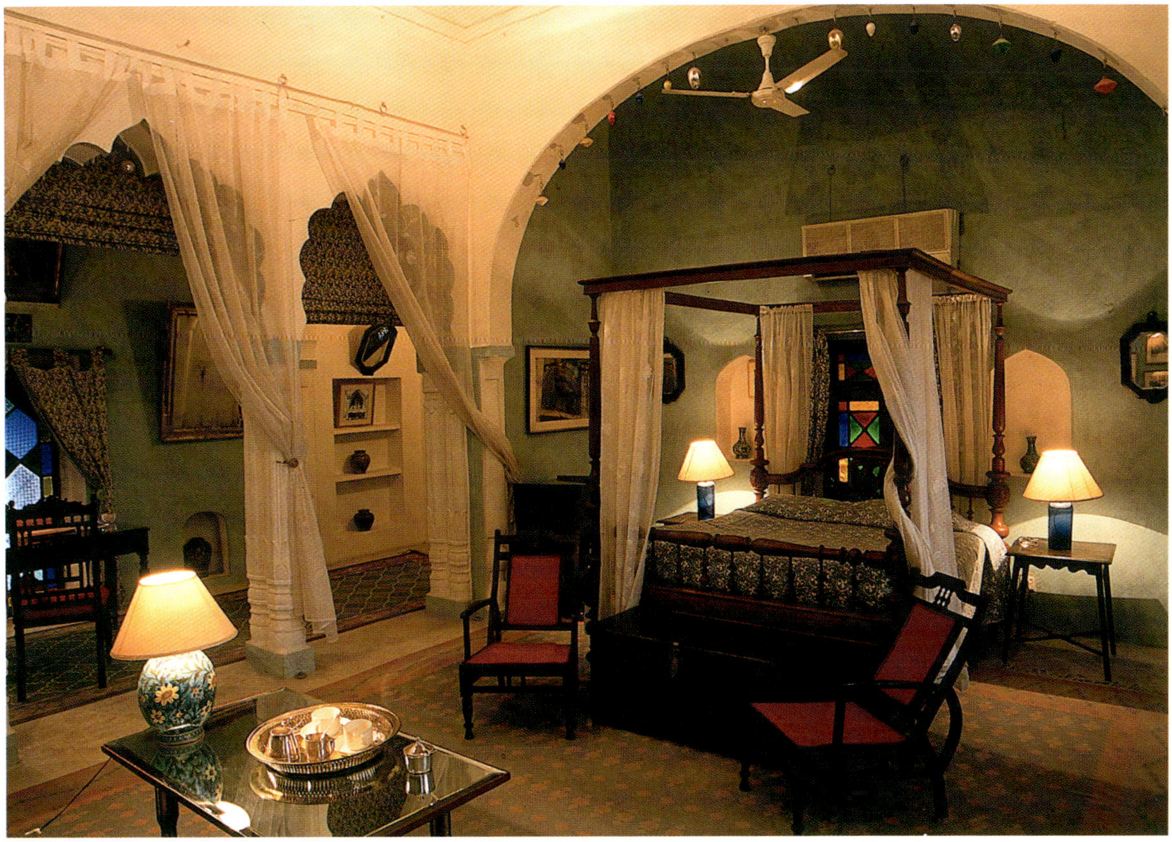

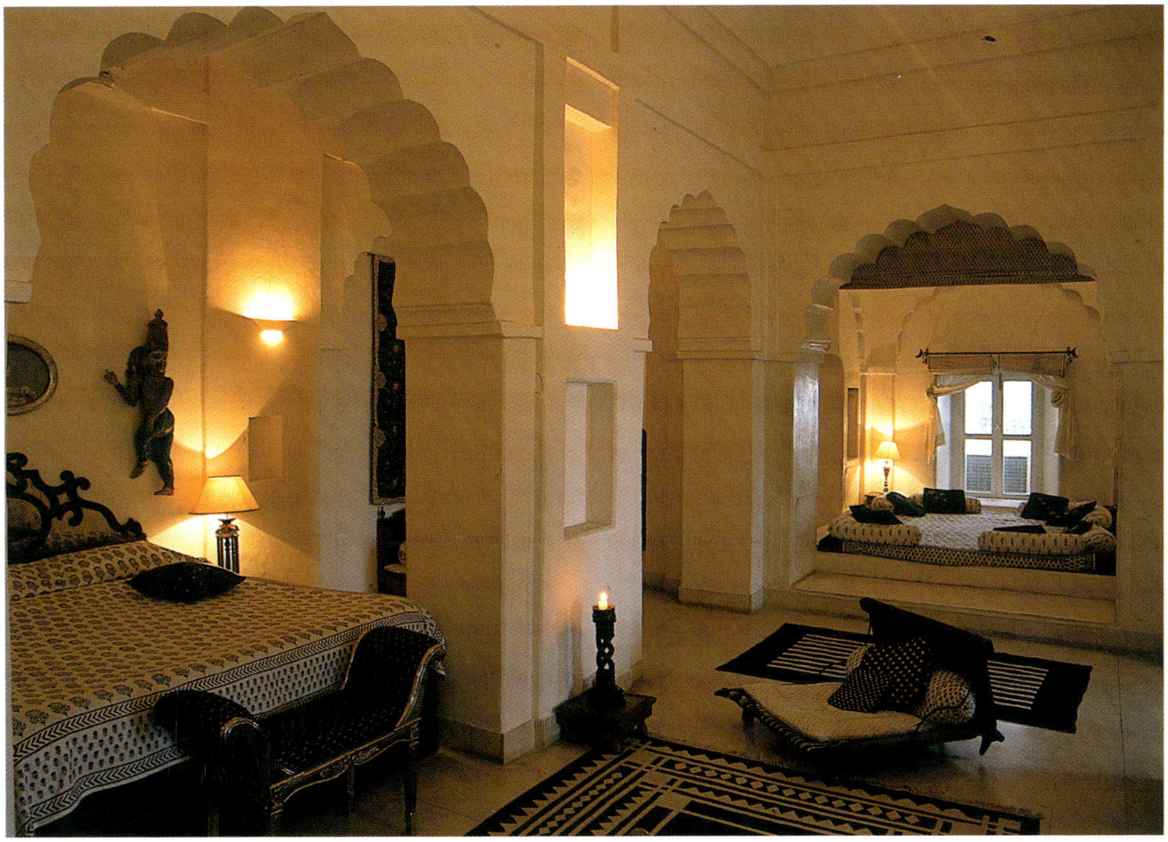

Bambora is just a little lost town some fifty kilometres southeast of Udaipur. Yet we are stopped in our tracks on discovering its mediaeval Karni Fort, gallantly perched on a hilltop. Our chateaux on the Loire better watch out! The fortress was in a wretched condition when the private secretary and great personal friend of the maharajah of Jodhpur, the thakur Sunder Singh, decided to restore it at a huge expense. Having inherited the gallant spirit of a true Rajput, he offered it as a gift to his wife who had fallen in love with the fort. After holding in check the Moghuls, today it is a quality hotel offering the comfort of 30 beautifully decorated suites and rooms. The marble swimming pool, in the midst of the gardens, is a favourite of the visitors. A family atmosphere reigns: the thakur, his thakurani wife Chanda Kanwar of Sodawas and their son Vicku greet their hosts with warmth and enthusiasm.

Welcome to Karni Fort

You cannot resist the charm of Karni Fort whose turrets rise up in the region of Udaipur. Ages ago this eighteenth-century castle was given to the Rana Sanwat Singh of Salumber by the maharajahs of Sisodias. Neglected and quite the worse for wear, the determination of the thakur Sunder Singh and his wife converted it into a charming stopover. Each suite is a jewel glorifying Indo-Muslim art.

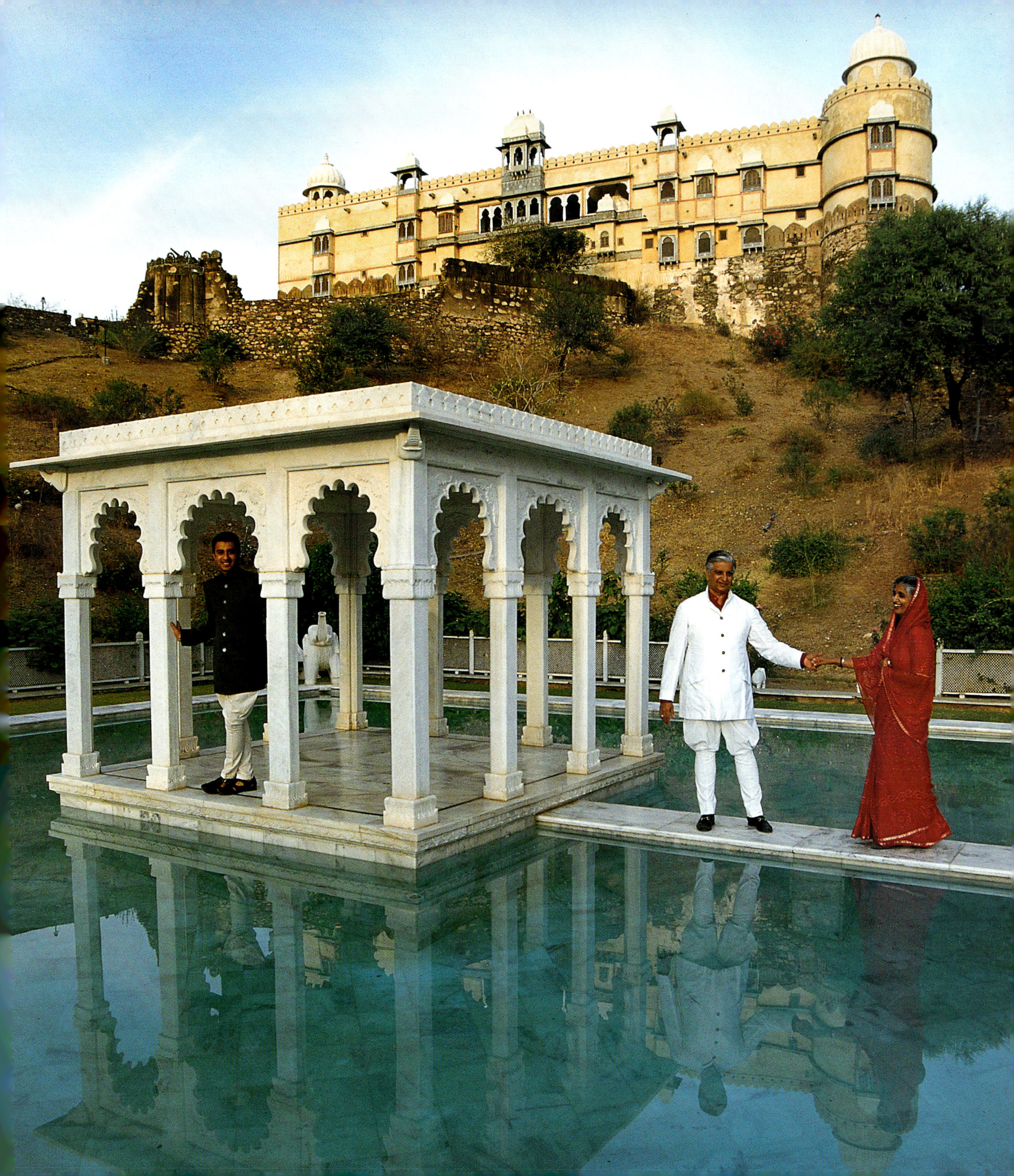

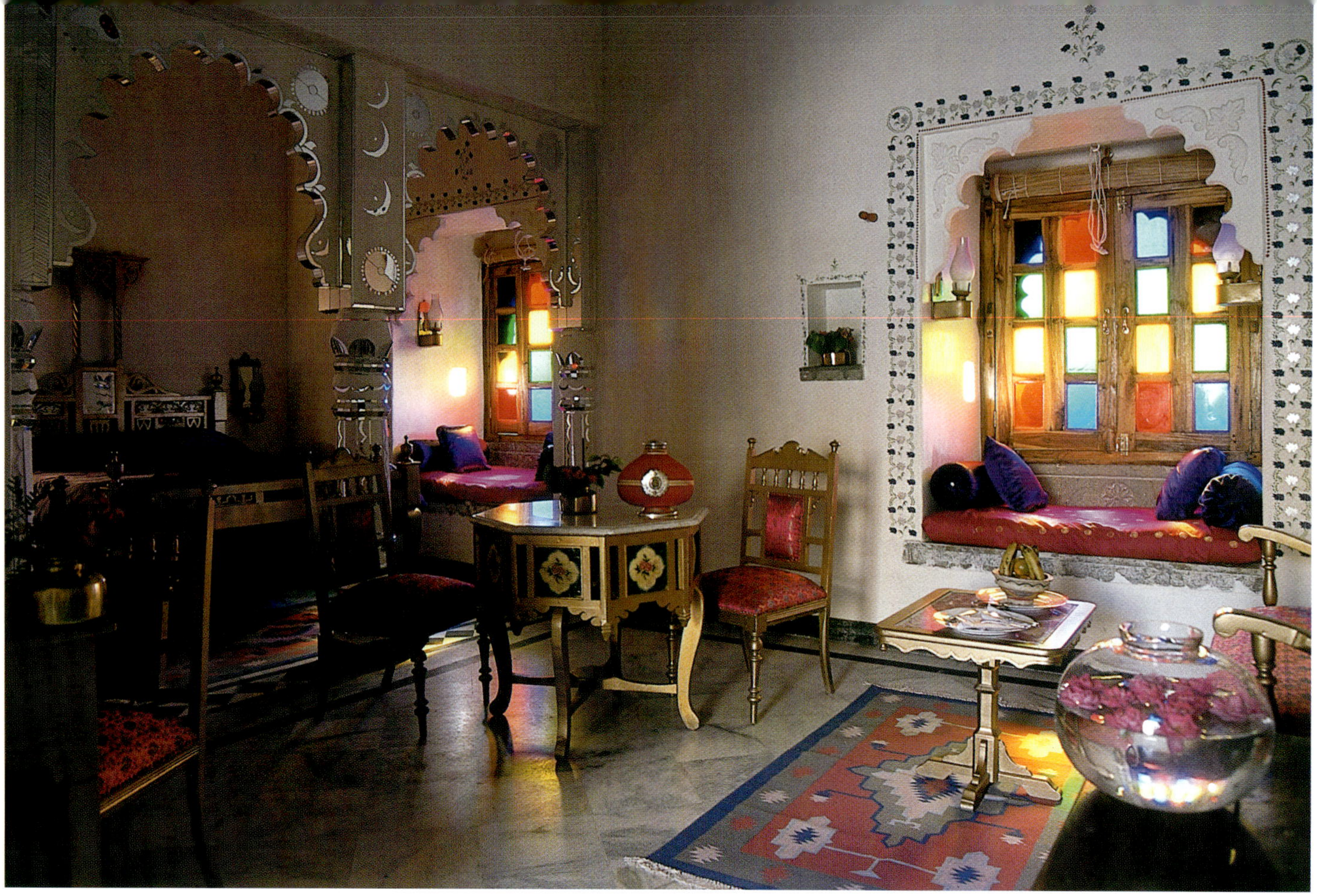

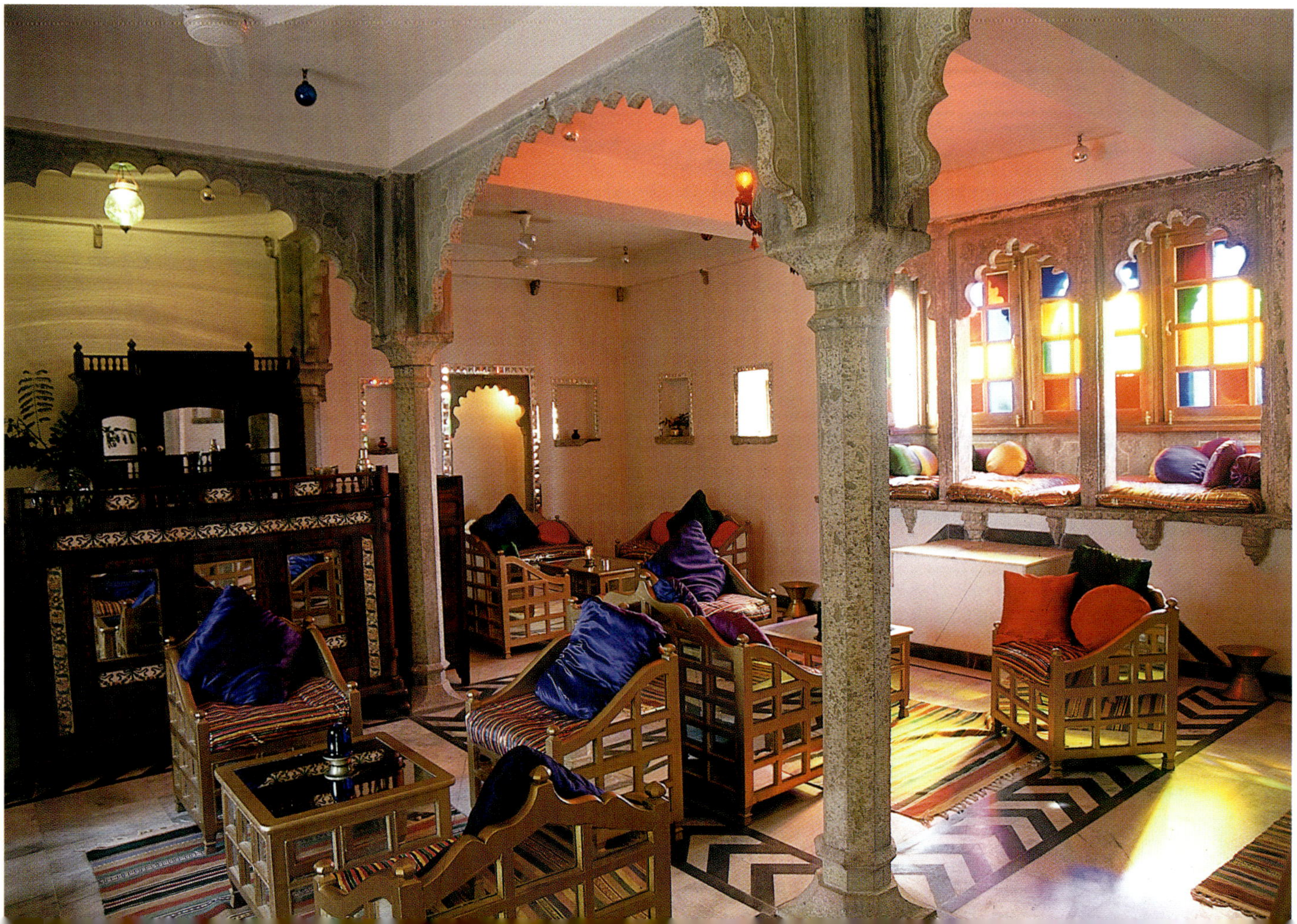

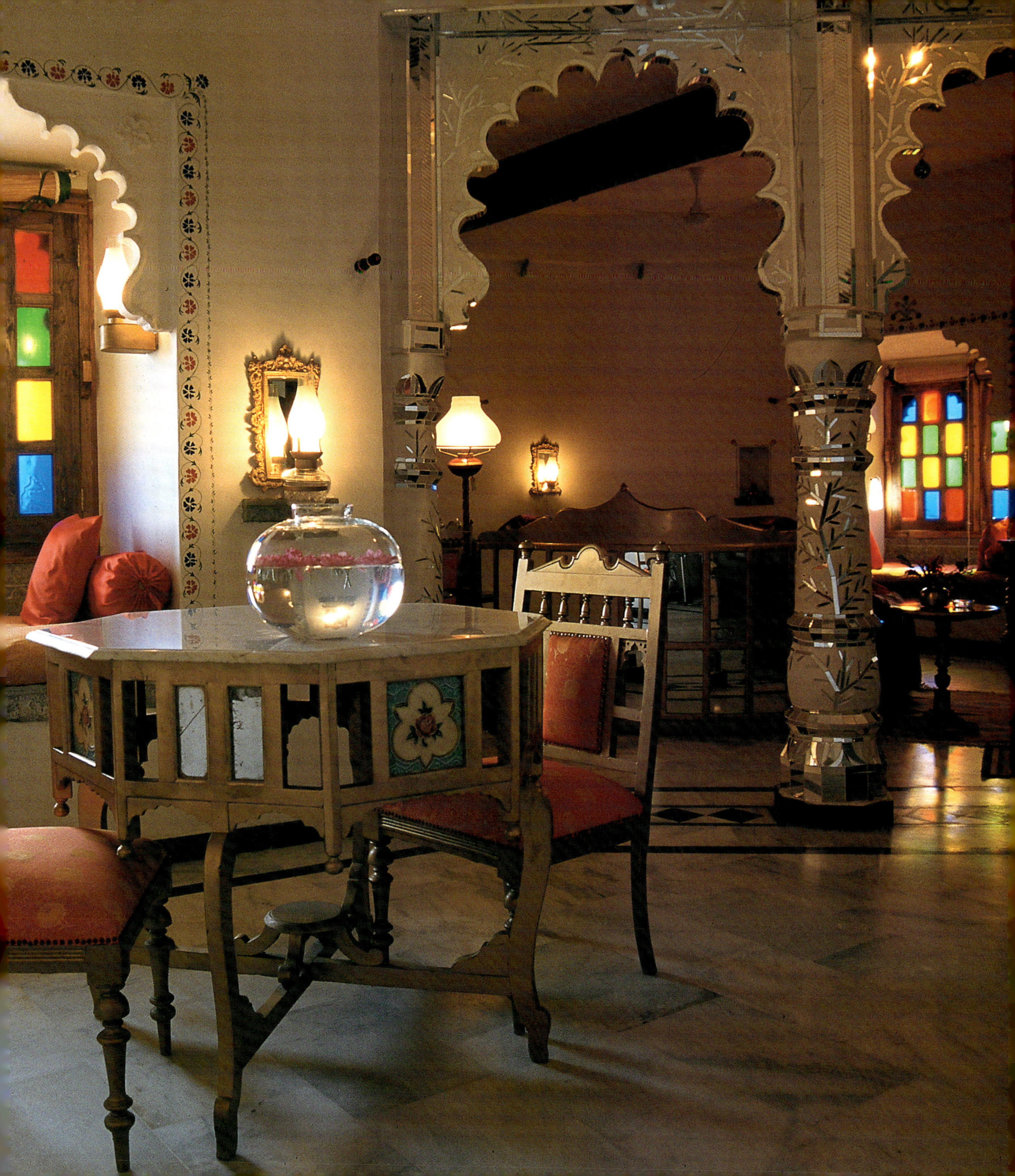

Welcome to Devi Garh

This lofty sixteenth-century Rajput fortress was converted into a minimalist palace-hotel thanks to the talent of its owner, Lekha Poddar. She loves architecture and decorating, and claims she is influenced by Asia, especially Japan. Opposite: The simplicity of the grand salon, former Durbar Hall where the rajah gathered his Court.

Even more outstanding is the new appearance of Devi Garh, the only minimalist palace in India. What more can you ask for? This is a rare address shared by jetsetters at trendy parties in Bombay and Delhi. A few carefully selected Indian families come and "religiously" have a cup of coffee just to see this unusual fortress. Is it a hotel or a palace? In any case it is not visibly advertised. Just the name Devi Garh with the logo of triangles inside circles informs the visitor leaving Udaipur. Actually, the hotel is known only to a small number of relatively wealthy tourists. Perched above the large town of Delwara, 28 kilometres northeast of Udaipur, this Rajput fortress does not appear to have suffered from the onslaught of time. The inside underwent a complete metamorphosis, and offers the privileged 23 suites in a refined style (if you have the choice, ask for suite 34, an utterly enchanting small duplex!). The decoration is both sober and highly sophisticated. For relaxation: outdoor swimming pool, Ayurvedic massage, yoga at daybreak..., 150 servants to pamper you during your stay. A dream! This desert castle that had resisted the assaults of the Moghuls had been completely forgotten and abandoned in 1960 by the family of a nobleman, Rajrana Khuman Singh. A few years ago, Lekha Poddar, an interior decoration enthusiast (and an extremely talented one) fell under its spell and designed this fabulous minimalist palace-hotel, for the delight of its guests and the people of the village who work here. She and her husband had seven dams built to bring water for the crops of the peasants in this desert region and a new road was put in so as to not disturb the villagers.

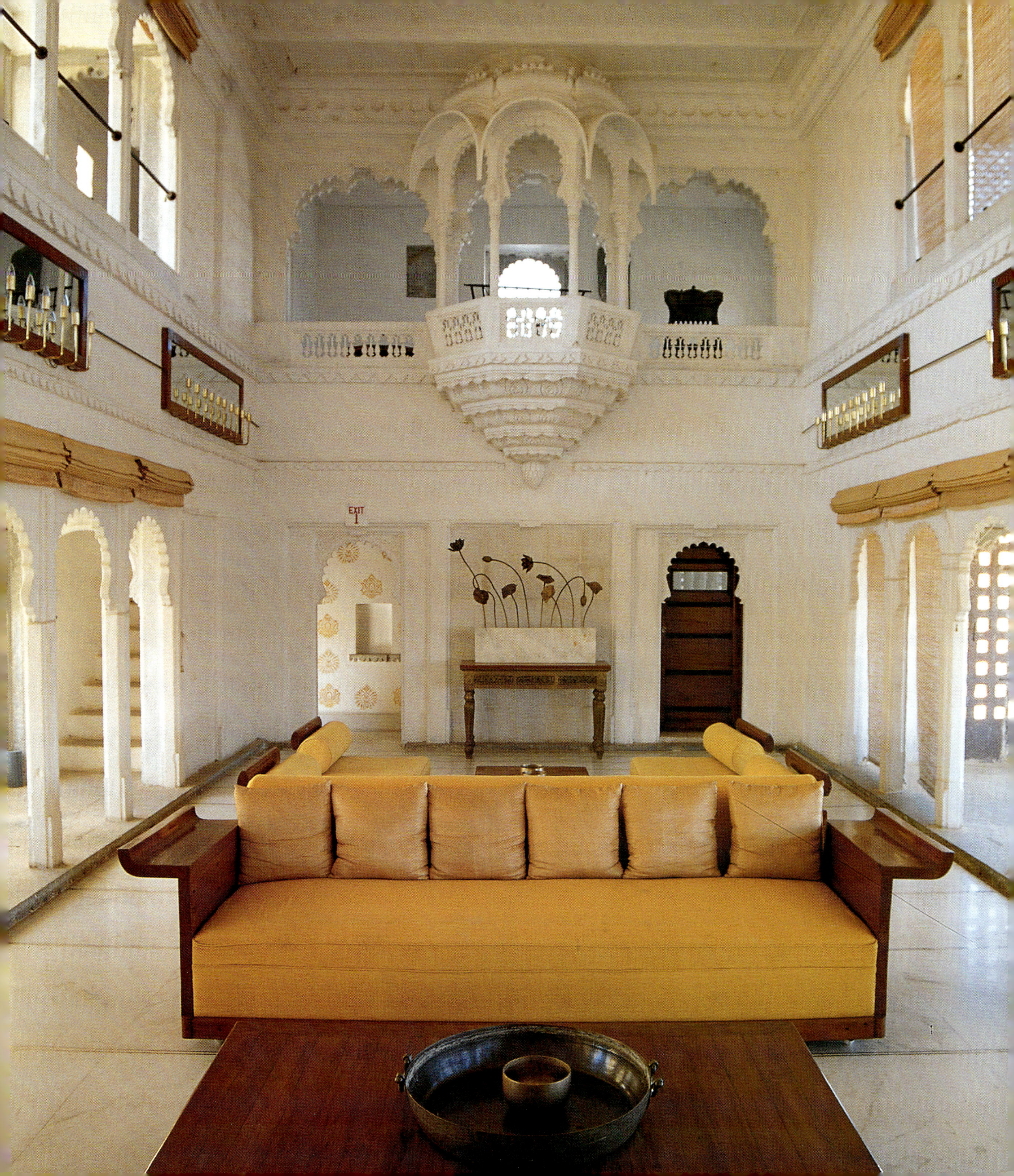
EXIT

Wherever you go in Devi Garh you will see immaculate white walls and sofas, yet each of the twenty-three suites has its own strong personality. Over the bed in Suite 43, there is a set of miniatures featuring the months of the year (above). Page 155, the Suite Aravali 34, with its wall covered with stylised lotus flowers.

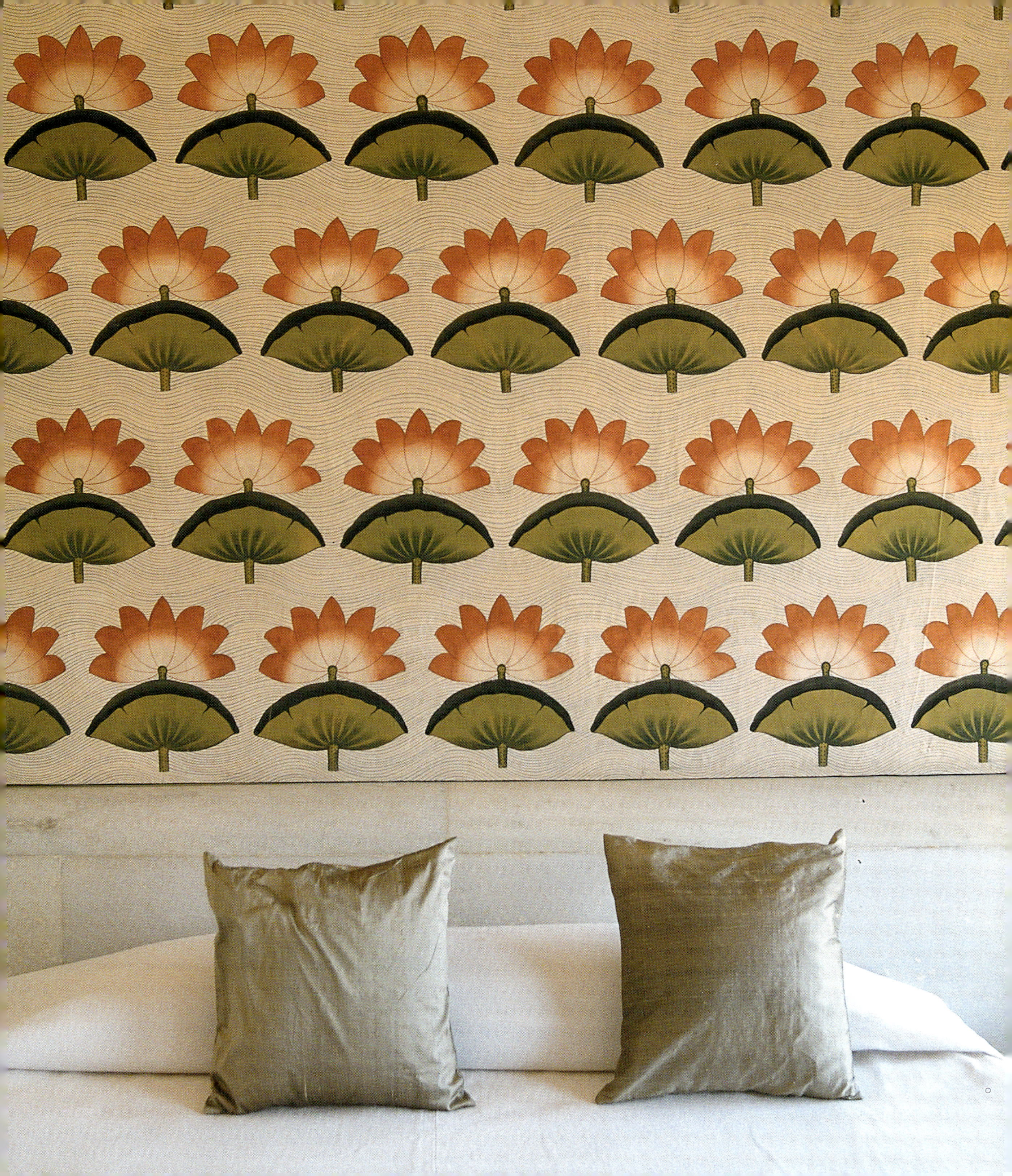

Devi Garh soon became one of the most popular addresses in India. Deserted in 1960, purchased and successfully "minimised" by the Poddar family in 1986, today it offers an atmosphere contrasting tradition and modernism. Festive atmosphere in the old palace of mirrors, the shish mahal.

157

The Samode Palace is another must for hedonists. Why not say so? It is supposed to be the most stylish palace-hotel in all of Rajasthan. Some forty kilometres from Jaipur, hidden in a narrow pass amidst the rocks of the Aravalli mountains, this palace built four hundred years ago is truly gorgeous. The owners, two aristocrat brothers, Yadavendra Singh and the rawal Raghavendra Singh, had the good fortune to inherit it from their ancestor, Prime Minister of the maharajah of Jaipur. After major restoration work, they opened the hotel in 1986, an ideal compromise blending the mellowness of time with ultra-modern comfort, featuring 43 rooms and suites of perfect taste. A beautifully designed outdoor swimming pool completes the ensemble. Occasionally, during banquets given in the former Durbar Hall, the fairylike bits of mirrors of the Shish Mahal sparkle once again as of old, lighting the amazing mural paintings evoking Shiva. Drums thunder, dancers whirl, brocades glitter. Eyes are wide open to enjoy every bit of the spectacle.

Welcome to Samode

Looming over a pass in the Aravalli mountains, the palace-hotel of Samode is the very essence of Rajasthani distinction, blending the patina of time with utmost comfort. The best address in Rajasthan!

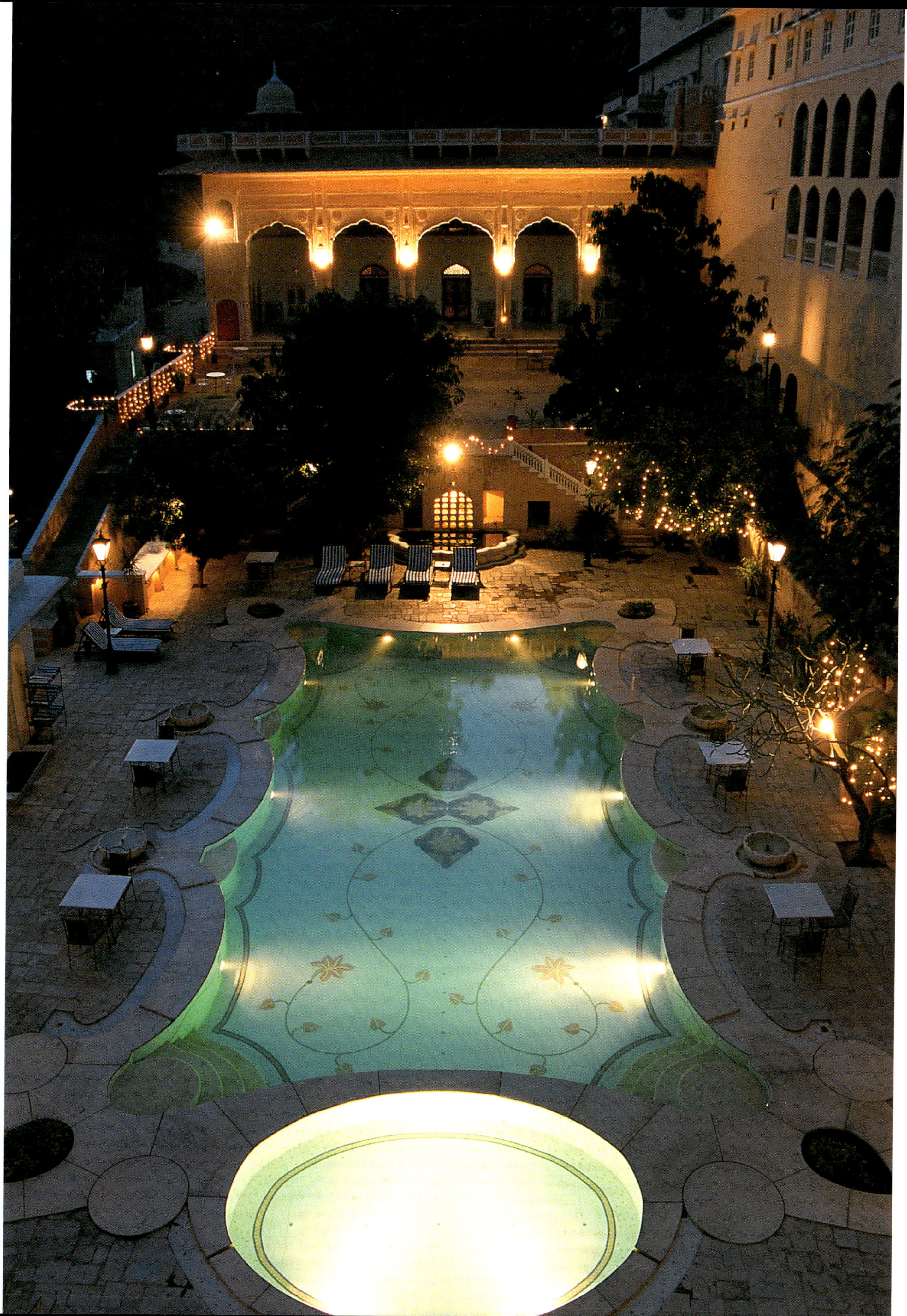

Gildings, paintings and fragments of mirror, the lounges of Samode are an incomparable summary of Indo-Muslim art in all its splendour.

Next double page:
Samode is a fine example of a successful renovation and is first of all a family affair. The two rawal (an aristocratic title) brothers, Raghavendra and Yadavedra Singh inherited this colossal, four century-old fortress from their ancestor, Prime Minister of the maharajah of Jaipur. They renovated and modernised it without losing any of its patina: the solid silver furniture comes from their grandmother, a Nepalese princess. Today Samode is an extraordinary hotel with great character. What would you like: tea or coffee?

161

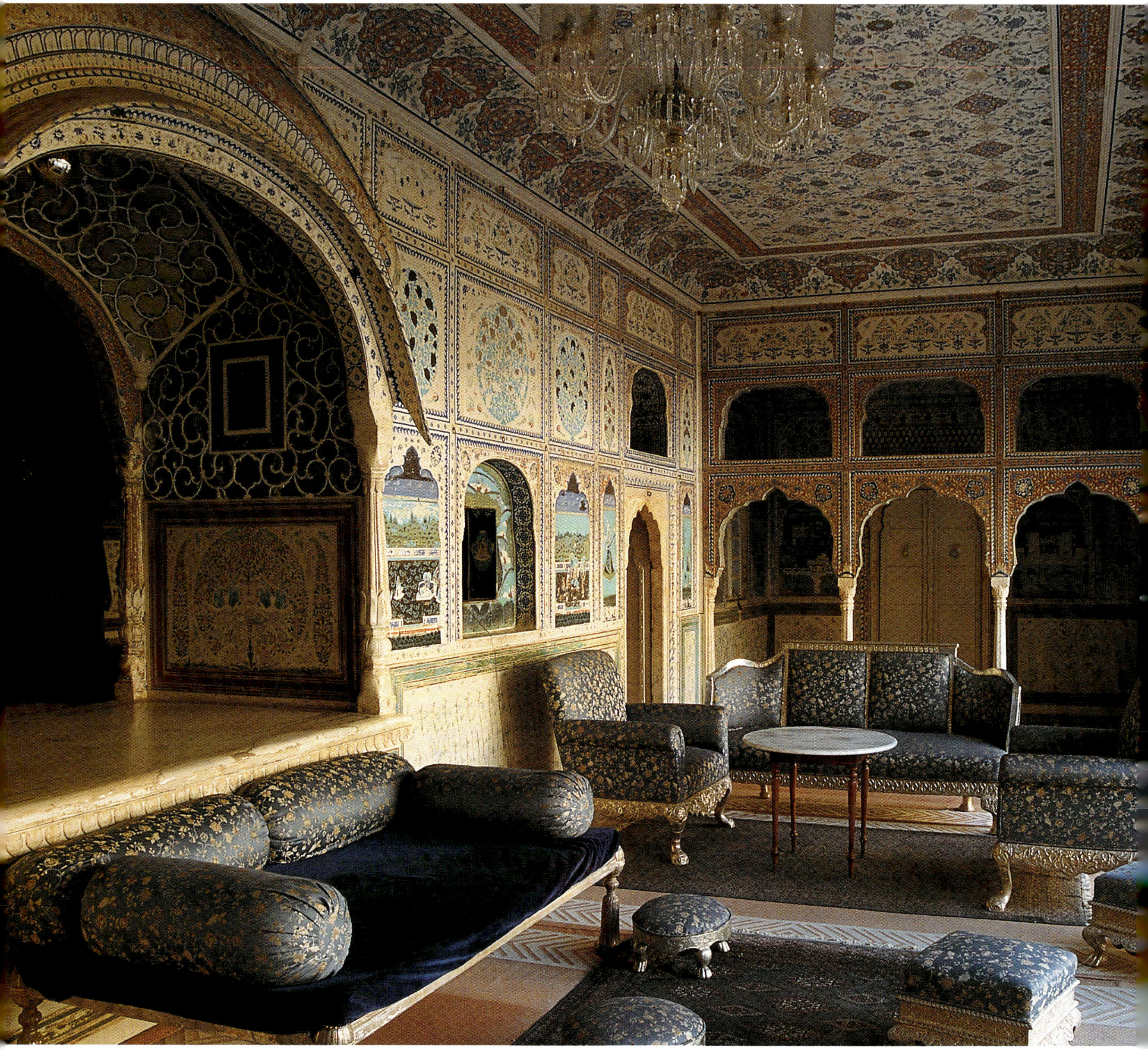

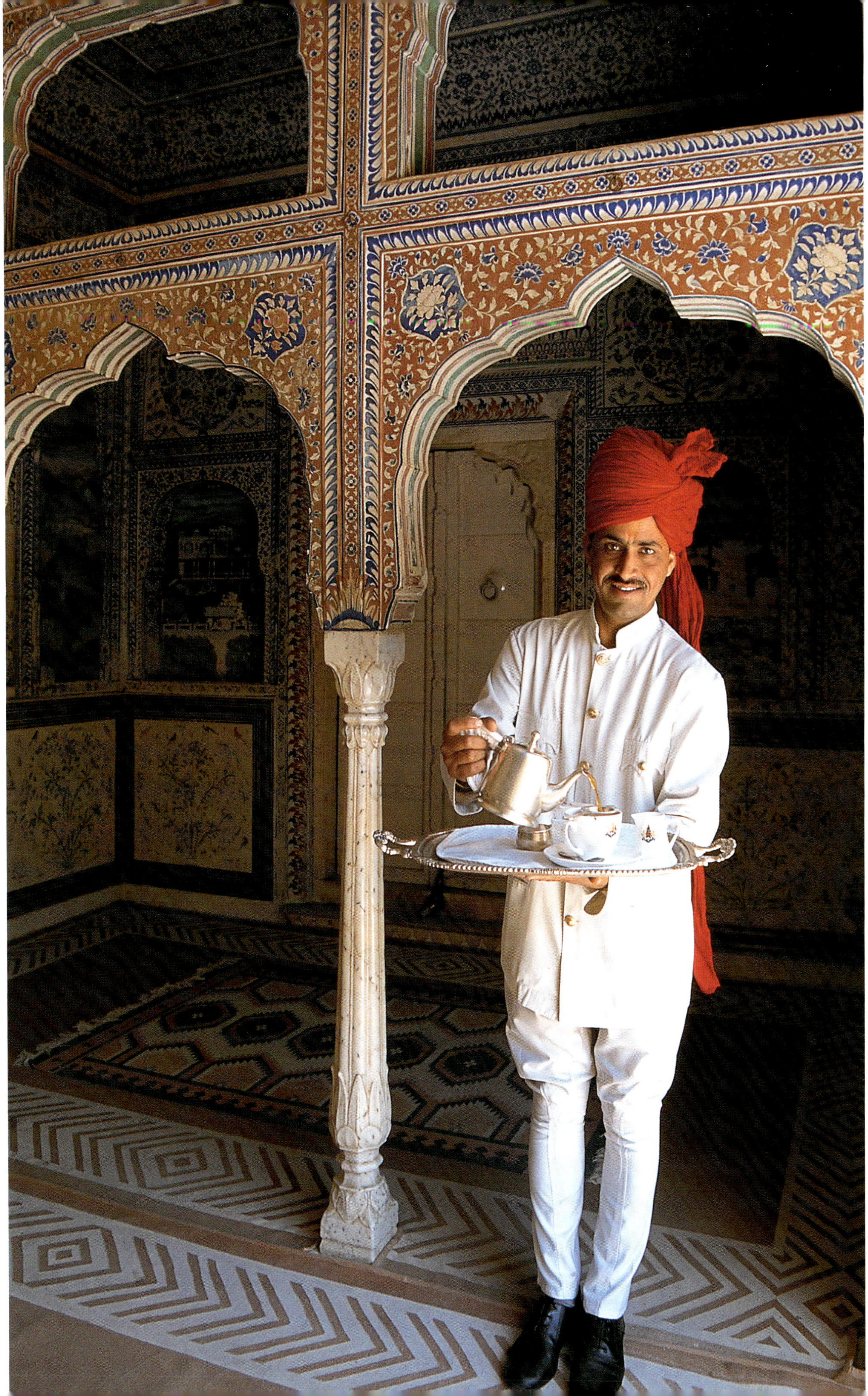

When the desert minstrels throng to Samode, displaying their adornments and jewellery, when the ancestral drums, the dhols, dholaks and other morchangs begin to resound in the durbar hall, when the women start the chari dance, holding a jug on their head, it all becomes a feast for the eye, like in the glorious days of the rawal Barisal.

Next double page:
From the enchanting interiors of the palace, most often inspired by Moghul art (page 167: the Samode Durbur Hall), to the ultra-cosy tents of Samode Baghs (left), Rajasthan exudes a unique life style. Refinement is truly everywhere.

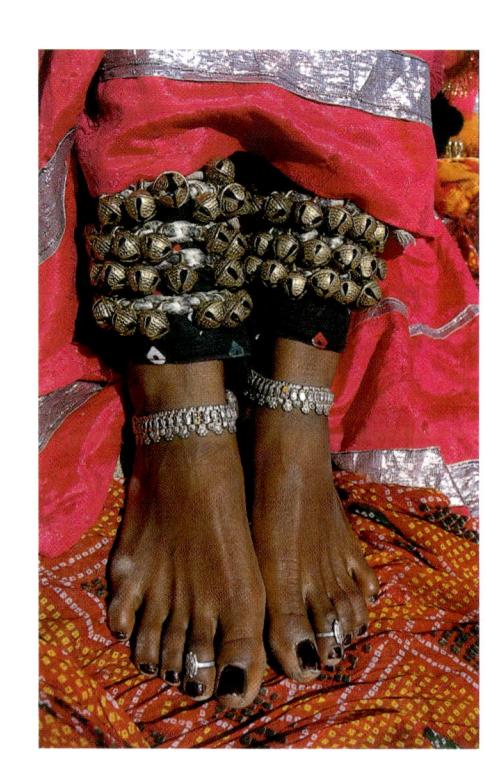

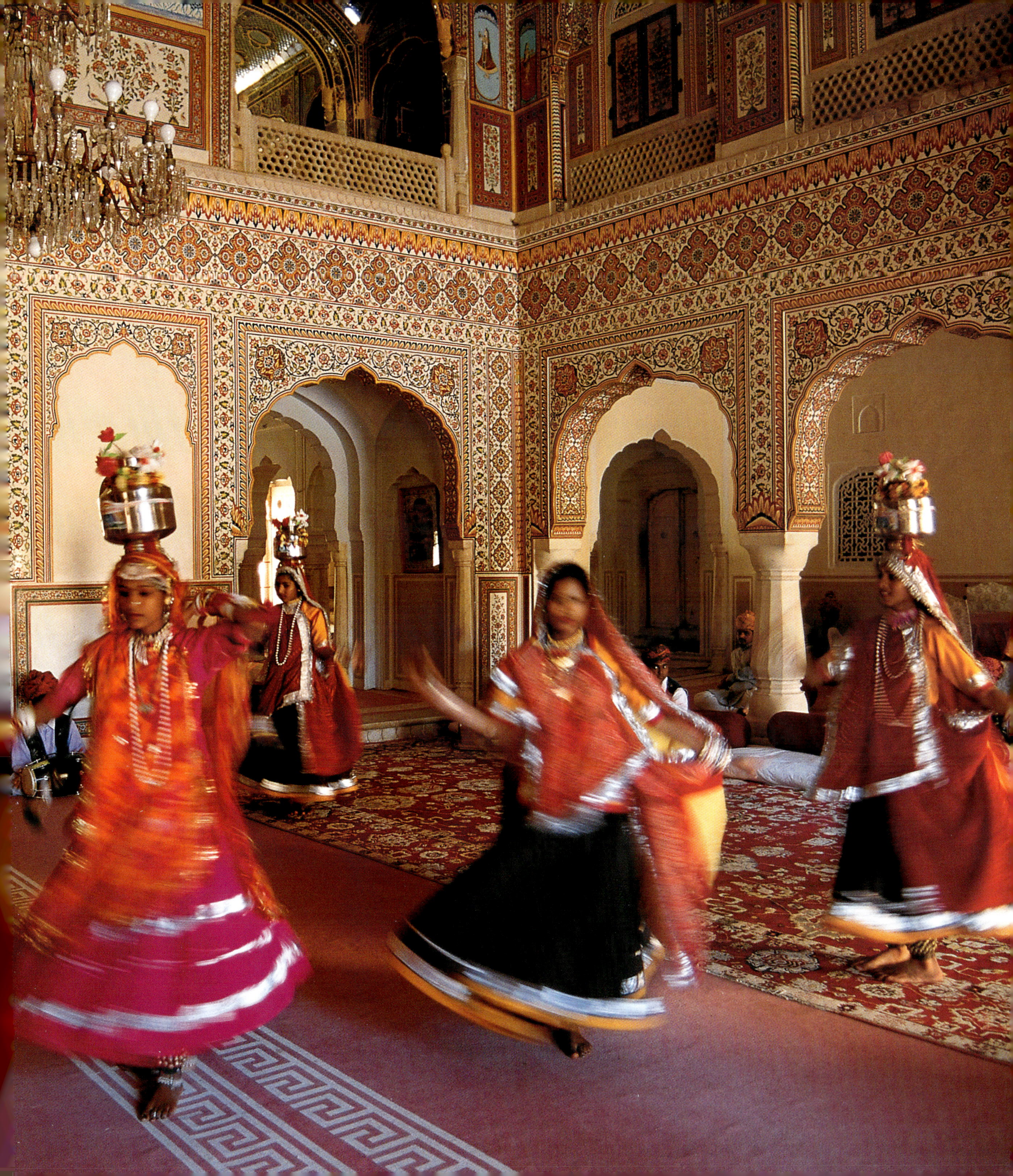

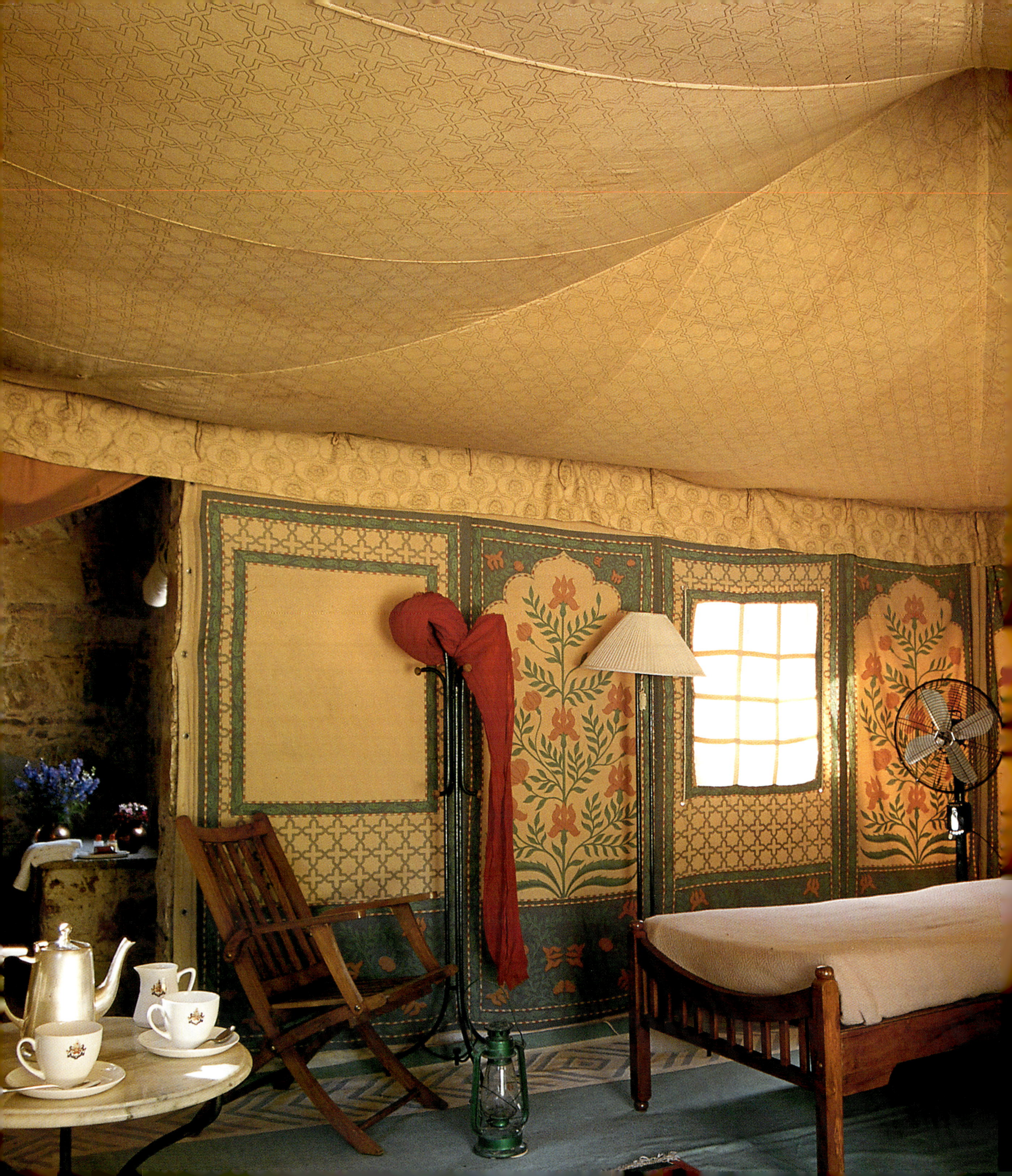

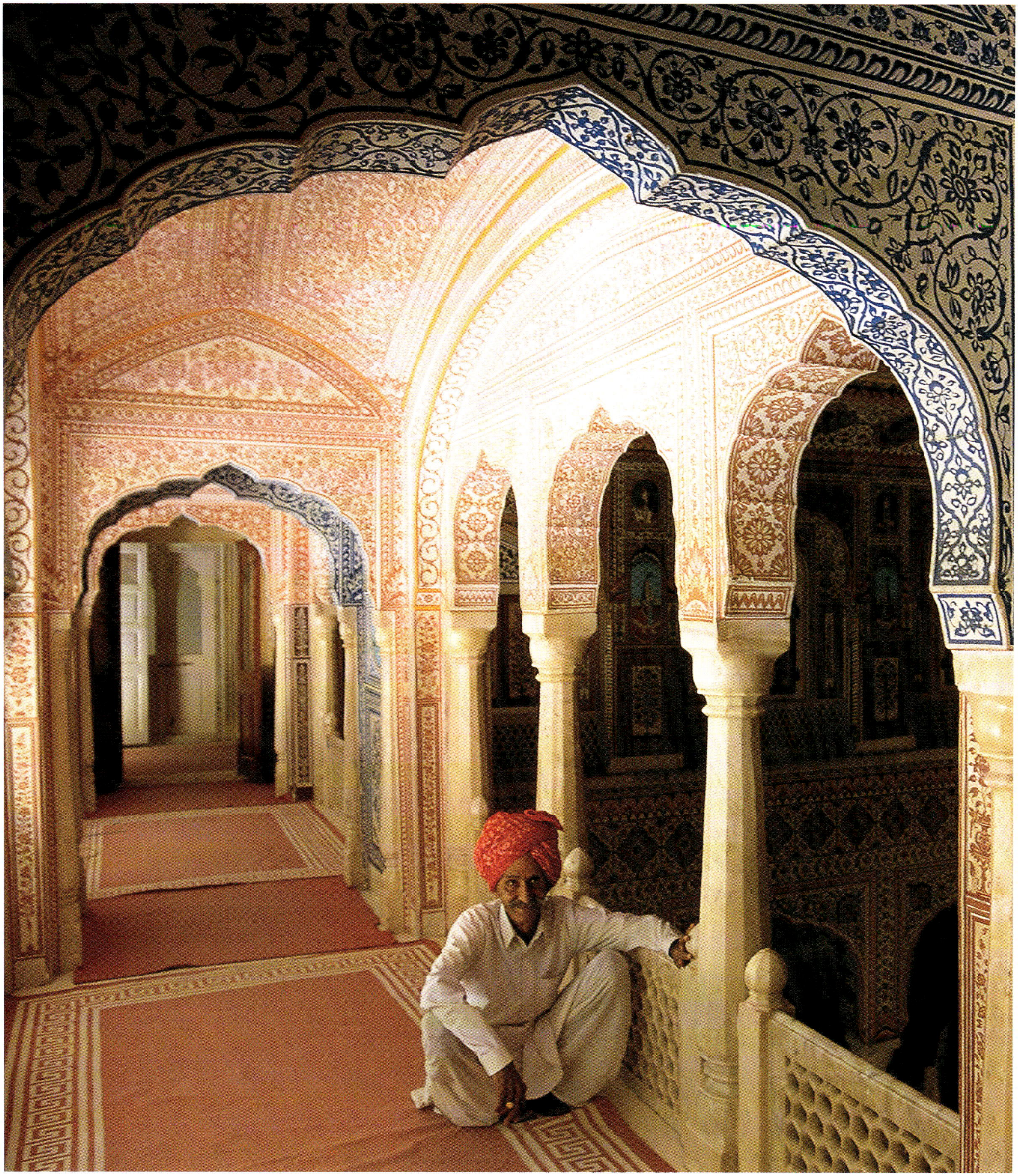

JAIPUR

Proud capital of Rajasthan, Jaipur, "the pink city", has its icon: the royal palace. It truly fires the imagination with a wild maze of courtyards and palaces giving it a singular cachet.

Mysterious Women of the Zenana

The sprawling royal palace takes up an entire section of the city. In the midst of this vast ensemble of pavilions, temples and museums intermingled with courtyards, the seven storeys of the Chandra Mahal are not open to visitors. They are the private apartments of the present-day maharajah, His Highness Sawai Man Singh II. The zenana, the very ancient, very secret quarter of the wives and concubines, is impenetrable as well. Just who were these women and how did they live? Gayatri Devi, in her book of memoirs, *A Princess Remembers*, recalls this phantasmagorical place. In 1940, at twenty-one years of age, she had just married the last reigning maharajah, father of the present maharajah, Man Singh II. Listen to Gayatri Devi's recollections:

"The part of the palace devoted to the zenana comprised a whole series of individual apartments. My own, decorated in shades of green and blue, was not different from the others, with its small square courtyard and durbar room, lit with blue glass lamps, onto which the other rooms opened. The year I was married, some 400 women still lived in this zenana. Relatives, widows lived there with their daughters, their servants and their personnel. There was also the dowager maharani and her suite of ladies-in-waiting, servants and cooks. Each of Jai's wives had entire suites as well. There were all the personnel of the other wives of the deceased maharajah, who could not be sent away after their mistresses died and therefore lived at the expense of the reigning family. The only surviving wife of the former maharajah presided this entire society. We called her Maji Sahiba, meaning respected mother. Even though I was Jai's wife, I almost always kept my face covered in her presence, and my usual place was several steps to her left."

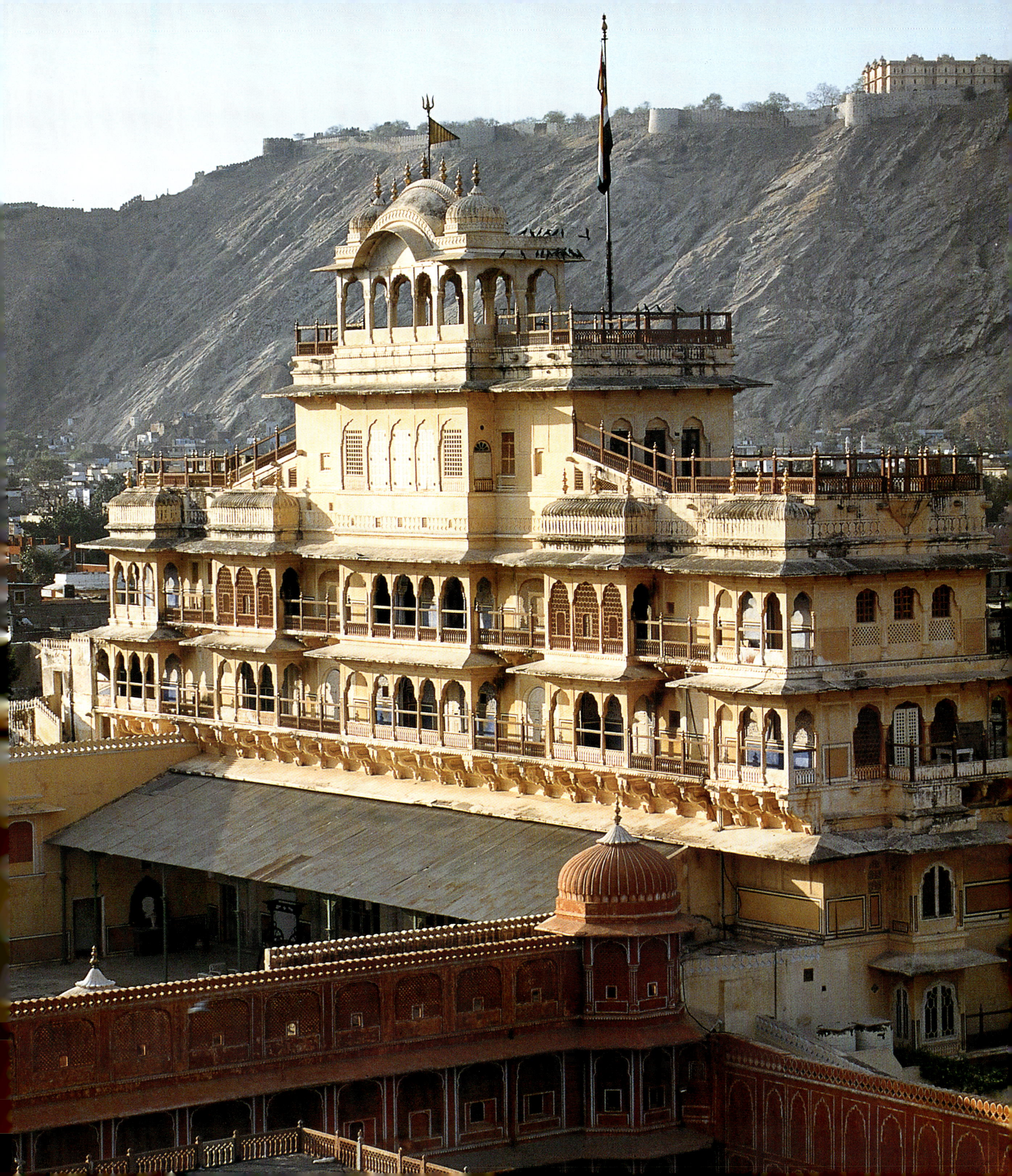

The Survivors

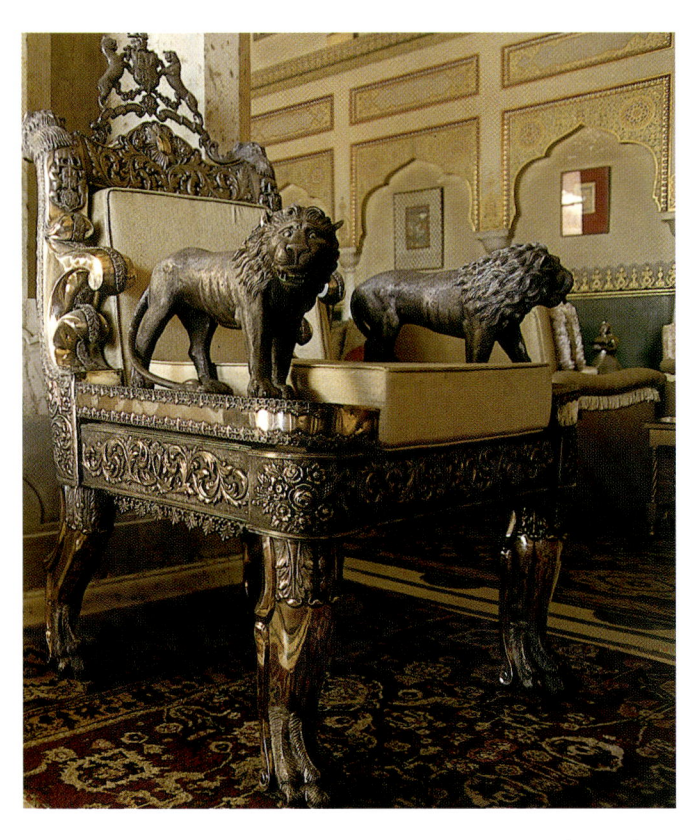

At the dawn of the twenty-first century there are but two left. Two very old women reign alone over the royal zenana of another era, far from tourist circuits, far from gossip, the only survivors of these 400 women, maharanis, concubines and servants. The others all died, decimated by the years that slipped by, just slipped by.

Everything has been said about these "women" condemned to the form of seclusion called purdah. Only "very special" envoys combed the cities and the countryside to seek out the most beautiful. Only the chosen ones were torn from their husband or their family before being forcefully locked in the zenana. It was fear of being chosen that made women take to hiding their face under a veil… Legend or true story?

At the time of the Independence, representatives of the new democracy came to solemnly announce to the recluse women of the Jaipur zenana that henceforth they were free. Free at last! They could go out and live as they liked… But no, they chose to live in their gilded cage. There are only two left today, living in the midst of this maze of courtyards, apartments and royal gardens. They are aware that when they die the zenana will be turned into a museum. But for the time being the maharajah takes care of them beautifully. A true gentleman!

His Highness is here. Like every morning, coming down from his private apartments, he crosses the lower palace courtyard, greets the passing tourists by joining his hands, and settles himself in his offices, recently refurbished in a slightly pompous Egyptian style. His secretaries have him sign notes; he speaks with his son-in-law Kunwar Shri Narendra Singh who administers the palace. He also graciously lends himself to a few photograph sittings. Simple families who come from Benares, Bombay and elsewhere ask him to pose in their midst. His Highness cannot say no. Elegance and panache! Now here we are in his office. Family photos, of his father and his ancestors all have their place. Like the one of Lady Di whose visit left such a lasting impression. A distinguished grandfather, who spends his afternoons in the palace gardens playing with his grandchildren and would not for anything in the world miss a polo match, he once was a great soldier and an ambassador.

A major monument in the history of Jaipur, overlooking the royal palace, the Chandra Mahal, or Palace of the Moon, houses the maharajah's private apartments. Moghul and Rajput ornamentation are combined, creating a contrasted decor. The Sukh Mahal, or Rest Lounge, contains lovely gold articles, silver furniture and a table signed René Lalique.

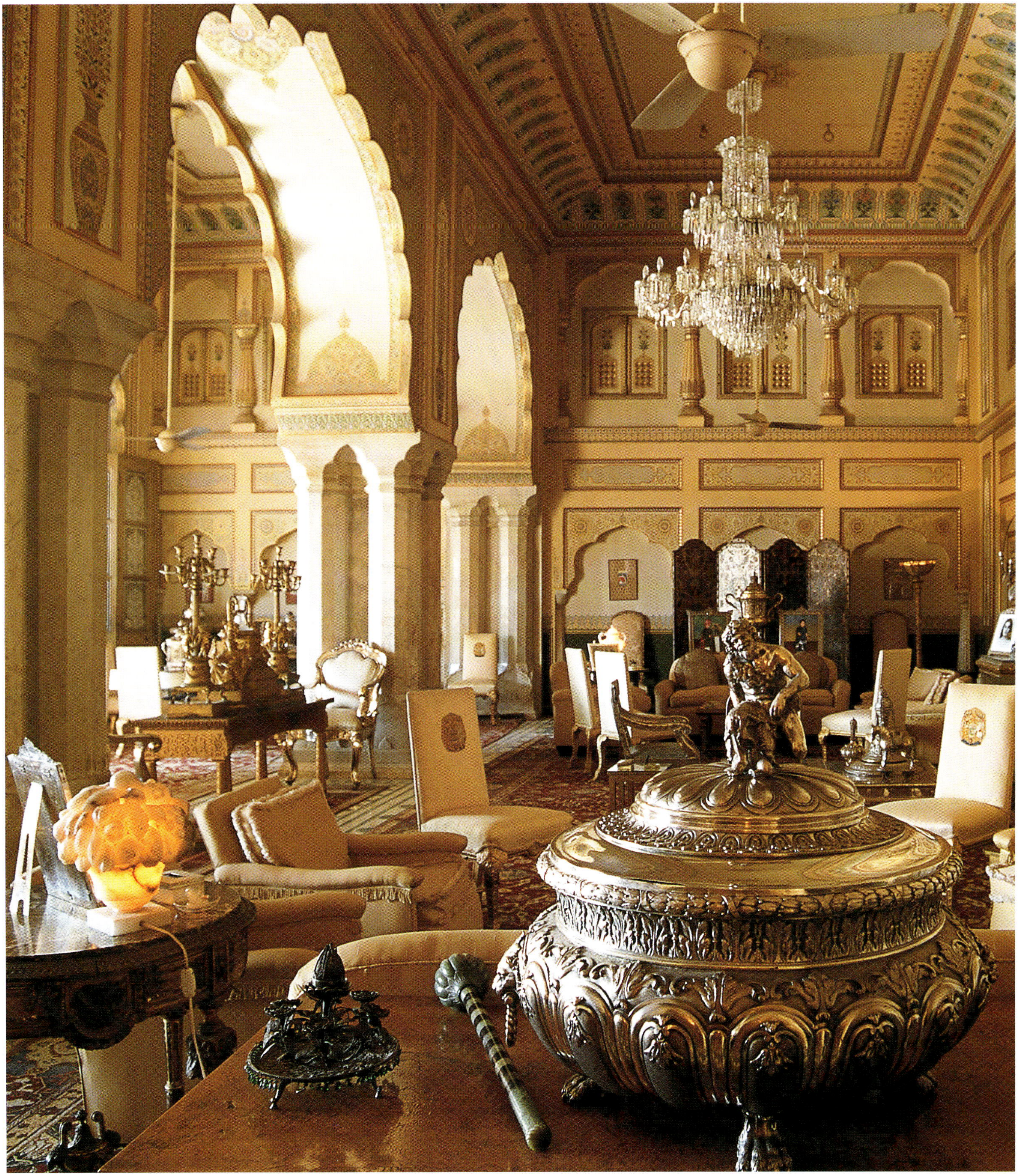

172

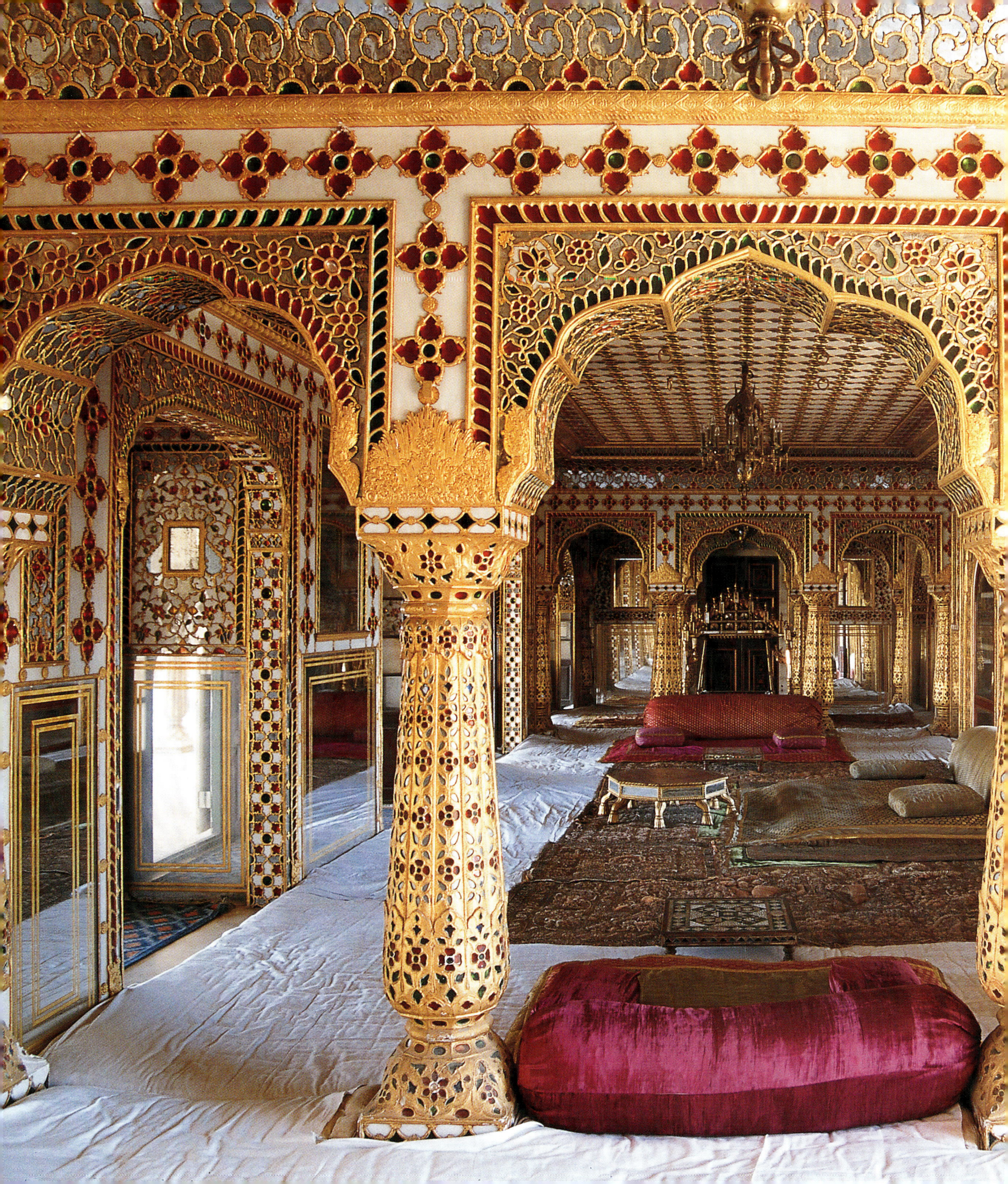

Preceding double page:
The fourth floor of the Chandra Mahal is entirely occupied by the fascinating Shobha Niwas, or Hall of Beauty, which well deserves its name. The walls, covered with stylised gypsum flowers and gold leaf, were done in the middle of the nineteenth century. Long before the British imported to India the very idea of furniture, the maharajahs lived on Persian rugs, cushions and fabrics. In the evening, when the candles and oil lamps were lit and placed on the floor, the atmosphere was even more captivating, each spot of light endlessly reflected in the fragments of mirror.

The Chandra Mahal

Only a few rare privileged people are allowed in the Chandra Mahal, the private palace of the royal family. On the ground floor overlooking Moghul gardens, the veranda, whose walls are graced with the portraits of the maharajahs of Jaipur and Amber executed by the German painter A. H. Mueller, is occasionally turned into a reception room for a wedding or elegant dinner parties. A long winding hall leads us up to the first floor. A terrace opens onto a vast apartment, the Sukh Niwas, the maharajah's drawing room, done over in Victorian style in the nineteenth century. Photos placed on the furniture evoke his favourite moments. You can see, for instance, Bill Clinton and his daughter vacationing in 2001. The winding hall also leads to the two most beautiful rooms of the Chandra Mahal: the Shobha Niwas, so dazzling with its mirrors inlaid in plaster and its antique rugs, and the Chhabi Niwas (Palace of the Moon) with its polished whitewashed floors and walls painted with white arabesques on a blue background. Grandiose art. Come on, just one more effort! From the terrace on the top floor, the view overlooks all of Jaipur surrounded by the Aravalli mountains. A faint hum rises from the city.

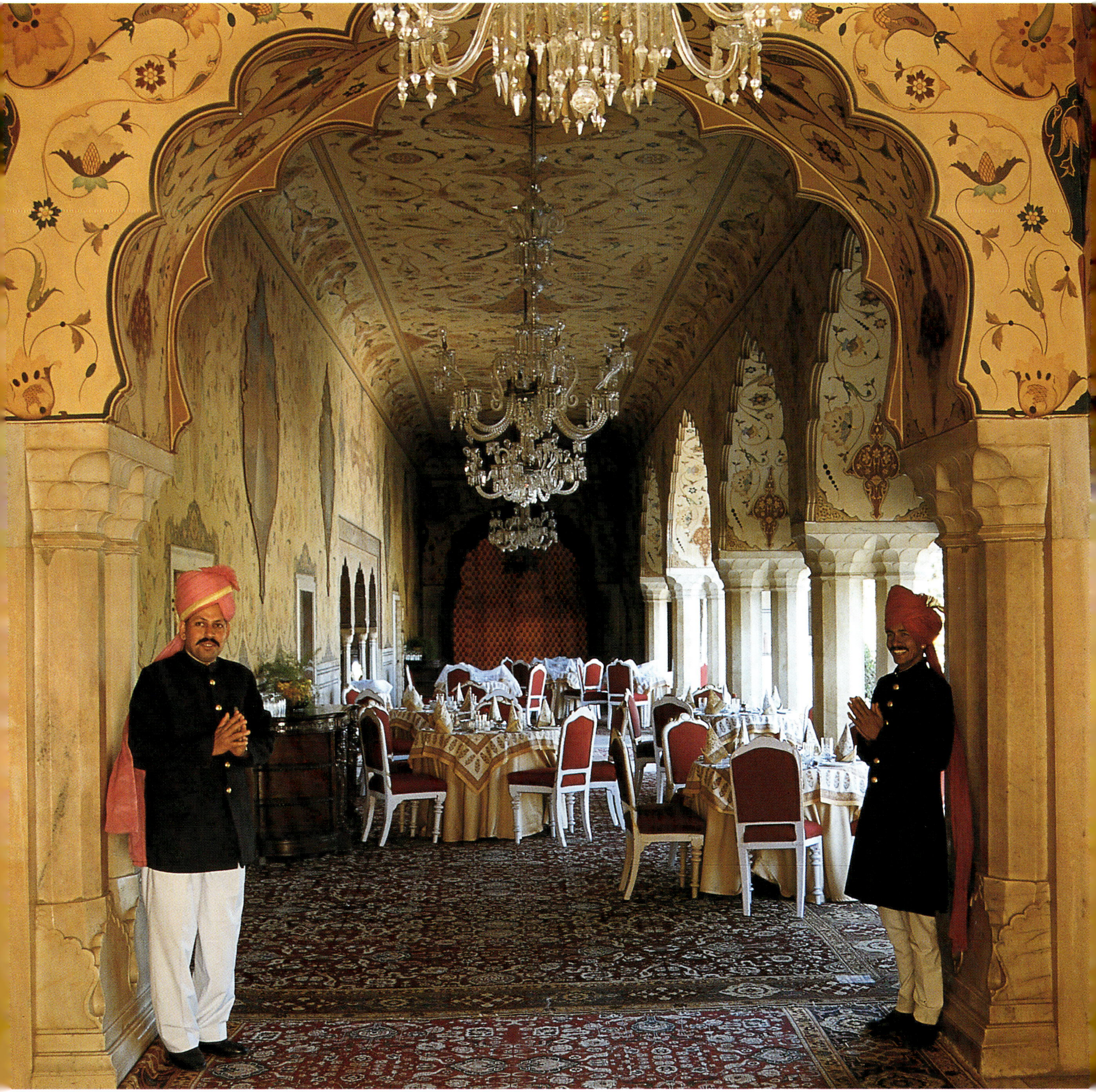

Arabesques and scenes from Indian mythology go well with the Bohemian crystal chandeliers.

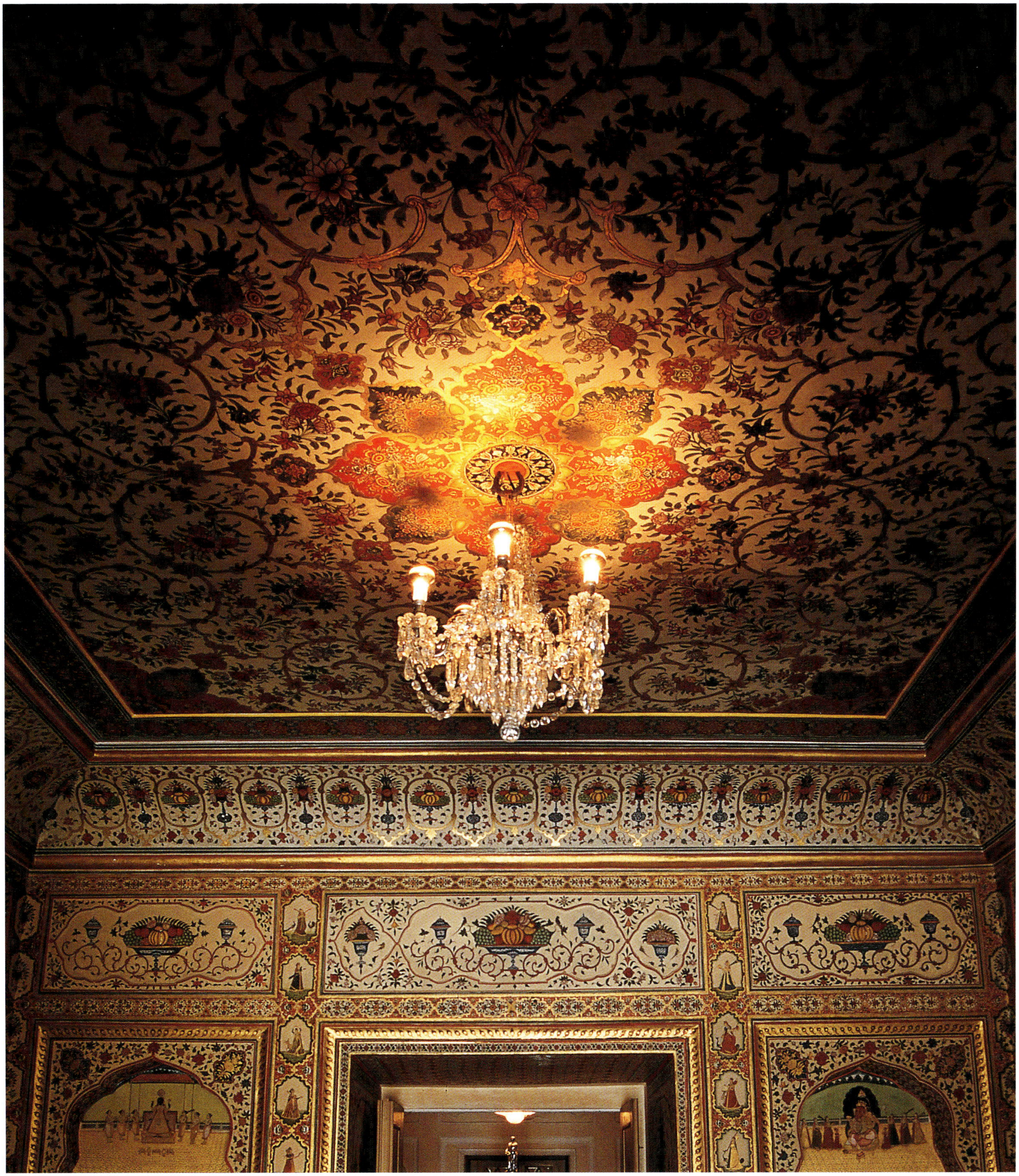

During the hottest days, the royal family would withdraw to the Chandra Niwas, the Palace of the Moon, with its pavement polished with eggshell. Liberally open onto the royal gardens, it let in even the slightest breeze. The blue and white motifs then appeared most "refreshing".

Alliance with the Moghuls

Vibrant with nostalgia, the capital of the Kachvahas maharajahs is incomparable. Designed in 1727 as a gigantic chequerboard with right-angle streets and buildings with aligned facades, the city preserves the memory of the maharajah Jai Singh (1699-1743) who drew up its layout. So he left his fortress of Amber nestled in the hills which had witnessed so many events when the Moghuls lorded over the land. At the time, the Rajputs' choice was simple: swear allegiance and thus save their kingdom or refuse domination and draw their subjects into a battle they could not win. The rajah Bhar Mal (1548-1574) chose the first solution. He became the faithful ally of the Moghul emperor Humayun, put his son in the service of the empire and gave his daughter to be the bride of the emperor's son, the very one who would become Akbar. Quite a stroke of luck for the Moghuls! On the road from Delhi to Ajmer, a pilgrimage town for Muslims, the site of Amber was strategic. To thank him Akbar gave the rajah the title of governor of the provinces and an armed troop. The alliance would last with the maharajahs Man Singh I (1589-1614) and Jai Singh (1621-1667), who won victory after victory serving the Moghuls.

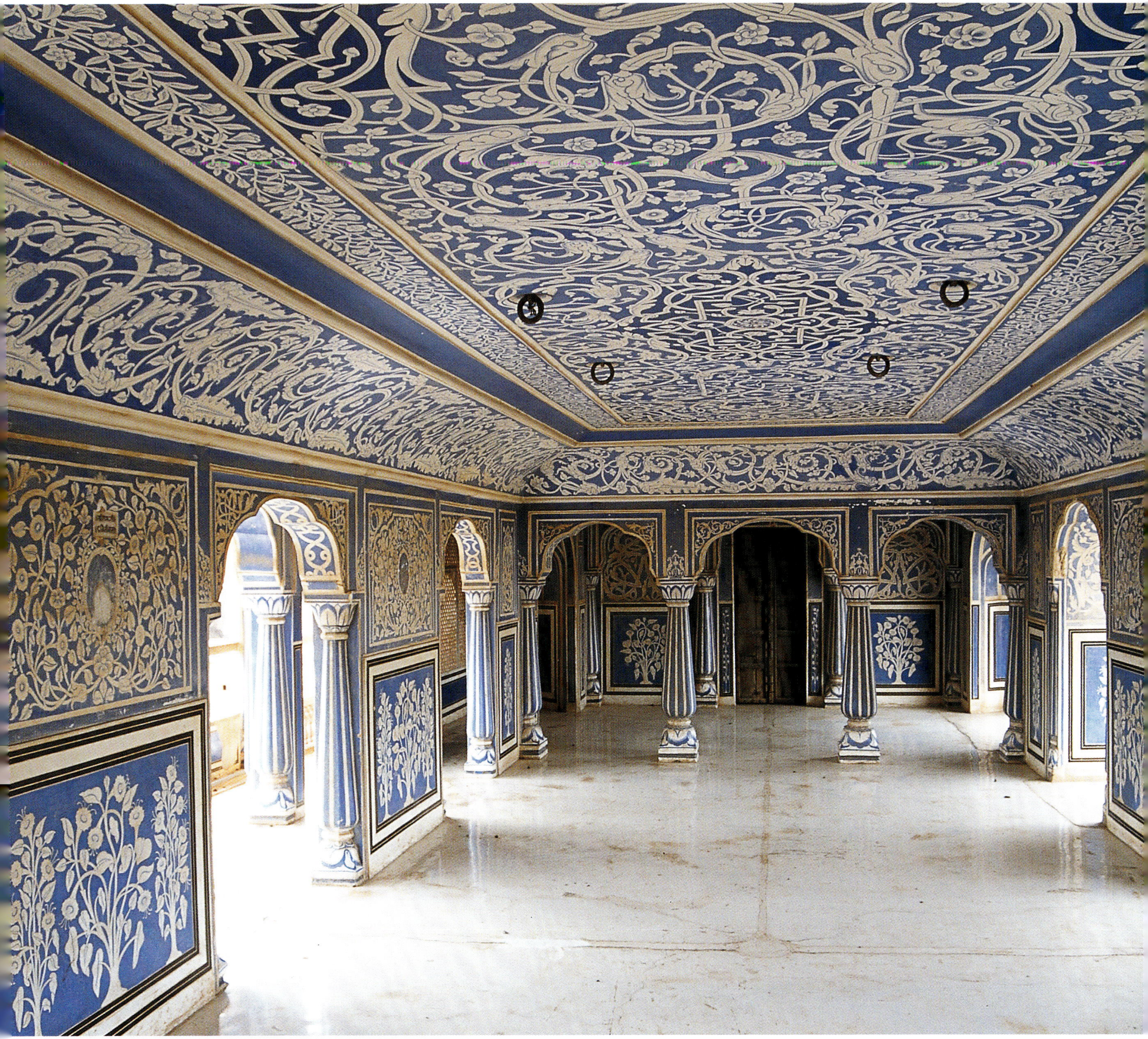

The City of Jai

A clever strategist, erudite and protector of the arts, the maharajah Jai Singh II was also fascinated by astronomy, as proved by the five observatories he had built in India, something revolutionary at the time. As for his city, he wished it to be ideal, calling upon the competence of the Bengali architect Vidyadhar Bhattacharya who was surrounded by the most prized craftsmen of the country. Work began on 17 November 1727, in conformity with expert astrological calculations. The division into quarters was borrowed from Hindu architectural treatises, respecting a chequerboard plan with right-angle streets. Nine quarters were formed, corresponding with the nine divisions of the universe. The houses overlooking the street were lower and cleverly set forward, with respect to the ones behind, thus creating wide terraces. Trees were planted and an aqueduct was built with drinking water wells here and there. The streets and alleys were attributed to the various crafts: jewellers, weavers and goldsmiths, thus encouraging trade. All that remained was to find a name for the city. It was found in no time: the maharajah lent it part of his own.

Jaipur, "the City of the Victory", was very prosperous until it was threatened by the Marathas. For protection, they chose the lesser of two evils: an alliance with the British, signed in 1818. A resident settled in Jaipur, which then was soon brought up to date. In 1876, the maharajah Ram Singh II (1835-1880) had all the facades painted pink in order to properly host the Prince of Wales and future Edward VII. This pink colour, delightfully old-fashioned and in the end very modern, is still Jaipur's fetish colour and is most becoming.

Designed in 1727 like a huge chequerboard, the city of Jaipur was divided according to Hindu concepts in nine districts, two of which were for the City Palace (royal palace). In the foreground, the Mubarak Mahal, the Palace of Welcome. On the right you can see one of the towers of the Jantar Mantar, the astronomical observatory.

*Opposite:
The Palace of the Winds, Hawa Mahal, reserved for the women of the zenana.*

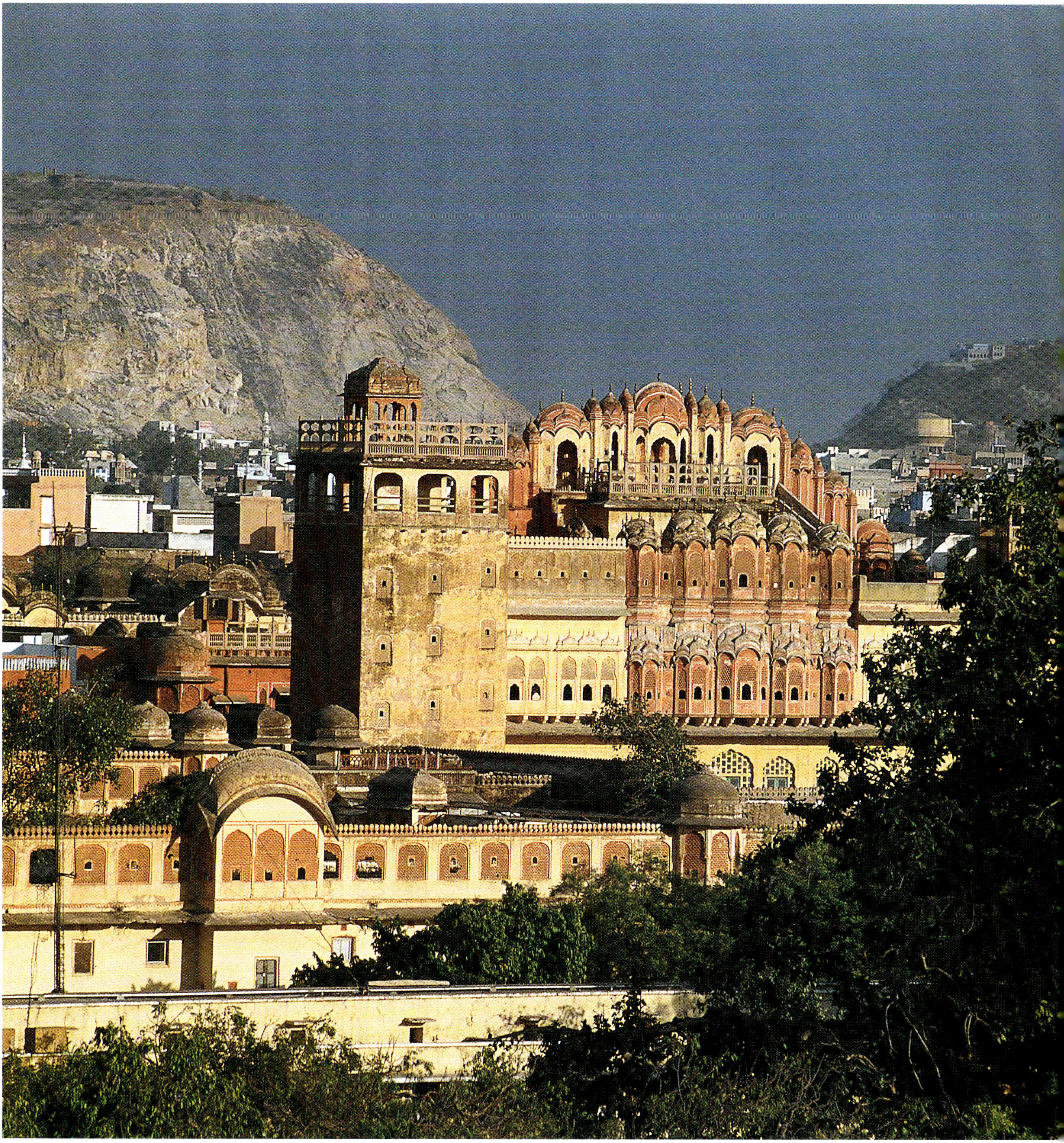

On entering the royal palace of Jaipur, we are told a thousand and one stories about princes. On the right, the strange astronomical monuments of the Jantar Mantar.

A Glamorous History

This pink city would be the setting for one of the most glamorous stories that ever took place in India. It all began like a fairy tale. Not having any children, the maharajah Madho Singh II (1880-1922) chose as his heir the young son of a local nobleman and distant cousin.

The new maharajah Man Singh was extremely good-looking, immensely rich, a polo champion and quite a socialite. He ruled from 1922 to 1949, when he decided to unite his country with the state of Rajasthan, Jaipur becoming the capital of the new state. But it was his third marriage, with an Indian princess, Gayatri Devi, that would occupy the society news and gossip of all of Europe. The magazine Vogue listed the princess among the ten most beautiful women in the world. Very popular, in 1962 she became a member of the Indian Parliament by a historic majority. Man Singh II died in 1970 in an accident on a polo field in Great Britain.

The City Palace

In the midst of this "pink city" with its deafening overpopulation, the City Palace is a haven of peace. We can rest, come round and begin to let our mind wander. For this palace, which Rudyard Kipling did not hesitate to call the "Indian Versailles", has retained unquestionable character and offers delightful surprises to lovers of Indo-Muslim art. Emblematic monument of the city, the Palace of the Winds, or Hawa Mahal, is the most poignant testimony of the era of the maharajahs to be found in Rajasthan. At the very end of the royal palace rise five storeys of pink facade pierced with slits and narrow windows overlooking the street. It is all just a trompe-l'oeil. Inside it is empty. This giant fretted screen, built in 1799, allowed the women of the zenana to be entertained by the processions going by in the street. We can just imagine dozens, hundreds of women, feeling languorous after a hot afternoon, climbing the inner stairways leading to the 61 covered balconies, these jharakha, closed by delicate jali (fretwork), to enjoy the poetry of everyday life.

Originally the City Palace took up two of the nine quarters or districts of the perfect city designed by Jai Singh II in the eighteenth century. This arrangement of palaces, courtyards, passageways and pavilions is surrounded by ramparts in which monumental delicately ornamented gates are carved out. Until recently, the Gate of the Moon (Chand Pol), leading into the Palace, was closed every evening. Protectors of the arts and often highly cultured, the maharajahs were also open to progress. If you have any doubts, just go and see the Jantar Mantar, the astronomical observatory with its 17 instruments in masonry that Jai Singh had built between 1728 and 1733 to obtain precise information for the calendar.

Overlooking the small Pritam Niwas Chowk courtyard and its majestic doors decorated with charming scenes (above), the Chandra Mahal or Palace of the Moon (page 185) houses the private apartments of the maharajah of Jaipur, Sawai Man Singh II.

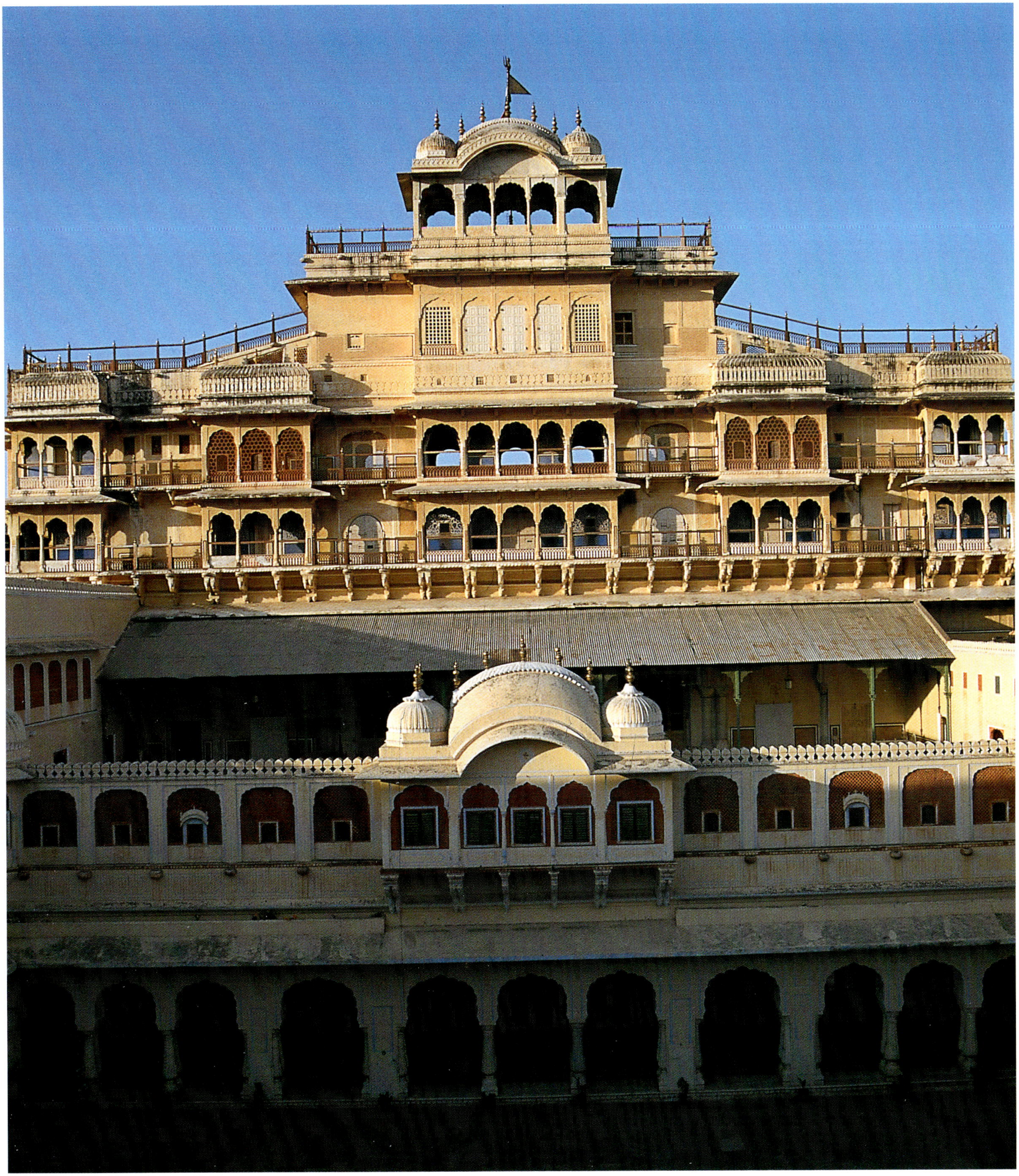

Constantly protected by a squad of guards with bright-coloured turbans and carefully tended moustaches, the Singh Pol, the Gate of the Lion, is framed by two marble statues of elephants. They commemorate the birth of the last maharajah, the long-awaited male heir. So much champagne flowed that the prince was nicknamed "bubble".

But it is time to enter the walls of the palace itself. In the middle of the first courtyard, the Mubarak Mahal, the "Welcome Palace", is worthy of our wonderment. This square marble pavilion, built in 1900, was meant to host official guests. Today, on the first floor, it houses a museum of royal costumes, which give us an idea of the lavishness of bygone days. The most impressive garb is perhaps the robe in Benares silk belonging to the maharajah Madho Singh I, a giant with a great beard who was two metres tall. A few steps away, another pavilion formerly reserved to the maharani (Maharani Palace) has a wealth of truly remarkable collections of Hindu and Moghul arms. Sensitive souls should forget for a few moments this deluge of daggers of all sorts, and linger over the exquisite decoration work of the jade-inlaid handles and the blades adorned with delicate arabesques.

We penetrate deeper into the world of the City Palace on entering the Singh Pol, the Lion Gate, guarded by statues of elephants. It leads into a second courtyard, surrounded by three storeys of fretted galleries behind which the maharanis could observe life in the palace. In the middle, the Moghul-style flat-roofed pavilion is the diwan-i khas, the private audiences hall. On the left, a passageway leads to another delightful courtyard, Pritam Niwas Chowk, where the maharajah has his offices. Take your time and examine the door leaves enhanced by decors of majestic peacocks fanning their tails. And look up at the seven storeys of this strange and elegant Chandra Mahal, palace of the moon. They are the maharajah's private apartments.

To delve once again in nostalgia, you must go toward the vast diwan-i am (public audiences hall) where the maharajahs gathered their durbar (assembly) of nobles. Persian and Moghul influences are magnificently reflected on the marble walls decorated with floral motifs. Here a sort of museum has been reconstituted to glorify the past, with a collection of handsome howdah (elephant litters), palanquins, rugs from Lahore, manuscripts, miniatures, not to mention gigantic chandeliers in crystal from Bohemia. It is one of the most beautiful former reception rooms to be found in Rajasthan.

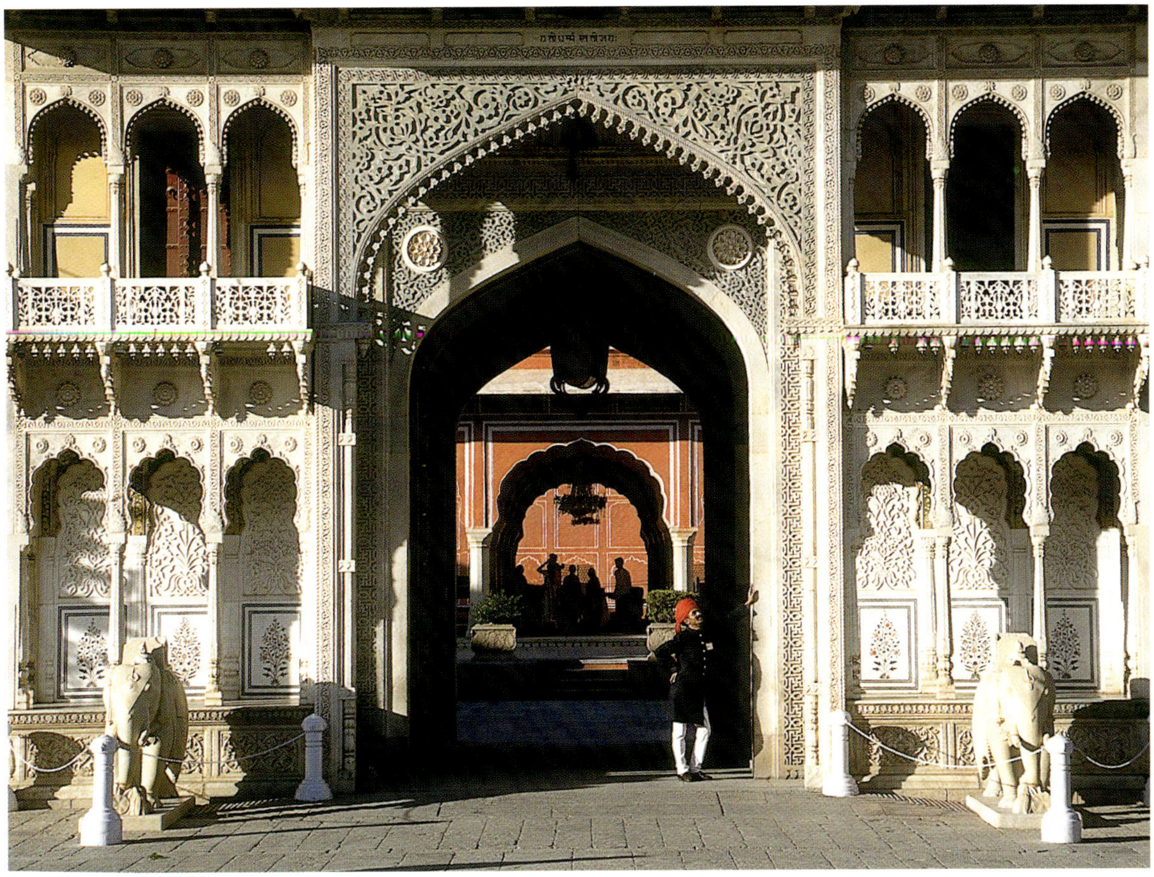

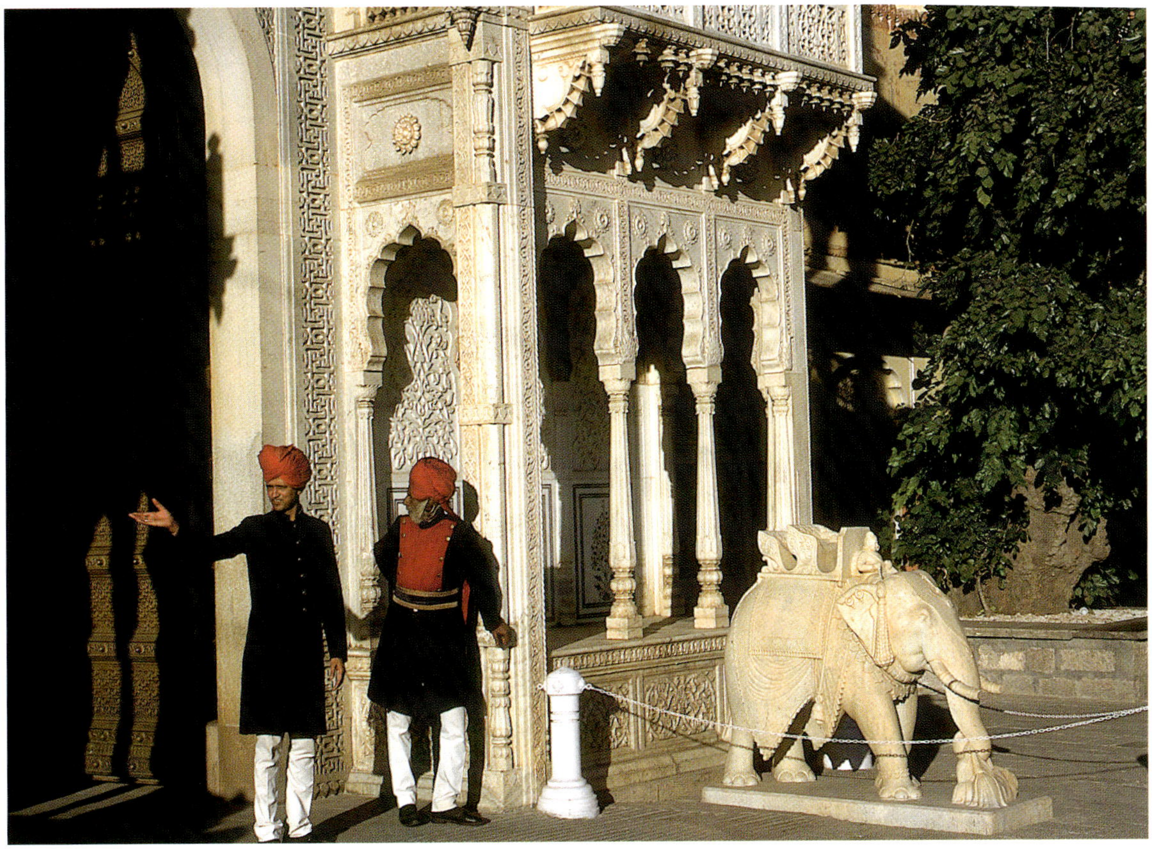

In front of the tall gates controlling the entrance to the royal palace; if you are sensitive to the poetic mood of a city you will enjoy strolling in the narrow streets and markets of Jaipur.

The Bazaars of Jaipur

*I*f overpopulation and traffic jams make crossing Jaipur quite a trial, the city in itself has not really changed greatly since its creation. There are the same delightfully old-fashioned pink on the facades and bazaars lined up according to the different crafts as in the eighteenth century. You can run into a few Europeans out for jewellery, precious stones and enamels. As for shopping, you cannot resist the odd maharajah shoes with pointed, up-tilted toes in the alleys of the Ramganj Bazaar or across from the Palace of the Winds. All these streets are crammed with shops. Go and catch a glimpse of the wealthy Indian women choosing a minakari, an enamelled gold jewel, at the jewellers of the Jauhari Bazaar. A piece of advice; it is on the way out of the city, in the direction of Amber, that you will find the best bargains in the workshops where they manufacture rugs, items in marble, blue pottery and shoes. But beware! Do not hesitate to bargain.

189

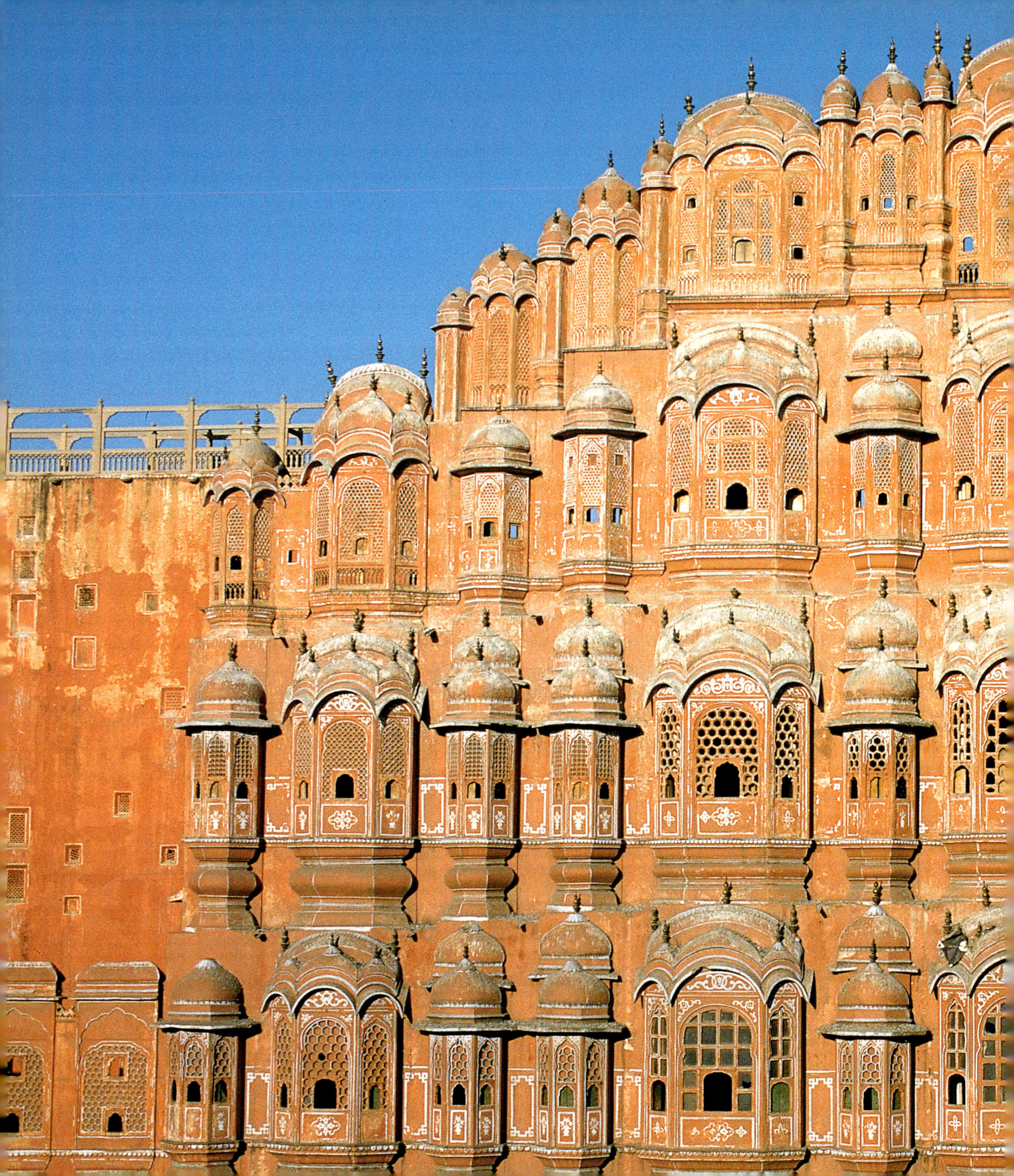

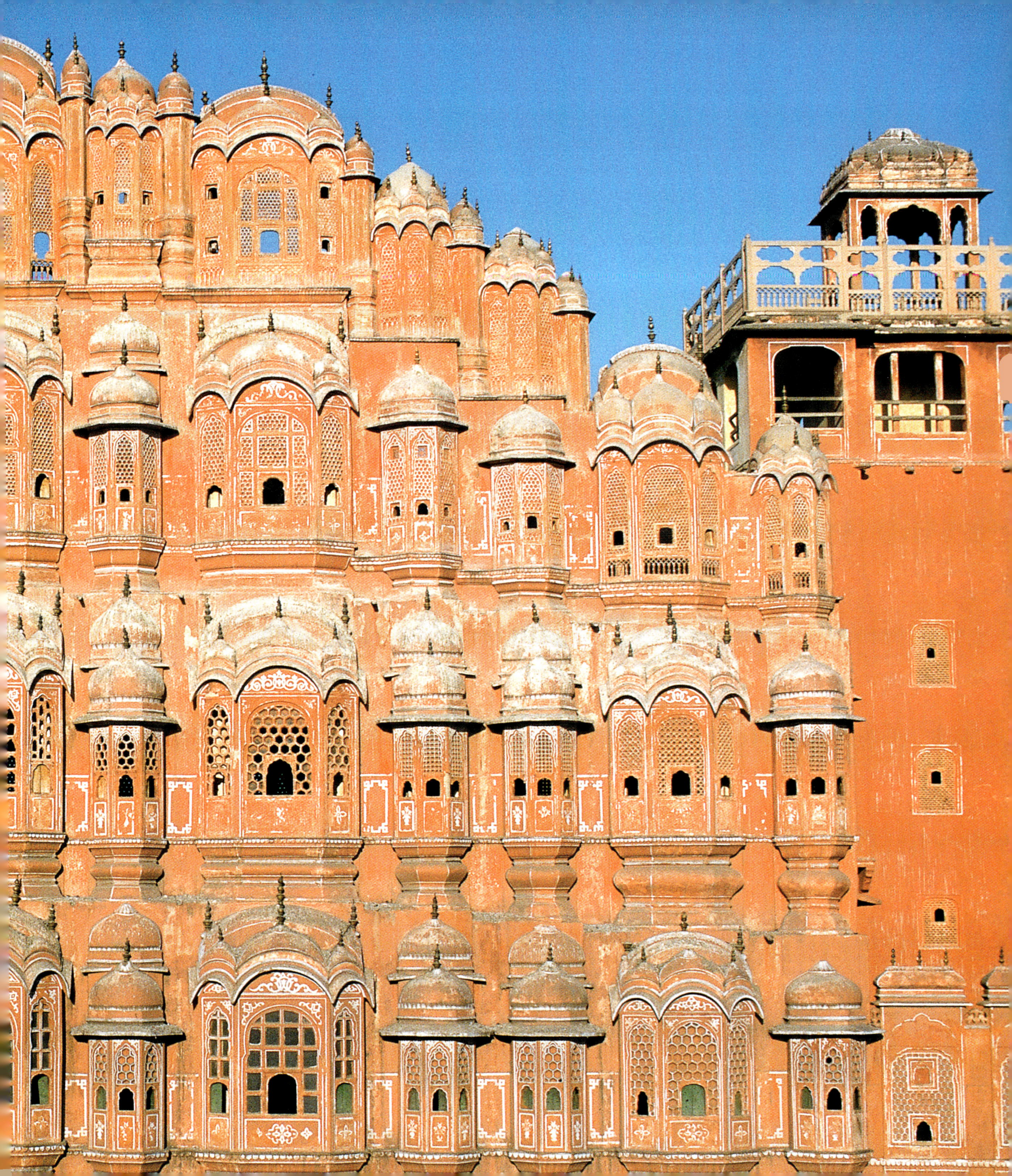

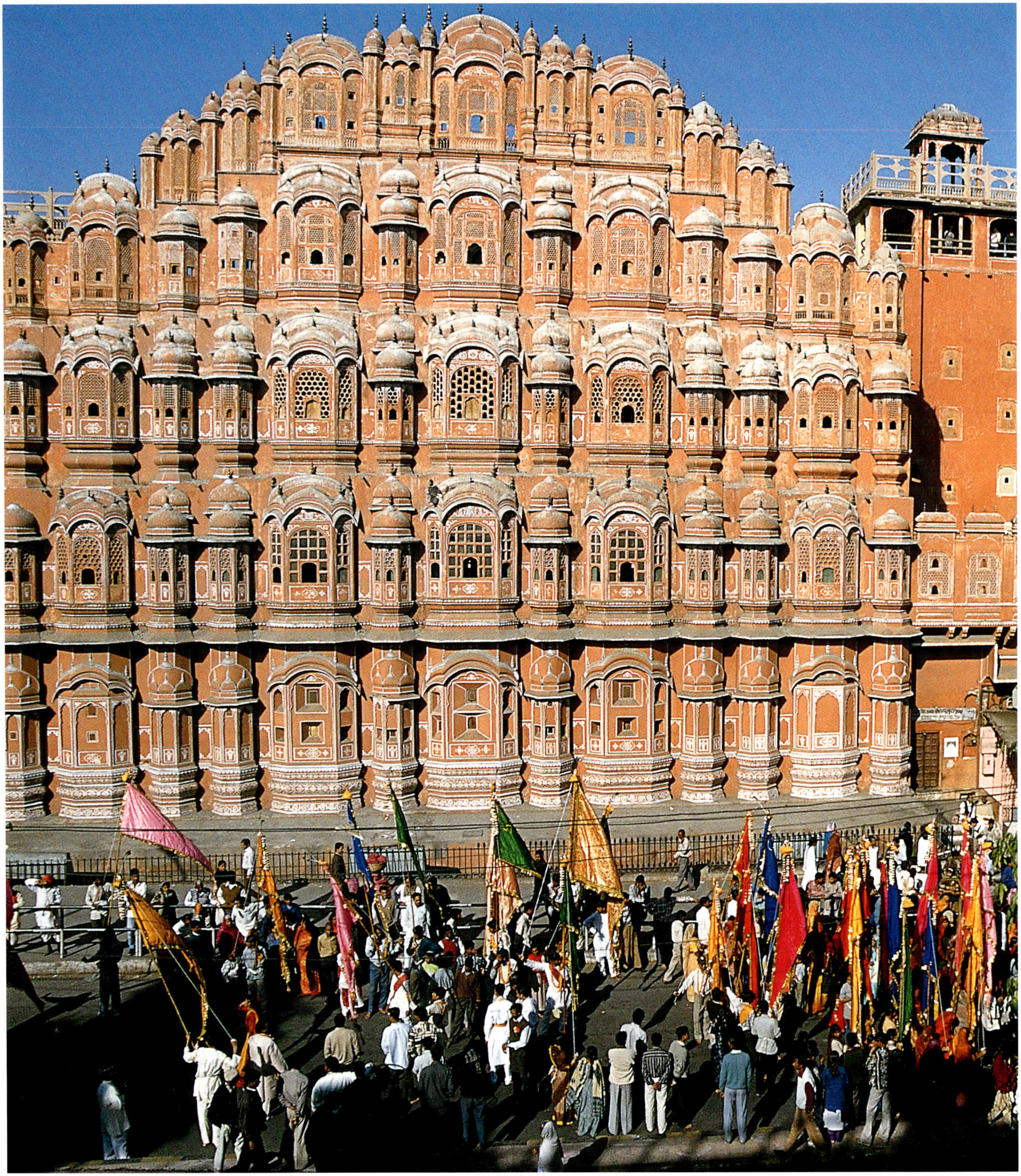

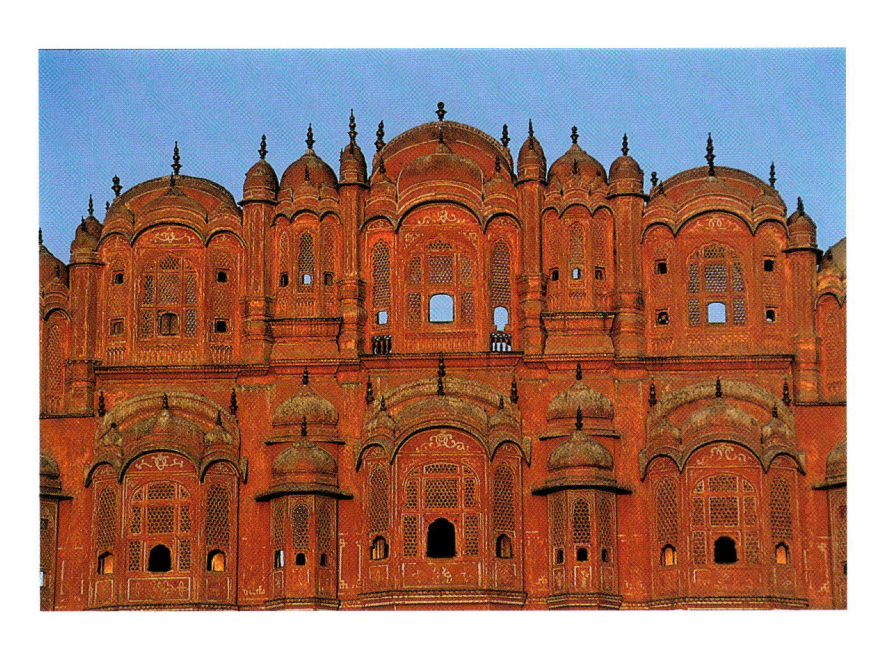

Emblematic monument of Jaipur and Rajasthan, Hawa Mahal, the Palace of the Winds, designed in 1799, displays its amazing reddish facade, perforated with 61 balconies called jharokha. Through mysterious underground passages, the women of the zenana (the name of their reserved quarters) could reach this fantastic gigantic screen (the inside is empty) where they could be entertained by the street scene. If you want to make sure the royal palace has not lost any of its soul or its mystery, just climb the stairs inside this truly strange palace.

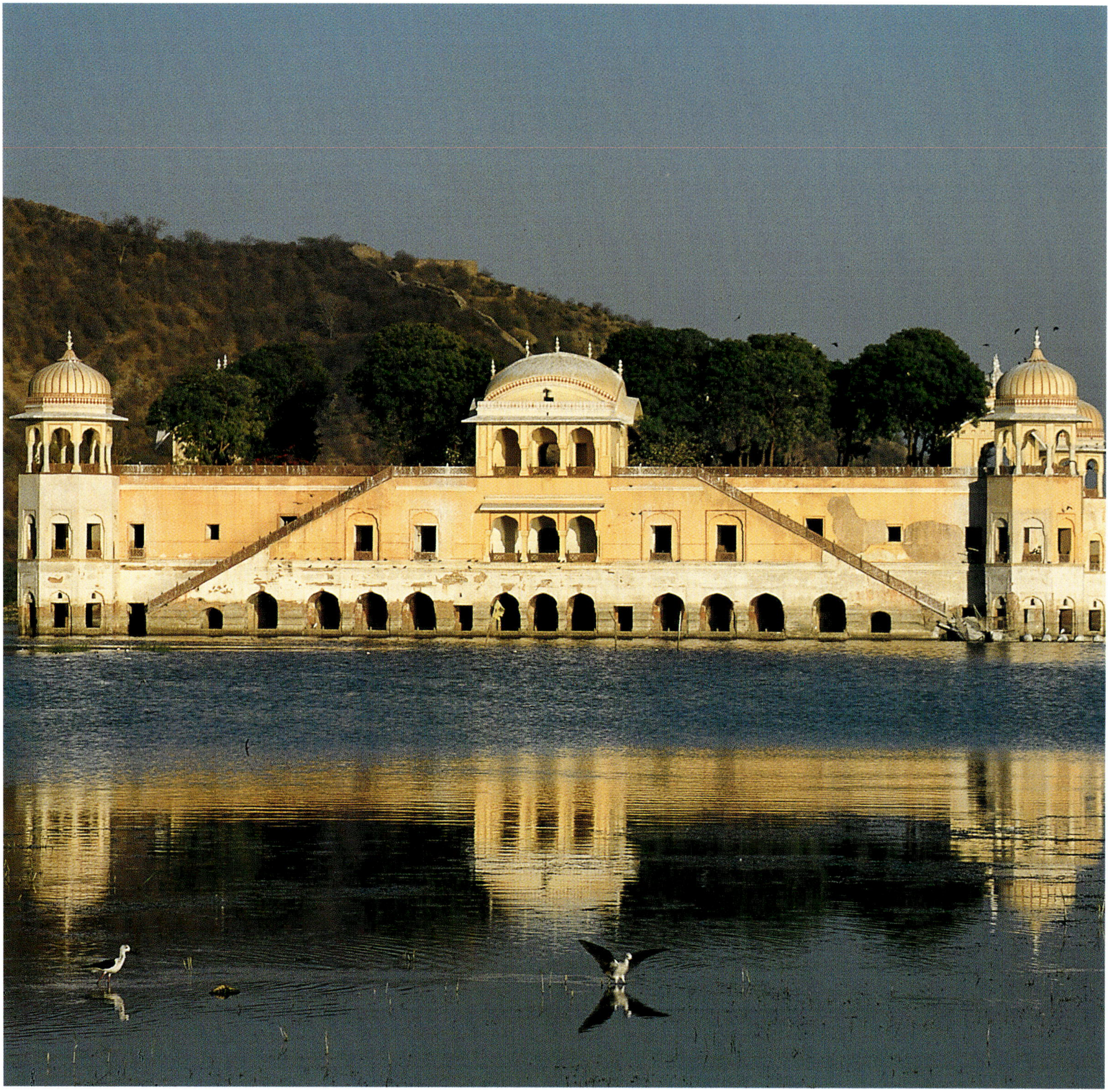

Each palace, each fortress brings back the memory of the time when Rajasthan was called Rajputana. Keen on hunting, the maharajahs would meet at the Jal Mahal (Palace of Water) to hunt duck in the middle of the Man Sagar lake (left). Above, the Rambagh Palace, former hunting lodge of the maharajahs of Jaipur, was the first palace in Rajasthan to be converted into a hotel in 1957 by Man Singh II.

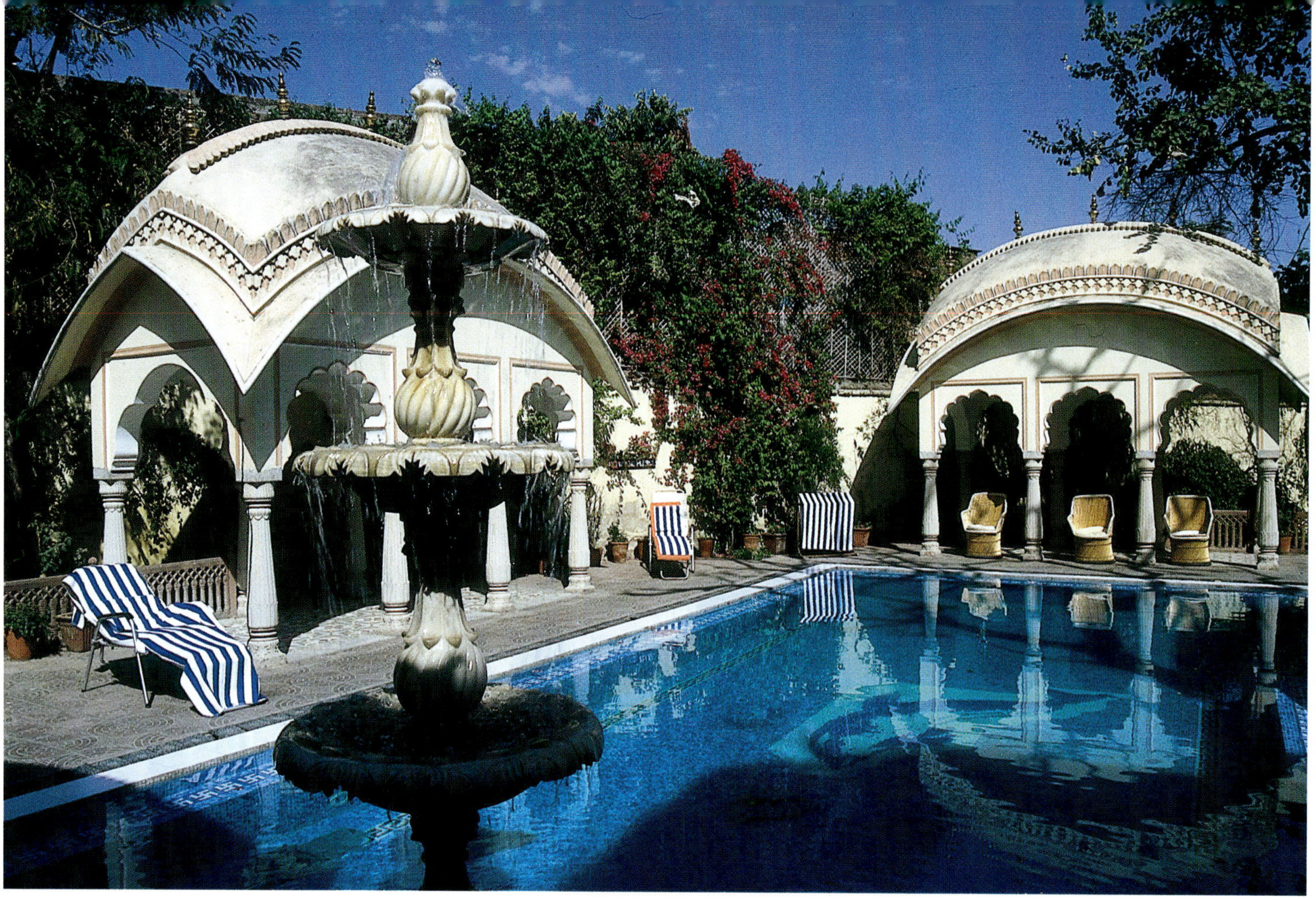

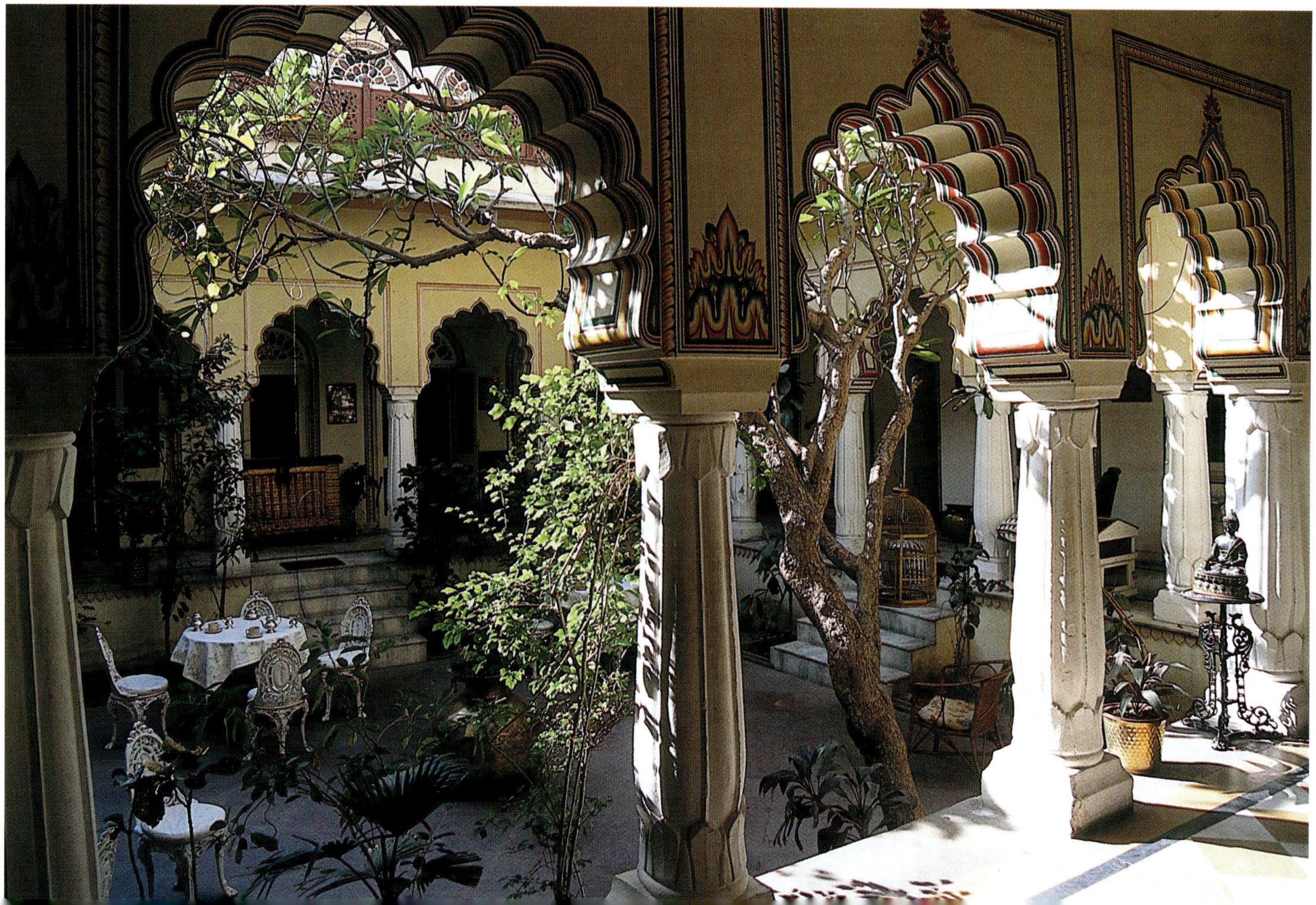

Right in the heart of Jaipur, Alsisar Haveli is a secret address. Descendent of the glorious clan of the Kachhawa Rajputs, the thakur (aristocratic title) Gaj Singh converted his family haveli, built in 1892, into a most inspiring hotel.

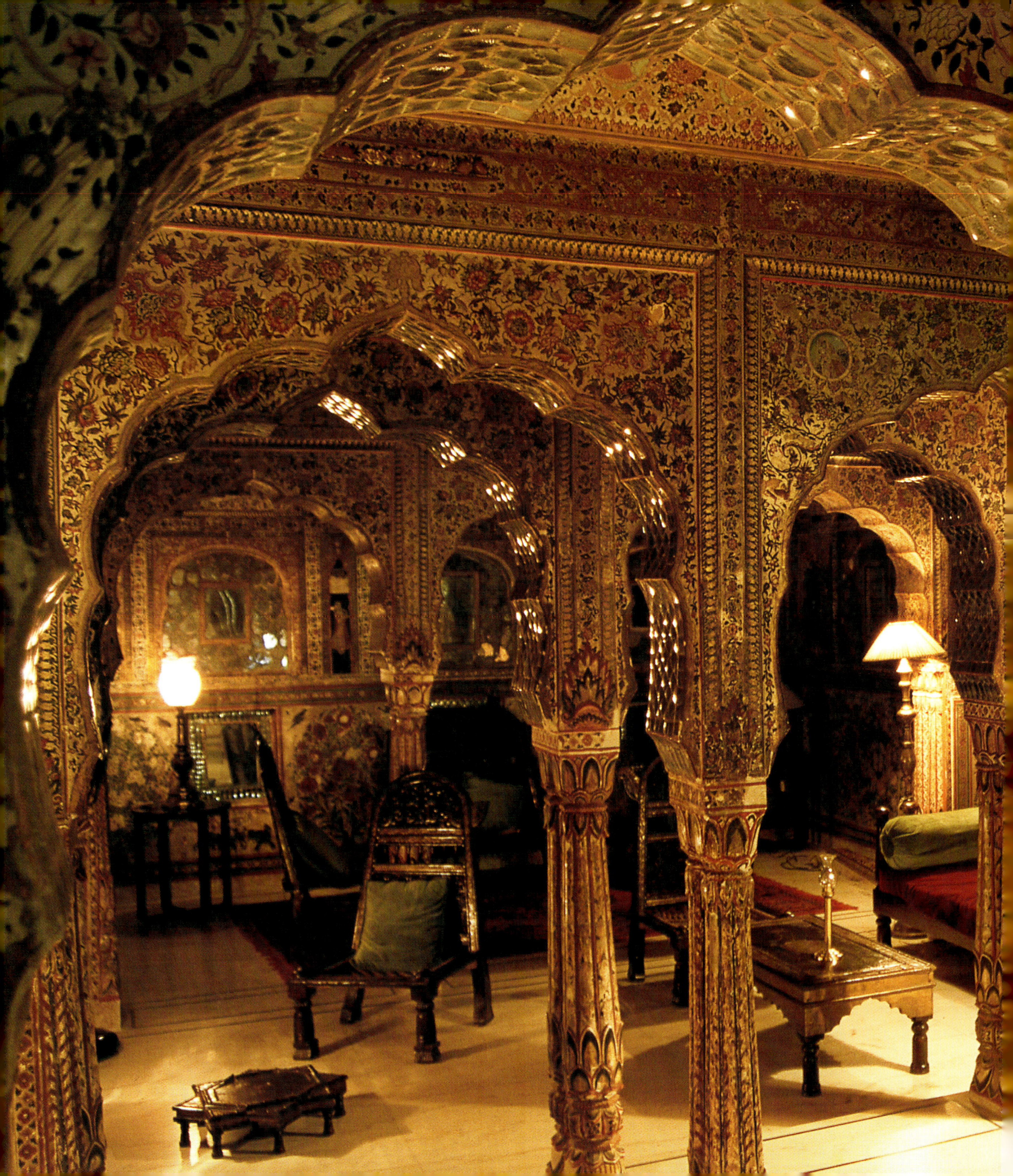

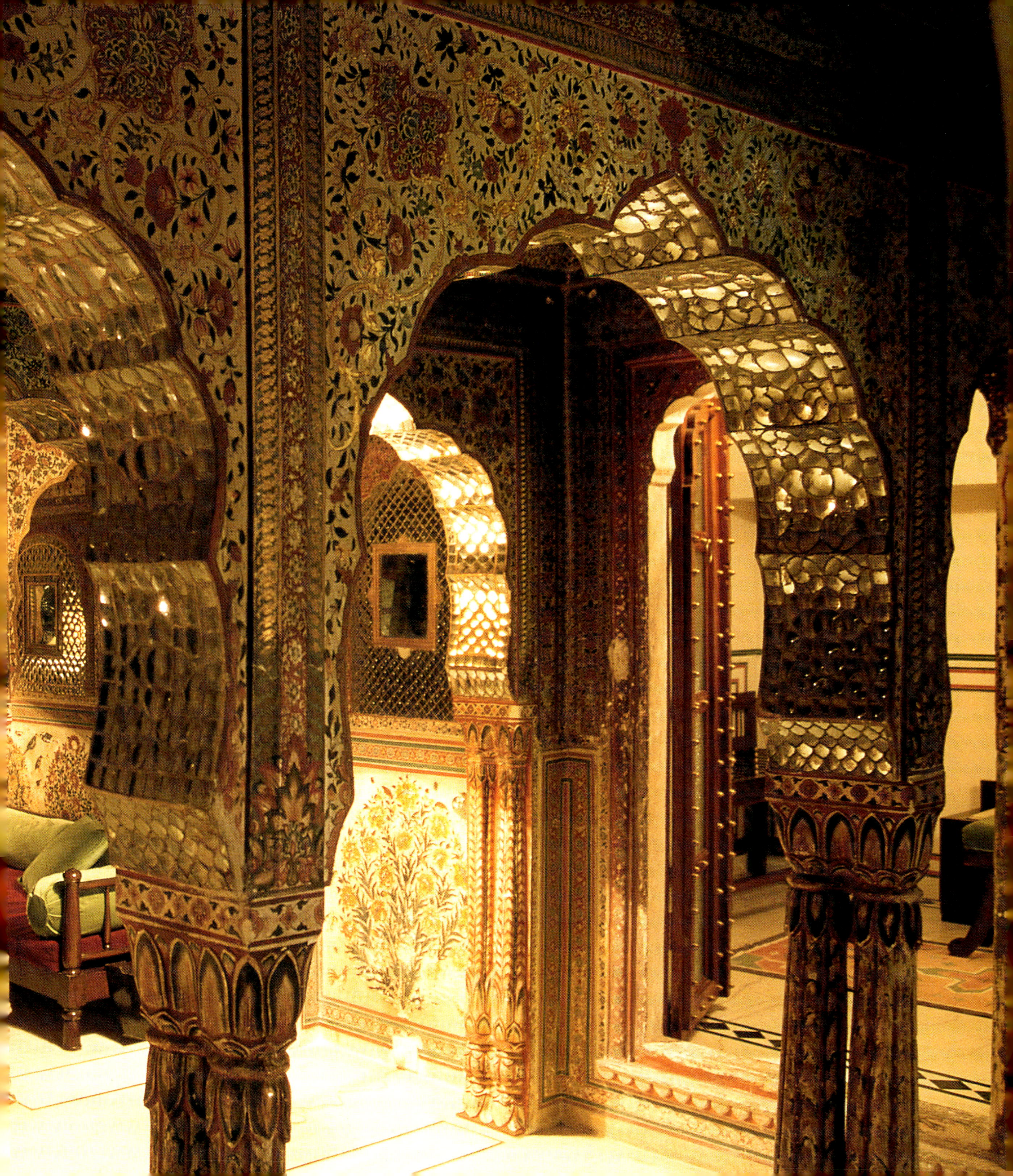

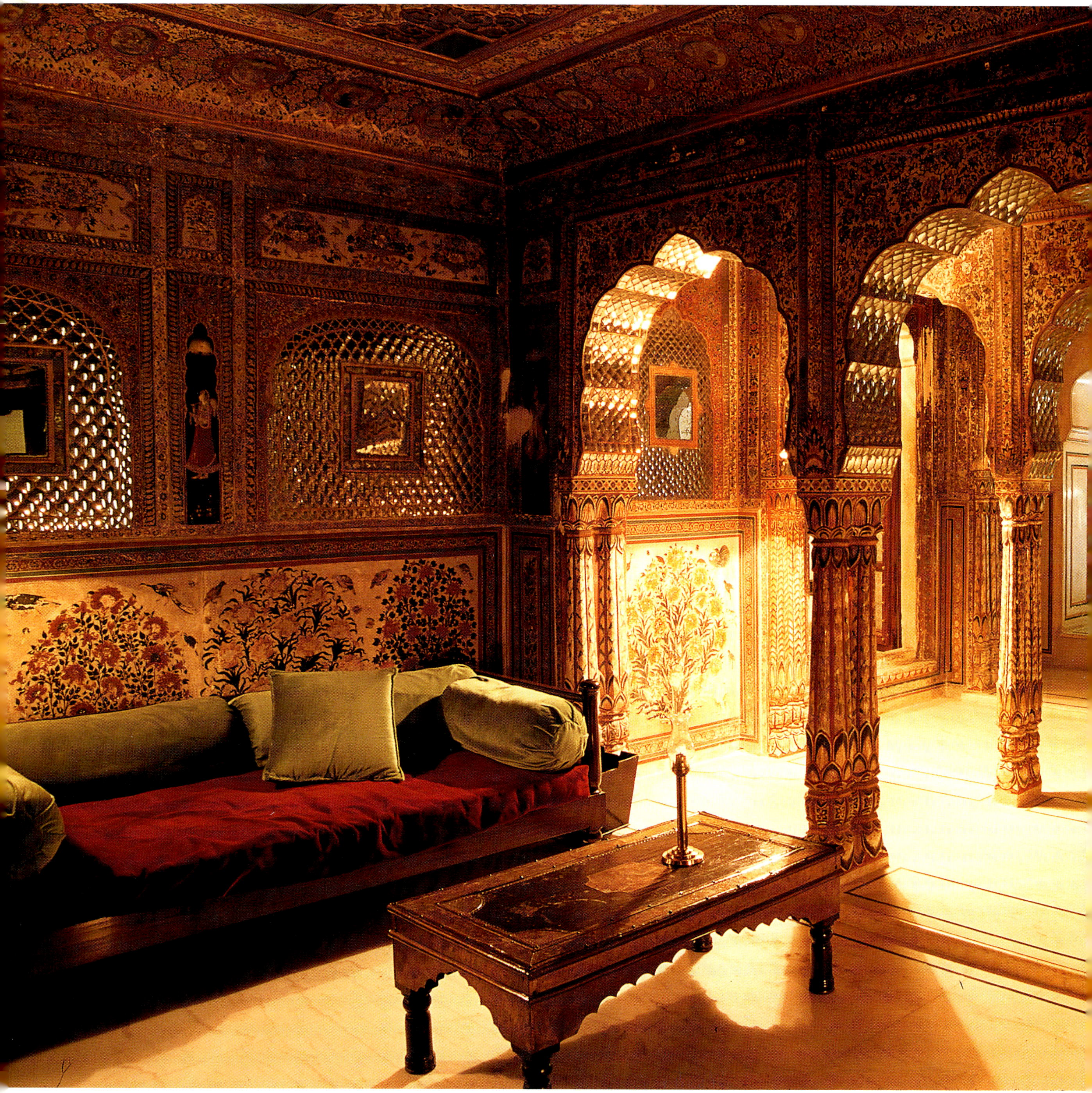

Pages 198 to 201:
Raghavendra and Yadavendra won their wager: the two young aristocratic-looking brothers decided to open to the public the residence of their ancestor, Prime Minister of the maharajah of Jaipur. Spending the night, even just one, in the "Little Mirrors Suite" of Samode Haveli, is sheer magic and will fascinate the most demanding visitors. Indo-Muslim art in all its glory…

THE FORTRESSES OF AMBER, JAIGARH AND NAHARGARH

Birthplace of the Kachhvahas dynasty, the fortress of Amber is nestled in the steep mountains some 8 kilometres from Jaipur. The road first runs alongside the Man Sagar lake where the Jal Mahal palace appears to be floating upon its surface. The maharajahs hunted duck here. A bit further on, atop a rocky hill, you discover Amber, encircled by ramparts, bastions and watchtowers rising on the surrounding hillsides. Impregnable in its heyday, today it succumbs to the pressure of tourism. This site enabled to control the road to Delhi, making it of great strategic interest in the distant past.

In the twelfth century, the prince Duleh Rai made it the capital of his kingdom. The citadel itself goes back to the sixteenth century under the reign of Man Singh II. It was reinforced and extended in the seventeenth century by Jai Singh who abandoned it toward 1733 to found Jaipur. Several steep paths lead to a row of massive gates commanding the entrance to the fort.

How would you like to take a promenade on an elephant's back? They are awaiting you. Down below, the eye is drawn to handsome Moghul gardens laid out in 1588 on an island. The last gate, Suraj Pol (Door of the Sun) opens onto Jaleb Chowk, a vast esplanade framed by buildings that used to be barrack-rooms. The poor elephants that

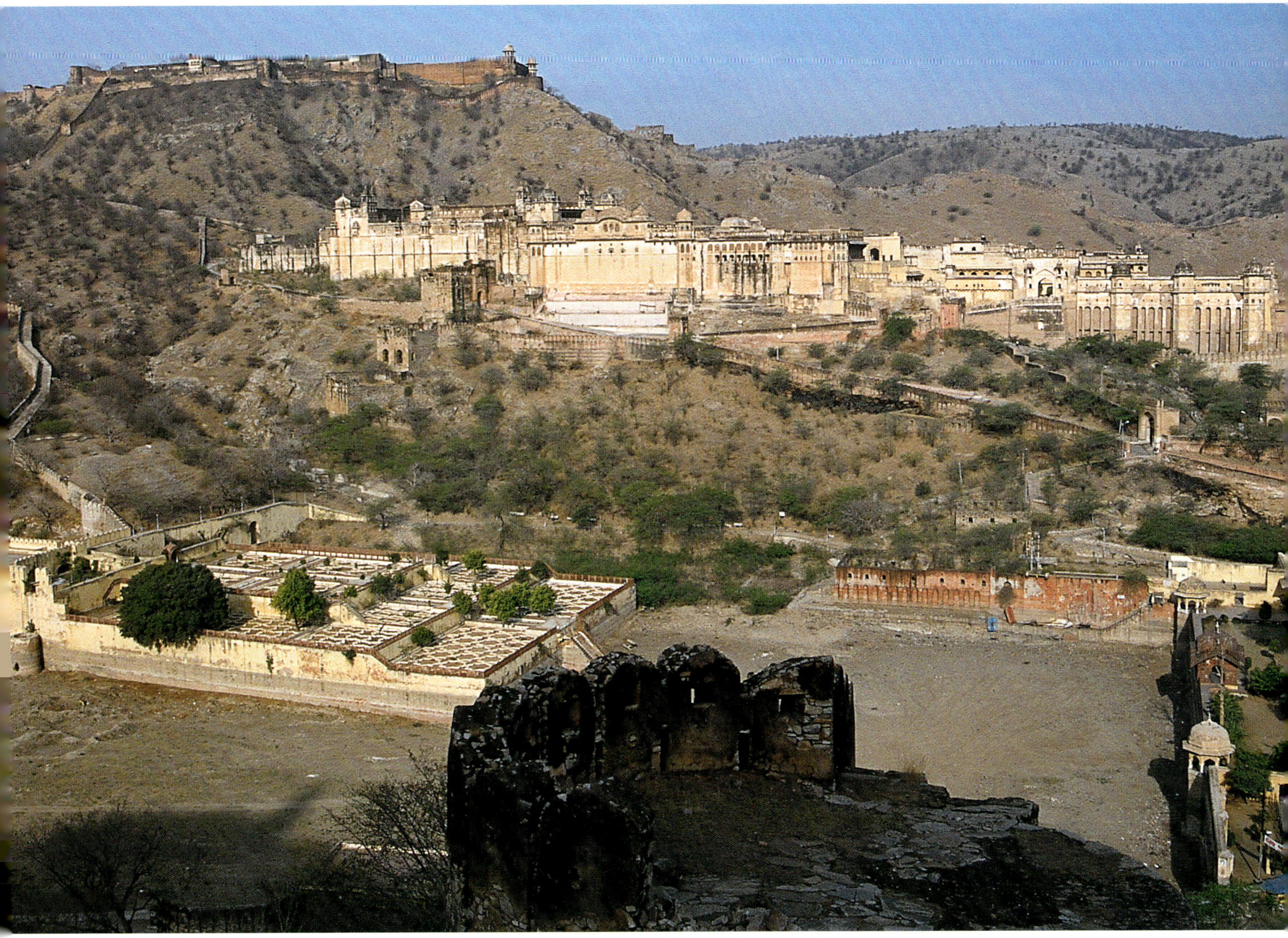

204

Pages 202 to 205:
The Fortress of Amber. When the rajahs of Amber finally decided to seek an alliance with the Moghuls instead of resisting them, they had the bright idea of embellishing their fortress with gorgeous palaces scattered with gardens designed in Moghul style, in the late sixteenth century and the early seventeenth. We are fully rewarded for storming the citadel. Architectural wonders lead the way on an exceptional promenade from the Gate of Ganesh (pages 204 and 204) graced with paintings with Moghul-style motifs.

brought the tourists are only too happy to finally get a rest. The cool air is conducive to exploring. A stairway leads to a small plaza in front of the diwan-i am (public audiences hall) which we recognise by its double row of red sandstone and marble columns supporting a vaulted ceiling. It is pure early seventeenth-century Moghul style. On one side a breath-taking view overlooking the valley below; on the other, the magnificent Ganesh Pol gate, installed in 1639, sparkles with its paintings and inlaid mirrors. A passageway leads to orderly Moghul gardens surrounded by the private apartments designed during the era of Jai Singh I.

You hardly know where to look standing in the midst of this mardana, the men's quarter. It is laden with treasures of Indo-Moghul art: the Sukh Mahal (Palace of Delights) and the Jai Mandir, a sort of small palace whose walls are inlaid with mirrors set in plaster. The ravishing Shish Mahal (Palace of Mirrors) is truly fairylike. In the central diwan-i khas (private audiences hall), we delight in these tiny mirrors combined with polychrome

The diwan-i khas, the private audiences hall, is recognisable by its multifoil arches and soaring columns.

*Pages 206 to 208:
Taken with the refinement of the Courts of Akbar and of Shah Jahan, the Rajahs of Amber enhanced their palaces with the loveliest Moghul devices, as in the Jai Mandir and the Shish Mahal where grandiose receptions were given: ceilings lit with floral decors and dotted with tiny mirrors, tympanums with bottle-shaped openings, polished whitewashed floors, elegant marble friezes, corbelled vaults…*

mosaics and painted arabesques. It is laden with the sublime Moghul details borrowed from the Iranian style: bottles big and small, bowls of fruit, bouquets, cypress trees… In comparison the zenana cuts a poor figure; dark windowless galleries alternating with austere palaces. Even though each wife had her own apartment, her hammam and her servants. But it is all slightly drab!

The mighty Kachhvahas Rajput warriors had it all planned. Up above, the fortress of Jaigarh, founded in the twelfth century, was the coffer, the armoury and the observatory. As for the fort of the Lion, Nahargarh, which overlooks Jaipur, Jai Singh had it built in 1734 to protect his new city. It is no longer needed. Foreigners these days only seek to conquer a change of scenery and dreams.

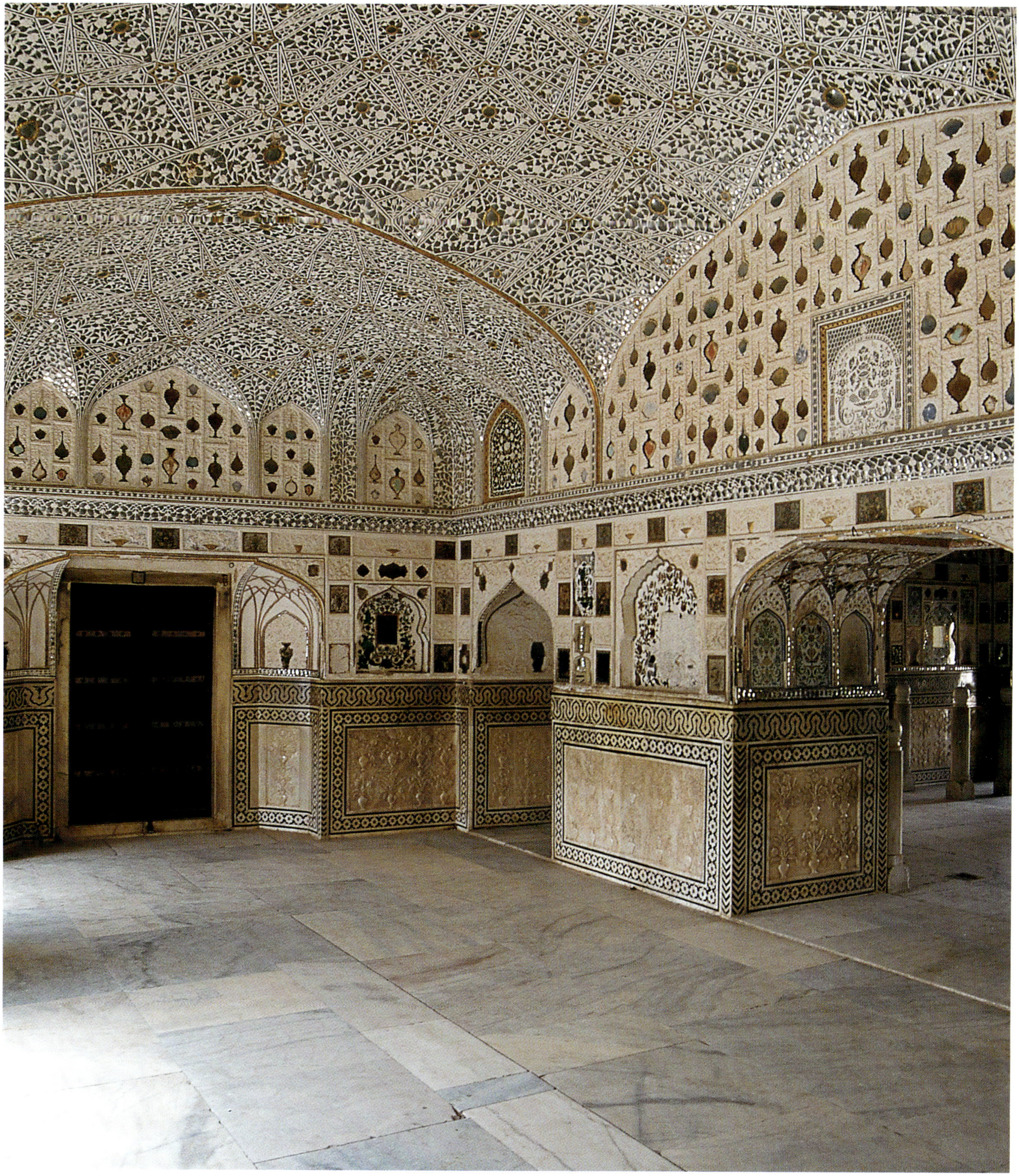

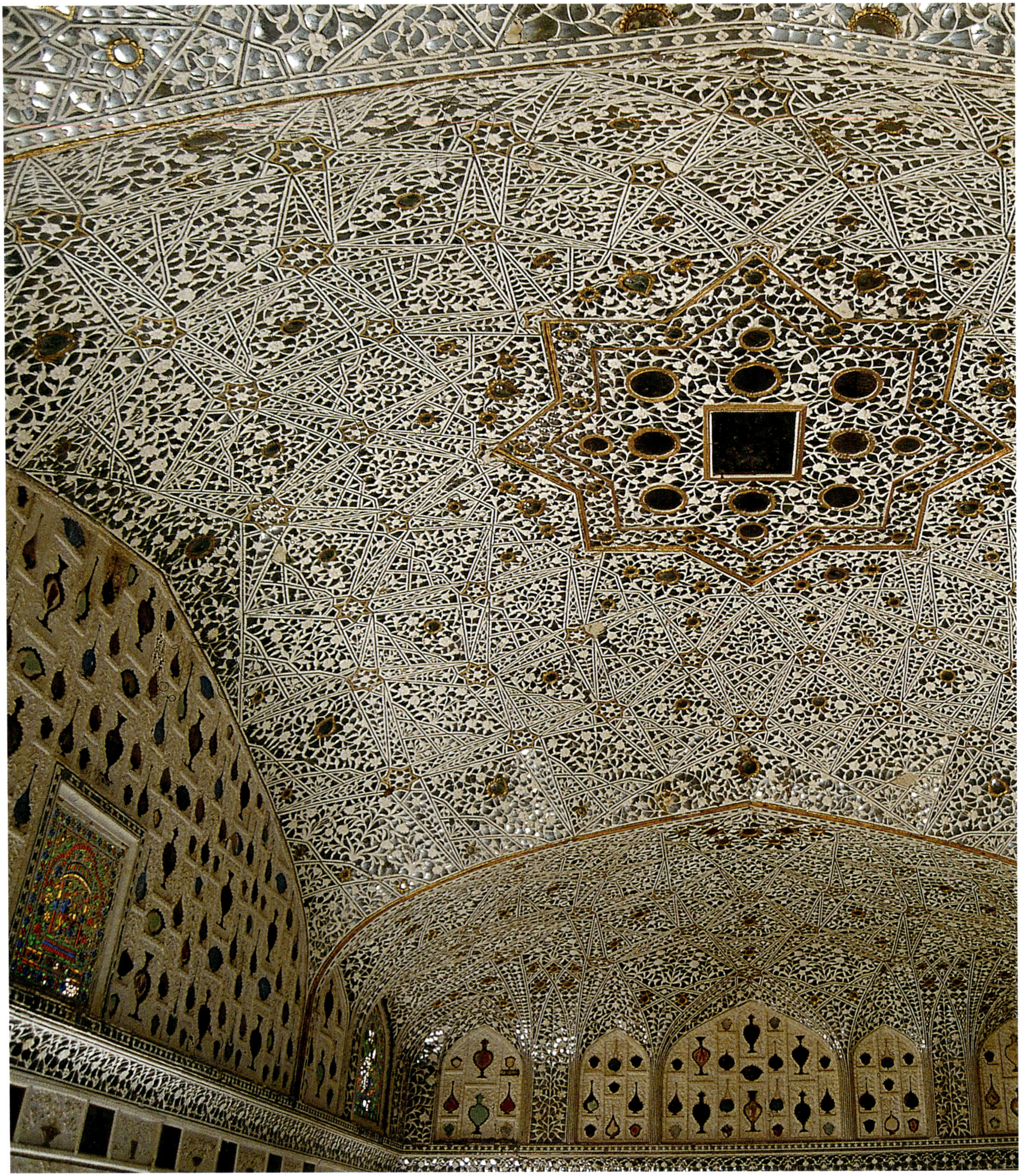

The cenotaphs of the Kachhvahas princes were usually built on the site of their cremation.

BIKANER

In the very heart of Bikaner, but withdrawn from its bustle, the Bhanwar Niwas haveli offers a muted, sweet atmosphere.

Connoisseurs claim the city contained five treasures: delicious sweets, the most robust dromedaries, exquisite jewellery, the cleverest tradesmen and the prettiest women in the region. Rather tricky to check it all out! As for architecture, experts all agree that the fort of Junagarh is the greatest prize and the best preserved of all Rajasthan.

Formerly called "Pearl of the Desert" because of the proximity of the Thar desert, or the "Red City" since it is built of red sandstone, etymologically speaking Bikaner is the city of Rao Bika. Son of the Rathor, the sovereign founder of Jodhpur, he decided in 1488 to create a new kingdom here. Akbar was on his way through, and the sovereigns became allies and took over the command of the Moghul armies. Peace allowed the city to grow, becoming a quiet stopping place and trading centre for the caravans after crossing the desert. The talent of its craftsmen, weavers and goldsmiths was known far beyond the borders of the state. But the new trade routes set up by the English in Calcutta and Bombay ended up by edging out the region. Yet toward the end of the nineteenth century Bikaner came back into its own. The breeding of dromedaries turned out to be of vital importance for the British armies in their clashes with the Afghans. And then there was the personality of the maharajah Ganga Singh, a model enlightened sovereign who during his reign, between 1898 and 1934, stirred an incomparable dynamism in his city, launching a major irrigation project to help the population and put an end to famine. His bravery is remembered by all. He founded the prestigious "Bikaner Camel Corps", fought in China and Somalia and won glory during World War I in France and Egypt.

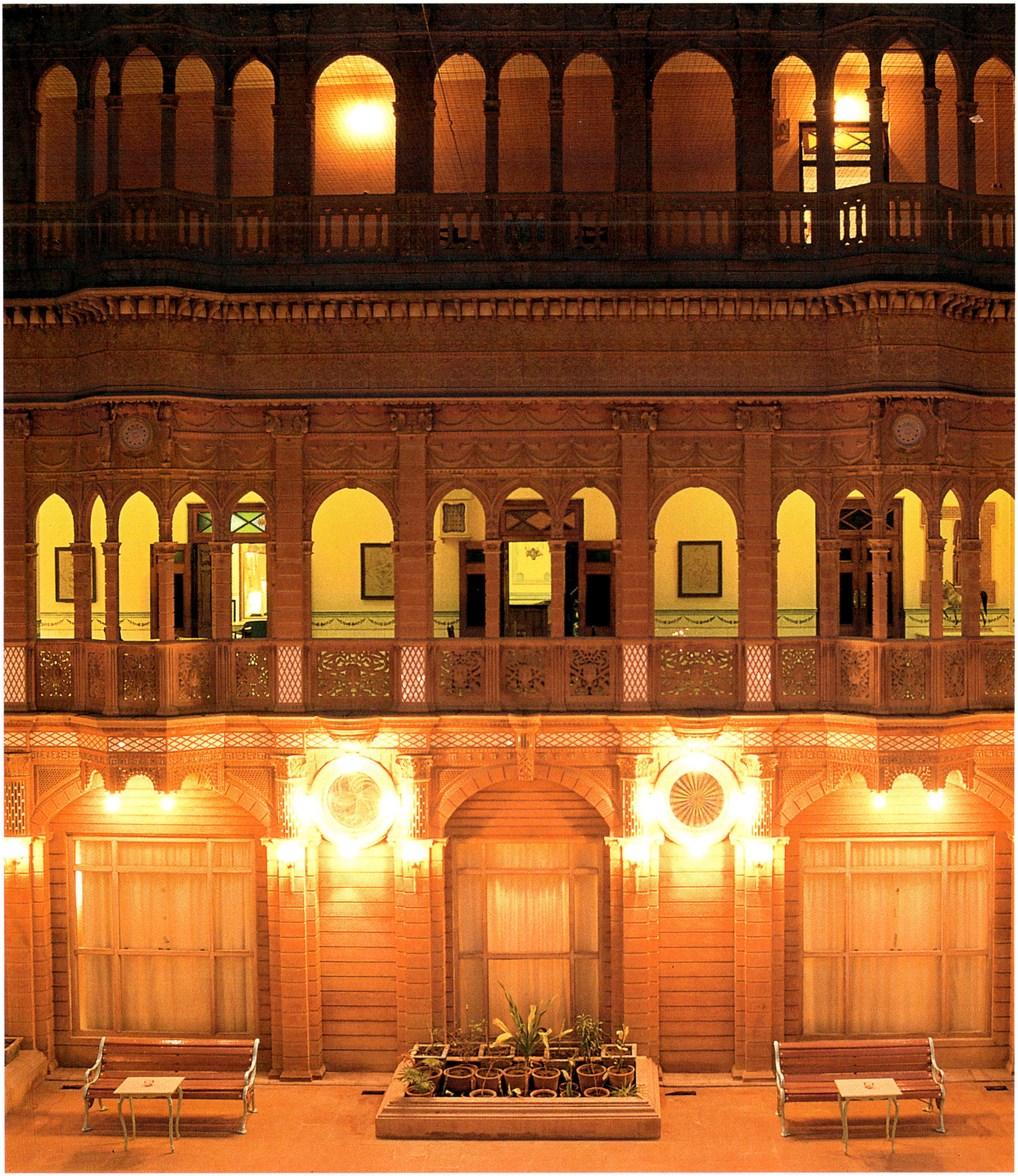

Connoisseurs claim the women of Bikaner are the most beautiful in Rajasthan.

Sunil Rampuria exquisitely renovated the family haveli that the best stone carvers of the land had built in 1927.

The Haveli of Bhanwar Niwas

The soul of Bikaner still dwells in the Middle Ages. It kept its mediaeval layout and the delightfully mercantile atmosphere of its bazaars. Let yourself be swept off your feet by the crowd in its maze of alleys. At a bend in the narrow Rampuria Street, you will be enthralled on discovering the incredibly carved façade of a haveli that has all the appearance of a palace. Its name: Bhanwar Niwas. Curiosity is an excellent foible that is often rewarded. Just try to go in: it will be the thrill of your stay in Bikaner. In the early evening, captivating Indian music echoes in the hallways lit by gilt torchères. Exquisite scents of pakaras and samosas (a kind of hot fritter) invite you to further exploration. Here everything merges superlatively to express richness and passion. Everything exudes charm and a sense of mystery. The dynamic owner, Sunil Rampuria, will be only too happy to tell you the story of this haveli, which is also that of his family, the Rampurias, a lineage of tradesmen practicing the Jain religion. Built in 1927 by his grandfather, the haveli was abandoned at the latter's death in 1947.

The Rampurias decided to move to Calcutta. However, a few years ago, one of them came back to Bikaner with his large family and converted part of the family residence into a very charming hotel. A great success! Today, 24 suites, each different, are housed in the former family apartments: stucco, marble, arabesque decors, marquetry, and mosaics surround splendid period furniture. Every morning, on the first floor of the haveli, the same pure, mysterious ceremony unfolds: when Sunil and his son, dressed in immaculate white robes, go into the small Jain family altar and perform with fervour the holy ritual, to the amazement of the guests.

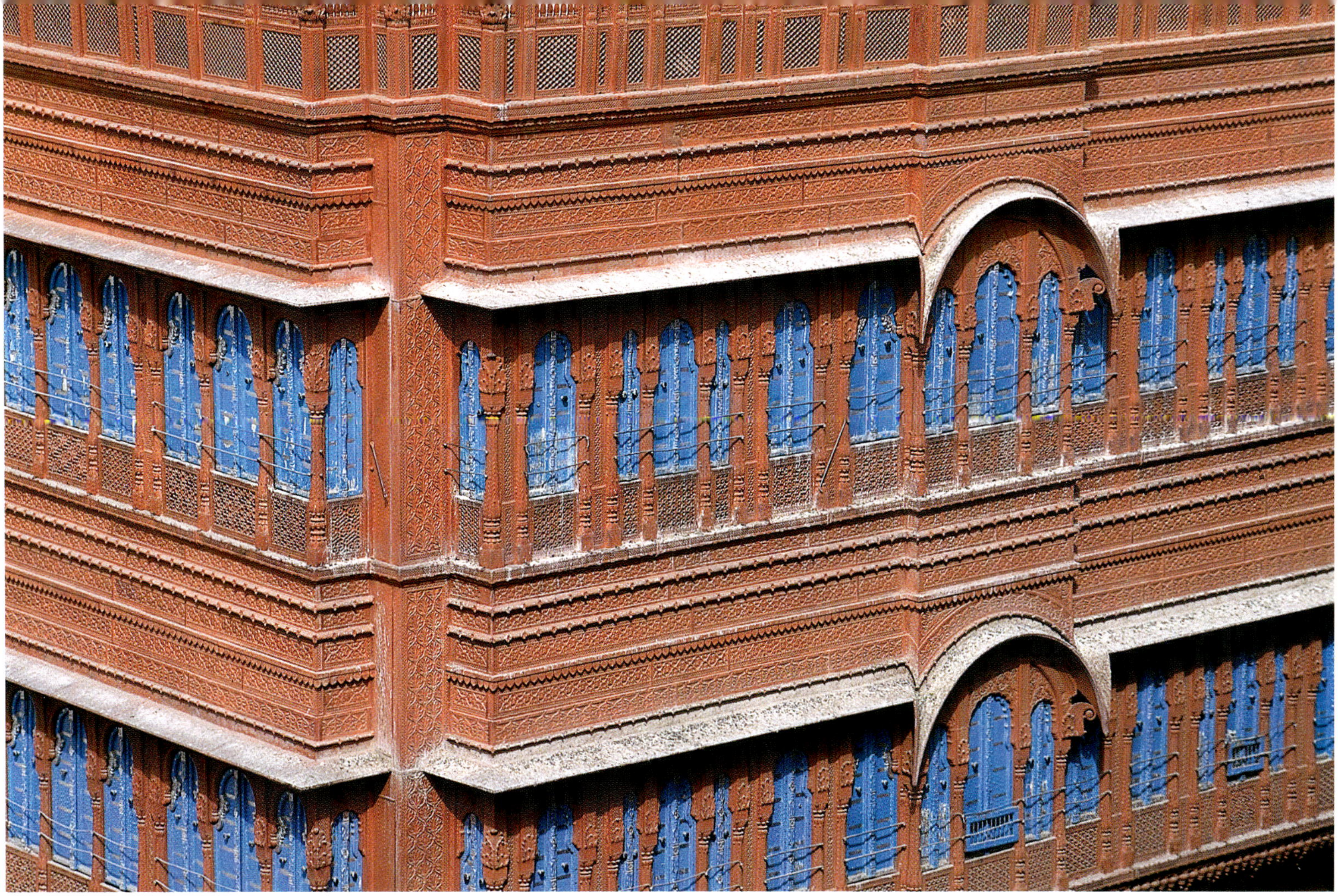
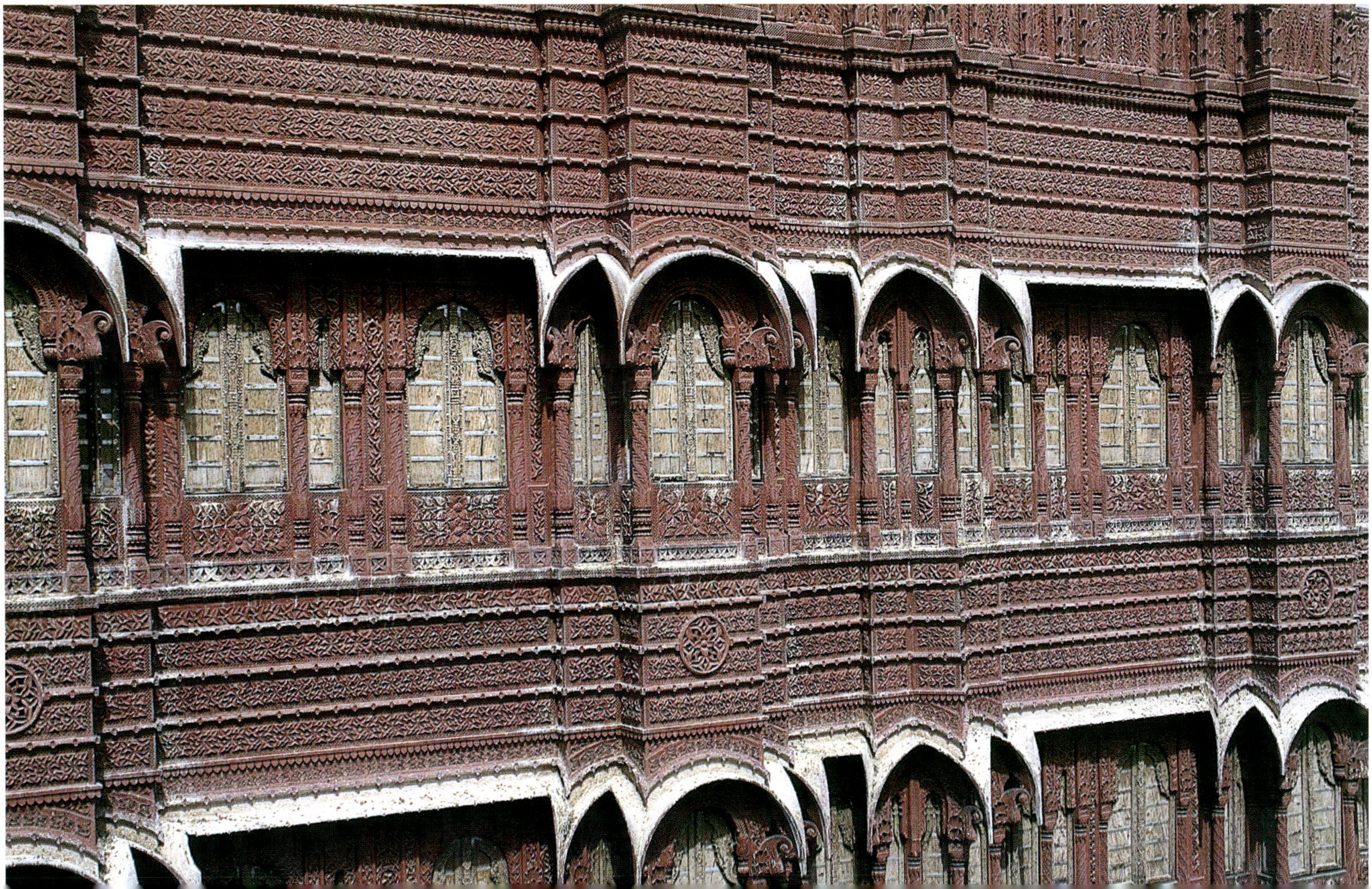

*The soul of the haveli is undoubtedly nestled in the
small Jain altar the family honours every morning.
The period furniture, colonial style, crafted in
Calcutta has been preserved in the suites.*

215

The Fort of Junagarh

Stalls rub shoulders around the five gates that used to close the city. Constructed under the rajah Rai Singh (1571-1611), the fort of Junagarh is perhaps the most interesting of all. Defended by a formidable red sandstone wall a kilometre long, marked by 37 bastions, it was never taken by the enemy. Three massive doors with defences against elephants regulated its access. The first courtyard is framed by a remarkable ensemble of palaces and courtyards paved in Italian faience. You just do not know where to look. Here is the diwan-i am (public audiences hall), built in 1631 by Karan Singh, with its ceilings and columns decorated with gilding and paintings. Over there the Anup Mahal with its wealth of decorations, paintings, mosaics, coloured tiles was the coronation room for the maharajahs. The Phul Mahal (Palace of Flowers) and the Chandra Mahal (Palace of the Moon), shaped like a crescent moon, are frequently closed to the public. Too bad! Their walls dotted with tiny mirrors are more beautiful. Further on, you will be hypnotised by the magnificence of the diwan-i khas (private audiences hall), an authentic symphony of gildings and frescoes, lit by mirrors from Belgium. A few steps beyond, you will be moved by the little Badal Mahal (Palace of the Clouds) that fits its name. The blue and white clouds painted on the walls are like so many prayers asking for rain.

Solemn symbol of the greatness of the maharajahs of Bikaner, the Fort of Junagarh never fell to the Moghuls, in part thanks to its colossal red sandstone walls, its moats and 37 bastions.

Unlike most of the other forts in Rajasthan erected at the top of a rock or a hill to protect them, Junagarh was built on the plain. The desert, reaching the city gates, was enough to dissuade potential assailants.

The red sandstone walls hide from sight magnificent halls and palaces, like the Lal Niwas, an unusual room with its colourful red and gold walls (page 218) and the Anup Mahal designed in 1669 (right), the prize of the fort. With its throne, its gildings and mirror mosaics, it was the maharajahs' coronation room.

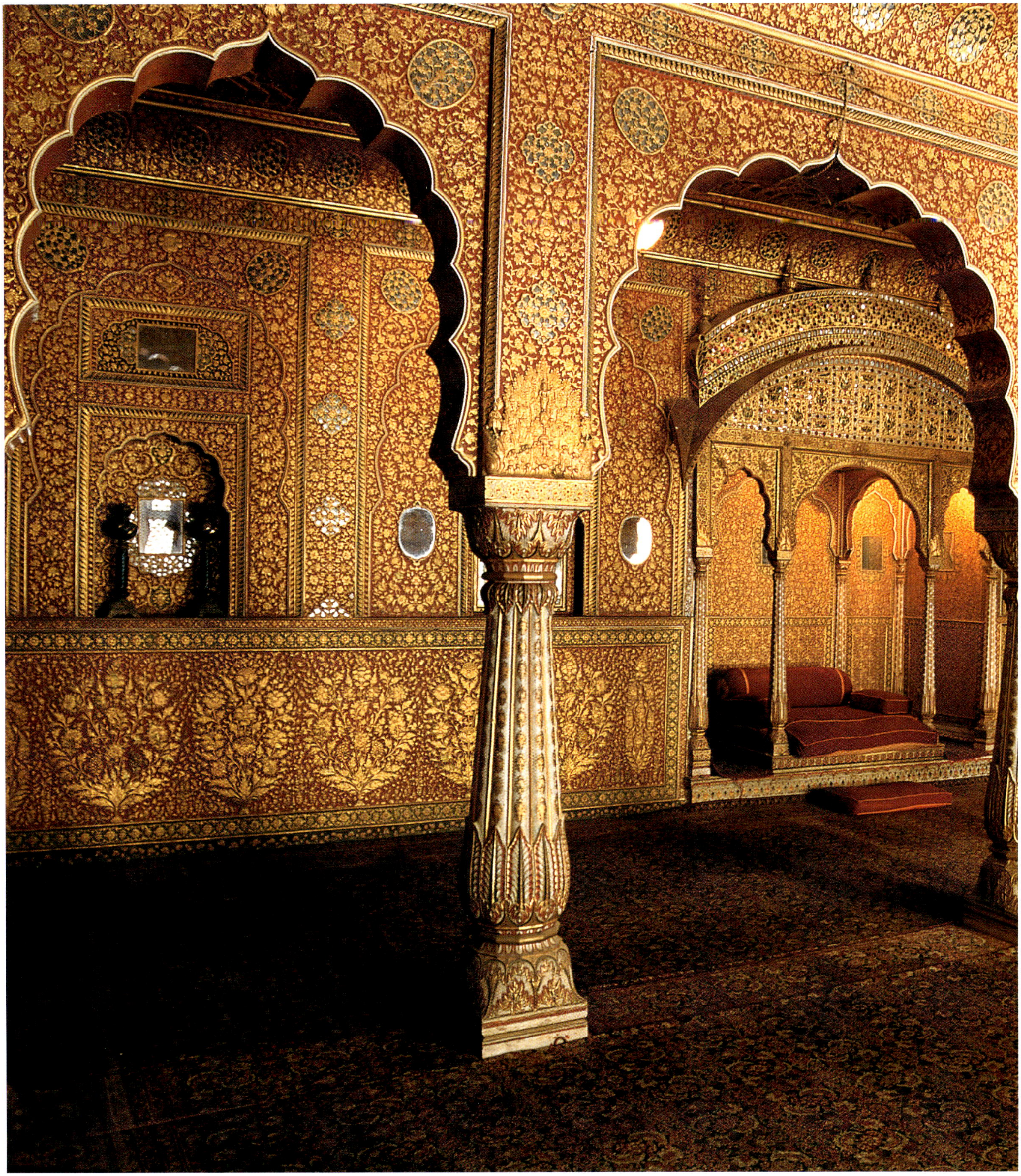

In this stucco-walled room for audiences, Anup Singh received in grand pomp.

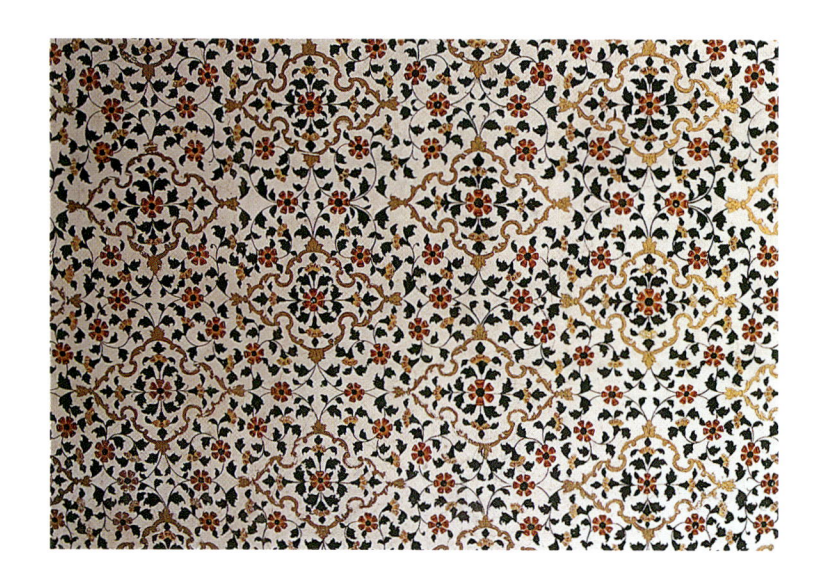

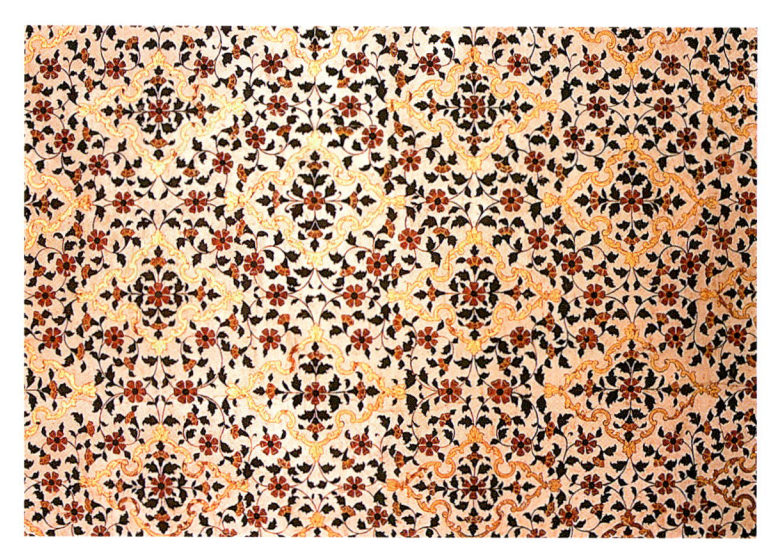

On the first floor of the fort of Junagarh, we are enthralled on entering the Gaj Mandir, the room of mirrors, which housed the king's private apartments, not far from the queen's room.

222

The precious Palace of the Clouds, Badal Mahal, covered with paintings featuring blue and white clouds, was for the children. Maybe to show them where to look for rain, so scarce in the desert!

The desert comes all the way to the gates of Bikaner. On very hot days the maharajah would withdraw in the small Palace of the Winds, Hawa Mahal, overlooking the terraces of the fort of Junagarh, elegantly covered with blue China earthenware tiles and dancing frescoes of Krishna.

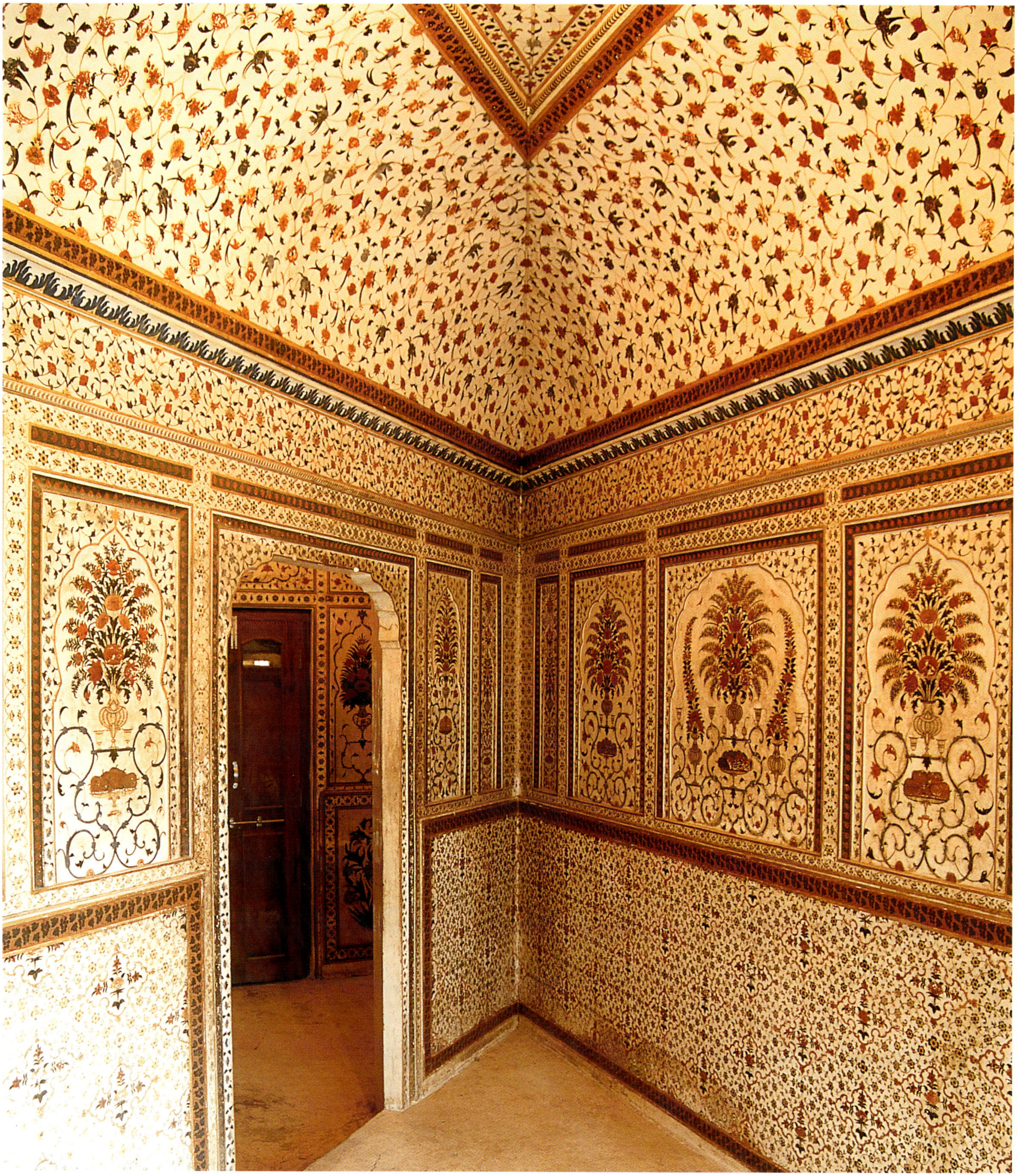

Such an unusual little room! The Palace of Flowers or Phul Mahal has recently been restored by young Persian artists. Their ancestors, called to the Court of the Rajputs of Bikaner, were the ones to adorn this room with Persian-style floral motifs.

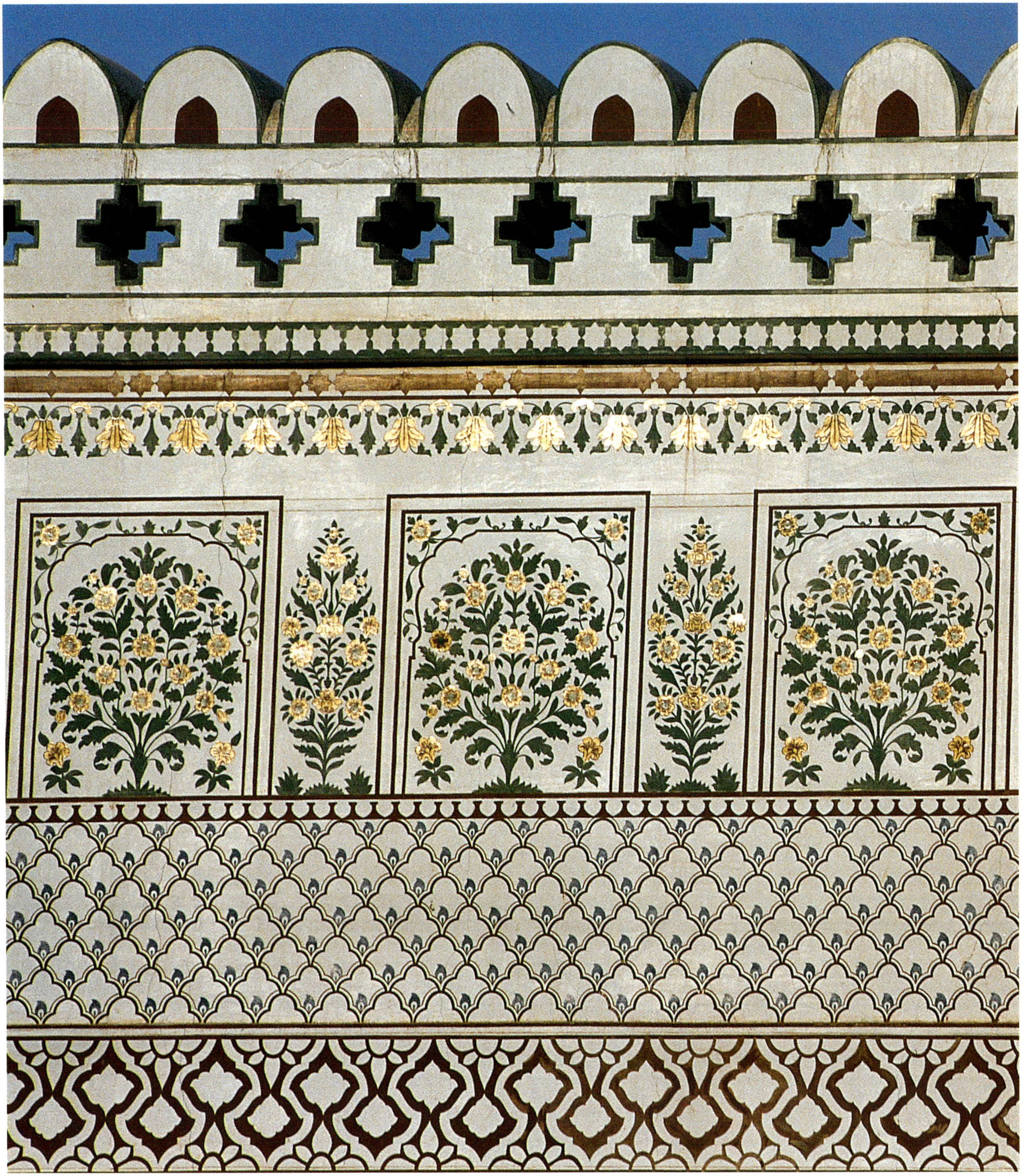

Bouquets, geometric patterns, Indo-Muslim decorative art endlessly unfolds its variations on all the facades and all the doors.

After bowing to the temple dedicated to Hanuman, on the first floor, you cross the Gaj Mandir with its walls inlaid with mirrors (you just never tire of them!), the Queen's room, identifiable by its beautiful ivory inlays, and the King's room. On the upper terraces, the Hawa Mahal (Palace of the Winds) has wonderful surprises in store with its outstanding China blue faience tiles featuring interesting bucolic scenes. The maharajahs had such good taste! During the hottest days, some of them surely retired here in amorous company!

The highlight in the midst of this insane maze of stairways and passageways is your next visit, the huge Durbar Hall. It contrasts with the sweetness of the Palace of the Winds. The last ruling maharajah, Ganga Singh, entertained here in great pomp. It is said that he had artisans come from Afghanistan to carve the red sandstone walls of the immense room and that it took them seven years. But just look at the result! Lace made of stone… Today Durbar Hall is a museum displaying articles and documents that belonged to the maharajah. If you have a longing for the past you will be enchanted.

The Lalgarh Palace History

In 1900 Ganga Singh decided to leave the fort, and had the Palace of Lalgarh built a stone's throw away. He called upon the British architect Sir Swinton Jacob. It took 24 years to build this symphony of red sandstone inspired by the Rajput style. While several members of the royal family reside in part of it, the rest was divided in two hotels: the "Laxmi Niwas Palace" and the "Lalgarh Palace". The rooms, which look about the size of a railroad station concourse, are arrayed around several courtyards where the guests can muse over the "exotic" colonial era. After a few lengths in the art deco swimming pool, you can go and explore the Trophy Room, the billiard room or the smoking room to get a taste of the "British atmosphere".

In the gardens you might run into the elegant princess Rajyashree Kumari, with her suite of secretaries busy taking notes. She is the great-granddaughter of the last ruling maharajah Ganga Singh, so do not hesitate to greet her. The princess, who divides her time between Great Britain which she calls her "adoptive country" and her native land, received us in her very cosy living-room: "I was born after the Independence", she explained. "So I do not feel the slightest nostalgia for the past. Times have changed

At Bikaner, the family of the last reigning maharajah, Ganga Singh, has transformed part of the vast palace of Lalgarh into a luxury hotel. They have retained private apartments where the Princess Rajyashree Kumari resides during her visits since her time is divided between Great Britain and India.

*With its dark pink sandstone towers, turrets, balconies,
chhatri and Bengali roofs designed by the British architect
Sir Swinton Jacob, the palace of Lalgarh is an eye-catcher.*

Warmed by the last rays of the sun, the imposing entrance to the Lalgarh Palace is a dazzling architectural symphony.

and it is a good thing for our country. I myself was given a modern education and was prepared for the great change. Of all my ancestors, Ganga Singh is certainly the most dynamic. He brought to his land the railroad, as well as an irrigation canal that allowed the development of agriculture and areas of greenery. During their reign, often very long, the maharajahs had to be committed to their people, far more than politicians who in our day make promises they usually forget once they are elected. And anyway, they are replaced before they have time to change anything at all."

The princess spoke of the work carried out by her father and member of Parliament, Doctor Kami Singh, who founded several charities. She sponsors a number of foundations which assist the poorest families: gifts for the dowries of the girls to be married and for the wedding ceremonies, gifts to orphans, purchase of equipment for hospitals, financial participation in the eye bank and in sending the poorest children to school as well as support for elderly women. With an abundance of photos, documents, items either amusing or touching, the museum of the maharajah Sadul Singh, nestled in the palace, sums up the glorious and slightly pathetic history of the princes. If you love nice little anecdotes, this is the place for you!

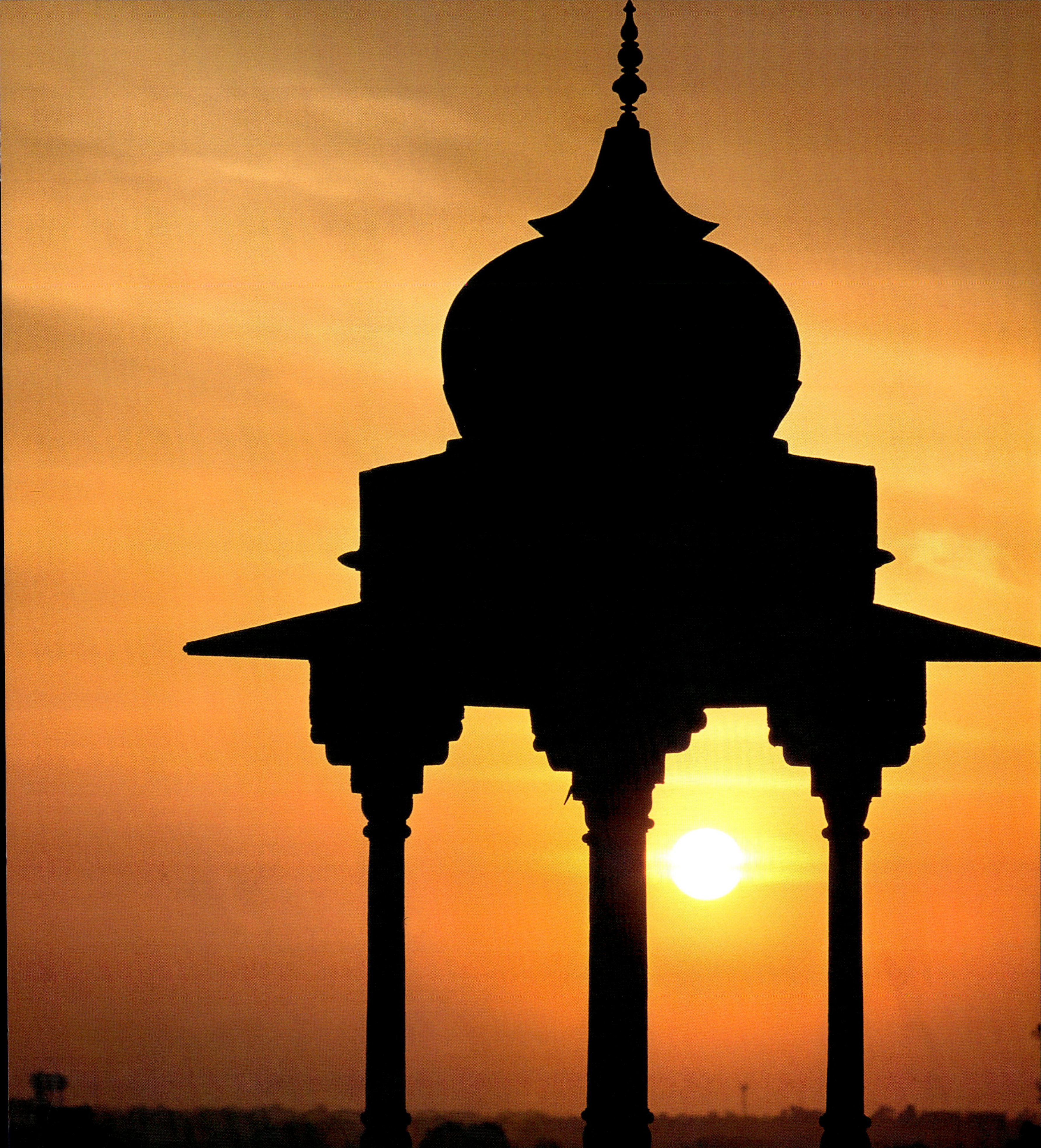

Bohemian crystal chandeliers, an old-fashioned gramophone, sepia photographs... With its smoking room and hunting trophy room, its durbar and its Art Deco swimming pool, the Lalgarh Palace will enrapture fans of bygone days. Once the setting for brilliant receptions given by Ganga Singh, today it is a decor for opulent weddings. A lasting tradition in Rajasthan as all over India; in most instances, the parents arrange their children's marriages.

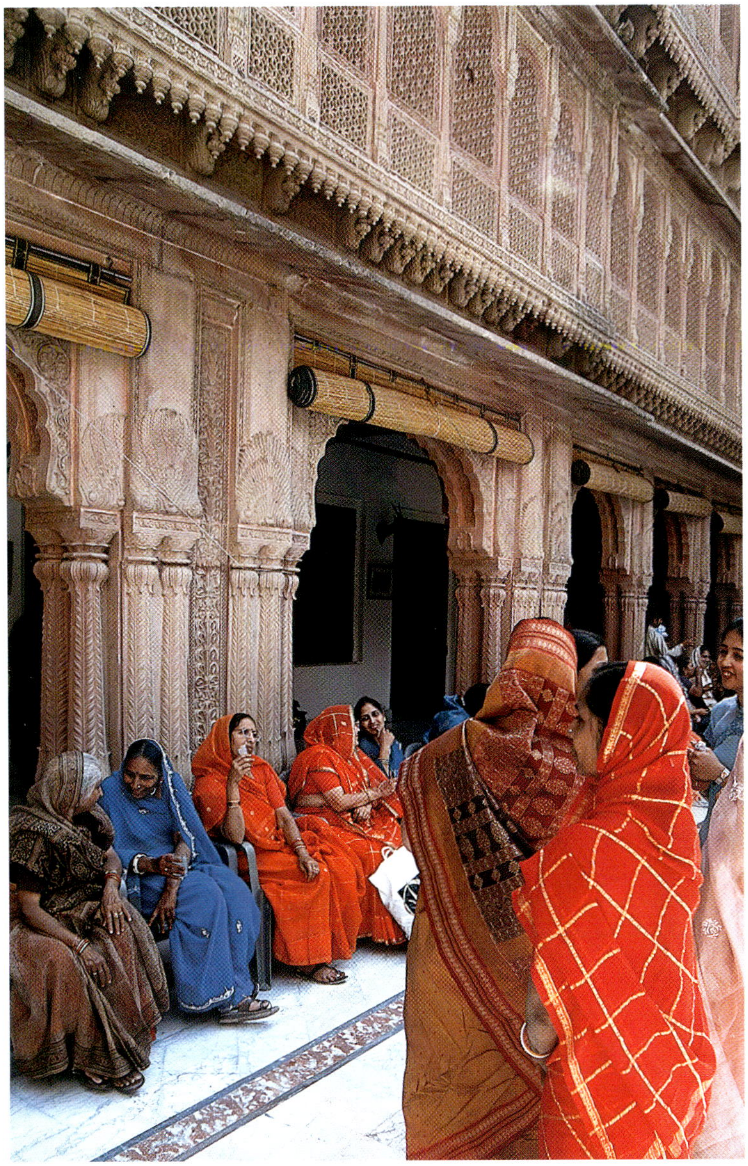
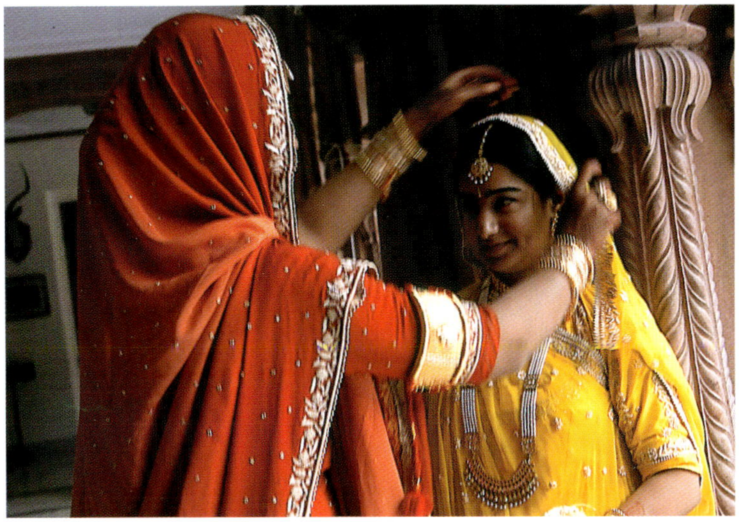
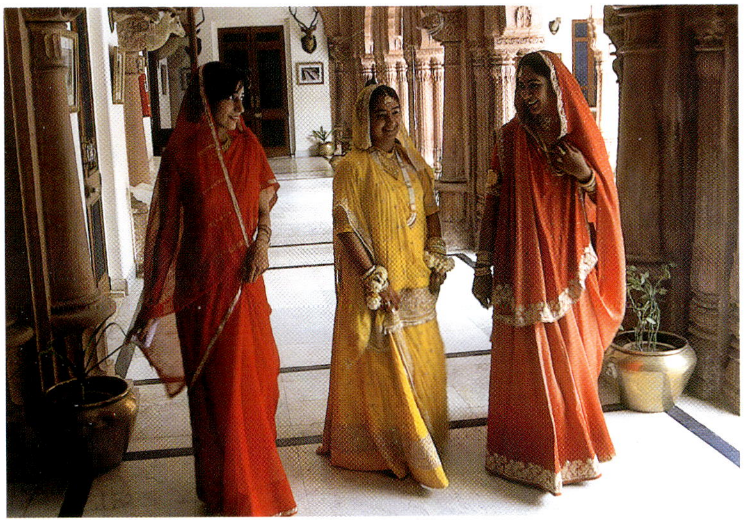
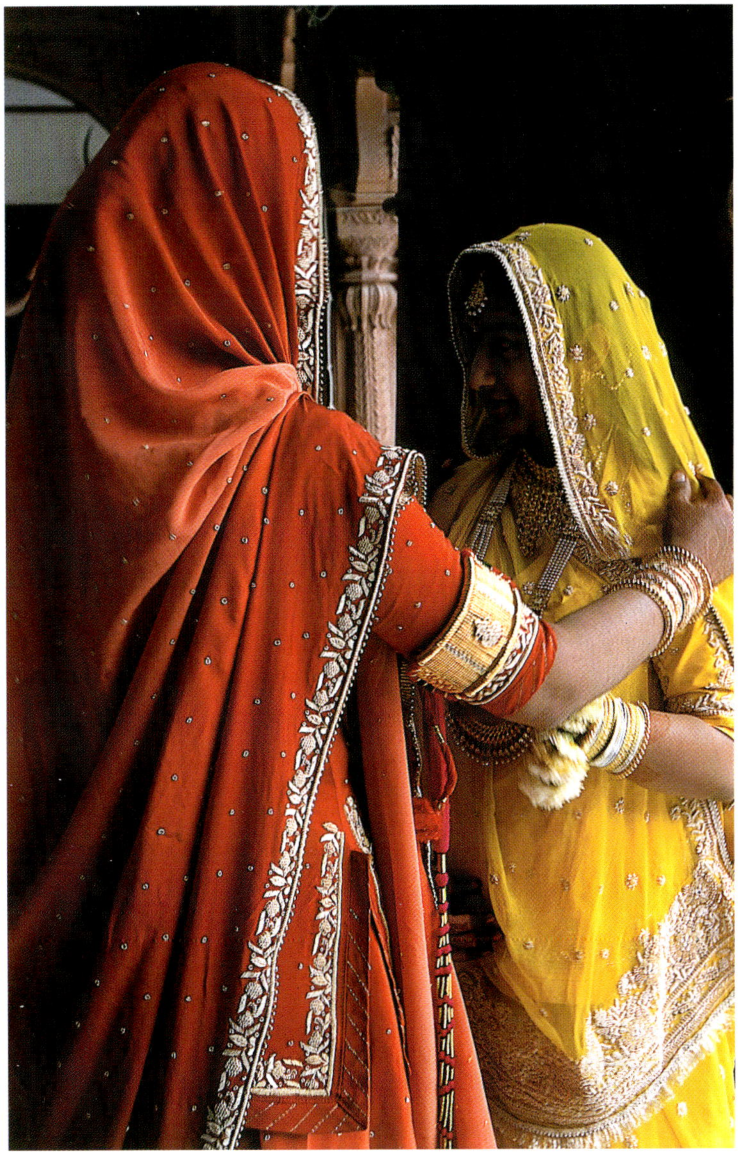

JODHPUR

Starting at daybreak the fruit and vegetable market of Sardar throngs with small stallholders. Tomatoes, spinach, ginger roots have no qualms about rubbing shoulders with the reddest peppers.

For someone who has the good fortune to fly over the city in the late afternoon, Jodhpur is like a heaven-sent present. The sun turns to honey on a stunning patchwork of bluish houses climbing the slopes of the imposing fortress of Mehrangarh. This tradition of the Brahmins to paint their house blue was borrowed by most of the population when they realised that the colour kept mosquitoes away.

Across from Mehrangarh another icon catches your eye: the Umaid Bwahan palace, considered the largest privately owned palace in the world. The dashing maharajah Gaj Singh II is expecting our visit. He lives with his family in one of the wings of the palace he converted into a hotel. What a hotel and what a destiny! Having mounted the throne at the age of four, in 1952, Gaj Singh II lavishly celebrated his jubilee in 2002. Heir to the famous clan of the Rathors that, according to legend, descends directly from Rama, he is supposed to belong to the "solar lineage". His ancestors were the ones to raise this lofty fortress of Mehrangarh which, if we are to believe Rudyard Kipling, "could only have been built by giants". Its name means "His Majesty's fort". It's a city within the city.

Residence of the Rathor maharajahs until the sixteenth century, today it is left to tourists and offers a striking view overlooking the city. Every tower, every hall, every bastion tells the story of the resistance to the Moghuls. Visionary and resolutely modern, the maharajah Umaid Singh, who wished to provide his descendants with greater ease, had a more comfortable palace built in a pure art deco style, Umaid Bhawan.

Between the two properties, the city is attractive with its vegetable market set up at the foot of the very British clock tower. But it is in the maze of narrow streets climbing up to the fortress that you will discover the most genuine quarter, with its low houses that have kept the poignant charm and the nostalgia of bygone days. Explore the inner courtyards, the passageways and the blue patios. Friendly families await you.

An overwhelming sight, the fort of Mehrangarh towers over the city which 120 m below it, displays its strange maze of narrow streets (next pages).

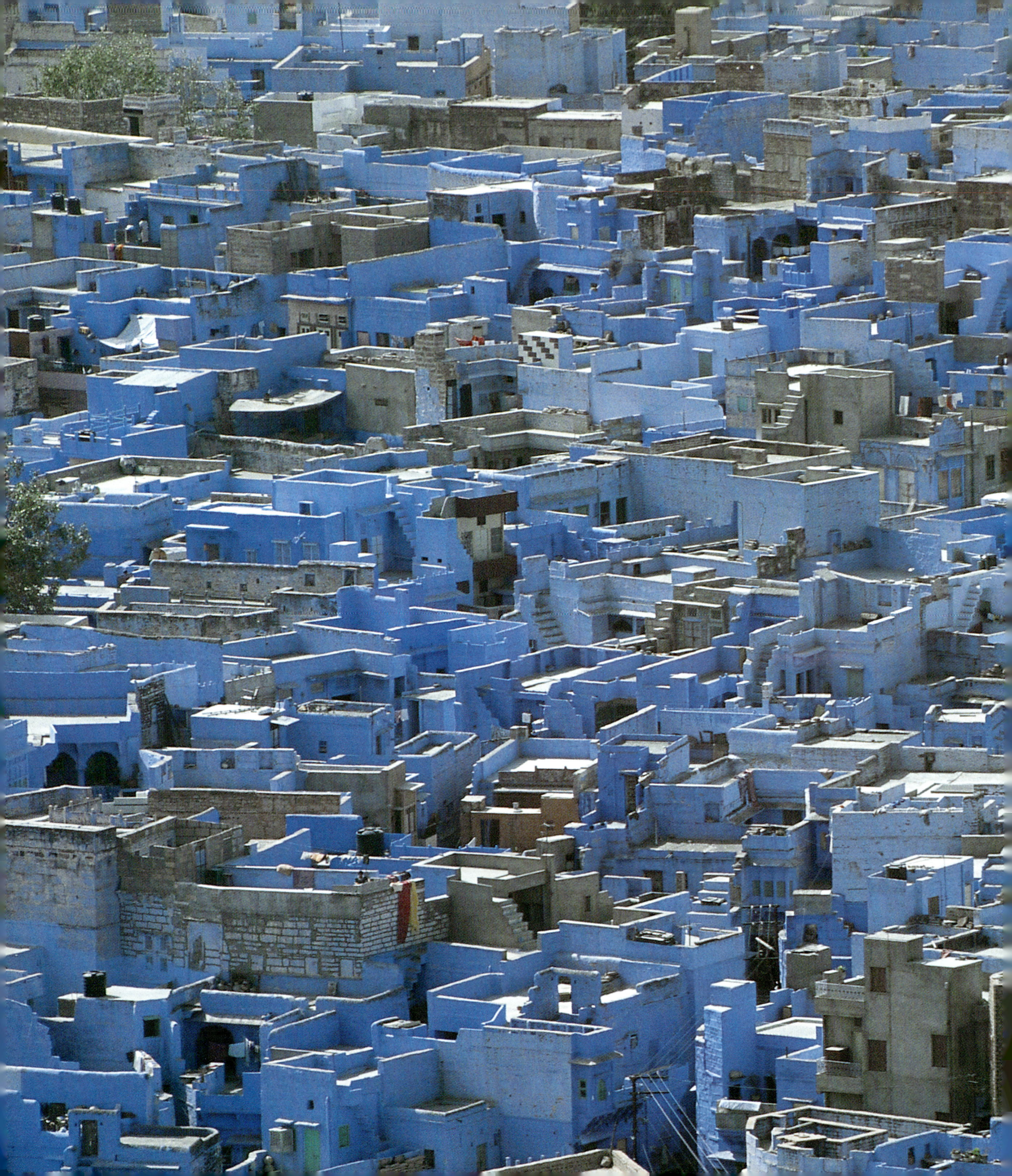

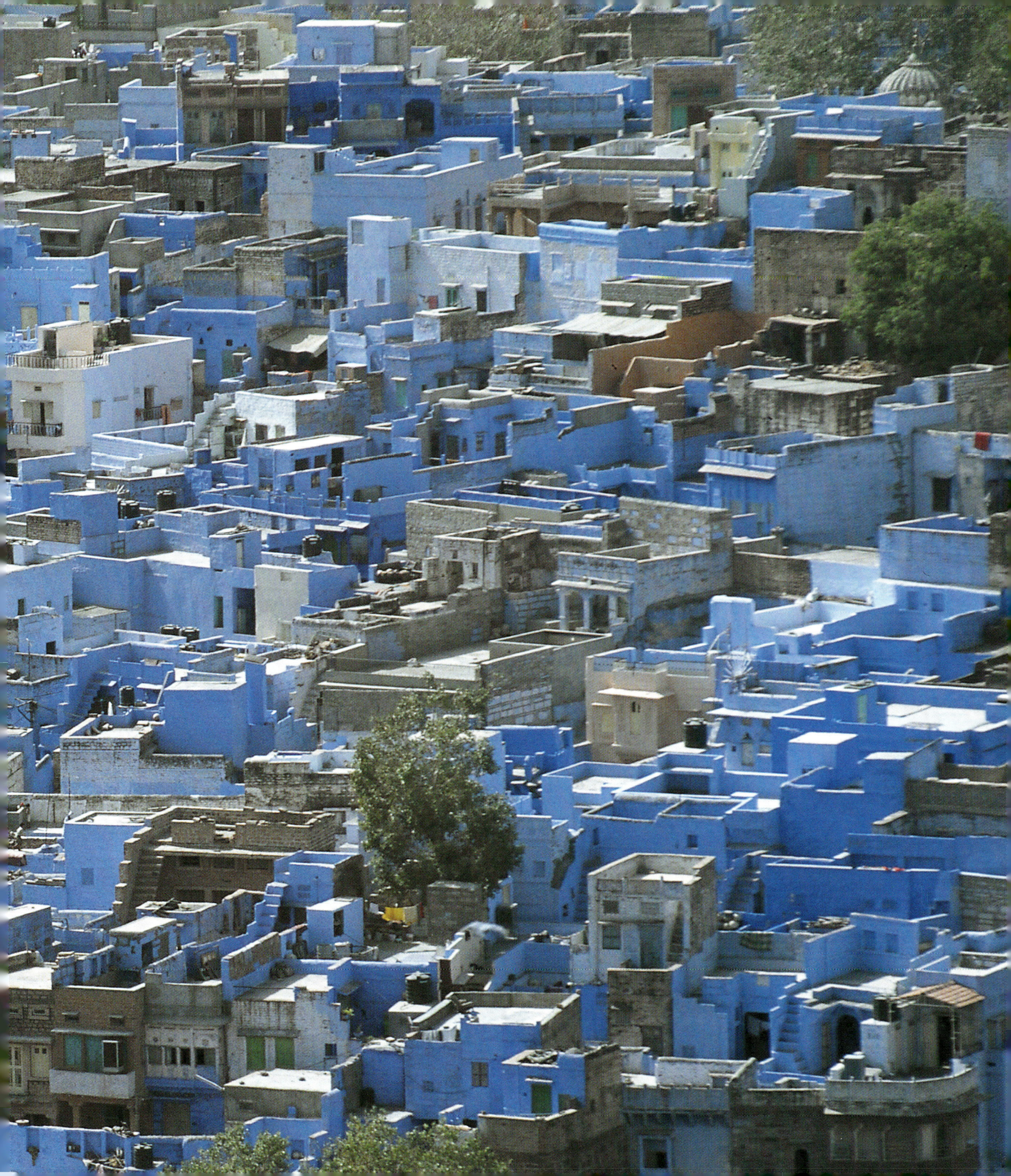

At the entrance to the fort, these handprints recall the sacrifice of the maharanis who became sati by choosing to immolate themselves on the funeral pyre during the maharajah's cremation.

History

Textbooks claim Rao Jodha founded Jodhpur in 1459. His clan, the Rathors, is supposed to descend from Rama, the famous hero of the Ramayana. Born in the valley of the Ganges, the ancestors of the reigning family came to this inhospitable region called Mewar, "Death Valley", to escape the warriors of Mohammed of Ghor. In 1527, Babur the Moghul defeated the army of the Rathors who were then forced to accept an alliance with Akbar (1556-1605). Later he took a Rathor princess for his bride. This historic agreement was maintained by the Rao Gaj Singh who helped Jahangir the Moghul to pacify the region. Subsequently, the emperor Shah Jahan (the one who built the Taj Mahal) granted the title of maharajah to Jaswant Singh, who mounted the throne in 1638.

Peace allowed the city and the arts to blossom. In the seventeenth century, Jodhpur was a prosperous city. But the excesses of the Moghul emperor Aurangzeb caused the Rajputs of various states to join forces to fight him. History stammers as the English tutelage was pronounced in 1818. The maharajahs were forced to unite. At the head of his proud Jodhpur lancers, Pratrap Singh (1845-1922) won fame for his bravery during World War I in Afghanistan, Egypt and China at the side of the British. In France as well in 1917, when at the age of seventy, near Cambrai he pushed back the Germans positions. At the Armistice, during a triumphal procession on the Champs-Elysées, he told his men: "This is our last campaign, children. It is time for us to go home." He died four years later at Jodhpur. At Cambrai they have not forgotten him, his moustache, his turban, his stylish jodhpurs or his courage.

Perched on a rock, the symbol and pride of Jodhpur, the fort can be seen from every house, from every terrace.

239

The Fortress of Mehrangarh

Perched on a rocky promontory, this impassive guardian offers a stunning panorama of the city unfurling at its base, 120 metres below, in a slow wave of blue roofs. Not less than seven gates give access to the fortress. Just think of all the fierce battles, the vain sacrifices to enter it! Near the one called the Iron Gate or Loha Pol, imprints of hands recall the renunciation of the sati, those wives of maharajahs who followed their defunct heroes in the flames of the pyre. Despite the defensive appearance of the fort, during its visit we are surprised by the refinement of the rooms, the most interesting of which are occupied by a museum containing a rich collection of silver litters for elephants called howdahs and ceremonial palanquins. On the first floor, you should linger in the Umaid Mahal which preserves colourful miniatures wonderfully illustrating the life of the maharajahs. One of them shows the maharajah Takhat Singh playing polo with the Court ladies. It is so amusing! And don't you just relish the little mirrors all over the place? Then go into the vast Takhat Mahal; its walls are dotted with ravishing miniatures of hunting scenes and mirrors making the room seem magic.

On the second floor, the Phu Mahal gives you a good idea of the maharajahs' lavishness! In fact this room was used as the Durbar Hall (grand reception room) by the maharajah Abhai Singh who lived in the eighteenth century. We are enchanted by the ceilings covered with gold leaf as well as by a lovely set of murals painted in the nineteenth century.

To resist the assaults of the Moghuls, the mighty Rajputs of the clan of the Rathors decided in 1459 to build their fortress in the region of the Marwar, the land of death, on this rocky promontory. And they named it Mehrangarh, "The Fort of Majesty".

As soon as you go through the last of its seven defensive doors, the wonders of Mehrangarh appear. Superlatives are needed to express the richness and passion of the Rathors, like in the Takhat Mahal room, adorned with scenes of the hunt and of mythology, mirrors, paintings and glass balls hanging from the ceiling.

Ceiling of the Zhanki Mahal at Mehrangarh.

With its gold leaf gilt ceilings, the Phul Mahal (Palace of Flowers) was used as the Durbar Hall, reception room, by the maharajah Abhai Singh (1724-1750).

Because of the size of the fortress, each maharajah could install his apartments wherever he wished. So in the nineteenth century, Takhat Singh decided that his bedroom would be in the Takhat Vilas, on the third floor. The best artisans carved the ceilings in marquetry and the painters adorned the walls of the room with their genius. As for the women, they waited like good girls in the other wing of the fort. Their favourite entertainment? Seeing without being seen. In the well-named Jankhi Mahal, "Palace of Glances", they could observe the passers-by through fretted sandstone screens or jali, with their many different designs.

The visit ends in glory with the Moti Mahal or "Palace of the Pearl", an authentic jewel designed in the sixteenth century to be used as the diwan-i am, the public audiences hall. You have plenty of time to look at the extravagant world of mirrors, inlaid in gold, covering the ceilings. In niches, oil lamps provided enough light during receptions. There is nothing missing in the decor: a silver throne for the great man and fretted screens through which the beautiful princesses could quietly swoon while watching their maharajah-hero manage the affairs of State.

*Three hundred and ninety-four rooms…
This is the rather extravagant work
the British architect Henry Vaughan
Lanchester completed in 1943. The
construction of the Umaid Bwahan palace
took fourteen years, providing work for
thousands of inhabitants of the region,
threatened with starvation.*

245

the trophy room, the swimming pool in the bowels of the giant and dinners by candlelight under the portraits of the former princes.

At the Umaid Bhawan there is something magic. If you question the maharajah's intimates, they will tell you it is because Gaj Singh II has showered his charm over the entire palace. With his wife and their two children, he resides in one of the wings of the edifice. They entertain us in their comfortable drawing room. Have the twenty-first-century maharajas just become businessmen? "I do not think so", Gaj Singh II distinctly replies. "We simply try to increase the value of our predecessors' possessions. You know, as for getting rich, I do not know of any maharajah who has become rich since the Independence. Our ancestors often brought prosperity to their region. Today, politicians make promises they only keep in part."

At the age of twenty-five, his son, prince Yuvraj Shivraj Singh, embodies the India of tomorrow. A generous India turned toward progress. After spending his youth at the Mayo College boarding school at Amber, then at Eton and Oxford, he acquired experience working in banks, in Switzerland, Great Britain and Hong Kong. For the past two years he has been happy to assist his father in running the hotel. "After years of boarding school abroad when I only came home on holidays I am glad to live in Jodhpur. I have travelled some in the world, I love France, and I love to ski in the Alps. But in Europe I think people are in too much of a hurry, they run after a form of happiness that is often too materialistic. In our villages, people are proud of what they have, even if it is not much, sometimes just a cow. It is this happiness, of being what you are, that I most appreciate in my people. As for myself, I am happy and proud to be the son of the maharajah of Jodhpur, fully aware of having privileges but duties as well. My family is very open-minded and we can talk about everything, even marriage. And I approve of the Indian custom which gives parents the right to choose their son's wife." There are a great many aspiring brides!

Right:
The maharajah Gaj Singh II with the maharani Hemlata Rajya in their private apartments. Gaj Singh, maharajah of Jodhpur, mounted the throne at the age of four and celebrated his jubilee in 2002. One of the most popular maharajahs in Rajasthan successfully converted part of his palace into a hotel.

Next double page:
The last great (gigantic!) palace to have been built in India, the Umaid Bhawan, described by a resounding list of superlatives, is proud of being or having been the largest private palace in the world. The central rotunda rises 32 meters above the ground.

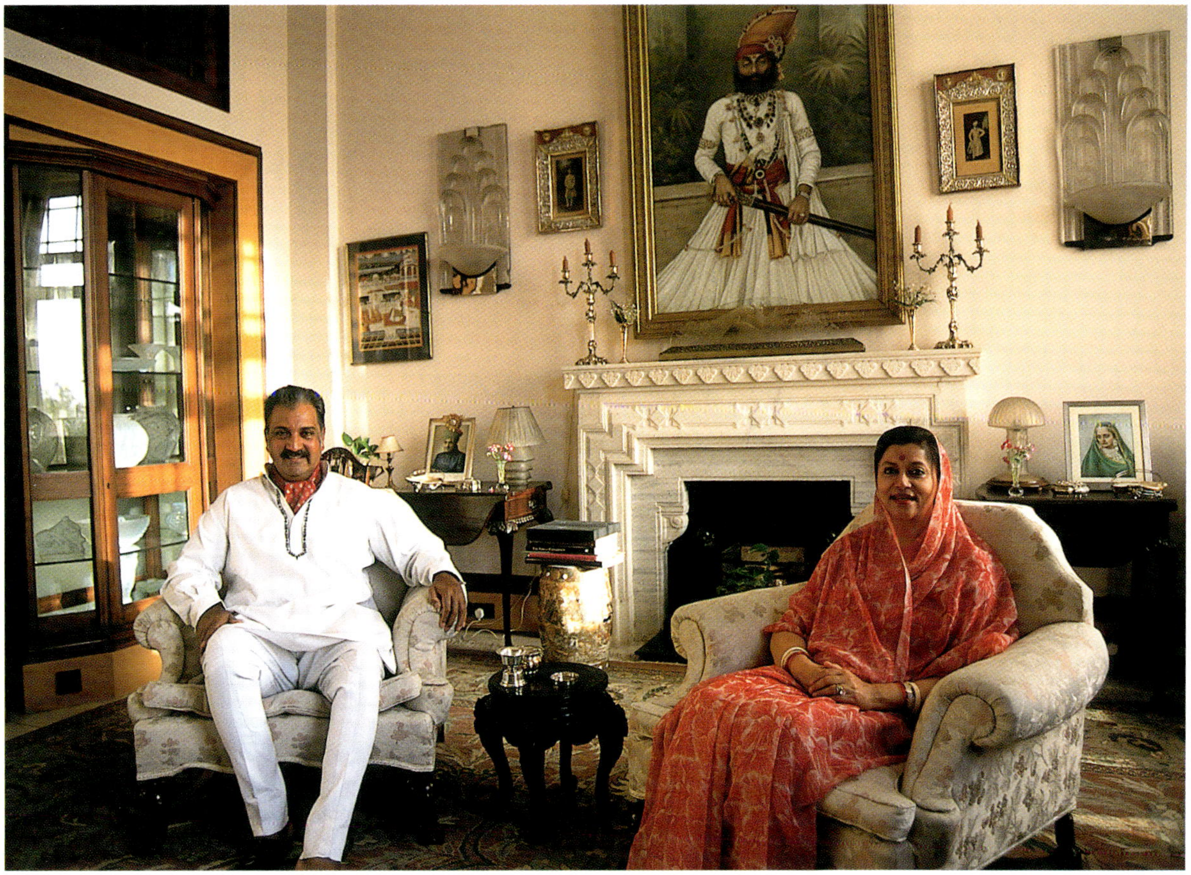

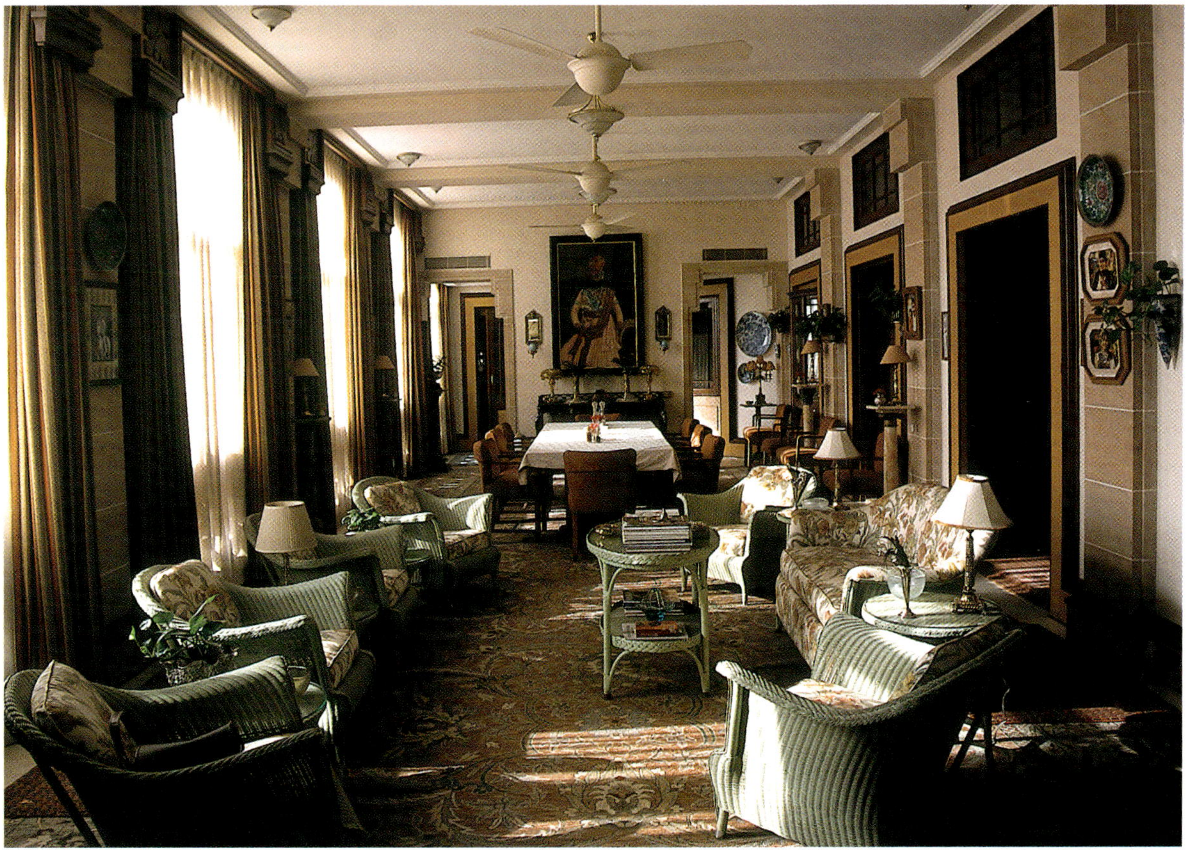

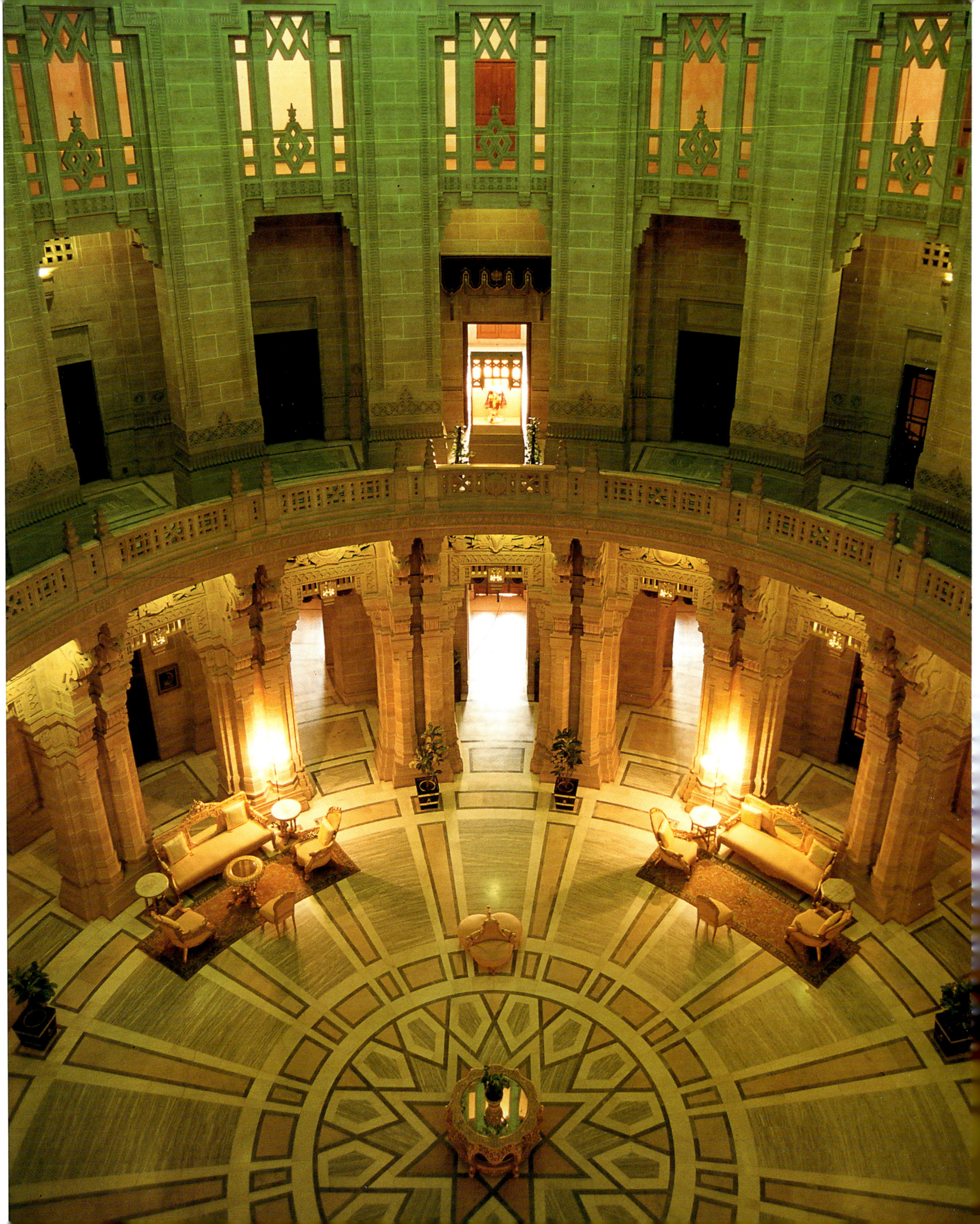

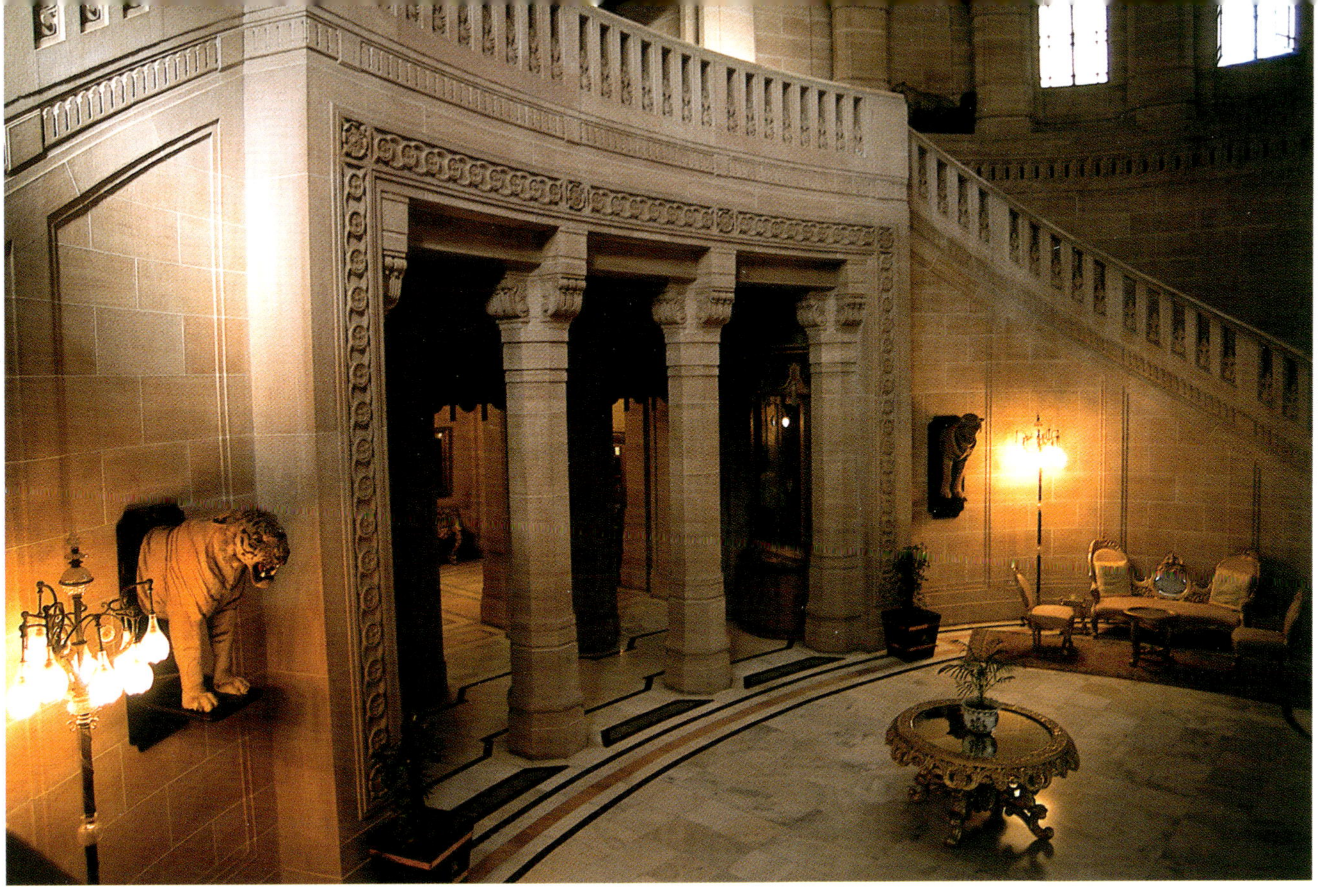

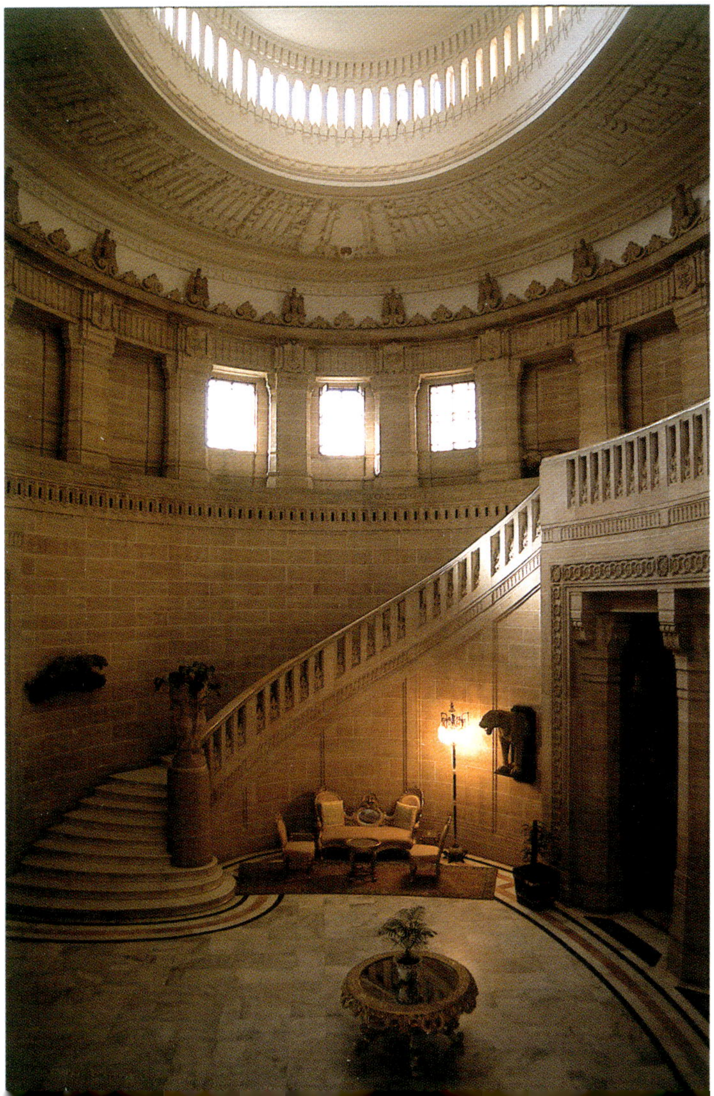

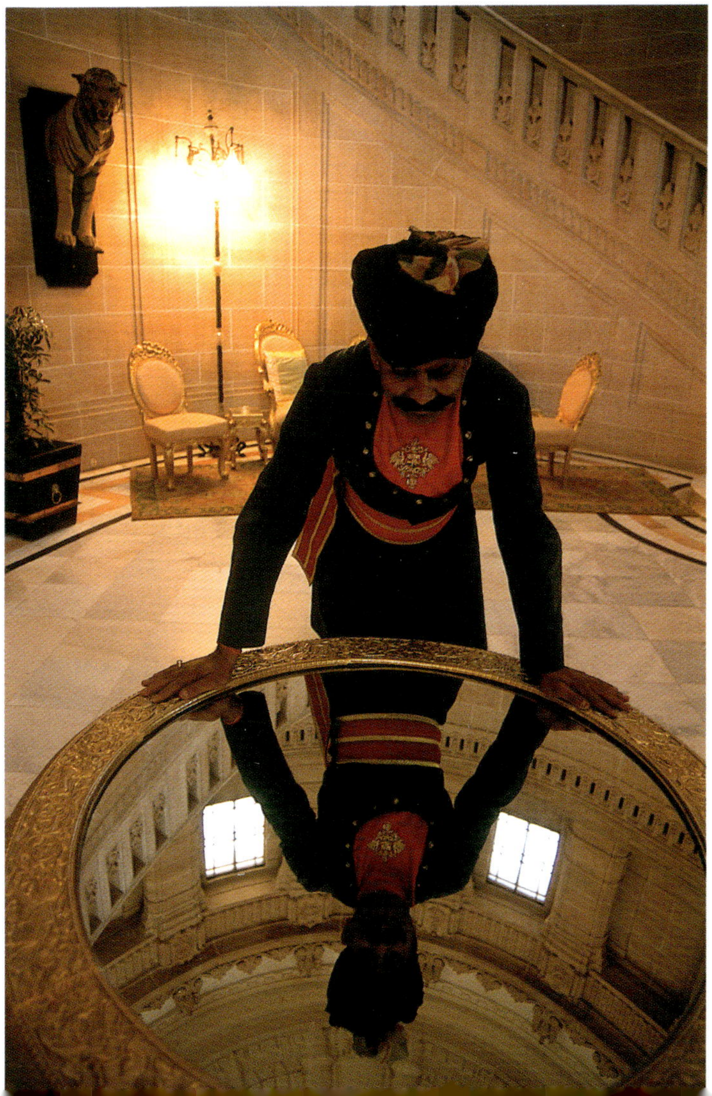

Among the countless suites the palace has to offer, the Maharani Suite, with its sofas upholstered in old pink, has become very trendy. It was decorated by a talented Polish designer, Stefan Norblin.

The bathtub of the Maharani Suite bathroom is a magnificent piece, made of pink marble from Italy.

The Maharani Suite, signed by Stefan Norblin.

RANAKPUR

Beautiful and Mysterious Jain Temples of Ranakpur

The temple of Ranakpur consecrated to Adinatha is the vastest Jain sanctuary in the whole country. Exuberant, daring demiurges, the stone carvers spread their talent over the 1.400 pillars of the temple, each one different. You swoon in front of the scrolls, floral motifs, lovely apsaras (dancer or musician goddesses) interwoven here and there, brushed with sunlight.

The concepts of Jainism are infinitely complex. Let that not worry us! Adepts of absolute respect for life and non-violence, the members of the Jain community are as secretive as they are refined, as elitist as they are generous. And their temples, as beautiful as they are mysterious, invite us to peace and meditation. Adinatha is the largest in the country and one of the holiest. Built in the fifteenth century by Dharnak Shah, later it was profaned and left untended until it was restored in the late nineteenth century.

Built on a cruciform design, for the neophyte the temple is an impressive maze of courtyards, passageways, rooms and chapels arranged around a central sanctuary. Fourteen hundred white marble pillars, carved with an endless variety, support the building. Wearing white robes as a sign of asceticism, sometimes even with a white cloth over their mouth to keep from swallowing an insect, with immense respect Jains draw near the central cella, that holds the four mysterious statues of Adinatha, to perform the sacred ritual.

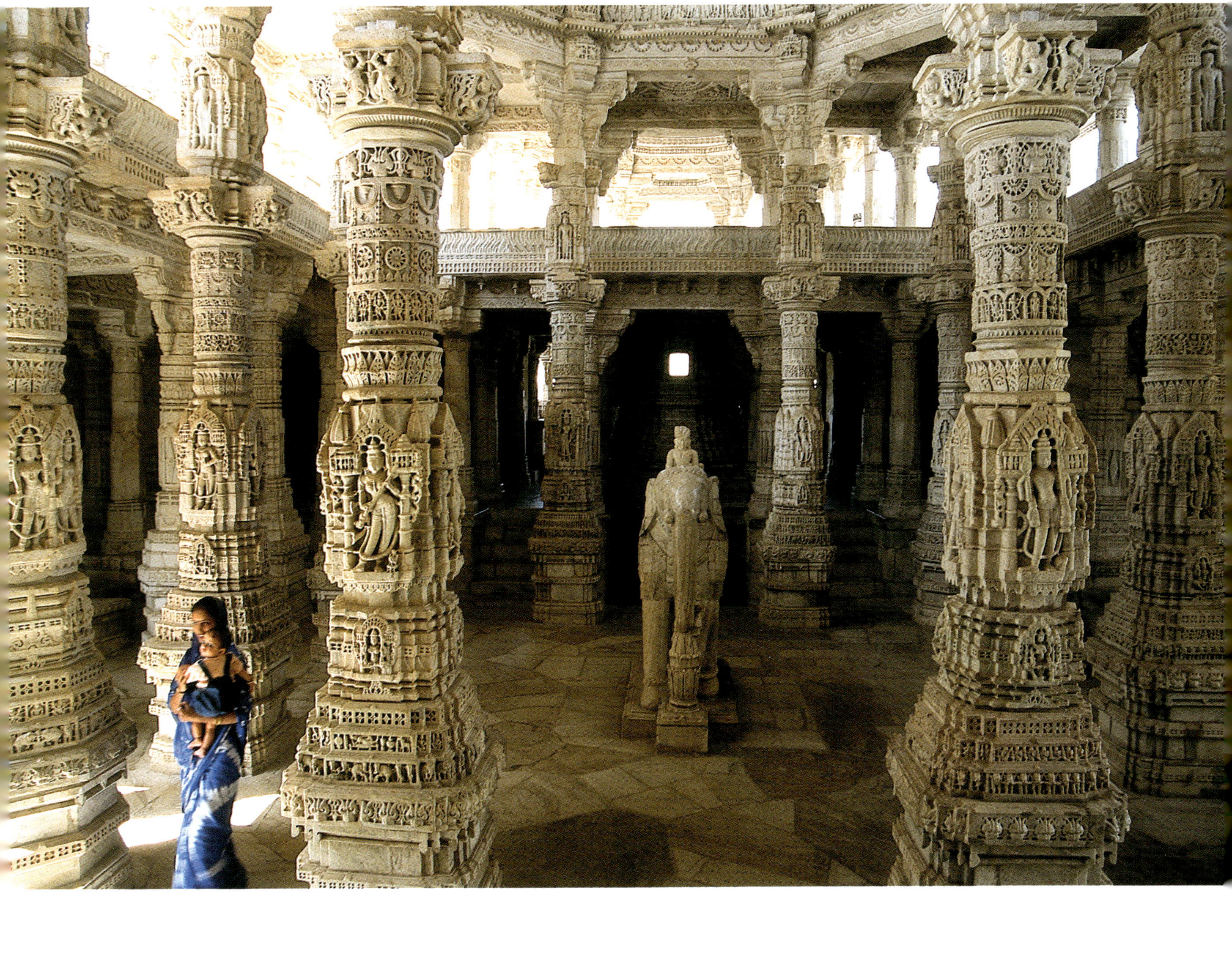

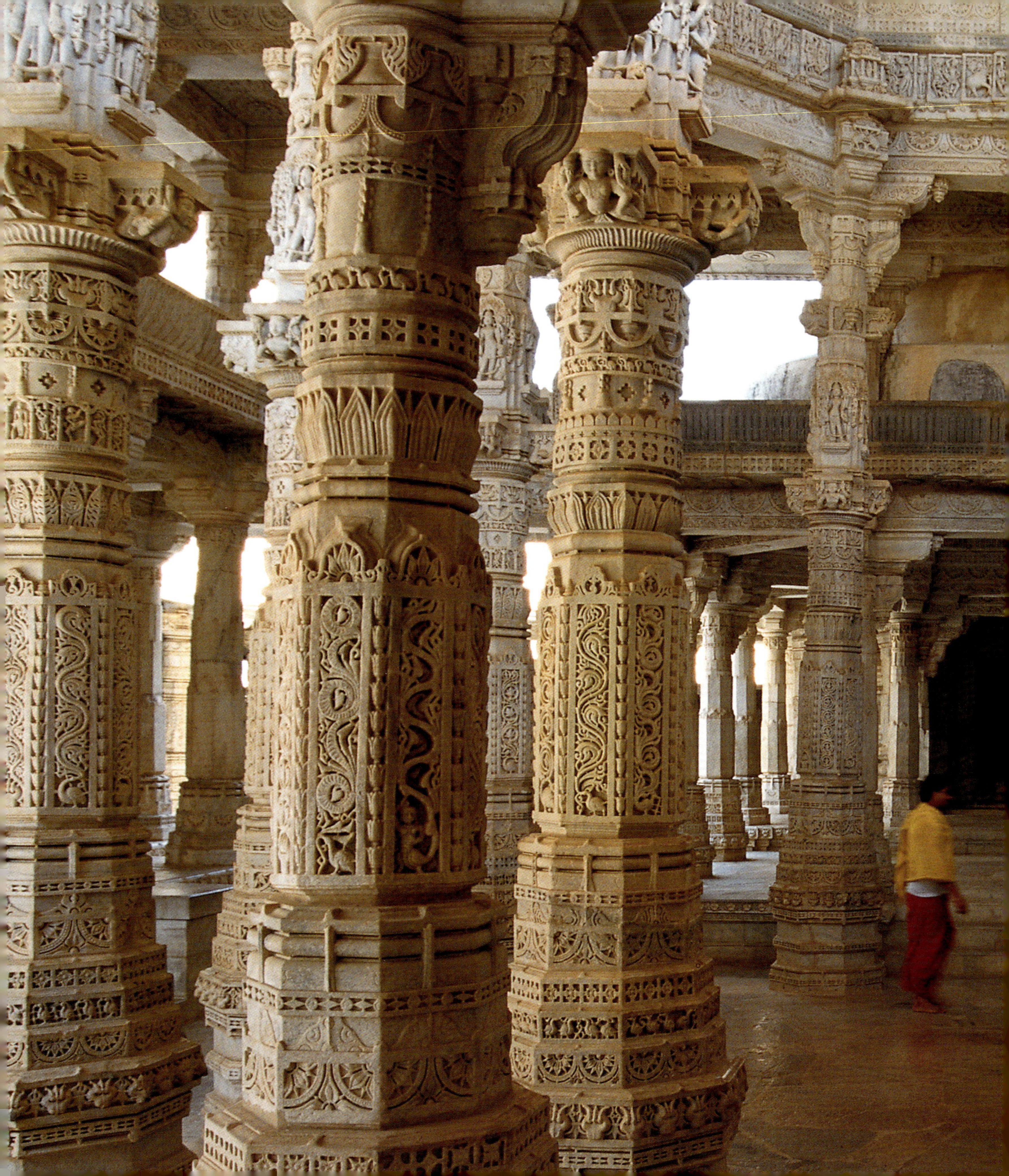

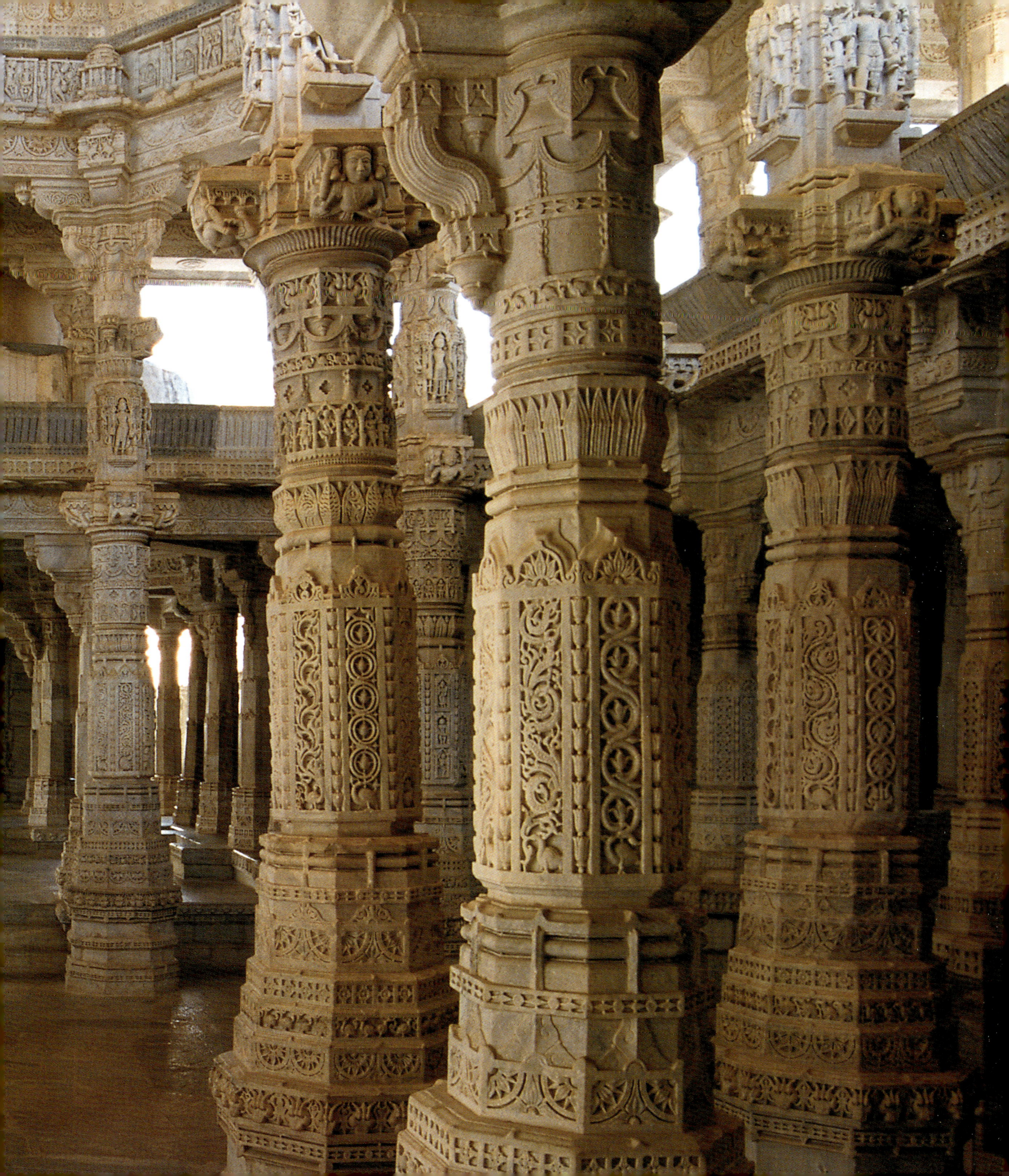

Everything is a feast for the eye in this marble jewel, the temple of Adinatha, from the entrance door, where scrolls and geometric motifs are lit by the sun, to the impressive dome decorated with sculptures of musicians and asparas.

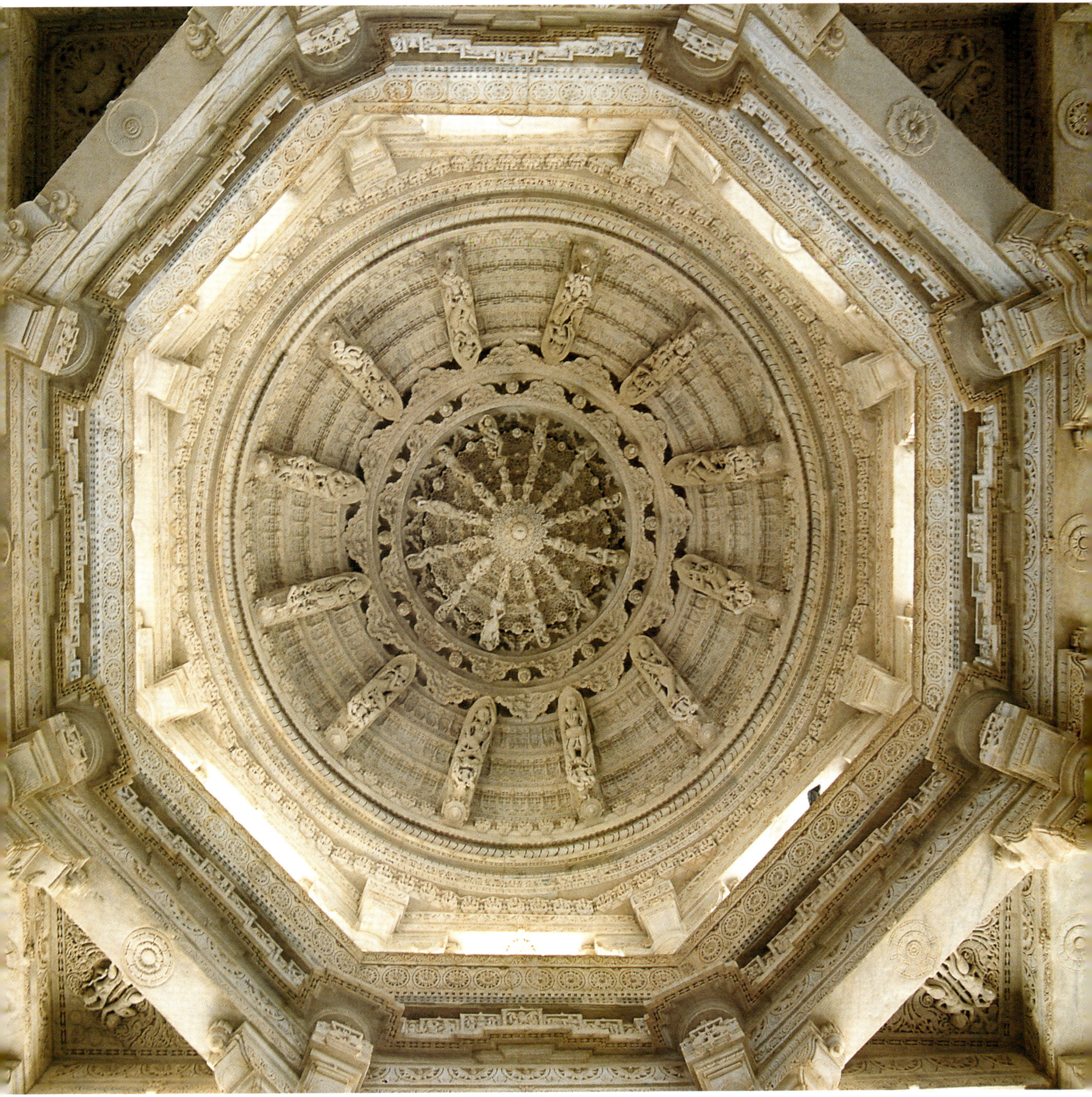

The sweet-scented narrow streets of the Shakhawati towns are graced with colourful frescoes, painted on the facades of houses called haveli, which means "closed place" in Persian. Alas! Today a great number of them have fallen into neglect. Nadine Le Prince decided to bring one back to life, in the town of Fatehpur (facing and following). A private visit to her haveli: if the first courtyard was accessible to visitors, the second was the women's quarters. Between the two, a chicane with a window protected them and allowed them to see without being seen.

SHEKHAWATI

A well-known Parisian painter, Nadine Le Prince brought her palette and brushes to this semi-arid, desolate region of brush and steppes northwest of Jaipur. The roads look like tracks where you run into humble towns encroached upon by the sands of the nearby Thar desert. In first appearances not very interesting, these towns are filled with enchanting houses called haveli, decorated with naïve frescoes which might have appealed to Facteur Cheval himself (the French twentieth-century postman and naïve sculptor). Alas! They all appear to be abandoned. Nadine Le Prince, who has been all over India since 1970, fell in love with one of them, nestled in the little town of Fatehpur, former capital of the Muslim dynasty of the nawab Qaimkhani before being controlled by the Hindu Raos. After quite a few ups and downs, our Parisian painter succeeded in buying in 1998, in her own name (only too proud of being the first foreign woman to be allowed to buy property in India!), the former residence of a thakur (noble) of the sultan, designed in 1802. She hired the best local craftsmen to bring back to life the wall paintings which tell the story of the house and the region. After years of effort, Nadine Le Prince's dream came true at last, and she opened a cultural centre in her haveli where Indian and foreign artists are invited to associate their inspirations.

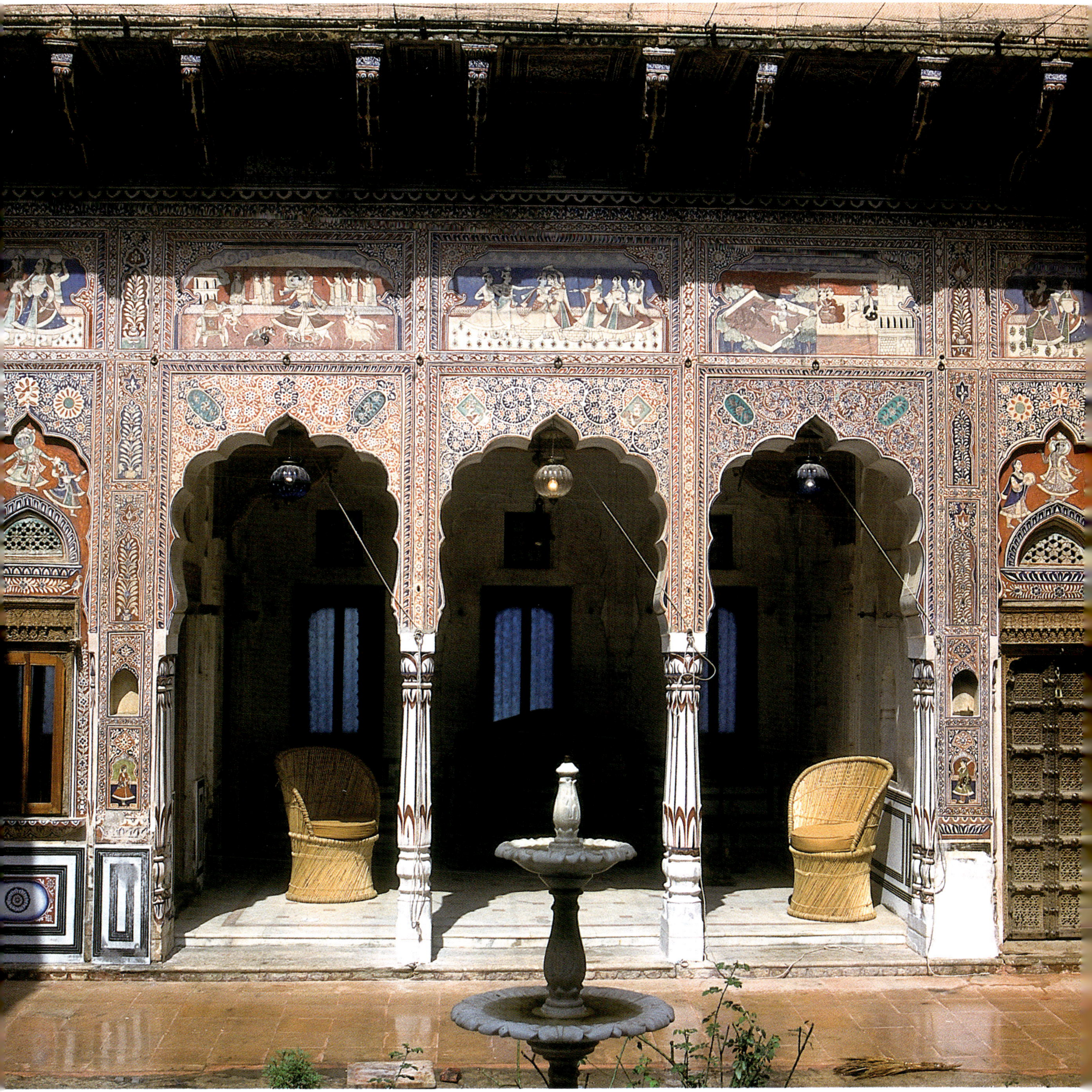

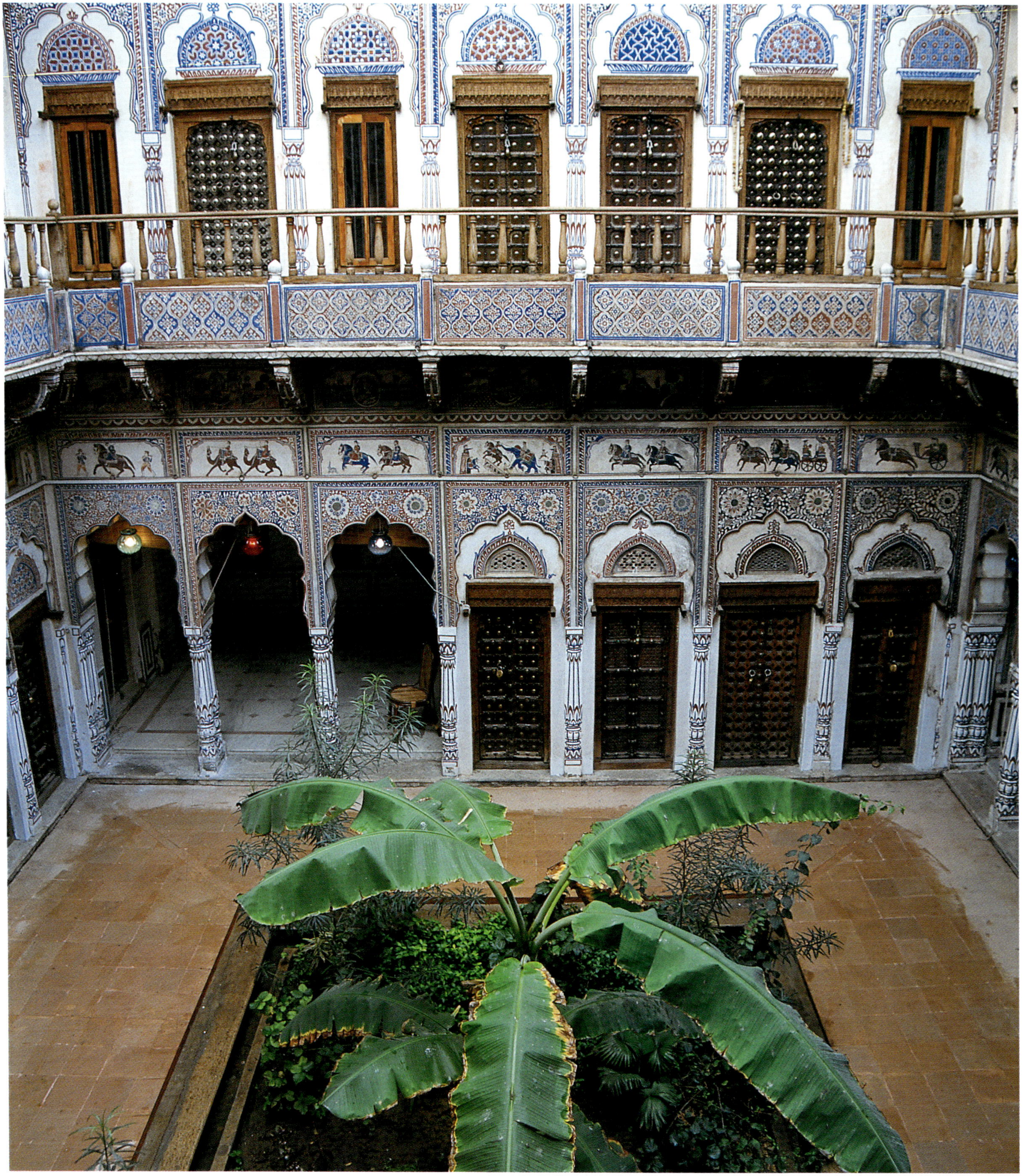

261

Nadine Le Prince's haveli displays painted scenes telling the story of the house and of the region. Marble dust, palm oil… Renovation took ages to restore their former appearance to the rooms and the reception courtyard with its niches where musicians performed every three hours for the guests. The result is grandiose: the ceilings resemble Persian rugs.

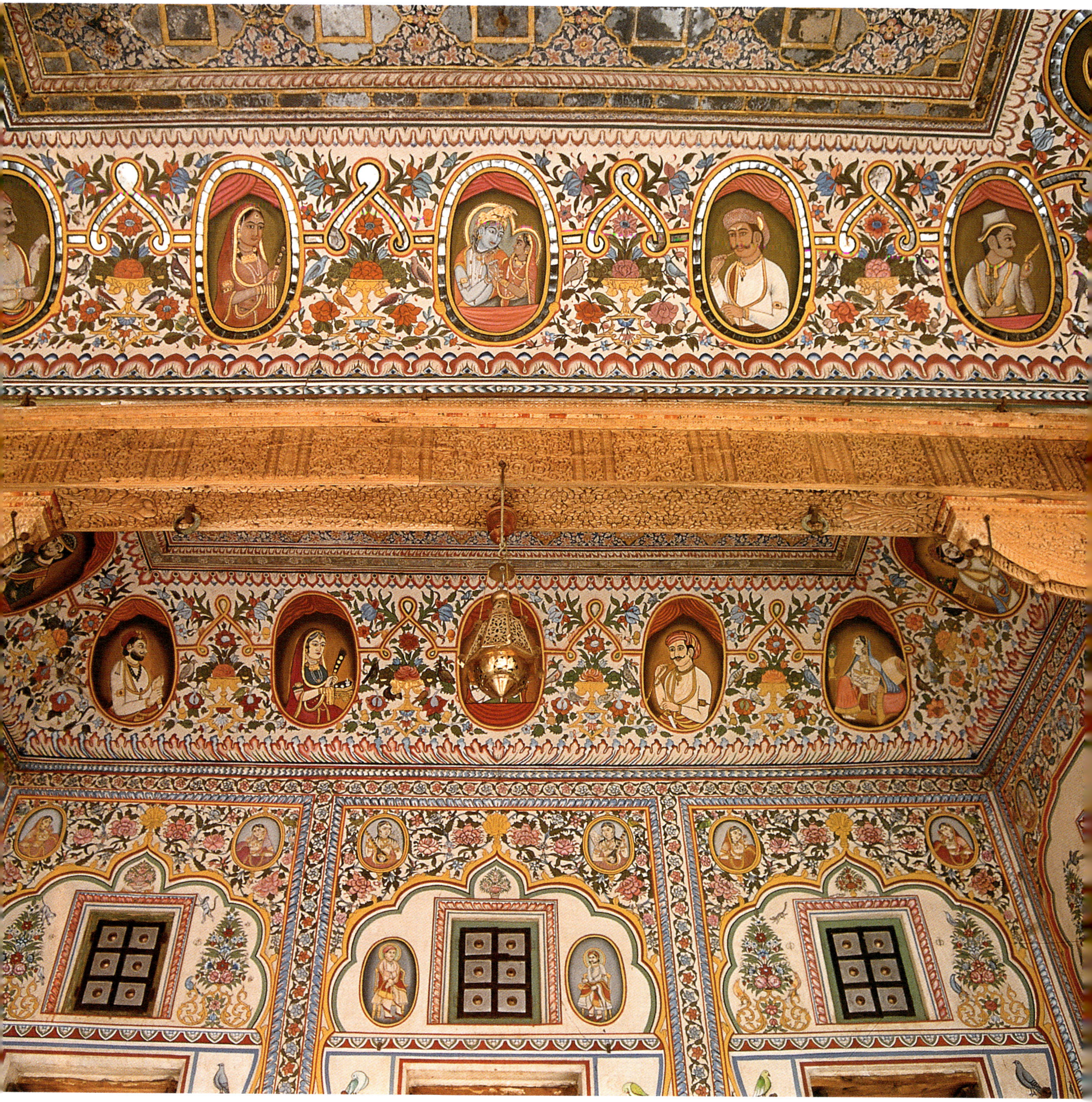

264

265

The Rich Merchants

*I*n this India of the twenty-first century, the wealthiest families often descend from illustrious merchants from Shekhawati. That is the case of the Tatas who for ages have manufactured the buses we see throughout the towns and the countryside here. The story of this region begins with a legend. In the fifteenth century, a local aristocrat, Mokul Singh, distant member of the family of powerful rajahs of Amber, was in despair because he had no heir. Attending a pilgrimage to the site of Vrindavan consecrated to the Hindu deity Krishna, a sadhu (wise man) he met predicted he would have a son if he began to collect sacred cows. So he did. Later, he met a Muslim saint who also promised him a son, on the condition he bathe him in the blood of a cow. His wishes were fulfilled in 1433 and the babe was finally bathed in the blood… of a goat. He was Rao Shekha who ruled the region and gave it his name. Akbar and his mighty armies appeared at the end of the sixteenth century. The Raos had no choice but to bow down and wait for the tide to turn. In the eighteenth century the maharajah of Jaipur regained control of Shekhawati then governed by Rao Sardul Singh whose sons would divide the towns and the land among themselves.

The paintings of the haveli called upon all the talents in the Shekhawati. When the baniya, the merchants who had become rich with the passage of the caravans, built them, they called the best artists who let their imaginations wander freely, between Indian mythology and the Moghul influence. The most precious frescoes were painted between 1830 and 1930. At a bend in a winding street of one of these towns, a few renovated haveli recall the glory of these art-loving merchants. The haveli of Ananda Lal Poddar at Nawalgarh, built in 1920, was restored to its beauty in 1980 thanks to the Poddar family.

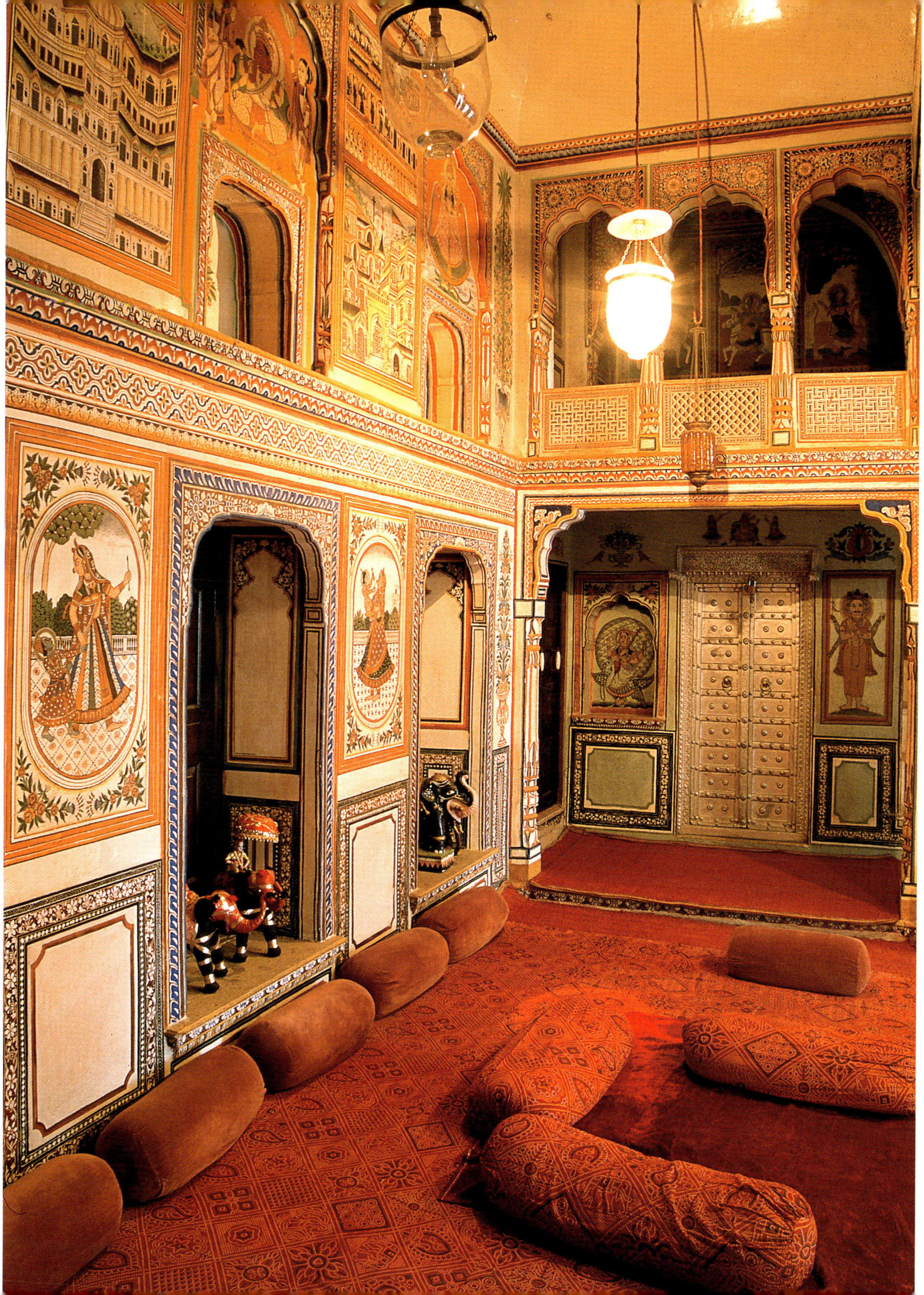

A school installed in a haveli.

It was at this time that the merchants known as baniya made their fortunes thanks to the caravans winding their way to Delhi, and passing through this strategic crossroads between India, the Middle East and China. The baniya, who excelled in the trade of wool, spices and sugar, amassed fortunes up to the nineteenth century when the East India Company and the railroad put an abrupt stop to the caravan route. Clever and hard-working, the merchants decided to leave Shekhawati for a new life, seeking their fortunes in Bombay and Calcutta. Since they had a real flair for business, they turned to the British and became rich all over again.

But they were homesick. So all over their native Shekhawati they scattered these haveli, palaces with two courtyards called chowk: the first open to visitors, the second being reserved to the family. They left the decoration up to local artists whose extravagant imagination was often influenced by Rajput painting and Anglo-Indian art. The latter immortalised on the walls the British railroad along with the heroes of Indian mythology, using the technique of painting on fresh plaster. The merchants wished to be art patrons as well and commissioned the decoration of temples, reservoirs, wells and schools.

And time flew by. Today the haveli appear neglected, often rented to modest families who live here for a rent of some 1.000 rupees a month, that is, around twenty euros. A few padlocked rooms are reserved for the owners who return once or twice a year or on the occasion of a wedding. Occasionally one of the family's children or a very old neighbour, for a few rupees, will open the palace doors to give a few gaping, spell-bound foreigners a look. Are you tempted to buy? First try to find a good detective. Because here nobody, truly nobody, will want to give you the name of the mysterious owner. A whole palace for a thousand rupees a month, who in the world would give it up for the first person to come along?

An intense sense of rapture takes hold of the visitor who enters these haveli of another era with their admirable interiors covered with naïve frescoes. Here, the Khedwal Bhavan Haveli at Nawalgarh.

Nawalgarh, Mandawa Jhunjhunu and Fatehpur have treasures to offer lovers of art. For just a few rupees, the custodians of these residences with their theatrical decors will show you a fascinating world that truly fires the imagination: Bhagton ki Haveli, at Nawalgarh.

271

Discovering the Haveli

Wandering through the streets of these little forgotten towns to seek out these abandoned palaces is a challenging treasure hunt. Sometimes with the help of a boy met on the street who claims he is a student in tourism, we set out in the villages with their charming narrow alleys. Aside from its Murarka, Jhunjhunuwala and Dami Dharka haveli, the village of Nawalgarh is especially known for its Ananda Lal Poddar haveli, which is now used as a school. Built in 1920, it was entirely restored in 1980, thanks to the backing of the Poddar family, settled in Delhi and Bombay and originally from Shekhawati. If purists judge the outside frescoes a bit too bright and showy, the initiative should be praised. Because the Indians who are aware of the beauty of these frescoes are rare.

Born in the town of Mandawa, Dinesh Dhabai is an exception. He just completed the restoration of a haveli he was able to buy in his home town. Talented artists renovated the house, converted into an absolutely charming hotel a few steps from the Castle Mandawa fortress-hotel which belongs to the descendents of Rao Shekha. Two ideal addresses offering a cosy haven from which to set out and explore the region.

Twenty-five kilometres northeast of Mandawa, a ramshackle bus will drop you off at Jhunjhunu. It has preserved a Muslim character owed to the domination of the Qaimkhani nawab for over 300 years. After stopping to look at the frescoes of the dargah (tomb) of Qamr ud-Din Shah, a Muslim saint venerated by the Hindu sovereigns, we will head for the Khatri Mahal palace, built in the eighteenth century, and the Modi and Tibrewala haveli. But only after not having been able to resist tasting a delicious korma (pieces of mutton cooked in a sauce with yoghurt, caschew nuts and almonds) or a succulent tikka chicken, marinated in spicy yoghurt, served in a tiny restaurant in the bazaar… Oh! It's so good. What about another spoonful?

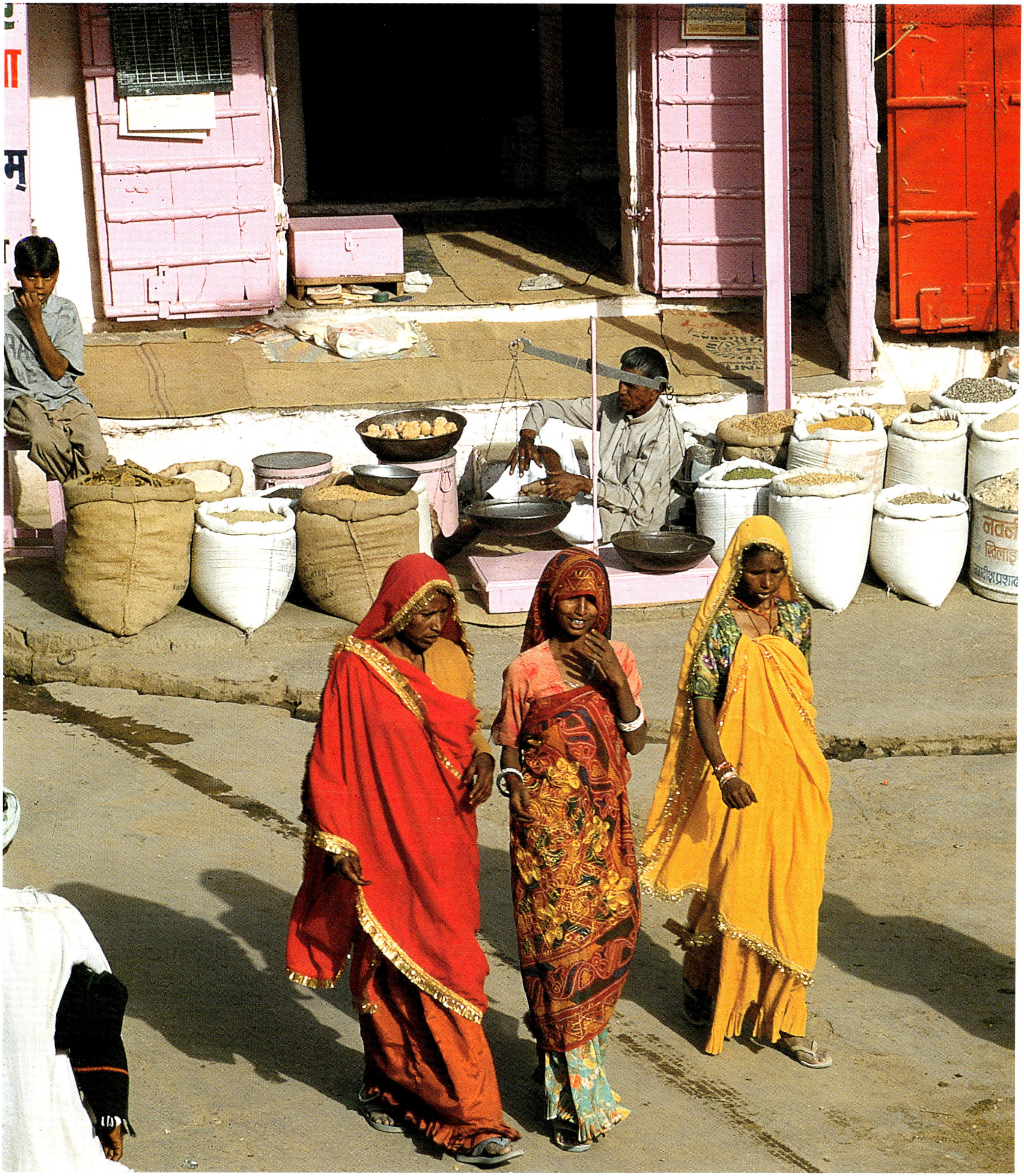

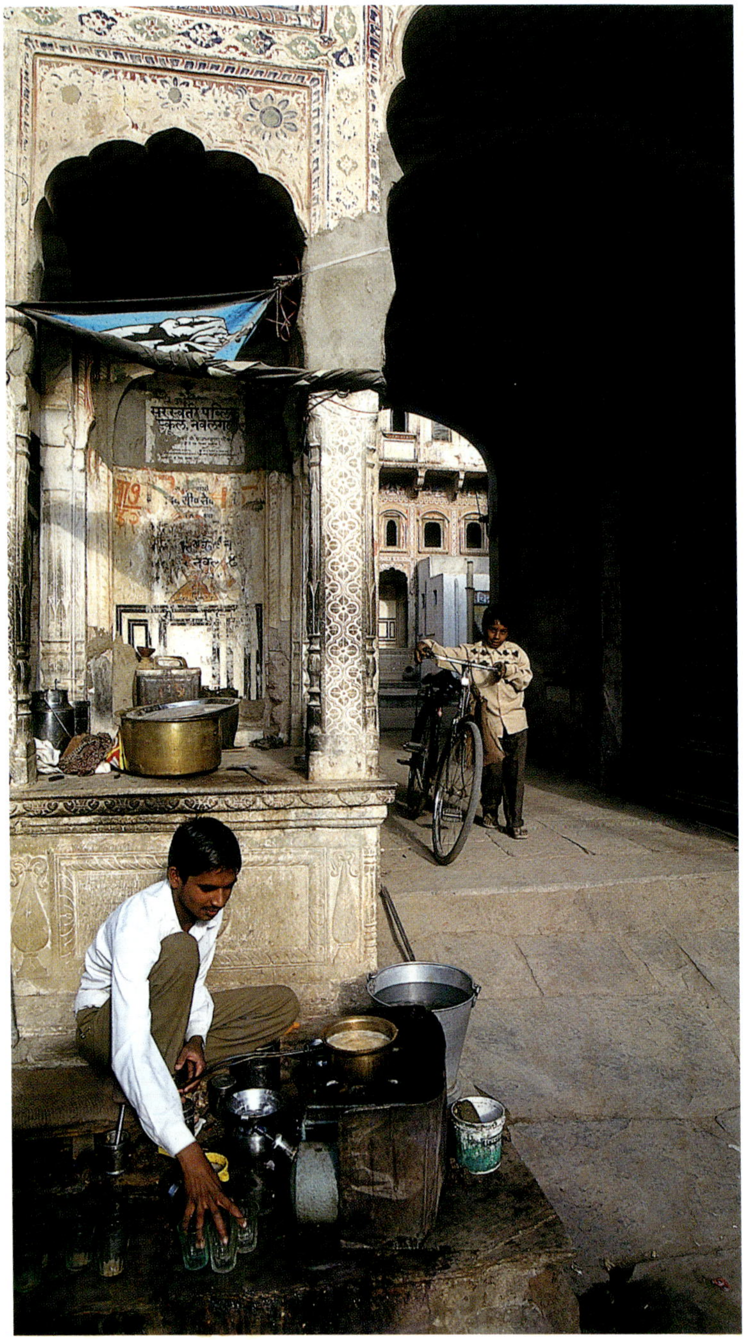

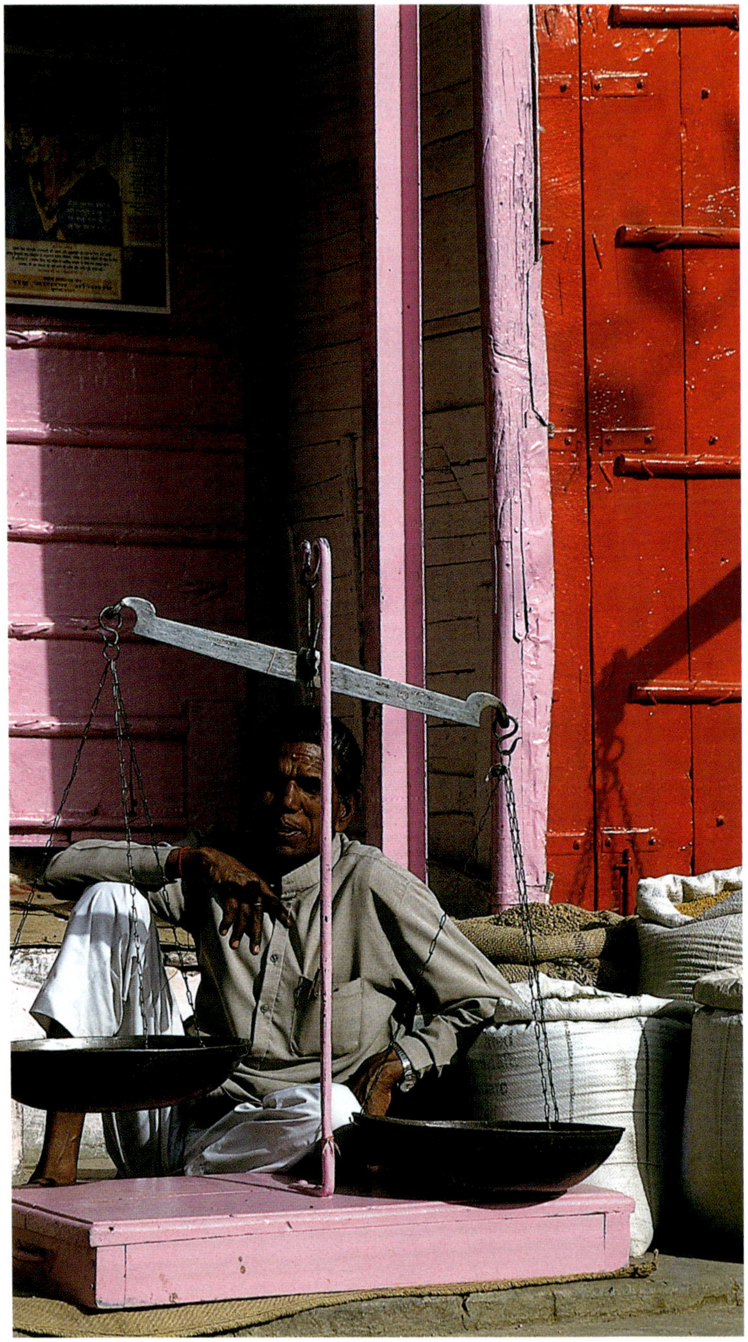

For centuries the Shekhawati offered its hospitality to a population of men and women who came to nourish the imagination of this land and to put down roots here.

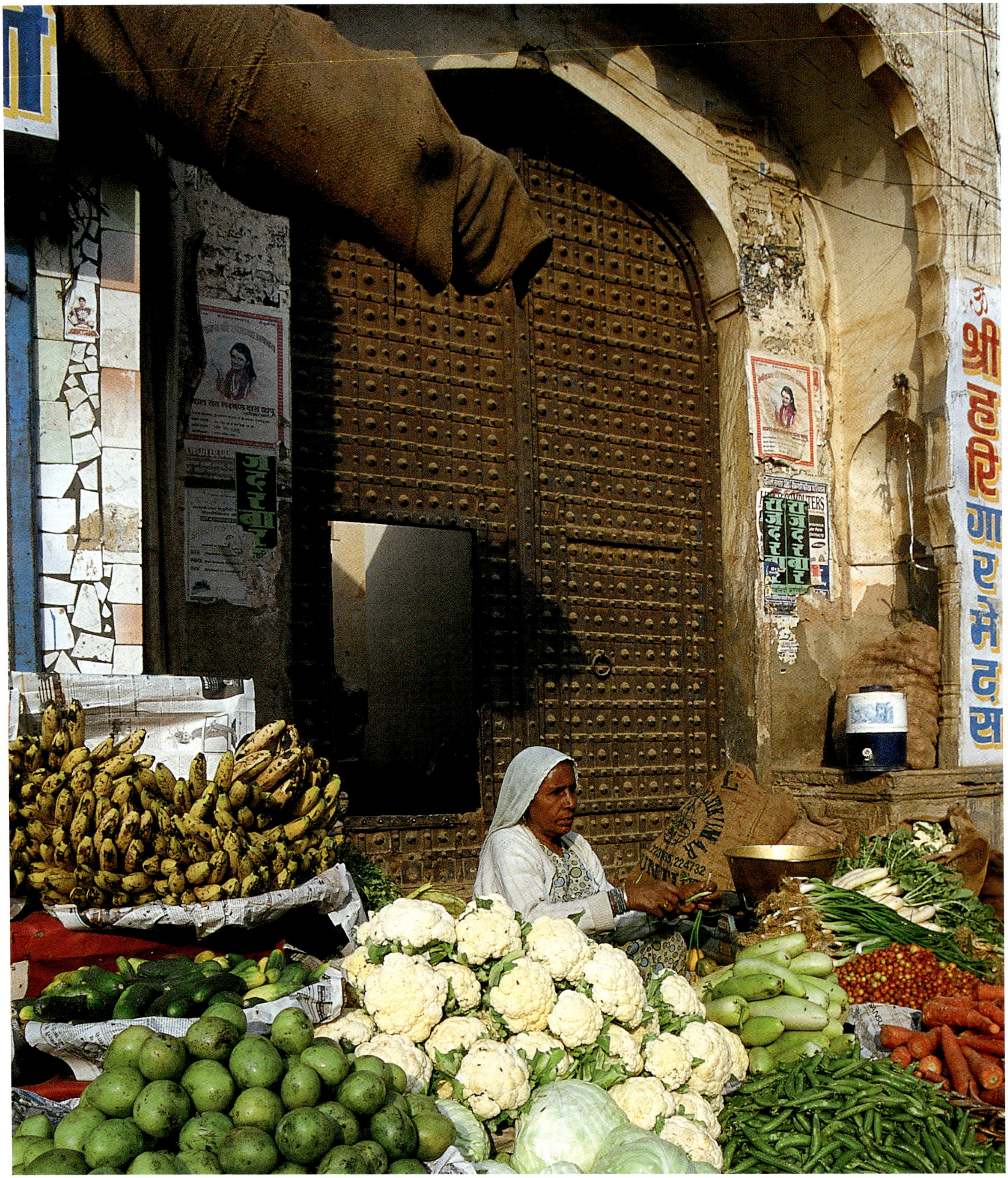

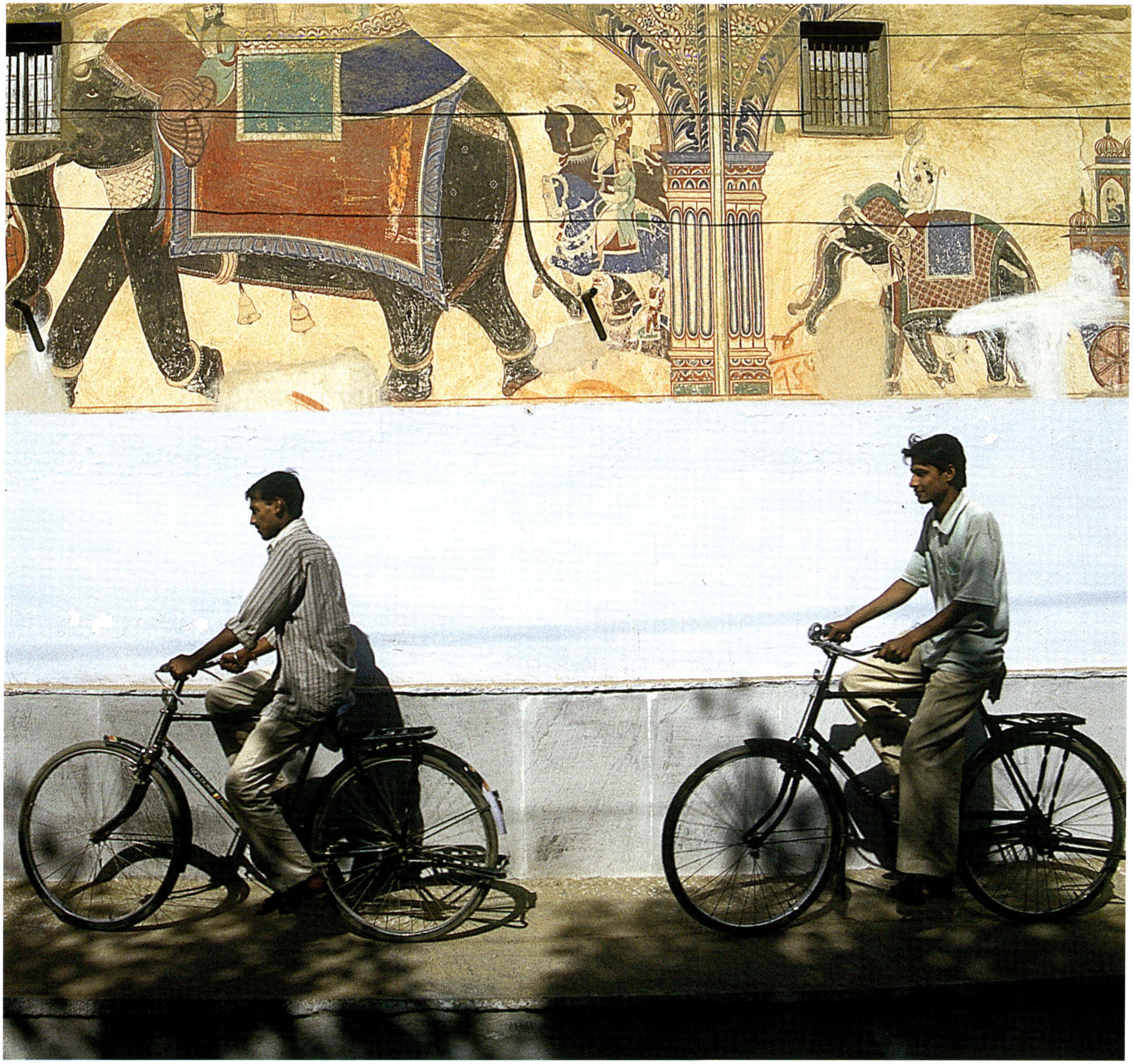

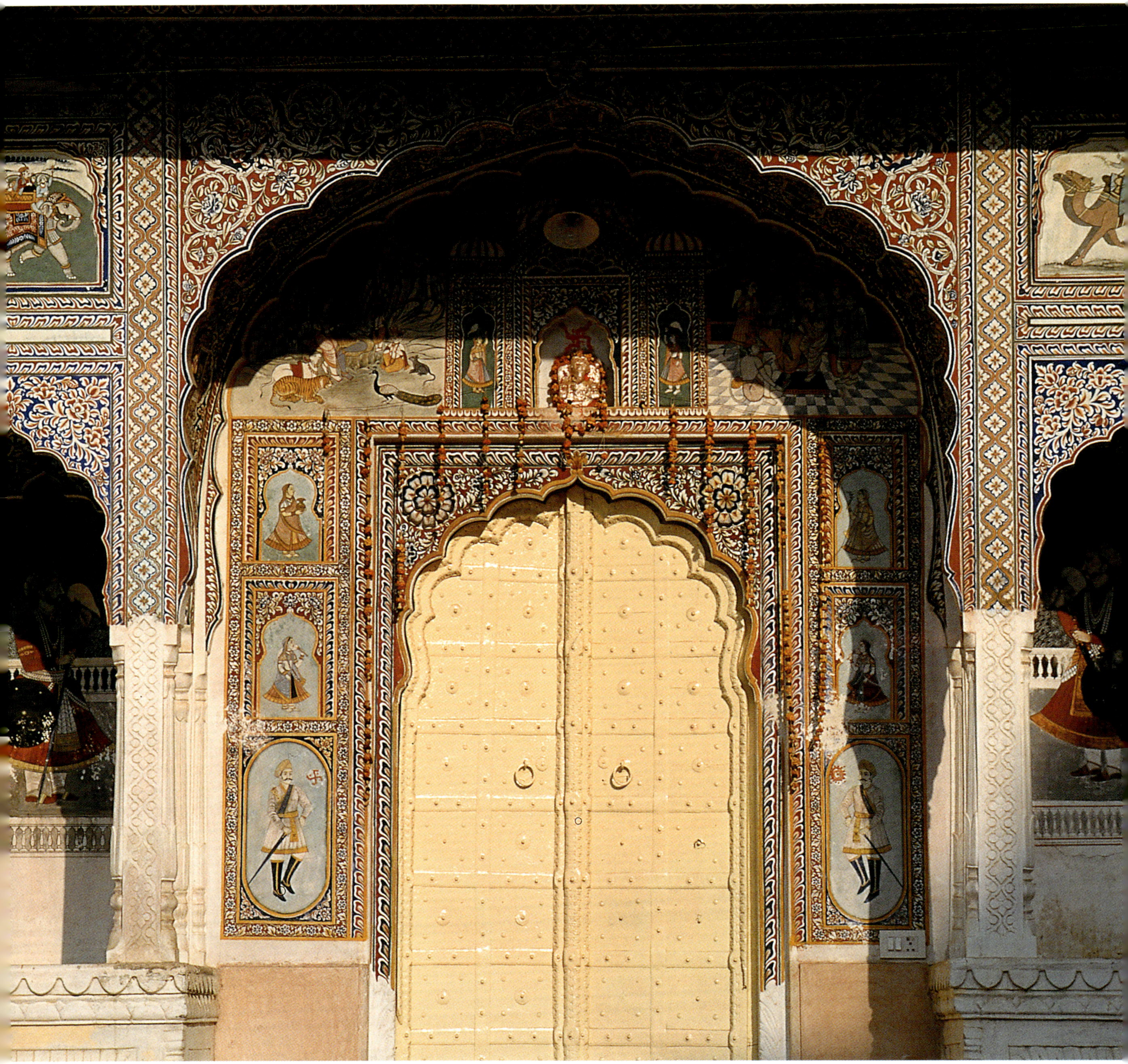

The town of Mandawa, with many haveli, will be forever linked to its eighteenth-century Rajput fortress. Its aristocrat owner, Kesri Singh, turned it into a sort of fortress-inn full of character and protected by a squad of moustachioed lancers.

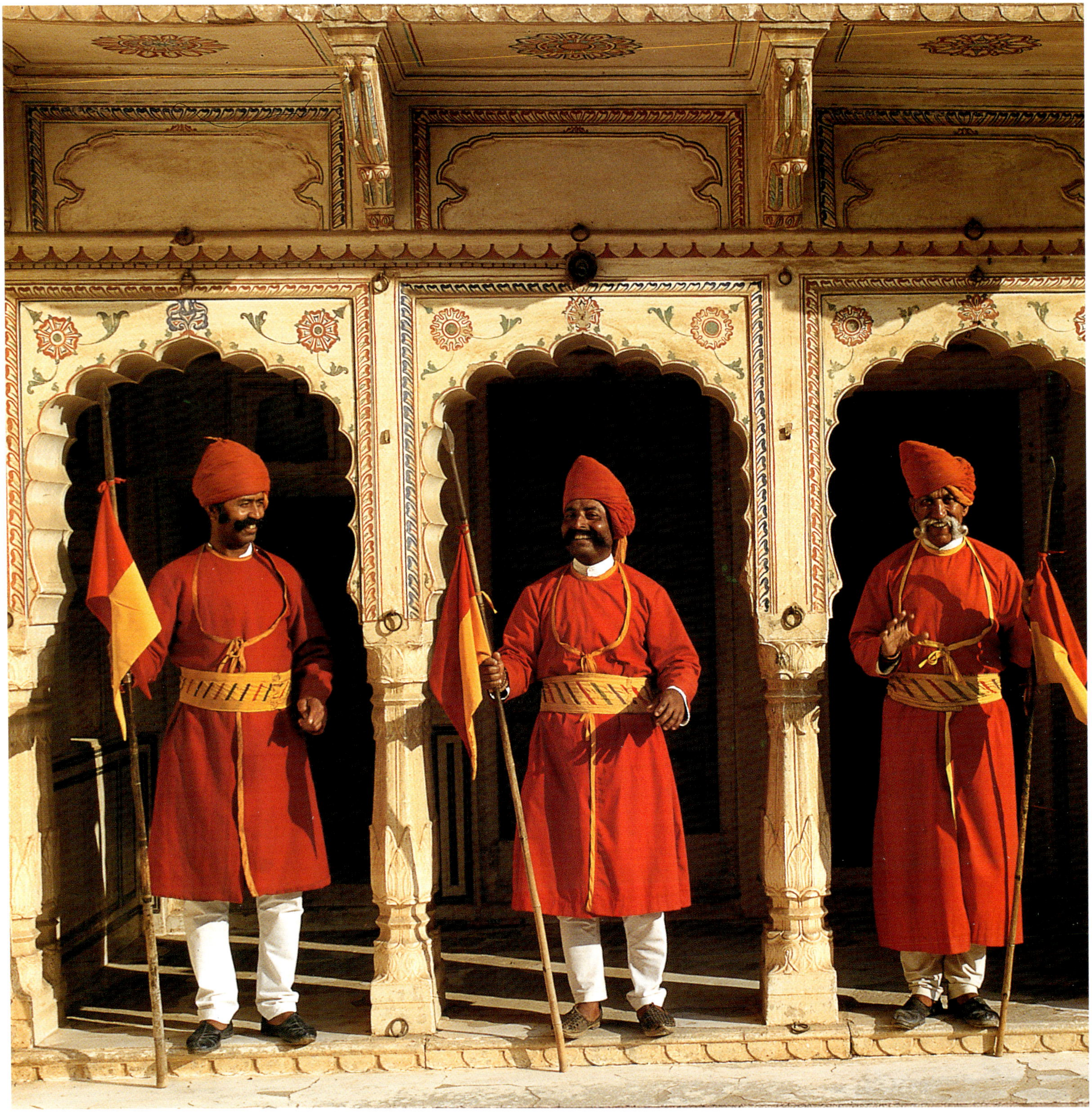

281

The frescoes of the salons of Mandawa castle give an idea of the virtuosity of the decorators who felt free to flaunt their talent and their inspiration.

283

With its walls covered with bits of mirror, its multifoil arches, its gildings and painted ceilings, the Palace of Mirrors, or Shish Mahal, asserts its Indo-Muslim style in the castle of Mandawa.

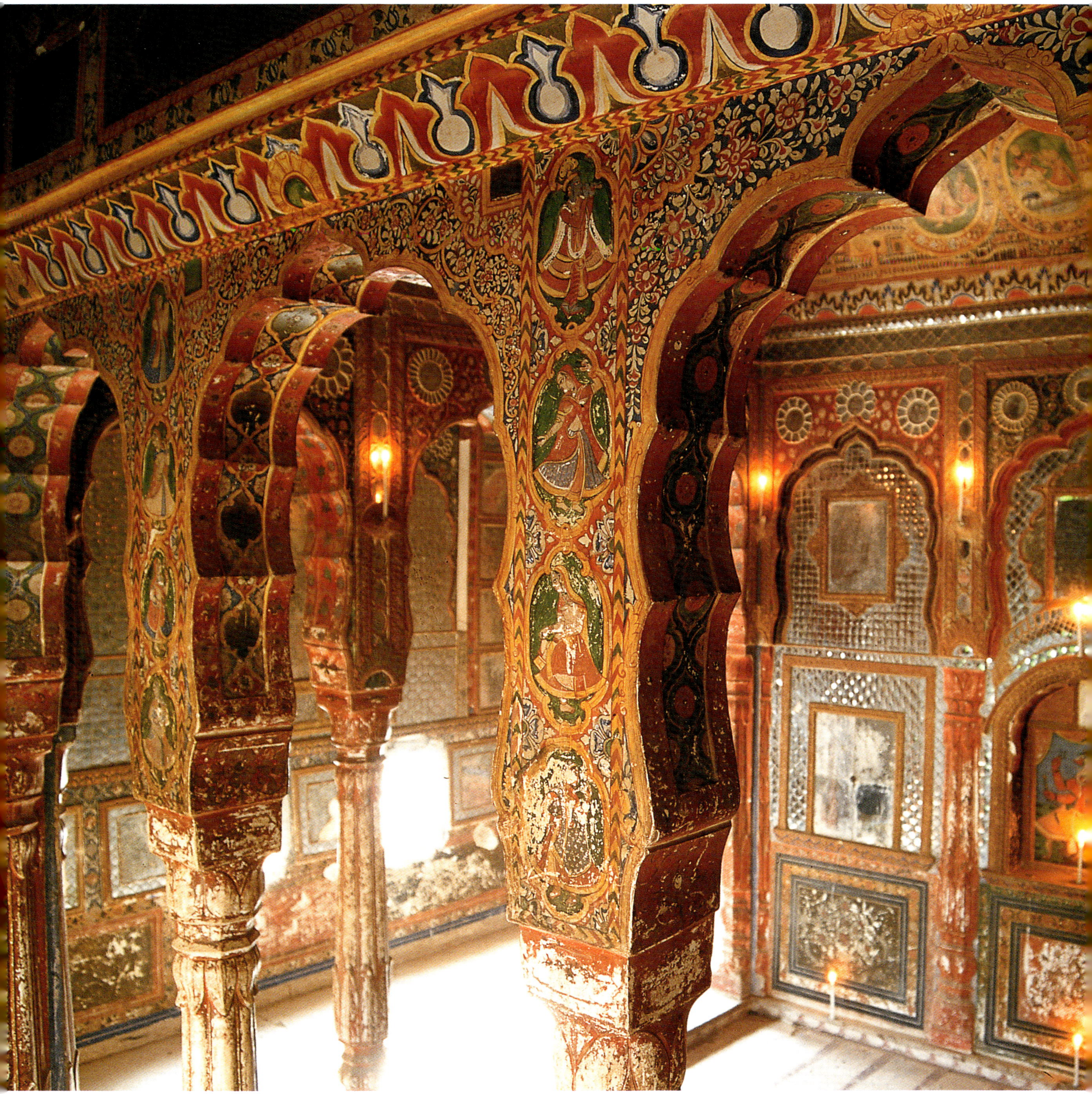

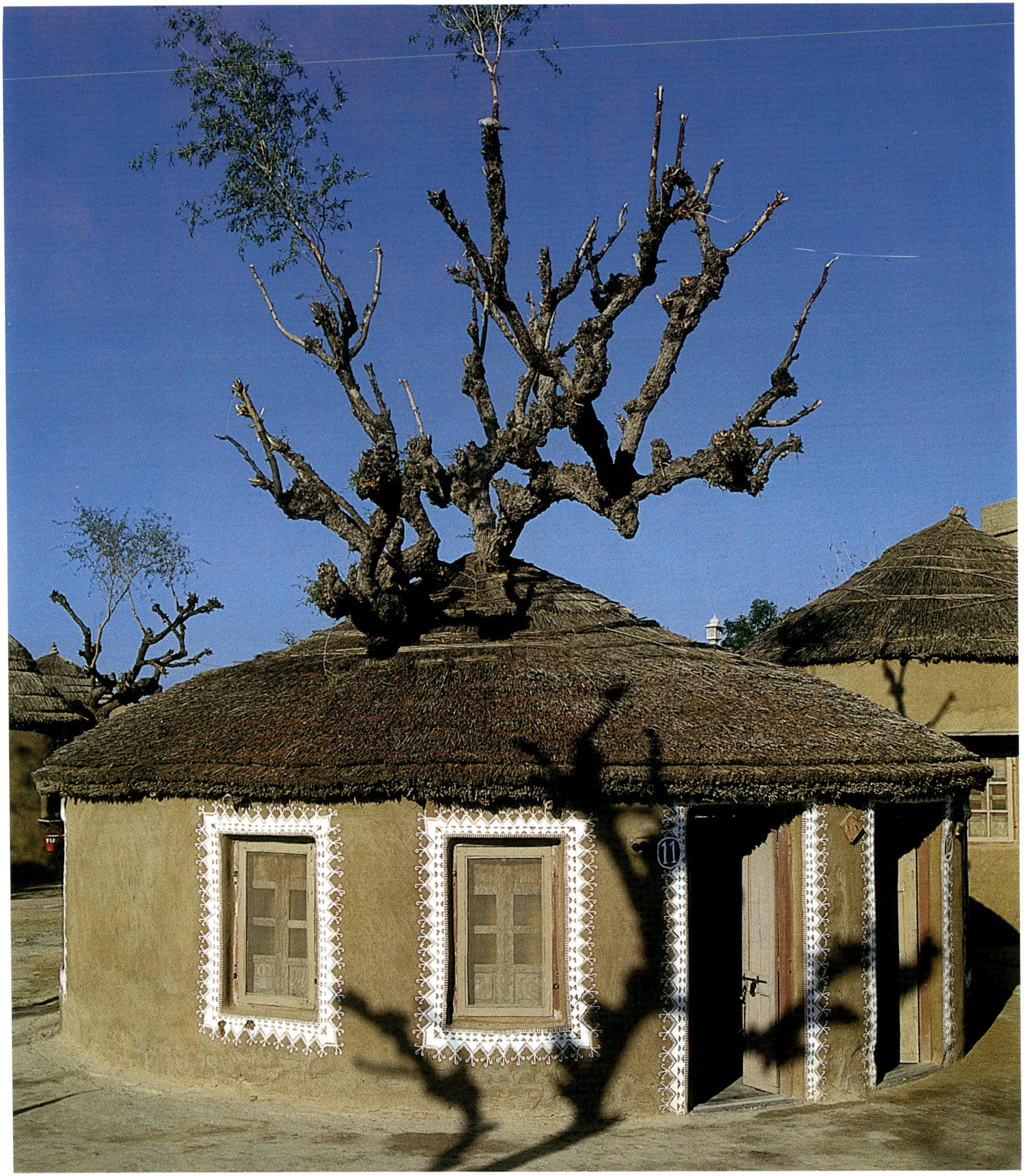
11

On the way out of Mandawa, Desert Resort has become a must for fans of eco-tourism and adobe architecture. The idea came to the owner of Mandawa castle, Kesri Singh: why not copy the earth huts of the desert folk, and offer them to travellers seeking authenticity? Brilliant! The architects Vasant and Revathi Kamath designed some very original houses that grew up on the edge of the desert.

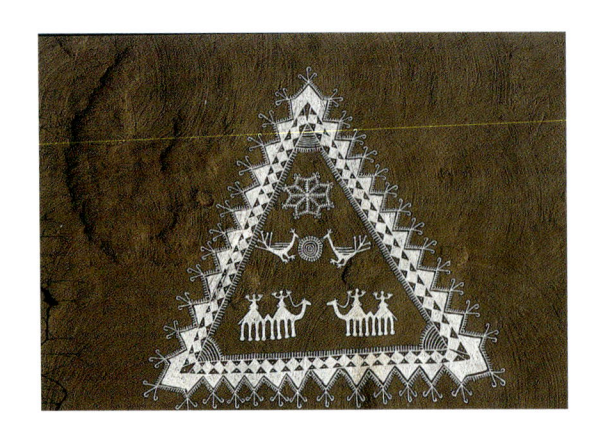

The Desert Resort decoration is signed by the women of the village. Good for them!

288

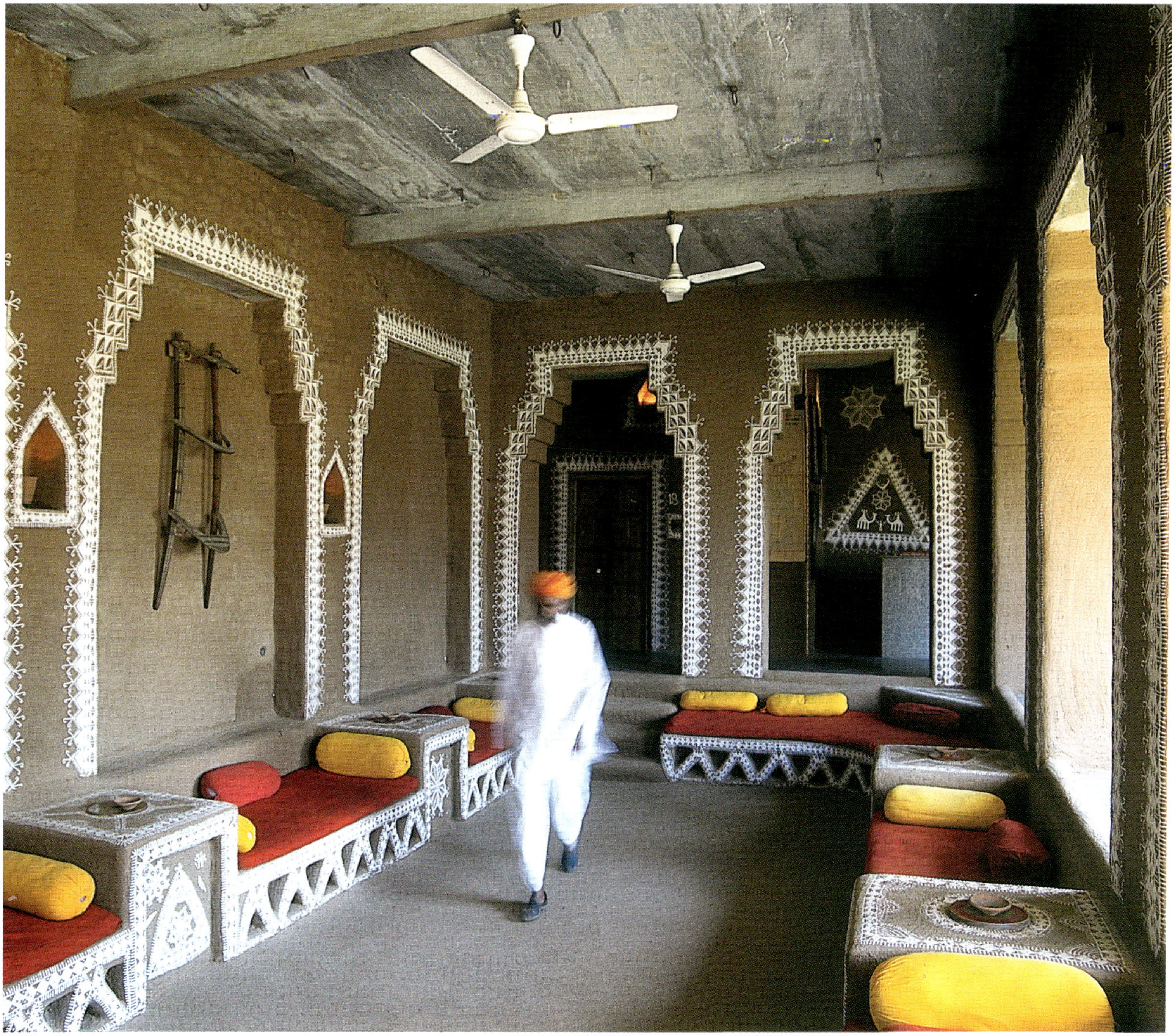

Born at Mandawa, a typical town in the Shekhawati, Dinesh Dhabhai fell in love with a haveli built some two centuries ago and practically in ruins. He bought it, undertook to restore it with passion and patience, piece by piece, and then opened a hotel, Mandawa Haveli, an utterly entrancing destination. Each of the delightful suites (page 293) bears one of the different names of lord Krishna.

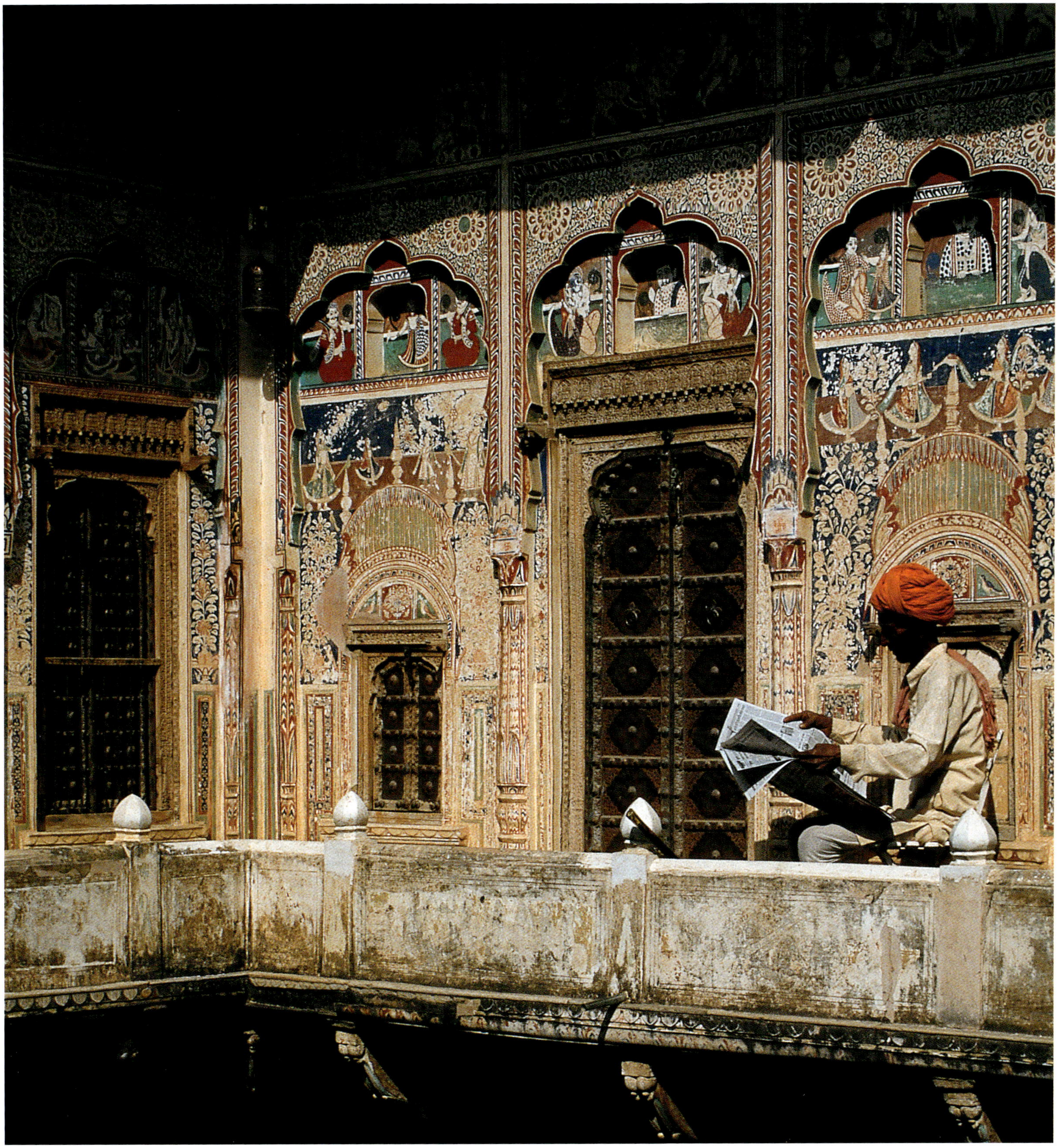

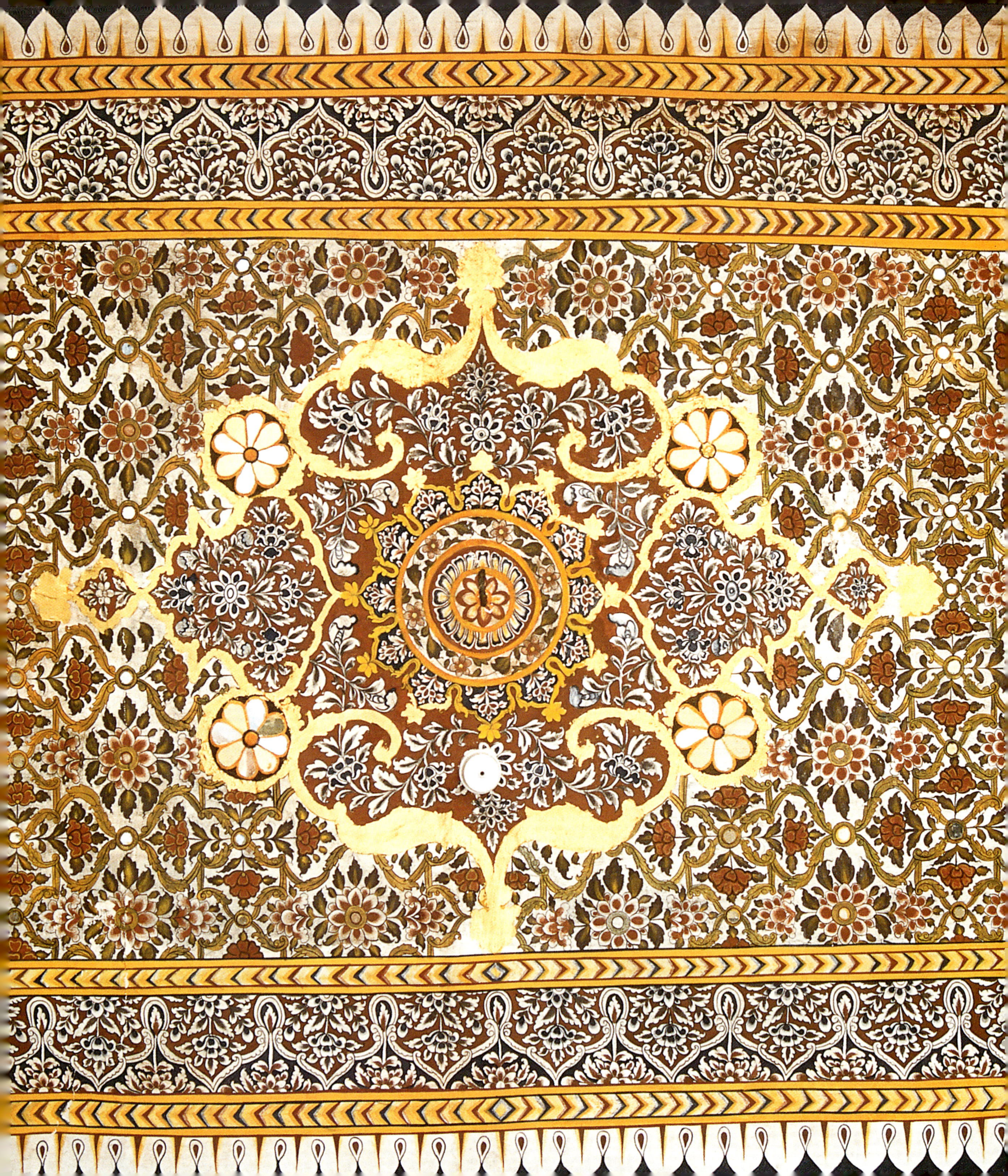

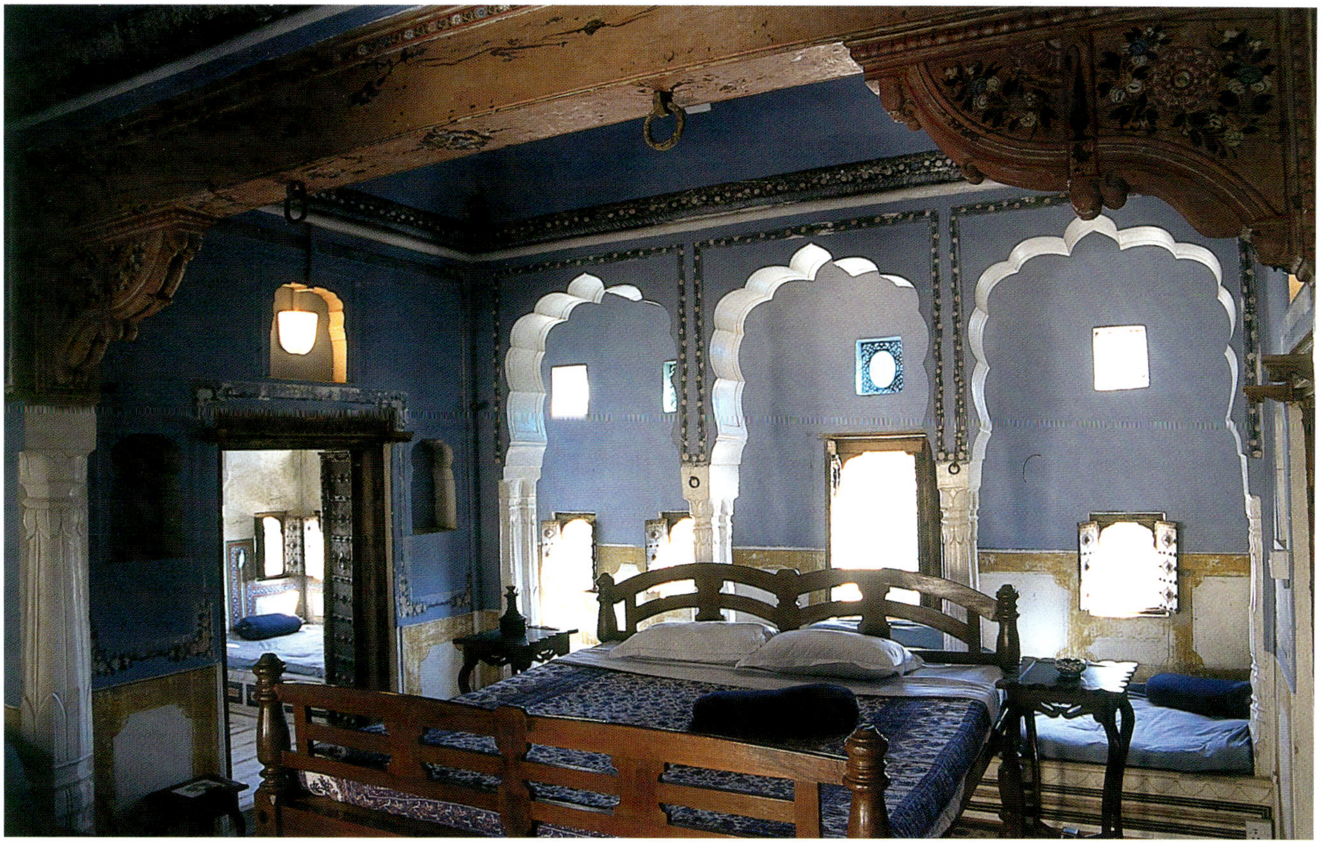

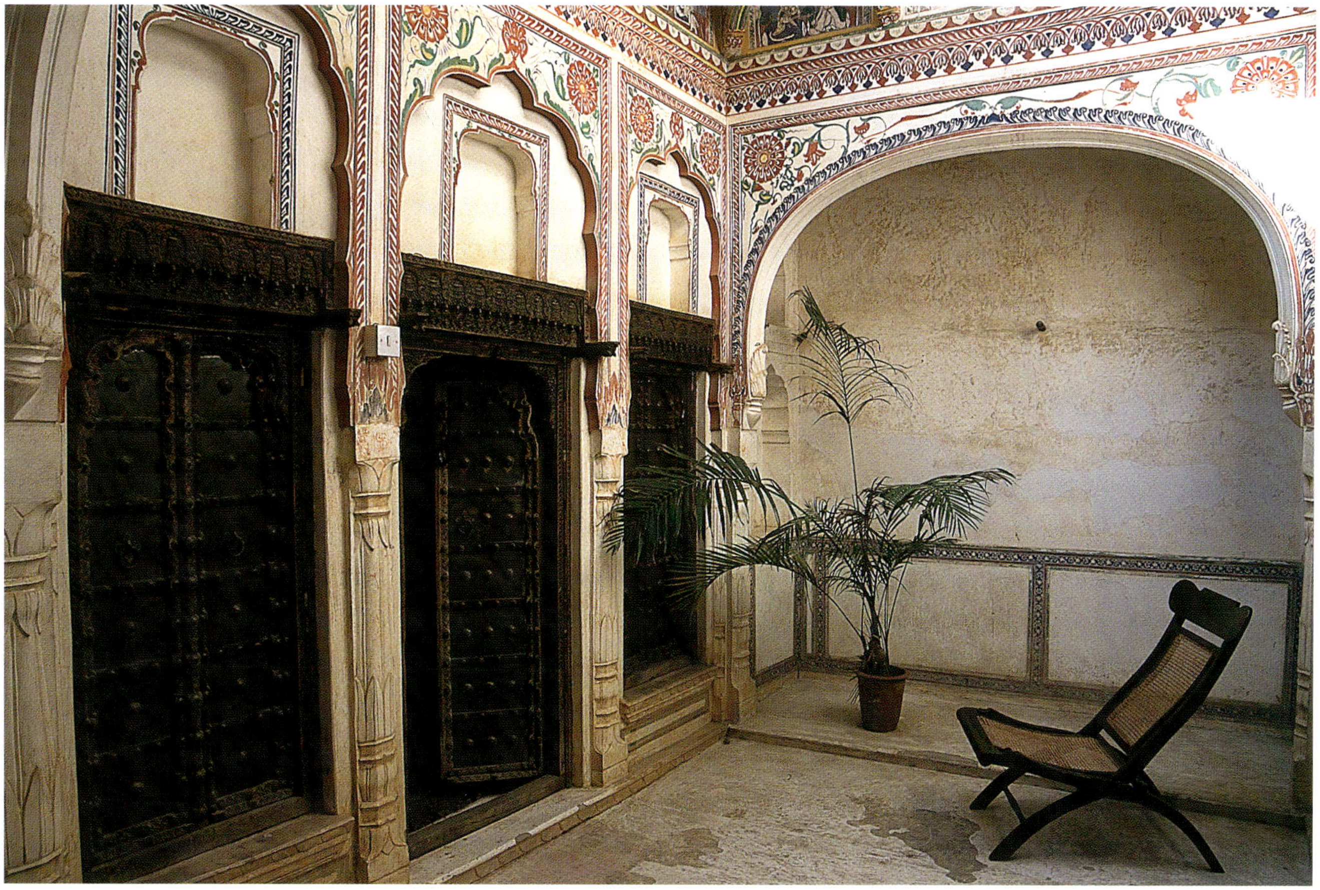

From the terraces of the palace of Khetri Mahal built in 1770 at Jhunjhunu, a town ruled for over three hundred years by the Qaimkhani nawabs (Muslims), you look out over the entire region. The dargah (sanctuary) of Qamr ed-Din Shah (page 295), a Muslim saint venerated by the Hindus, is worth a detour.

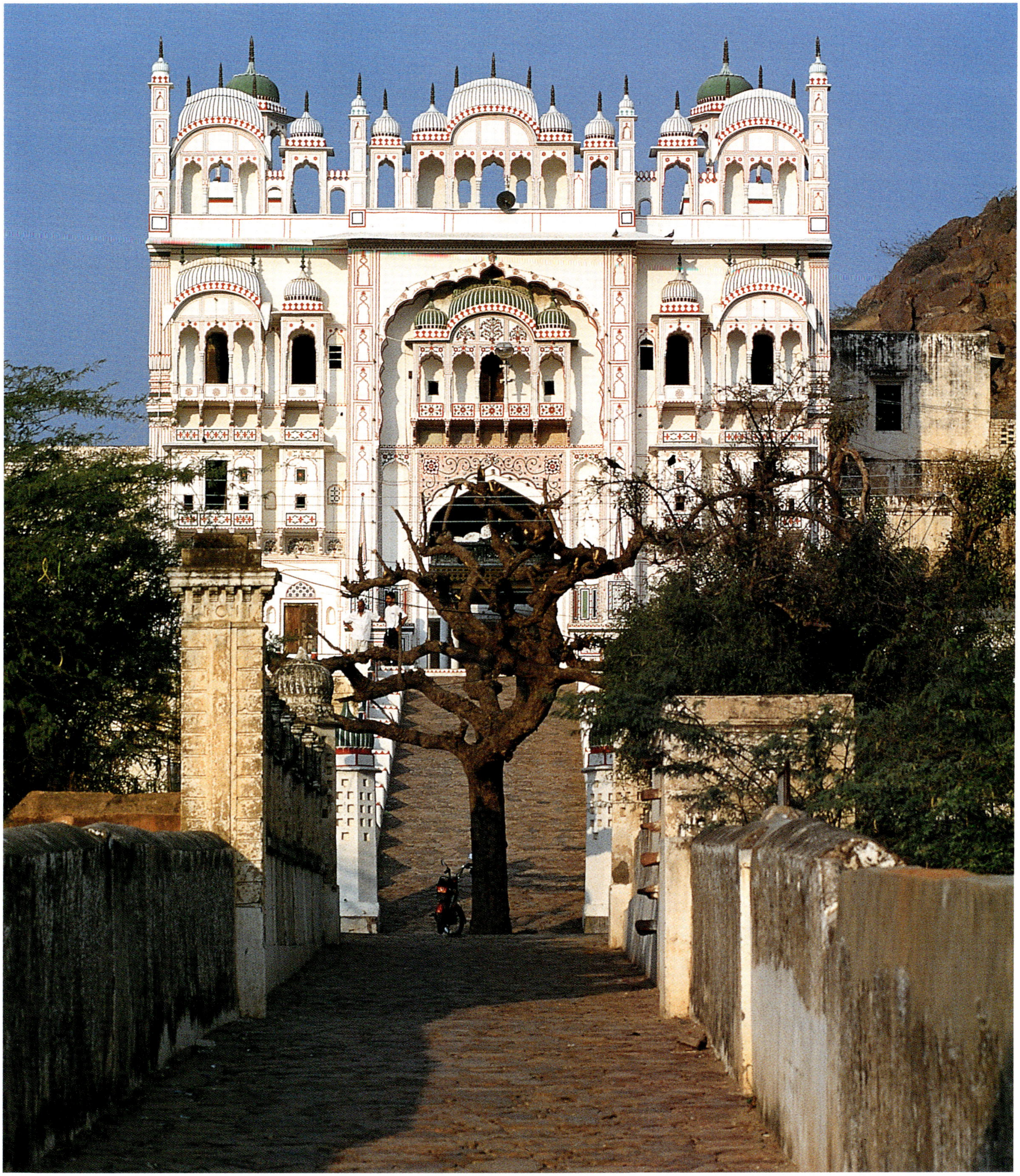

The owners of the haveli, who made their fortunes in Calcutta or Bombay, usually entrust their house to one of the local families who insure its upkeep in their absence. They will come back once or twice a year or for a wedding.

*Page 297:
Haveli Modi at Jhunjhunu, built in 1896.*

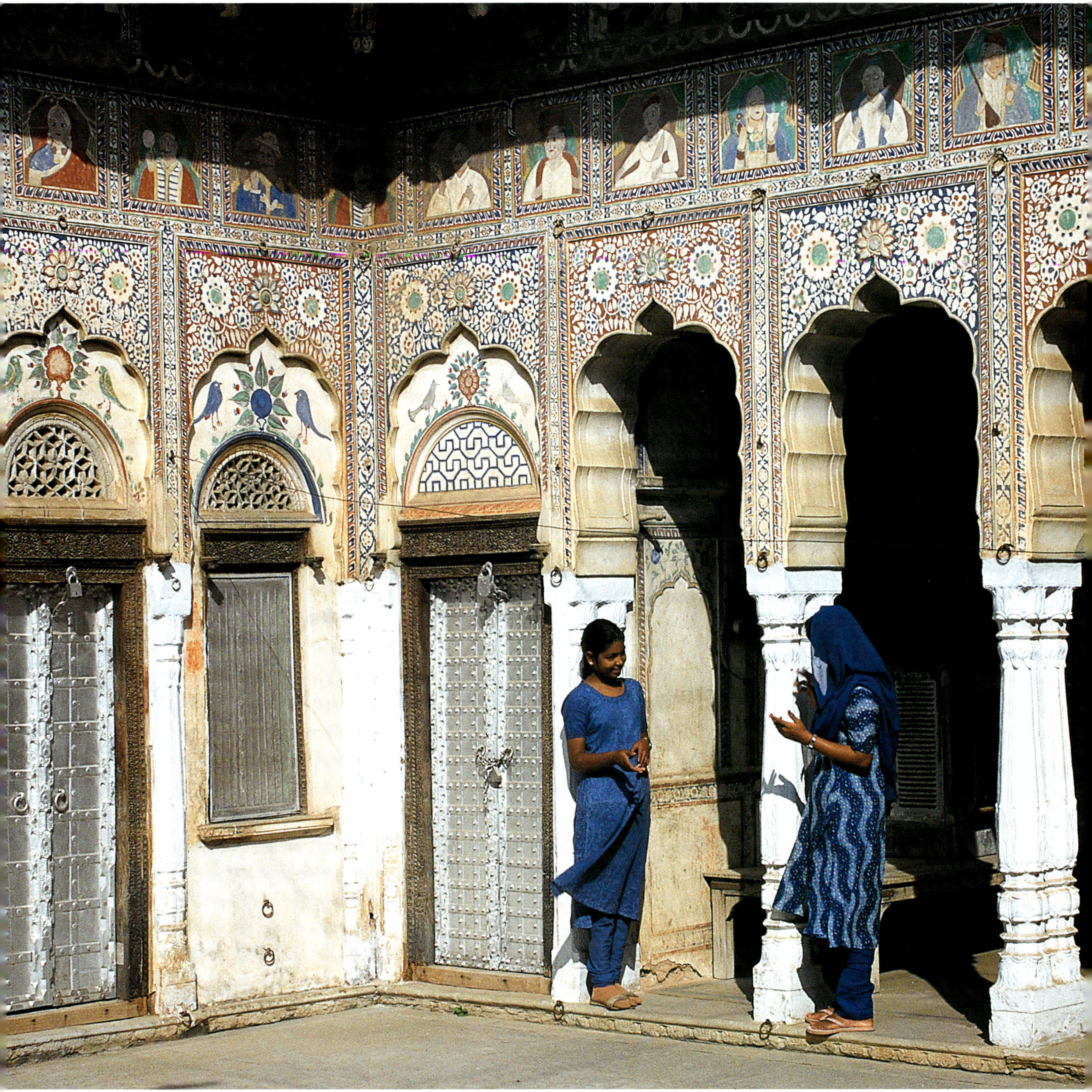

HINDU PUSHKAR

*I*f the days of caravans have long been over, every year the famous camel market of Pushkar recreates one of the last great desert gatherings. During the first moon of the month of Kartik, between October and November, from all over the land long columns of dromedaries converge toward this great event that for a few days brings the region back to life. Frequently the winter arrives like an unexpected guest. The camp is set up on the edge of the city which grows from 11.000 inhabitants to 200.000 visitors. It is a fairground in the midst of the desert with camel races, fanfares, games and the big wheel.

But for all true Hindus, Pushkar is something far grander than just an animal fair. It is a holy place. All year round, entire families come to spend a few days by the most venerated lake in all of India. Surrounded by palaces and temples, it is called Tirtha Raj (the king of holy places). According to legend, a lotus petal falling from the hands of Brahma, the creator of all things, formed its design.

Even if the oldest temples were razed to the ground by the Moghul emperor Aurangzeb at the end of the seventeenth century, the city remained an indispensable sanctuary for Hindus, rather like Benares. From morning to night, men and women perform their ritual bath all along the steps, called ghat, and do their devotions with the assistance of the Brahmans. A sight that is not devoid of poetry, especially at nightfall when the processions wind their way to the temple of Brahma, the only sanctuary in the country dedicated to this Hindu divinity. Lit by a brazen moon, the reflections on the lake turn a deeper blue, the mountains grow a more fiery red, the desert dust more golden. Some November evenings, the uncanny ringing of bells and cymbals in the temples, the hoarse moaning of the camels and the sacred drums prolong the inebriating pulse of the greatest celebration of the camel. In India religion is never mournful.

During the traditional camel fair in Pushkar, a holy city for every Hindu, the desert girls don all their jewellery and are more alluring than ever: long skirt gathered at the waist (ghagra), short bolero (kanchli), ample blouse (kurti) and colourful veil (orhni).

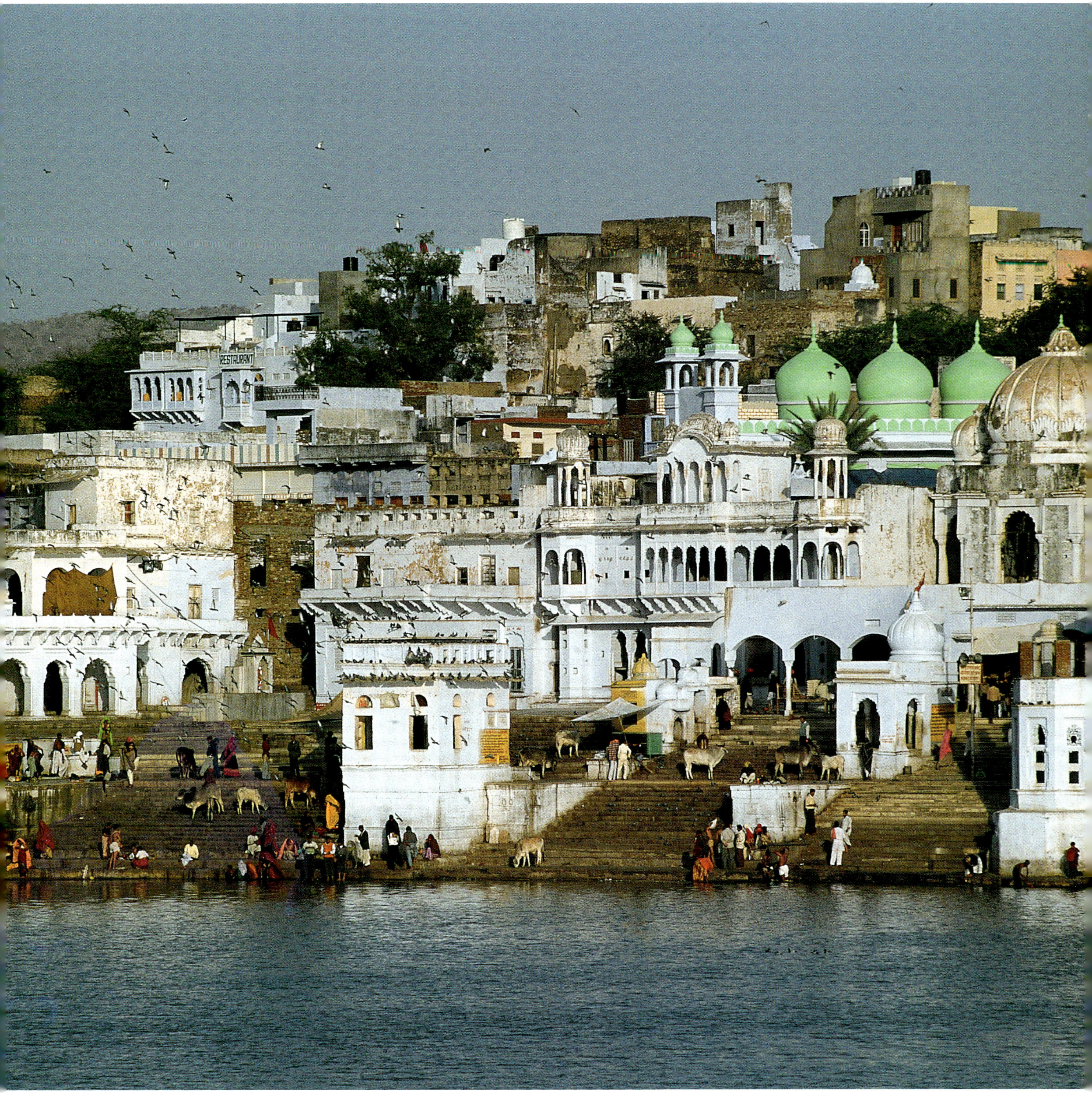
RESTAURANT

For every Hindu, Pushkar is still one of the most venerated cities of all. Its lake is said to have been designed in the spot where a lotus petal had fallen from Brahma's hand. If the mixture of styles of the palaces and residences on the shores of its lake are intriguing, it has a unique soul and a special atmosphere when pilgrims come to perform their devotions and bathe in its waters.

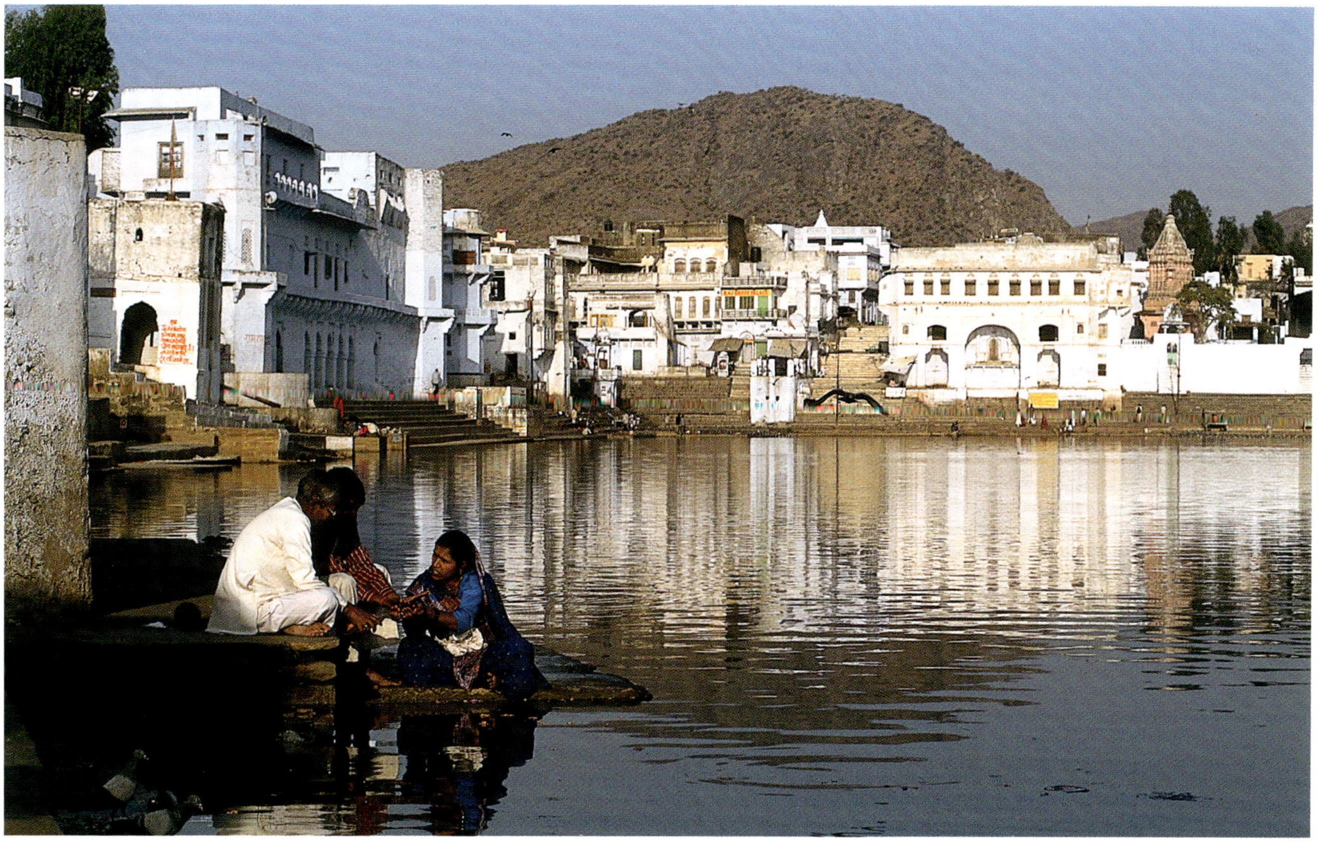

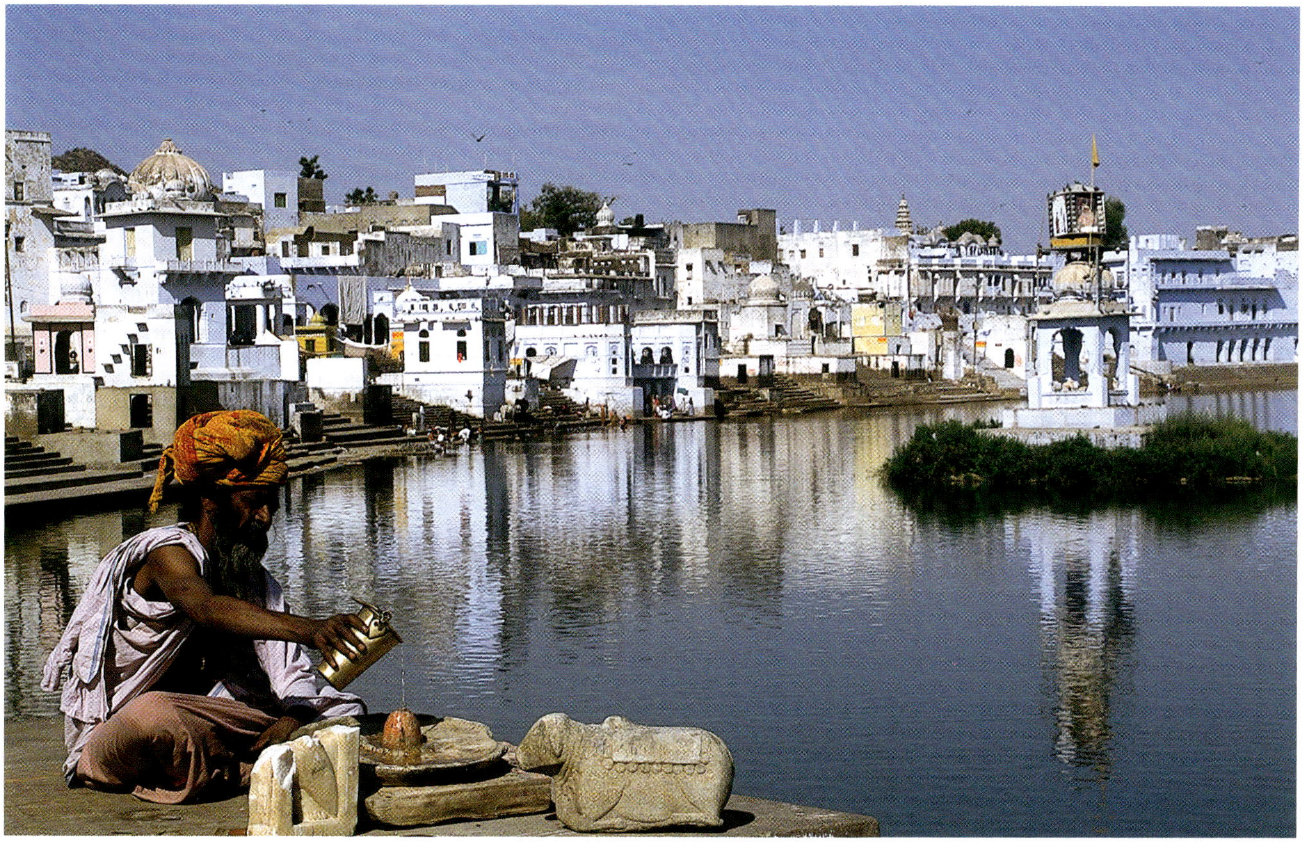

In matters of dress, the colour and prints of the fabrics allow to distinguish to which of the various communities the women and men belong. For men, the turban (pagdi) and moustache are the indispensable attributes of Rajput panache and pride. "He who stays awake runs away with the pagdi of he who sleeps", says a famous proverb of the Thar desert.

303

Whatever your age, you will be enthralled by the delicacy of the Adhai-din ka Jhonpra mosque in Ajmer, built in the early thirteenth century. It is one of the most ancient relics of Islamic India.

MUSLIM AJMER

An important religious centre for all the Muslims of India, the dargah (sanctuary) of the Sufi saint Main ud-Din Chisti is the heart of the city. Some claim seven pilgrimages to Ajmer equal one to Mecca. Others say that a wish uttered in front of the famous dargah will be fulfilled within the year.

The Burraq Manzil hotel is in the best location in town. Right across from the monumental green and white door that opens onto the famous mausoleum, or dargah, of the Sufi Khawaja Main ud-din Chisti. It is packed almost all year round. "The saint's tomb attracts thousands of Muslims from all over the country and even from Pakistan", claims Rahman Burraqui who warmly greets us on the first floor of his hotel. He is proud to bear the title of Haji after performing the holy journey to Mecca. "My family decided to move to Pakistan in 1947. But I chose to remain here. I am loyal to my country, India."

Every year on the occasion of the celebration of the Urs commemorating the saint's death, pilgrims gaily throng the streets of Ajmer to come pray before the most revered Muslim sanctuary in all of India.

Nothing remains of the fortress erected by the Rajput king Ajai Pal in the seventh century. The Afghan Mohammed of Ghor sacked the city at the end of the twelfth century. On its ruins, a pious Muslim, Main ud-Din Chisti (1142-1236), vested with the mission of spreading Islam in Northern India, settled at Ajmer, which became a pilgrimage site. In 1556 the Moghul emperor Akbar made it a Muslim centre in Rajput territory, enhancing it with a palace where his grandson, Shah Jahan, occasionally resided.

The old city is steeped in a very poignant charm during the pilgrimages. Going past the mediaeval gate (Delhi Gate), the flow of pilgrims climbs the main street, Dargah Bazaar, lined with souvenir shops and stands overflowing with rose petals. After entering a very

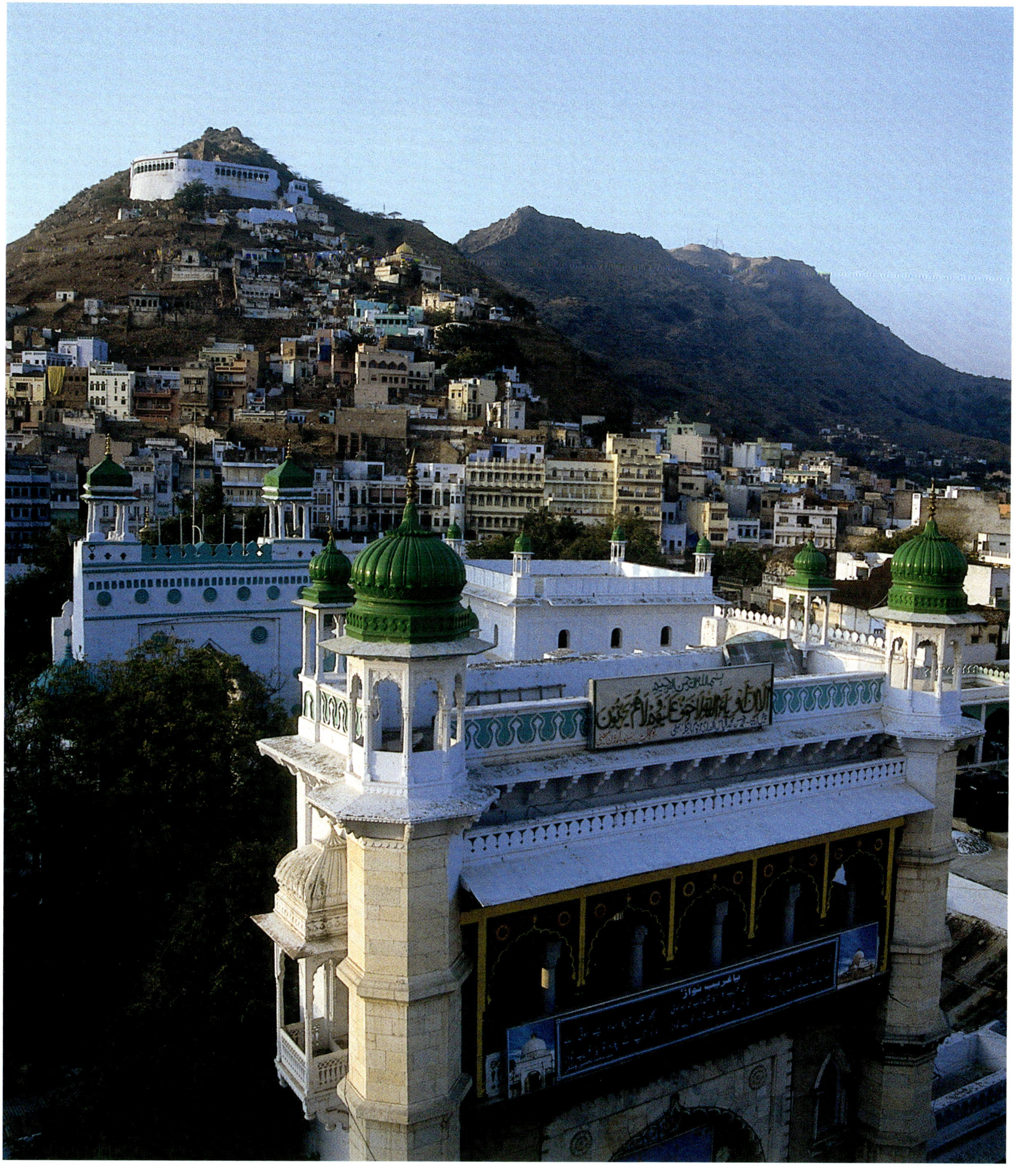

tall green and white door crowned with two minarets, the crowd converges on a vast esplanade. Identifiable by its white marble dome, the famous dargah is in the middle of a courtyard thronged with the faithful who are praying and strewing rose petals. The atmosphere is relaxed and friendly.

But for the eldest, the pilgrimage would not be complete without a visit to the very pure mosque named Adhai-dinka Jhonpra (translate "the hut of two and a half days"), not far from the dargah. One of the oldest mosques in the country, since it supposedly goes back to the twelfth century. Its resemblance with the Quwwat ul-Islam Qutab Minar mosque in Delhi, begun in 1193, is indeed striking. The facade of the prayer room, added on in the thirteenth century, features seven Tudor arches, enhanced with inscriptions from the Koran and truly remarkable arabesques. The prayer room inherited pillars made of three superimposed columns brought from twelfth-century Hindu and Jain temples. There are also the inscriptions delicately carved in the stone. What do they mean? Nobody knows. Perhaps they are Persian… In the late afternoon, when the muezzin calls to prayer, the last faithful and the sun leave the mosque. It retains its mysteries!

Ajmer is proud of the Adhai-din ka Jhonpra mosque (the hut of two and a half days) erected in the thirteenth century in a sublime mountain setting. It marks the height of Islam in India and of the reign of the Afghan sultan Mohammed of Ghor. It fully expresses the history of Islamic art. If the two minarets rising above the central arch have almost disappeared, the seven Tudor arches of the prayer room form a unique ensemble. The facades are admirably covered with wonderfully carved Koranic inscriptions and arabesques. The carved pillars of the prayer room were "borrowed" from Hindu and Jain temples in the region.

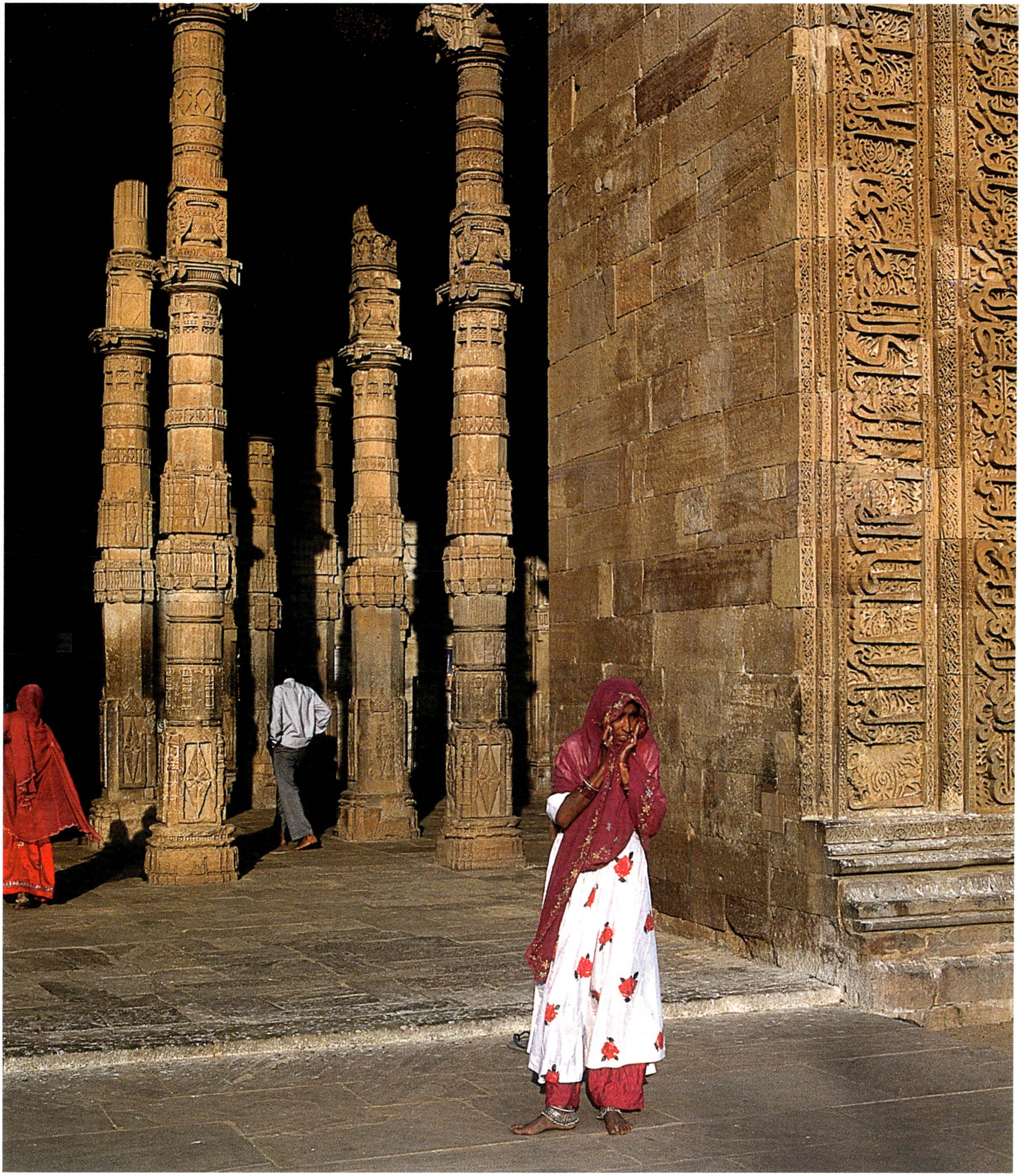

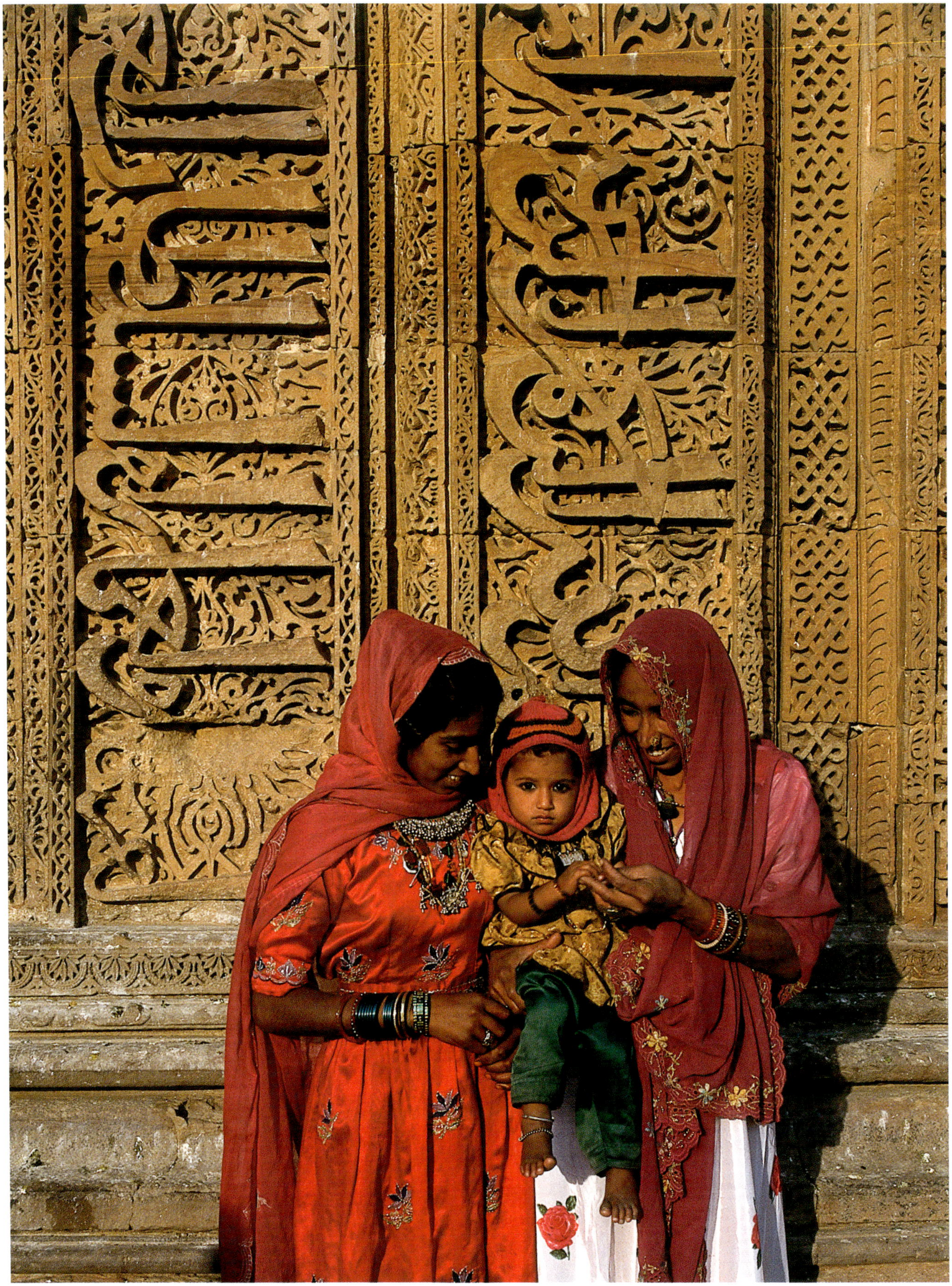

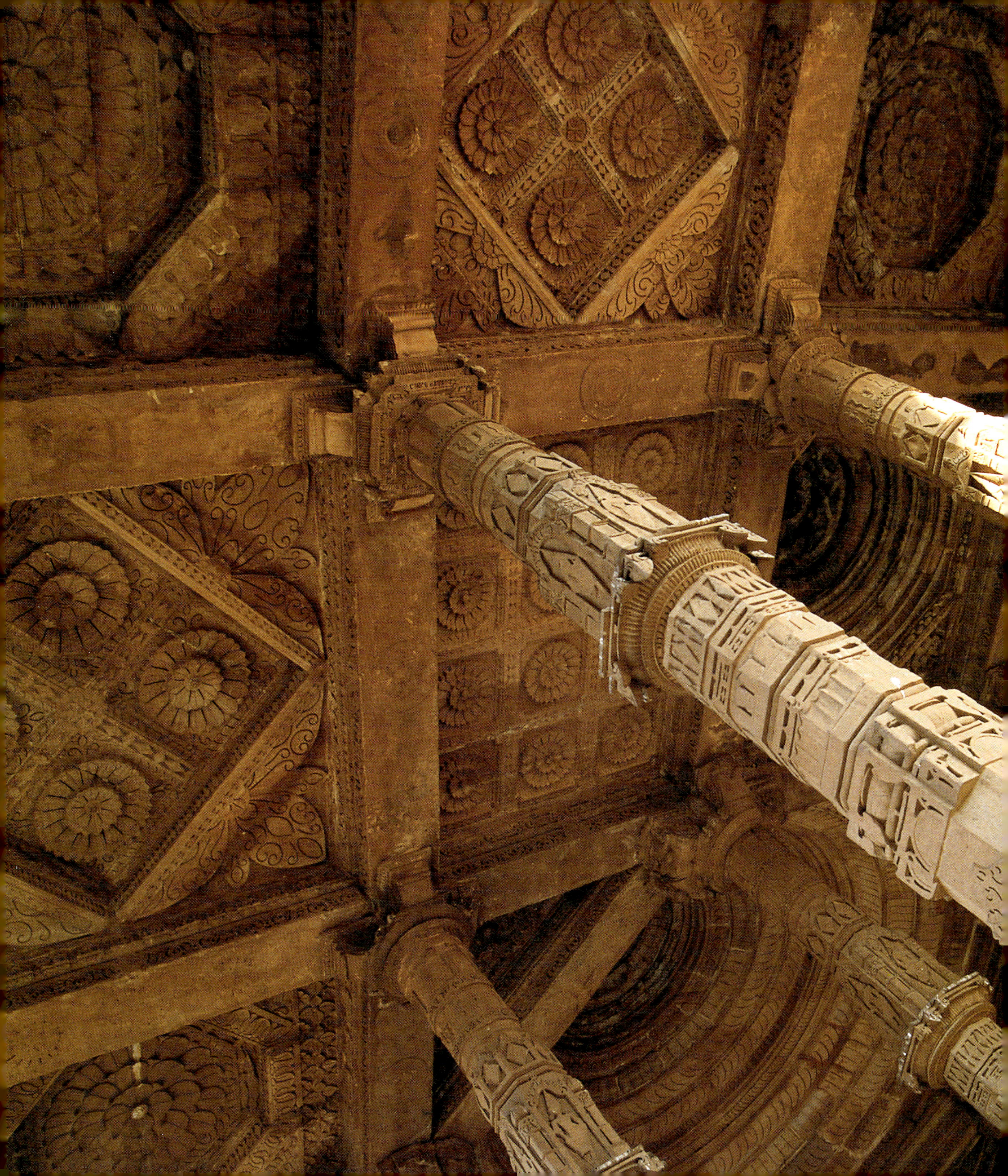

At the edge of the desert, on the borders of Rajasthan, the citadel of Jaisalmer that retained its incomparable mediaeval layout rises like a mirage.

JAISALMER, THE HONEY-COLOURED CITADEL

On his way to China Marco Polo is said to have dropped off his trunks here. The first road in 1928, the first railroad in 1968… At the end of the journey, at the end of the desert, at the end of Rajasthan and India, almost at the Pakistani border, this imposing fortress is like a reward for the seeker. With Jaisalmer, the desert has its land, and the traveller his refuge. Time here is different, it does not "go by". It is offered you and it lets you savour it. Living for a few days in the citadel, forbidden to every motor and open to every dream, living a few star-lit nights in a old palace whose narrow windows overlook the desert as far as you can see, it is all sheer ecstasy. You can spend days and days here without tiring of it. Under these ramparts, the lower city offers its most endearing aspects: an immense maze of streets crisscrossed by sunlight, dotted here and there with splendid houses called haveli where the stonecutters, the Silavats, virtuosos of the chisel, used their genius to carve lacy facades.

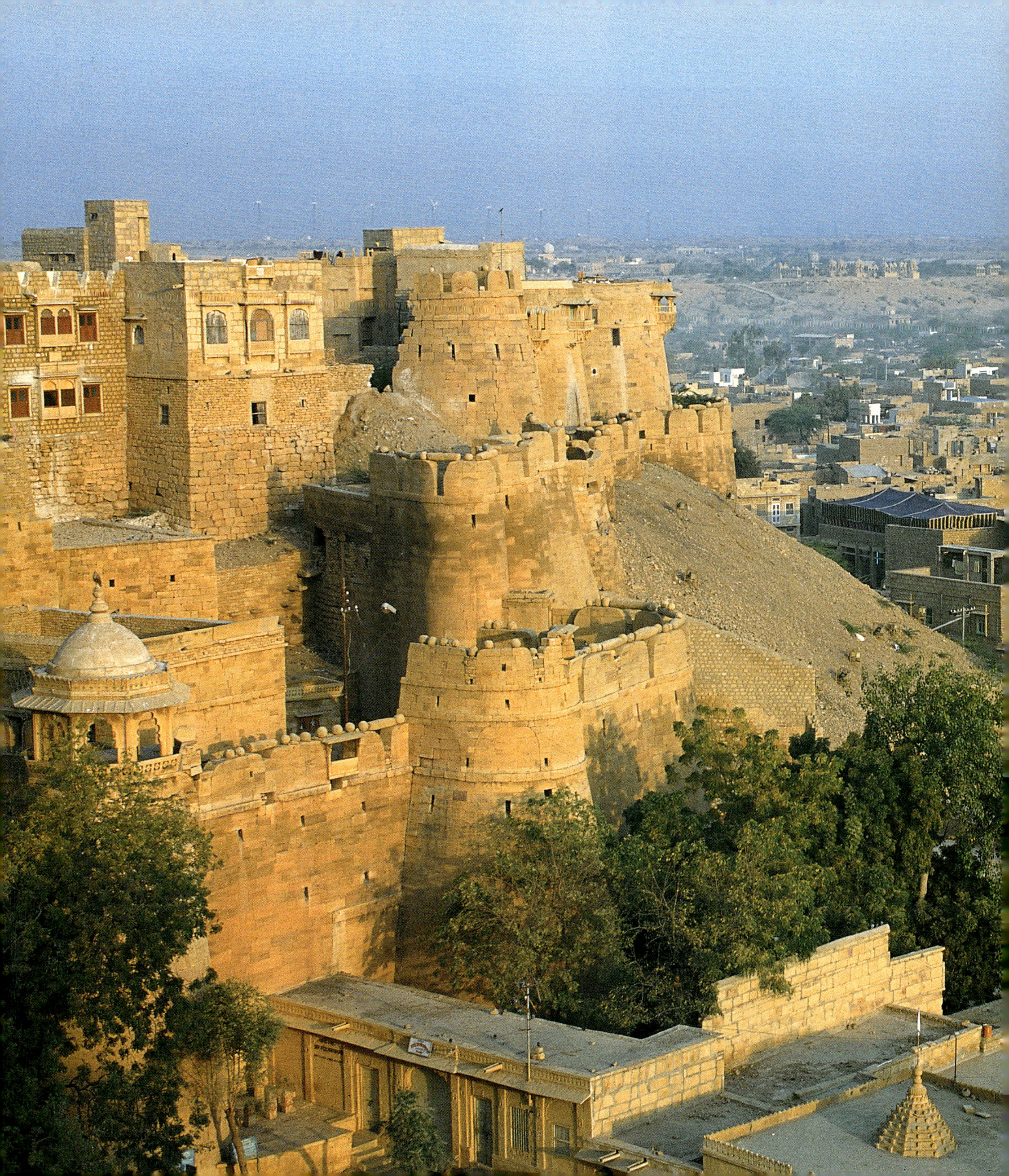

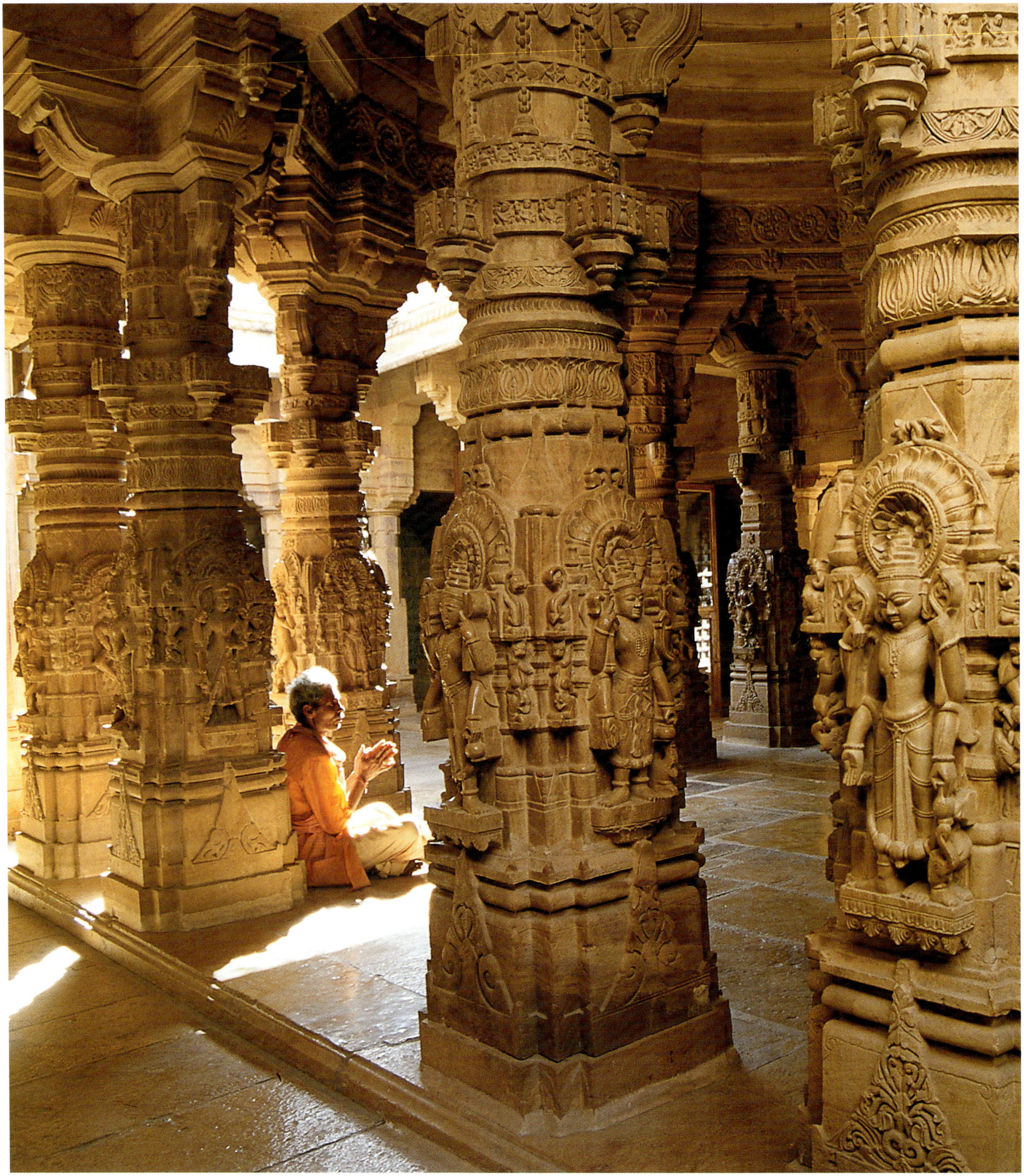

History

The interior of the citadel, perched in the midst of the desert, has in store some wonderful surprises: the Shree Jagdish temple which belongs to an ensemble of seven temples built between the twelfth and the fifteenth centuries (page 312) and the Raj Mahal royal palace lifting up its covered balconies (jharokhas) (page 313).

This lofty capital of the sands, the colour of honey, encircled in Vauban-style ramparts and overlooked by towers, was built in 1156 by the king Rao Jaïsal, a Rajput of the Bhatti clan, "race of the Moon". The citadel tells the story of these princes, rather fond of brigandage and known as "the desert wolves", who did not have any qualms about ransoming pilgrims on their way to Mecca. To embellish their jewel of a city, they taxed the caravans stretched out for miles nearby, connecting Egypt, Arabia Persia and Central Asia, and looted the goods being delivered to the markets of Delhi. Believing they were invincible, they even attacked the caravan of the mighty sultan of Delhi, Ala ud-Din Khilji. He lost his temper and besieged the city in 1314, patiently. The siege lasted eight years. Rajput warriors are proud. Rather than surrender, they preferred the supreme sacrifice, the terrible jauhar. Dressed in the traditional saffron-coloured robe, they launched a heroic, hopeless assault on the enemy while their 24.000 wives immolated themselves. Destructive folly! The eighteenth century would be one of compromise and prosperity. The maharajahs accepted the imperial rule and trade blossomed. The princes and rich merchants built palaces and haveli at the foot of the fortress. The arrival of the British would put an end to the days of rich caravans.

In the citadel, each house, each corner has a story to tell. From the terraces of the Killa Bhawan hotel, the view over the desert and the bastions of the honey-coloured walls is boundless.

The Citadel

Tightly held by its stone carapace and towering some one hundred metres over the lower city, the fort valiantly resisted the onslaught of time. Its dimensions are gigantic: a double row of walls ten metres high broken by 99 curved bastions. To really get the measure of the fort, you have to climb a long steep paved ramp passing under four gates: Akhai Pol, Suraj Pol, Ganesh Pol and Hawa Pol. The esplanade you reach is evocative of mystery and mirages. You wander with your nose in the air through the narrow streets flanked with handsome palaces, houses, ruins, stalls, hotels and gorgeously decorated Jain temples. Thanks to the absence of traffic, the citadel has preserved a soul and a unique atmosphere, highlighted by the royal palace raising its seven storeys of carved stone. On each side, you overlook the desert as far as you can see.

315

The Haveli in the Lower Town

Getting lost in the passageways of the lower city is like travelling back through the centuries to the days of the caravans that brought the city a fantastic expansion. Everything was traded, everything was bought: rugs from Herat (Afghanistan), scimitars from Damascus, stallions from Arabia, silks and spices. Up to the nineteenth century, merchants and bankers had these architectural treasures called haveli built by brilliant stone carvers. Shall we set out to discover them? Let us try to open the door of the Slim Singh haveli. What luck! We run straight into a large family, none other than that of the intriguing Salim Singh Mehta who had the haveli built. For a few rupees, the youngest tell us the sad story of their ancestor appointed diwan, meaning Prime Minister, in 1815. The man was immensely rich. To house his seven wives and two concubines, he hired the best artisans. His haveli was unique and at each storey it grew wider, the top level graced with a portico upheld by carved stone corbels. Blue domes elegantly crowned the building. Bursting with ambition, the diwan planned to raise his palace by two extra storeys. But the rawal, the sovereign of Jaisalmer, was rather touchy. He had them torn down for the royal palace to remain the tallest edifice. The highlight of the visit is nestled on the top storey, in the theatre reserved for the diwan. The ceilings were covered with tiny mirrors so Salim Singh Mehta could keep an eye on his enemies. But in the end danger came from within; he would be stabbed and poisoned by his own wife. What a fate!

During a stroll in the winding streets you may chance upon the sublime Patwon ki Haveli and its soaring stone facade, graced with 60 balconies or jharakha sometimes closed by jali, lined up in rows. This haveli was to be the showcase of Guman Chand Patwa, a rich Jain merchant who owned over 300 shops from Afghanistan to China. He planned the building to live there happily with his five sons. Construction began in 1805 and lasted fifty years.

Beneath the lower city, the small lake of Gadi Sadar offers the photographer one of the loveliest shots of Rajasthan with the citadel of Jaisalmer in the background, mellowed by the sun. Created in the fourteenth century, this lake was the main water reservoir of the city. We notice an elegant little stone edifice featuring a gate called Tila ki Pol. It was commissioned by Tila, the prince's favourite concubine. Chronicles of the time claim the jealous wives (and we can understand!) wished to have Tila's work demolished. She found a way out by adding to the building a small temple consecrated to Krishna, and that protected it from jealousy!

In the lower city of Jaisalmer, lined up in rows and striated by the sun, the palaces called haveli, carved by the finest stonecutters, tell the enthralling tales of the desert merchants.

Patwon ki Haveli belonged to five Jain brothers who made their fortune trading jewellery and delicate brocades.

A stroll in the intricate streets of the lower city of Jaisalmer is like travelling back through the centuries to the days when it was the stopping place of the caravans crossing the desert.

Seen from the lake of Gadi Sagar which reflects the famous Tila ki Pol gate, the citadel appears even more impregnable.

Next double page: A stone's throw from Jaisalmer in the dunes said to be "of Sam", the desert children quickly learn how to train dromedaries.

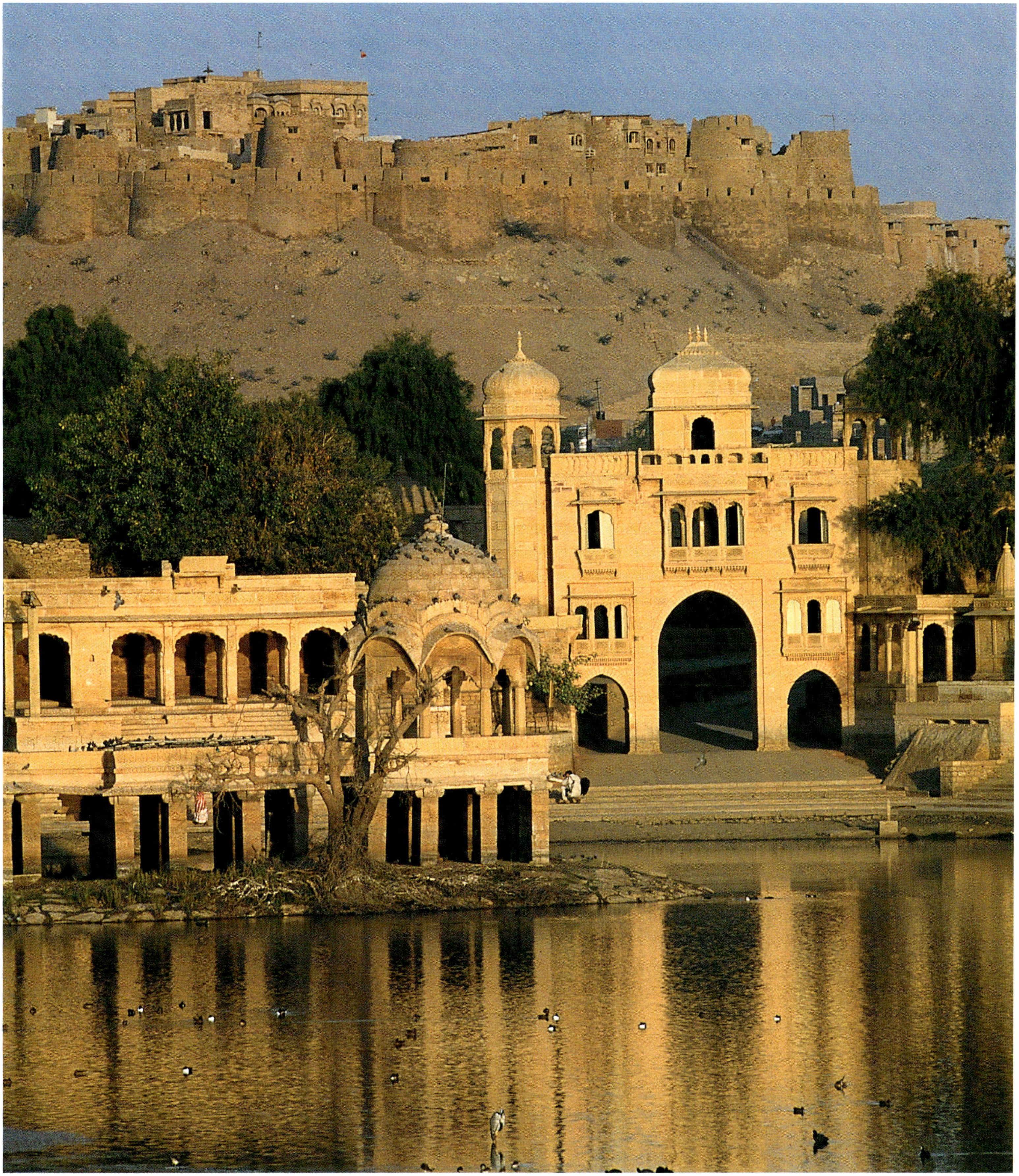

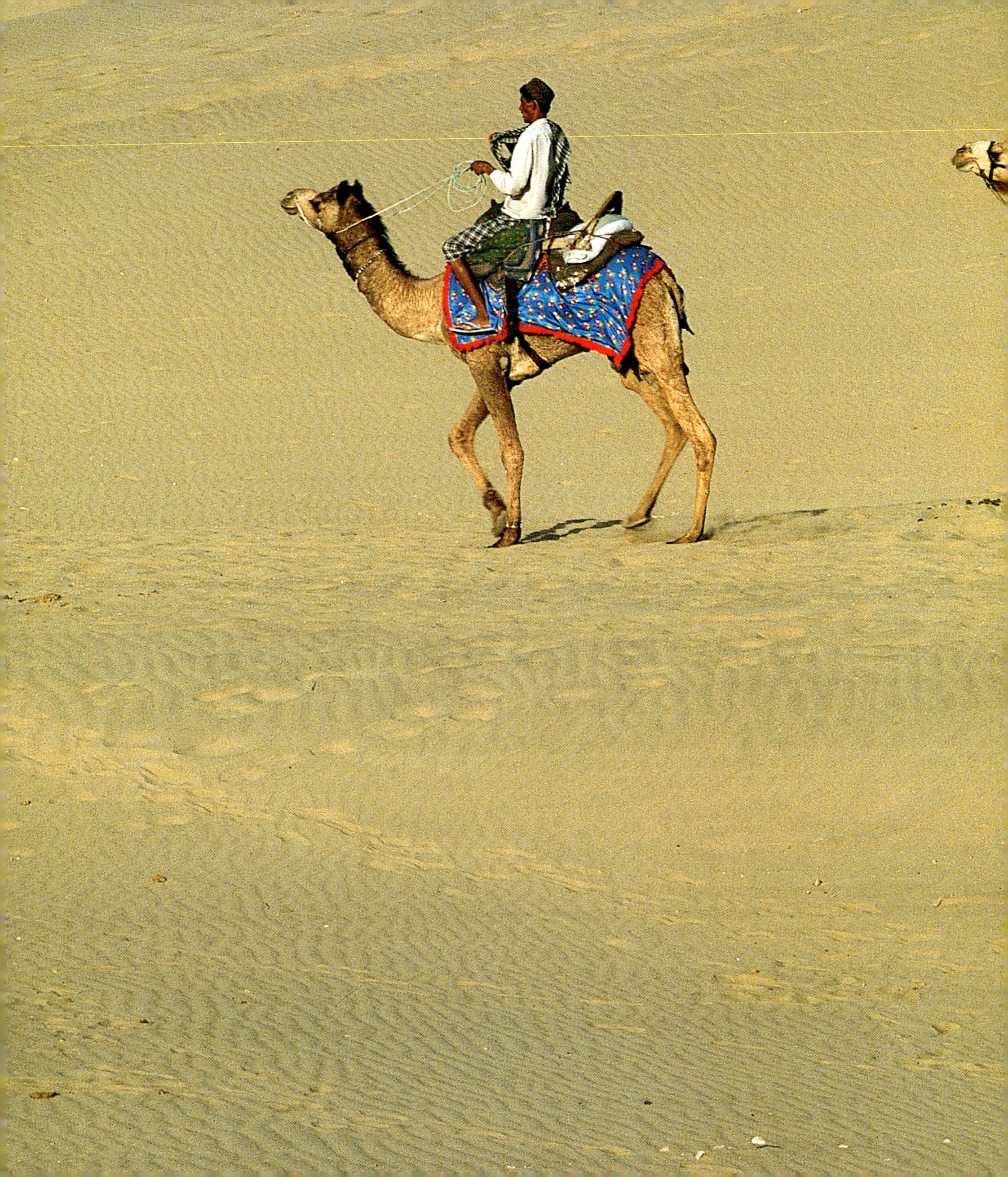

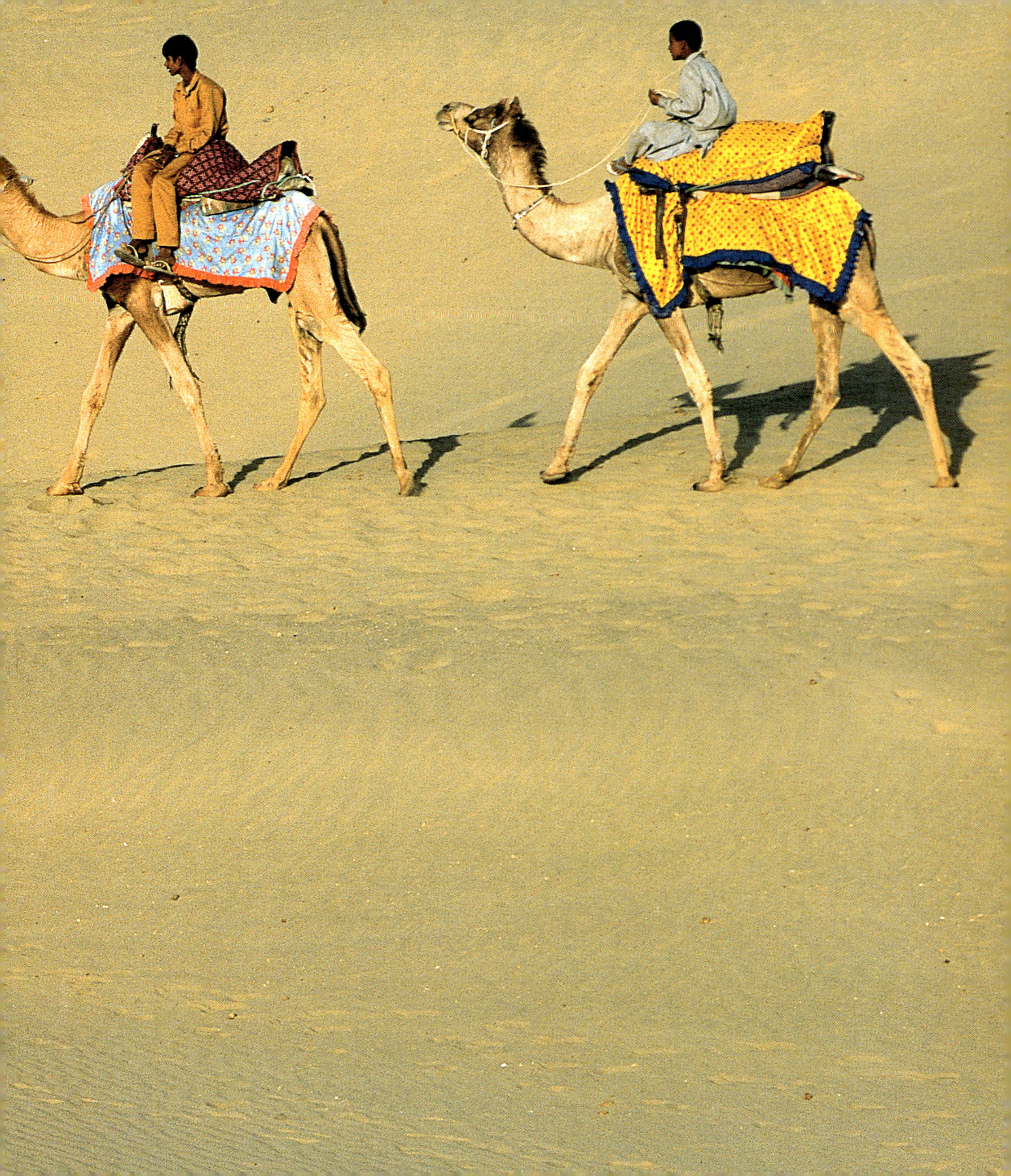

UDAIPUR, "THE CITY OF DAWN"

"His Highness" is up in the Air!

The viceroy Lord Northbrook, visibly won by the city, described it in these words: "Take a lake the size of Orta and some hills slightly lower and of a lighter hue; put the walls of Verona on the lowest slopes and add one or two forts, scatter about a few isles smaller than the ones on Lake Garda, face the palaces and domes with marble… Pile half-a-dozen French chateaux onto the city and complete it all with a piece of Venice." Lord Northbrook had obviously been all over!

Even for those who are not viceroys, Udaipur is often their favourite place in Rajasthan. You are happy to put down your suitcases here, to take a rest, to cool off. Indeed "the City of Dawn" contrasts with the rather austere fortresses of the region. Night and day the hotel terraces overlook a truly idyllic landscape. You just yield to the enchantment of these white marble palaces that seem to be floating upon a quiet lake framed in wooded hills. While you are having your breakfast on one of the terraces, if your eye is suddenly caught by a small aircraft circling over the royal palace, there is a very good chance the maharana Arvind Singh Mewar is at the commands. When he is not sitting in front of his computer managing his six palace-hotels, discussing plans with his precious British collaborator and friend Sabina Bailey, or sponsoring a charity fund, "His Highness", "Shriji" for his intimates, is in the air. He bought himself two small planes, Czech-made Microlites. His latest passion. He has some others: a sweet wife, his children, his city which he returned to after his studies in Great Britain and the United States (with a stop off in Chicago where he learned the hotel business).

The private apartments of the maharana occupy a charming pavilion built in 1860, the Shambu Niwas, set in the midst of the gardens of the royal palace (City Palace). On entering we discover a very European decor with antique gilt furniture, paintings and rugs, all with prestigious signatures. On one side, is an ultra-modern kitchen (the maharana is a remarkable cordon-bleu). A few servants quietly attend to their work. A stereo set is on a table (His Highness is a great lover of classical Indian music). There is a veranda at the back with a few sofas and gusts of wind come in. In short, a decor that inspires a certain nostalgia… Is that the right word, nostalgic? Arvind Singh bluntly replies: "Not in the least. My ancestors had to deal with the Moghuls who invaded us and the British who occupied us. Today the Indian people are free. Nothing matches freedom."

The maharana is the head of one of the richest hotel empires in India. But he thinks of the future, wishes to extend the small airport of the city to give more foreigners the chance to discover Udaipur. He also would like to develop a top level university and continue to encourage the arts as his ancestors did. And what proud and daring ancestors! They were the only Rajputs who resisted the Moghuls, thus winning for this bravery the title of maharana, greater than a maharajah!

With its elegant royal palace and its Lake Palace that appears to be floating on Lake Pichola, Udaipur charms, amazes…

History

The city was designed in the sixteenth century, but it goes quite a bit further back in time. The founding dynasty of the Sisodyas supposedly fled the Gujarat besieged by the Huns in the sixth century, seeking refuge in this region called Mewar in the seventh century. A century later, the king Bappa Rawal had the citadel of Chittaurgarh built. It was the capital of the Mewar for eight centuries, until the Moghuls arrived. Akbar was not fond of running into opposition, so he destroyed the citadel in 1568. The maharana Udai Singh II escaped and, following the advice of a hermit, founded Udaipur in this region where he hoped to be left in peace. His son, the maharana Pratap Singh (1572-1597) was finally crushed by Akbar at the battle of Haldighati in 1576, some thirty kilometres from Udaipur. Wiser, his heir Amar Singh (1597-1620) chose to treat with Akbar's son, Jahangir. A peace treaty was signed at last. But when the Moghuls' decline began, the city was threatened by the Marathas hailing from the south. The maharanas were forced to accept British rule in 1818.

Indians are not the last to enjoy getting lost in the maze of the City Palace of Udaipur, the capital of Mewar, that unfolds courtyards, terraces, palaces, zenana…

Emblematic figure of the region, overlooking Lake Pichola, the royal palace extends its facade over more than 500 metres.

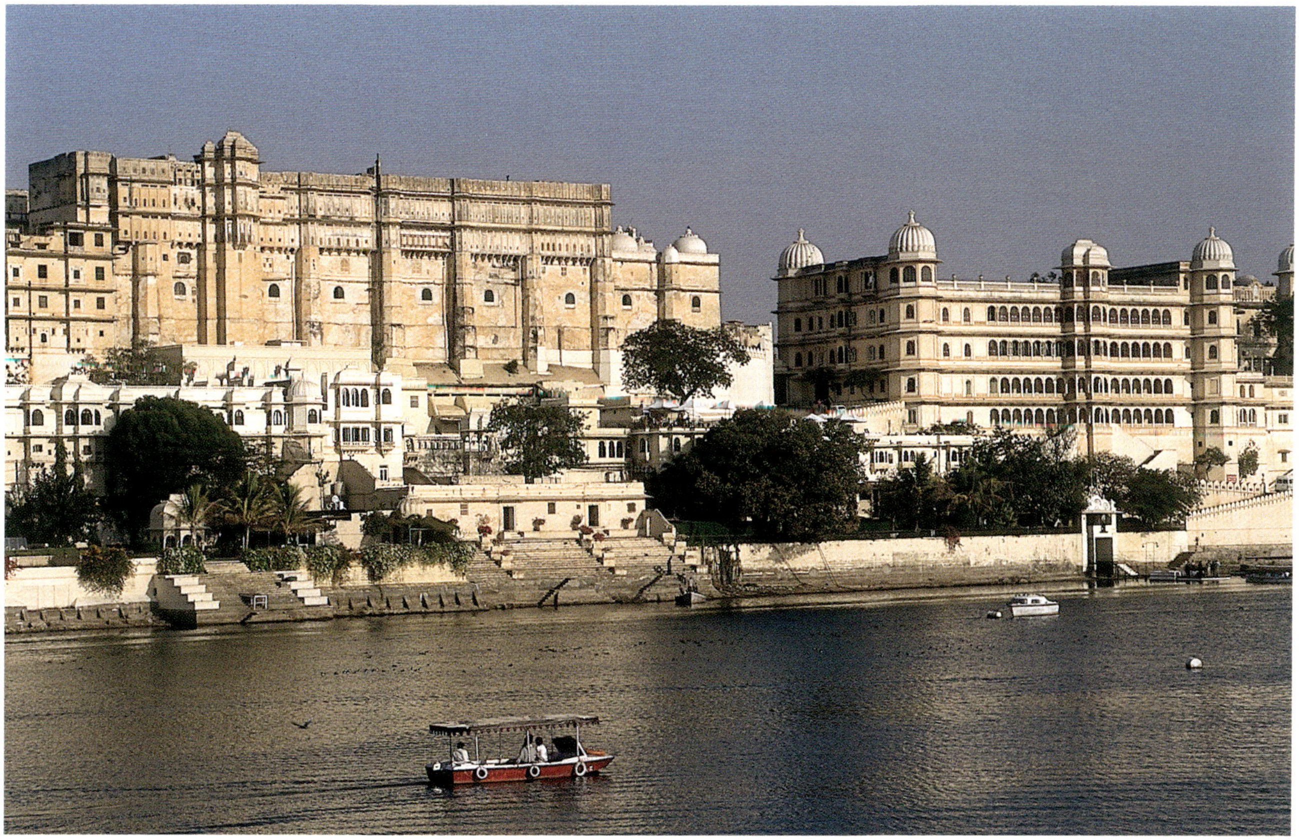

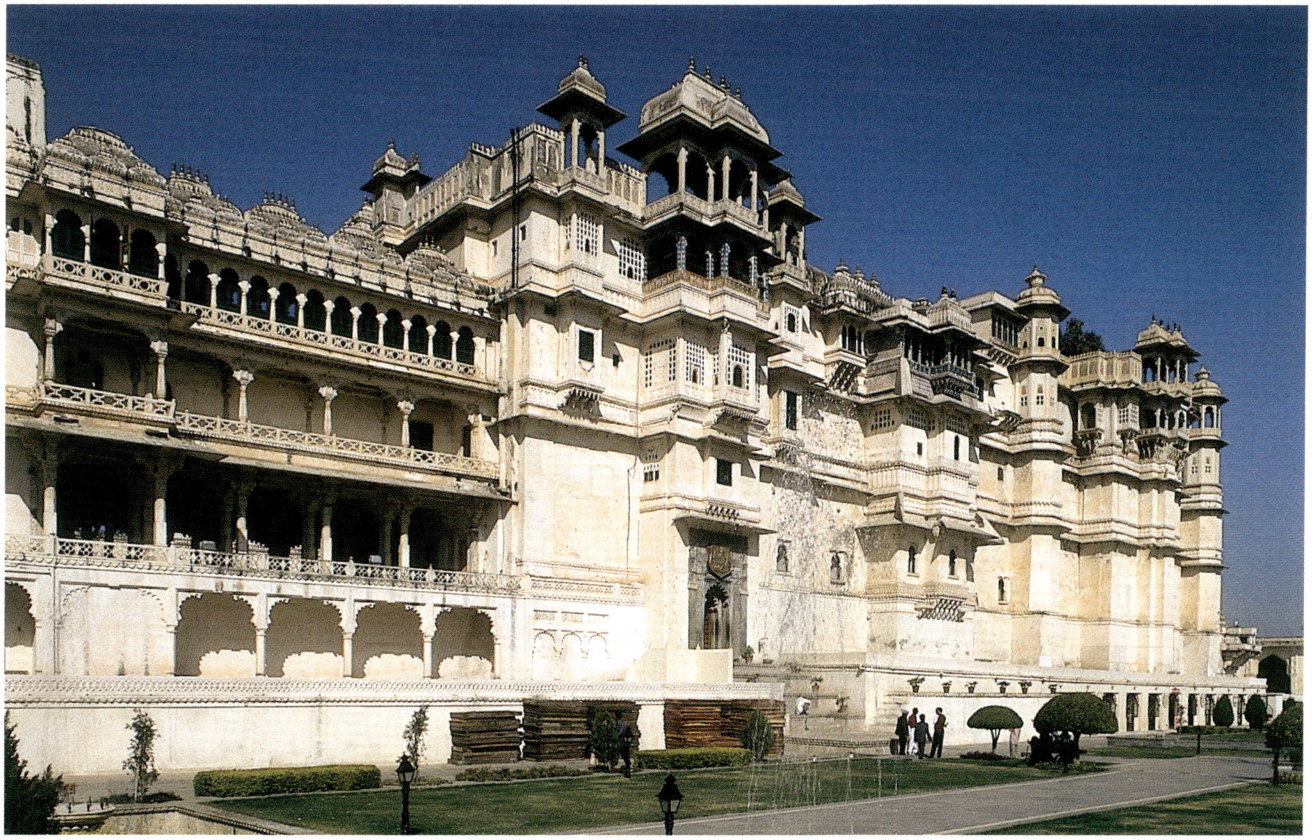

The Royal Palace

Astroll in the narrow streets that climb up and down the old walled city holds in store a multitude of surprises. The shops are bursting with textiles, brocades, and paintings on silk and paper that are good-humouredly wedged next to one another. In the upper part of town, the City Palace (royal palace), said to be the biggest in all of Rajasthan, offers an unrestricted view of Lake Pichola. It is actually several connected palaces, assembled between the first half of the sixteenth and the early twentieth centuries that form an impressive 500 metres-long facade. Rajput and Moghul styles are blended for the neophyte's pleasure.

You should first explore the Dikush Mahal (the Palace of the Joyful Heart) built in the seventeenth century and peer at length over the incomparable miniatures of the room called Chitran ki Burj. Not bad either the Delft faience tiles in the Chini Mahal gallery. Further on, an incredible little palace covered with tiny mirrors. A dazzling array! In this true maze, you should not miss one of the courtyards called Mor Chowk, decorated in the nineteenth century with mosaics and peacocks fanning their tails. Stunning! Again further on, you will not resist the charm of the Manak Mahal and its walls studded with semi-precious stones. But it is not fair! This boundless luxury was reserved to men, while the women waited patiently in the famous zenana, the women's quarter. You reach the Queen's Palace overlooking Lake Pichola. The beautiful queen had all the time in the world to muse over the Lake Palace.

Leaving the Palace, and so as to "digest" these treasures of old, you can go and enjoy a "cup of tea" in the gallery of the Palace-hotel Fateh Prakash. The service is elegant, the teapot silver. Living in style! With as a premium at your feet the Lake Palace which appears to be floating on the lake… The Fateh Prakash was created by the maharana Fateh Singh who ruled between 1884 and 1930. The oldest of the Rajput princes, an ardent defender of ancestral customs, they say he had even banned from his city automobiles, typewriters and European women whose necklines were too low! However, do go and take a look at the reception room, the durbar hall. The ceilings uphold gorgeous chandeliers overflowing with Bohemian crystal. Simply mind-boggling!

To completely bowl you over, the Shiv Niwas Palace awaits you. Converted to a hotel in 1982, the former residence of the royal family has preserved its class with several truly enthralling suites, formerly occupied by VIPs: Queen Elisabeth, Jacqueline Kennedy and the Shah of Iran. In 1983 they even shot a famous James Bond film, Octopussy, and Indians are crazy about it! The authors' favourite?… the imperial suite, with its circular room, its multifoil arches and pink marble bathroom.

The private apartments of the maharajah of Udaipur, Arvind Singh Mewar.

Next pages:
An extravagant mosaic of architectural influences is scattered over the halls, rooms and corridors of the City Palace of Udaipur, built between the sixteenth and the twentieth centuries. Rajput and Moghul styles merge delicately for the visitor's pleasure in the Kanch ki Burj (page 328, top) and the Moti Mahal (page 328, bottom), an exquisite palace of mirrors, both built in the seventeenth century. The entirely blue Bhim Vilas (page 329, top) was designed at the request of the maharajah Bhim Singh in the late eighteenth century. Page 329, bottom: The Chini Chitrashala gallery is decorated with blue ceramic tiles from Holland.

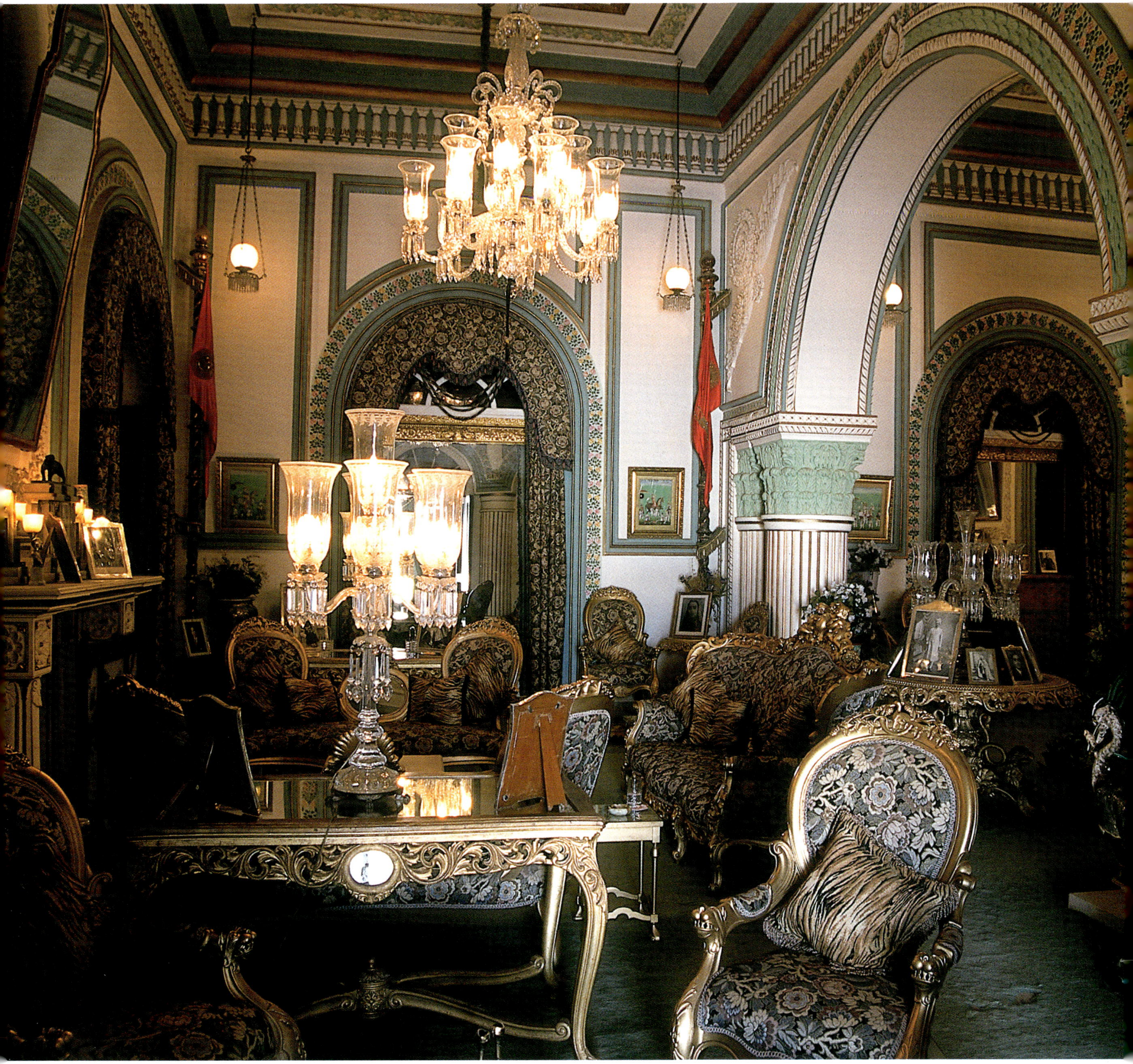

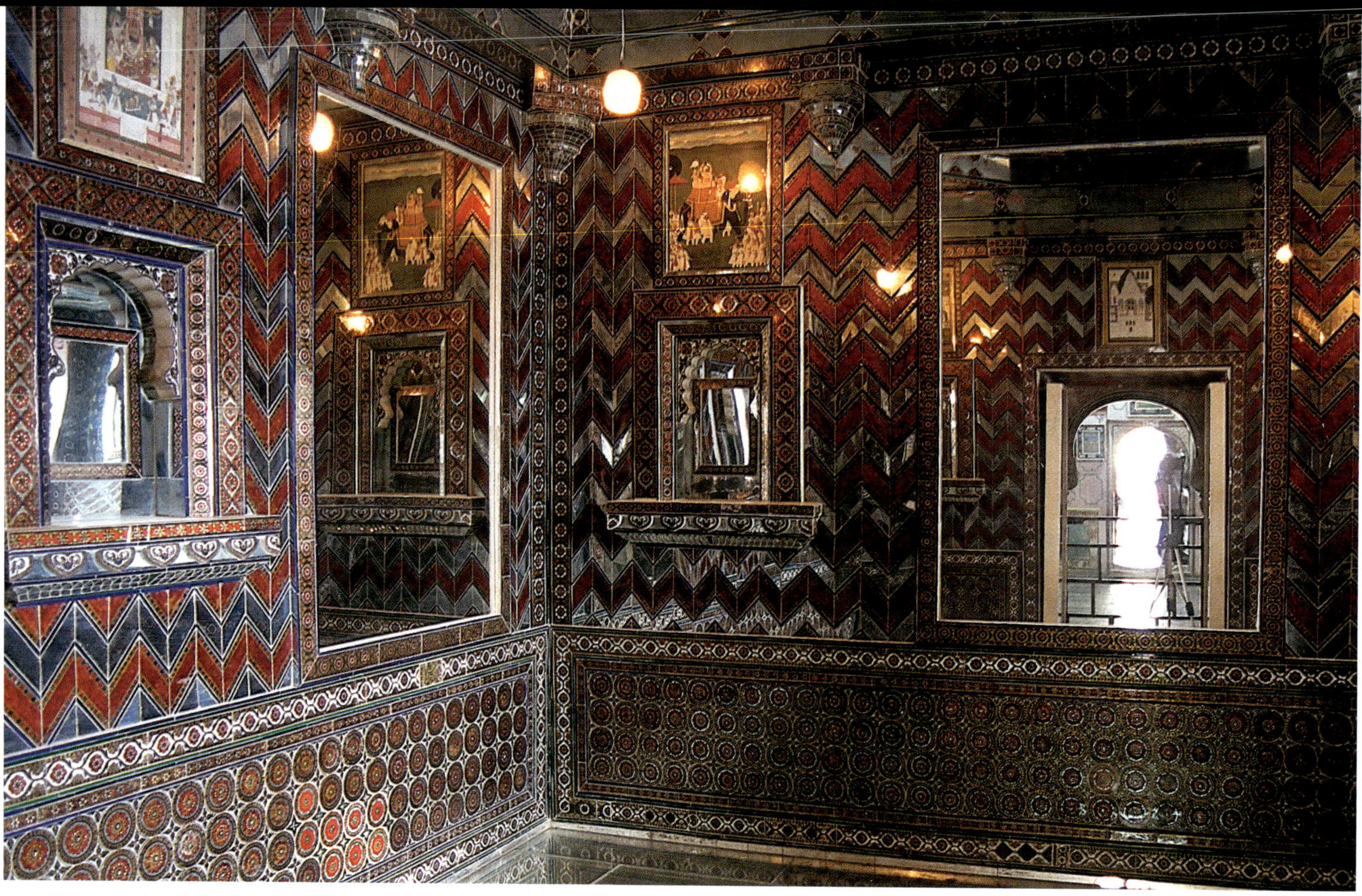

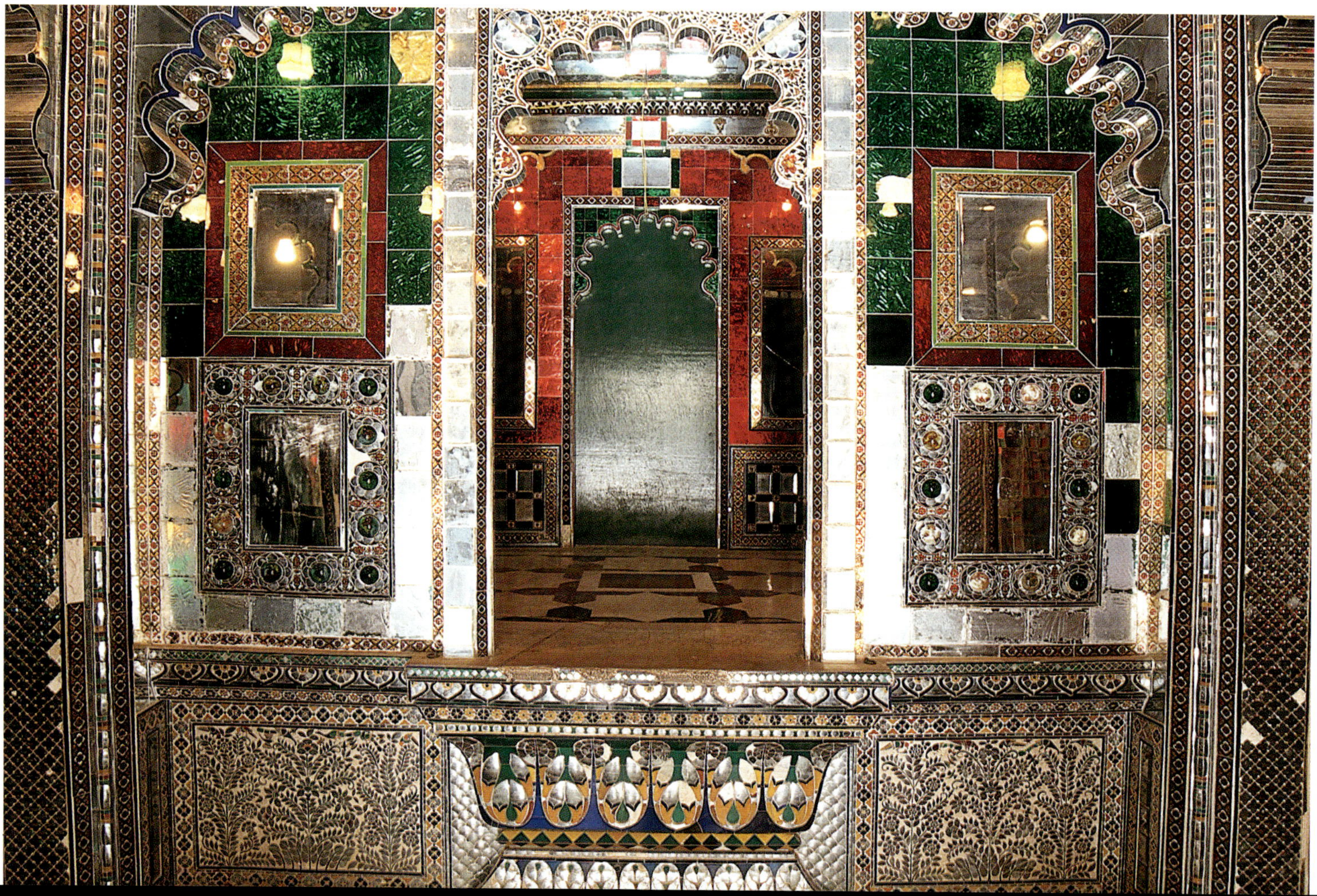

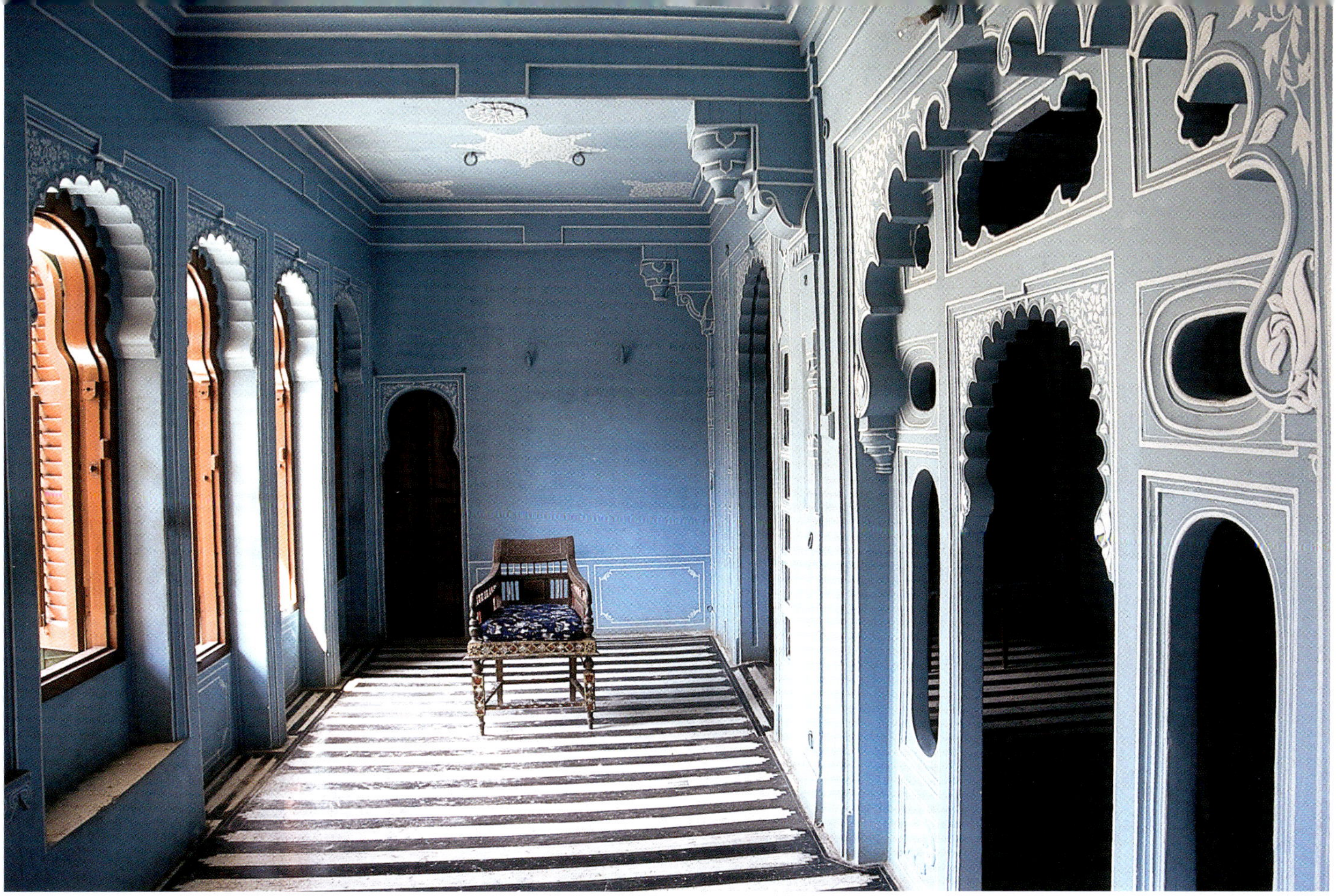

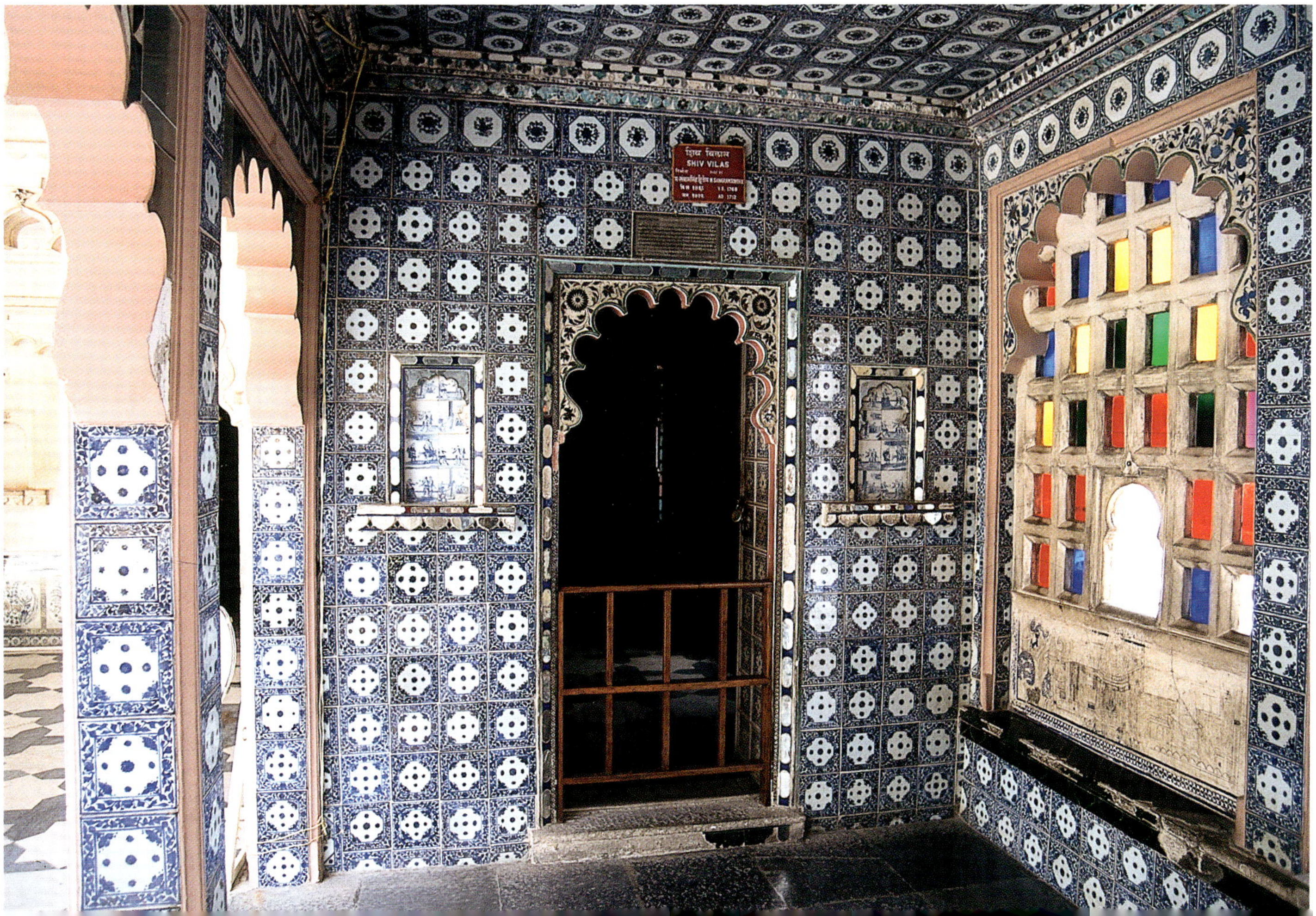
SHIV VILAS

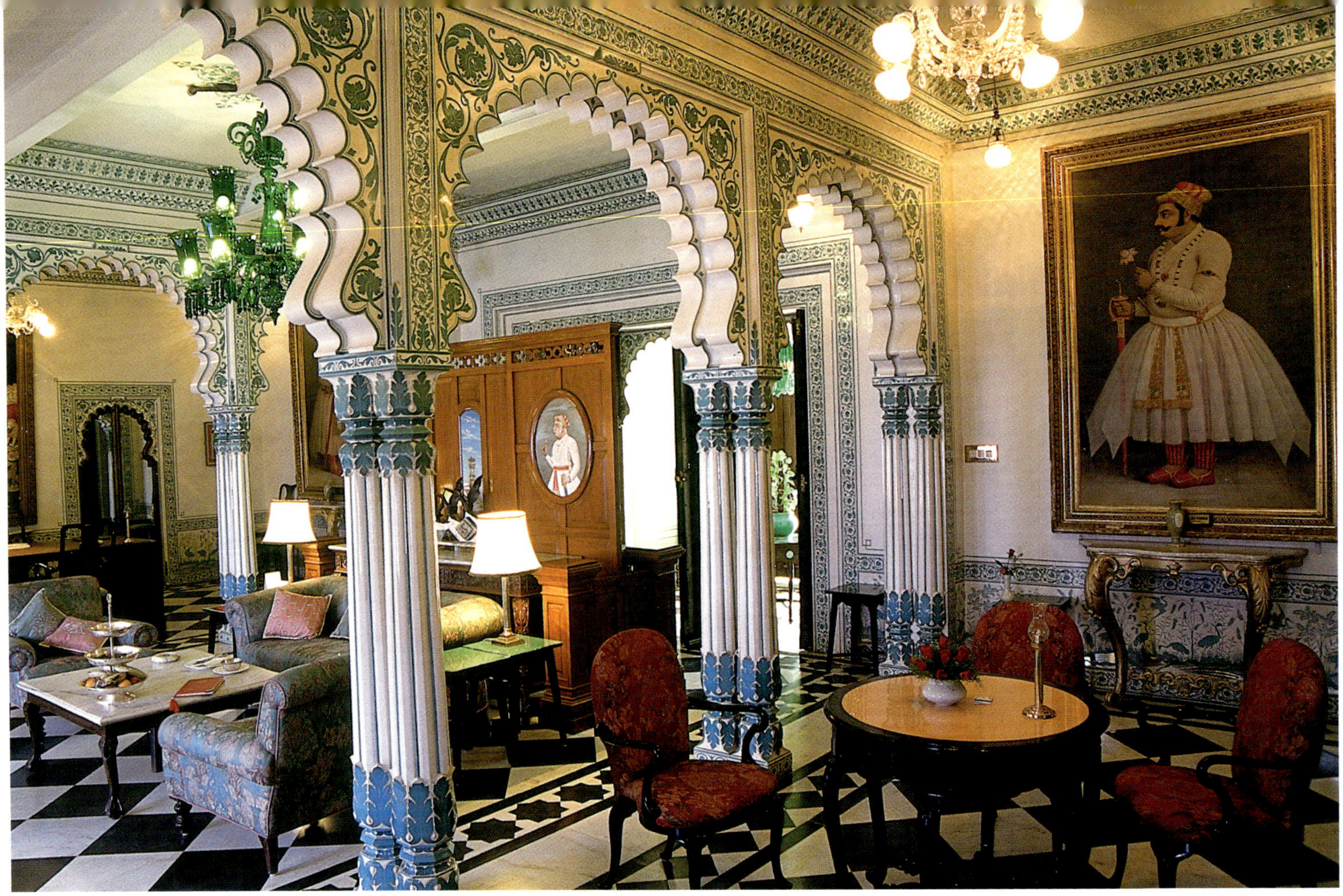

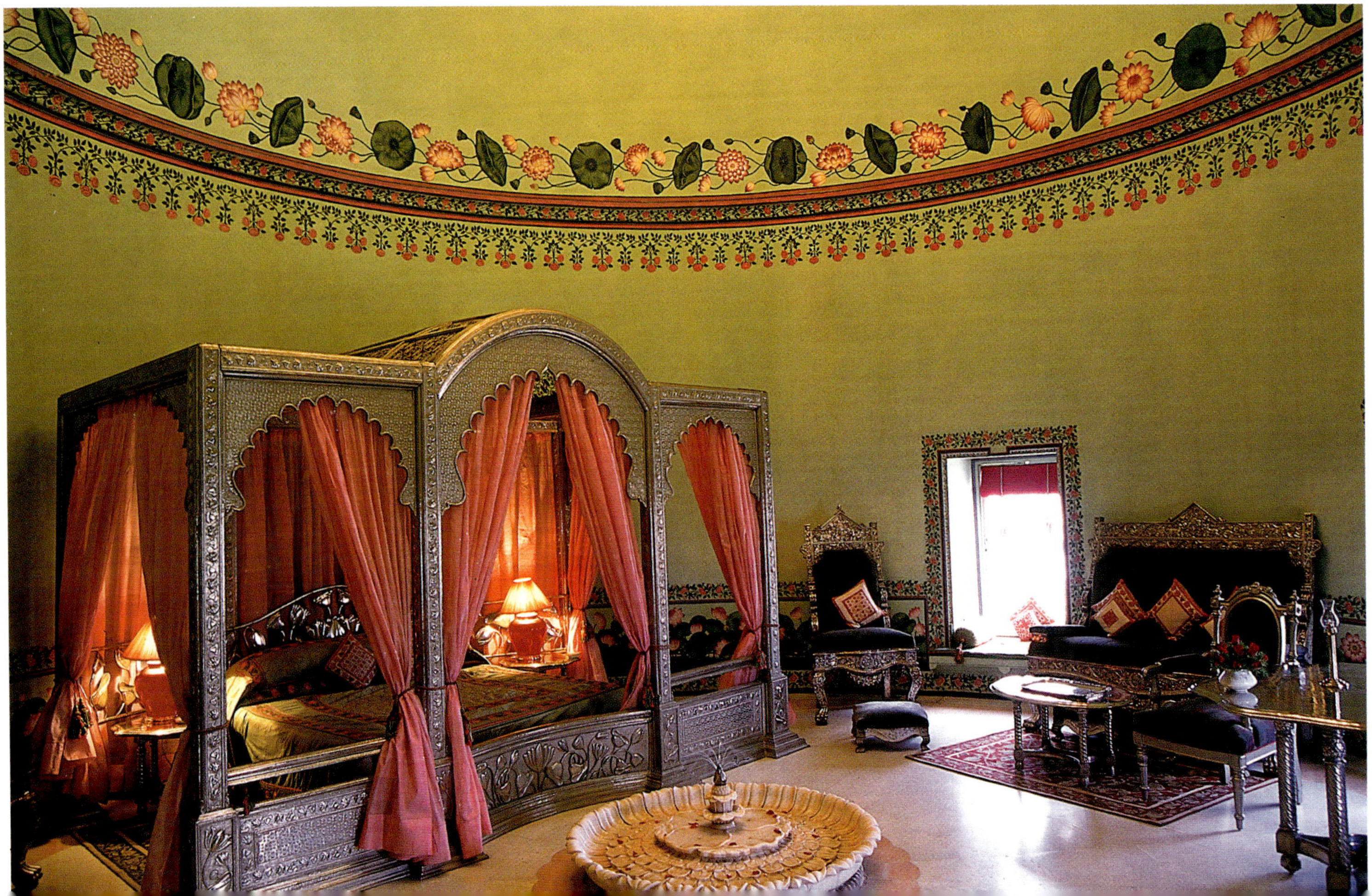

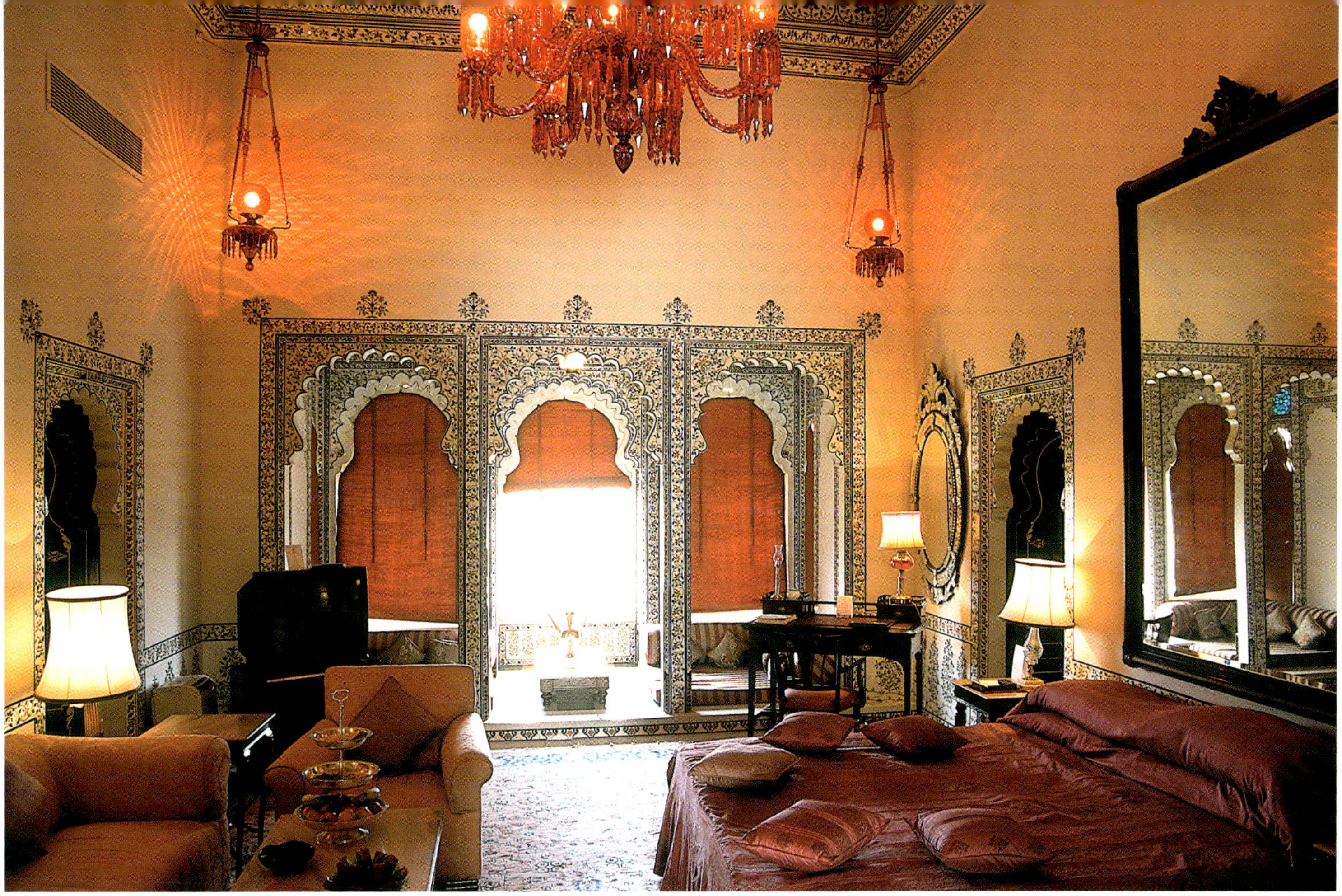

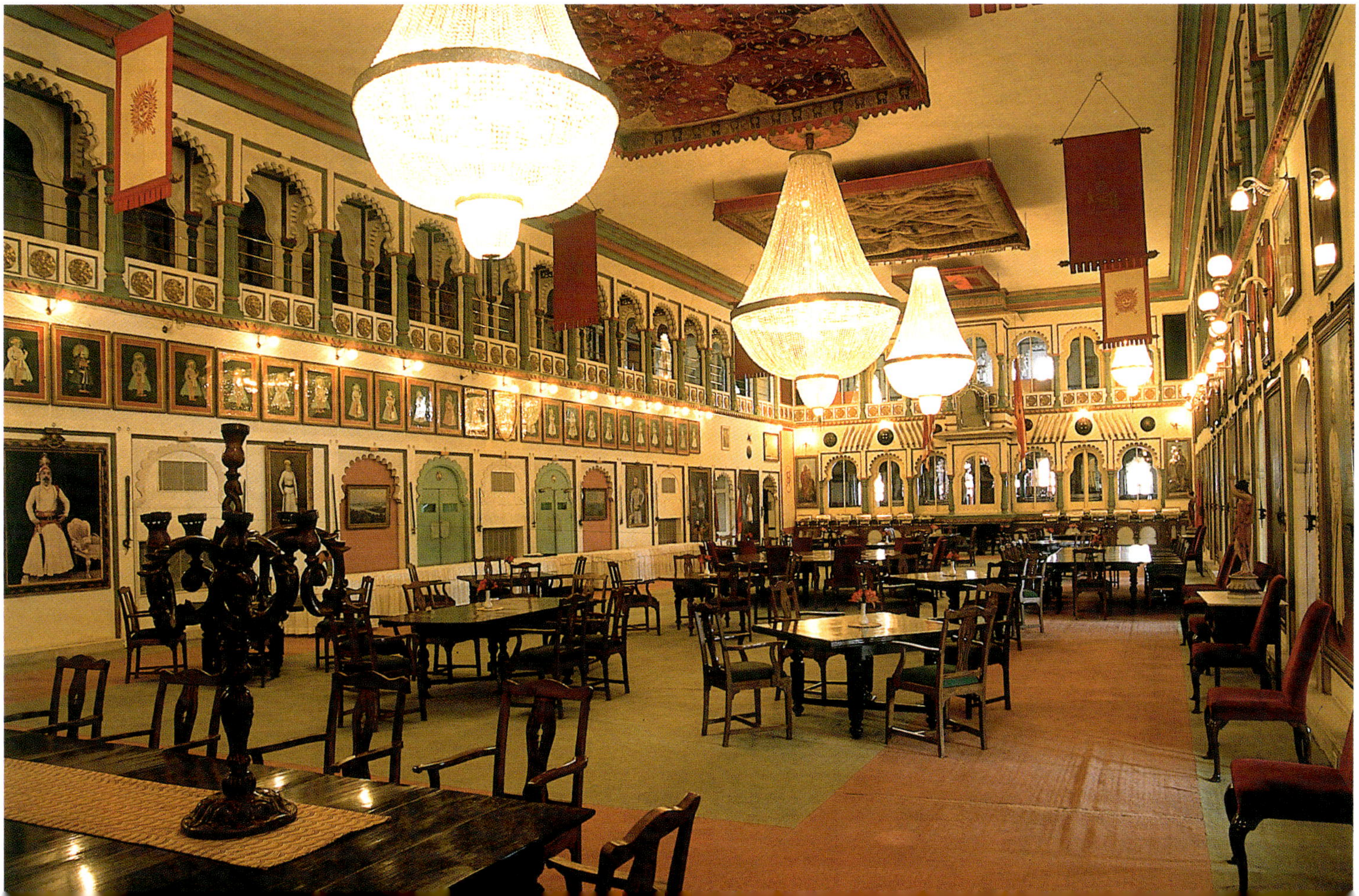

Preceding pages:
The suites of the Shiv Niwas palace are truly royal, with all their multifoil arches, gilding, marble, delicate fabrics (page 330, above: Imperial Suite; page 331, top: Royal Suite). As for the Durbar Hall of the Fateh Prakash Hotel, with its Bohemian crystal chandeliers and gallery of portraits of maharajahs, it was the setting for gorgeous receptions (page 331, bottom).

The Magic of Lake Pichola

Lake Pichola has its icons; two islets bearing palaces that incite romantic hearts to fantasise. The more distant is sheathed in mystery in the early morning mist. Conceived in 1622 by the maharana Karan Singh as a setting for lavish banquets, the Jag Mandir is named after his son Jagat Singh (1628-1652) who altered it to his taste. History tells us that the future Moghul emperor Shah Jahan, the one who gave the world the Taj Mahal, found shelter here when he fell out of grace with his father Jahangir.

Property of the maharana Arvind Singh, the palace is occasionally the setting for stylish weddings christened "royal". To dream and dream over and over again, nothing matches the old chronicles that transport us into the gentle world of the Jag Mandir. In those days: "Nobles came here to listen to the storytellers' tales, spending their days lost in the vapours of opium and rocked by the cool lake breezes wafting the delightful scents of the thousands of lotus flowers covering the surface of the lake; and when the effects of opium wore off, they could open their eyes again and contemplate a landscape whose enchantment was even far greater than what opium could inspire. It was in this atmosphere that the princes and the clan chiefs enjoyed themselves for two generations, neglecting the rattle of arms for a voluptuous idleness." You cannot weary of it!

Like a parenthesis in the city of Udaipur, Lake Pichola and its palaces still have an incomparable cachet. Above, the island of Jag Mandir.

Opposite:
With its grandiose suites and its delicious restaurant, the Lake Palace on the island of Jag Niwas offers visitors the enchantment of a timeless hotel.

Bottom:
The Kush Mahal Suite.

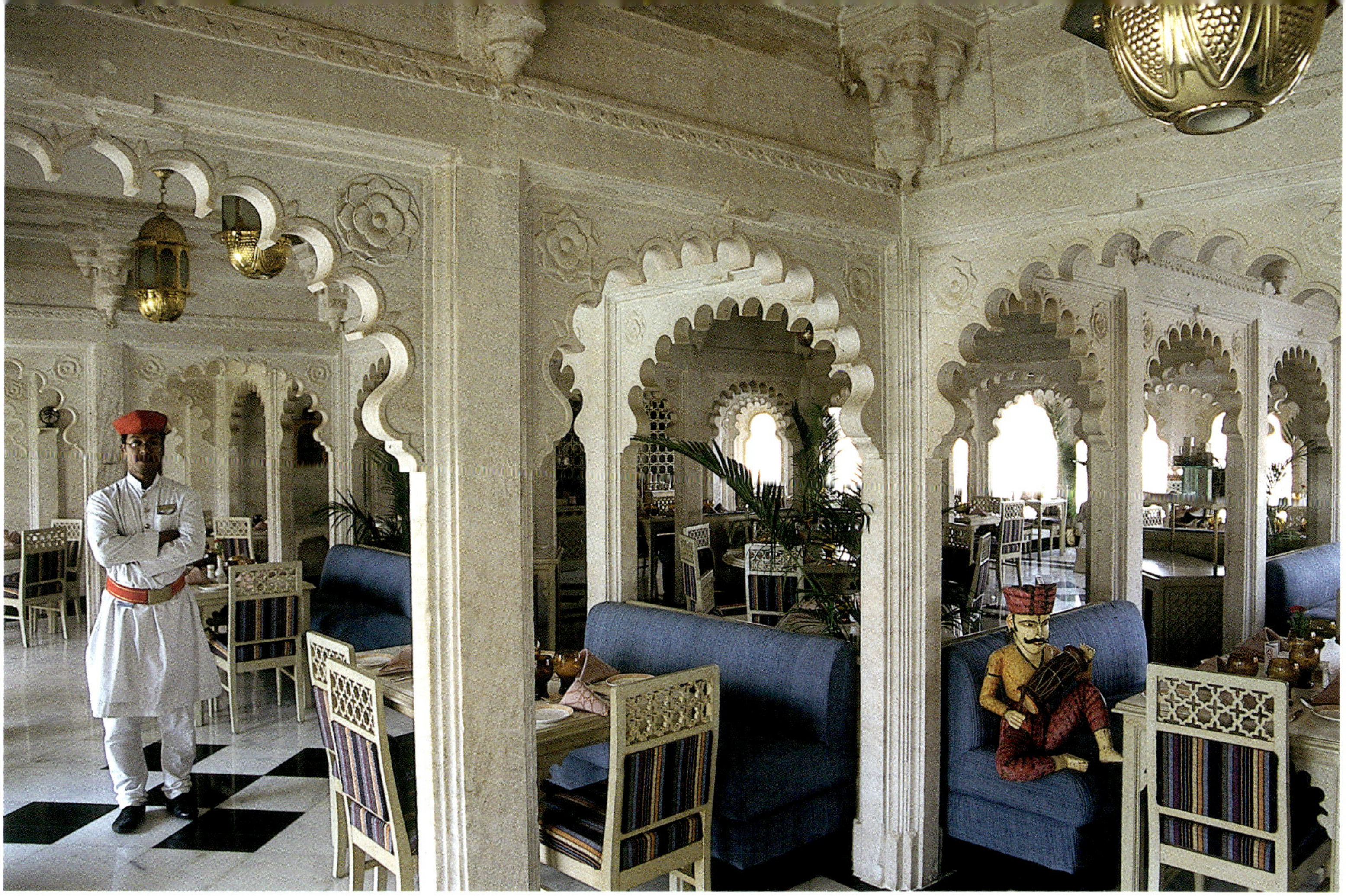

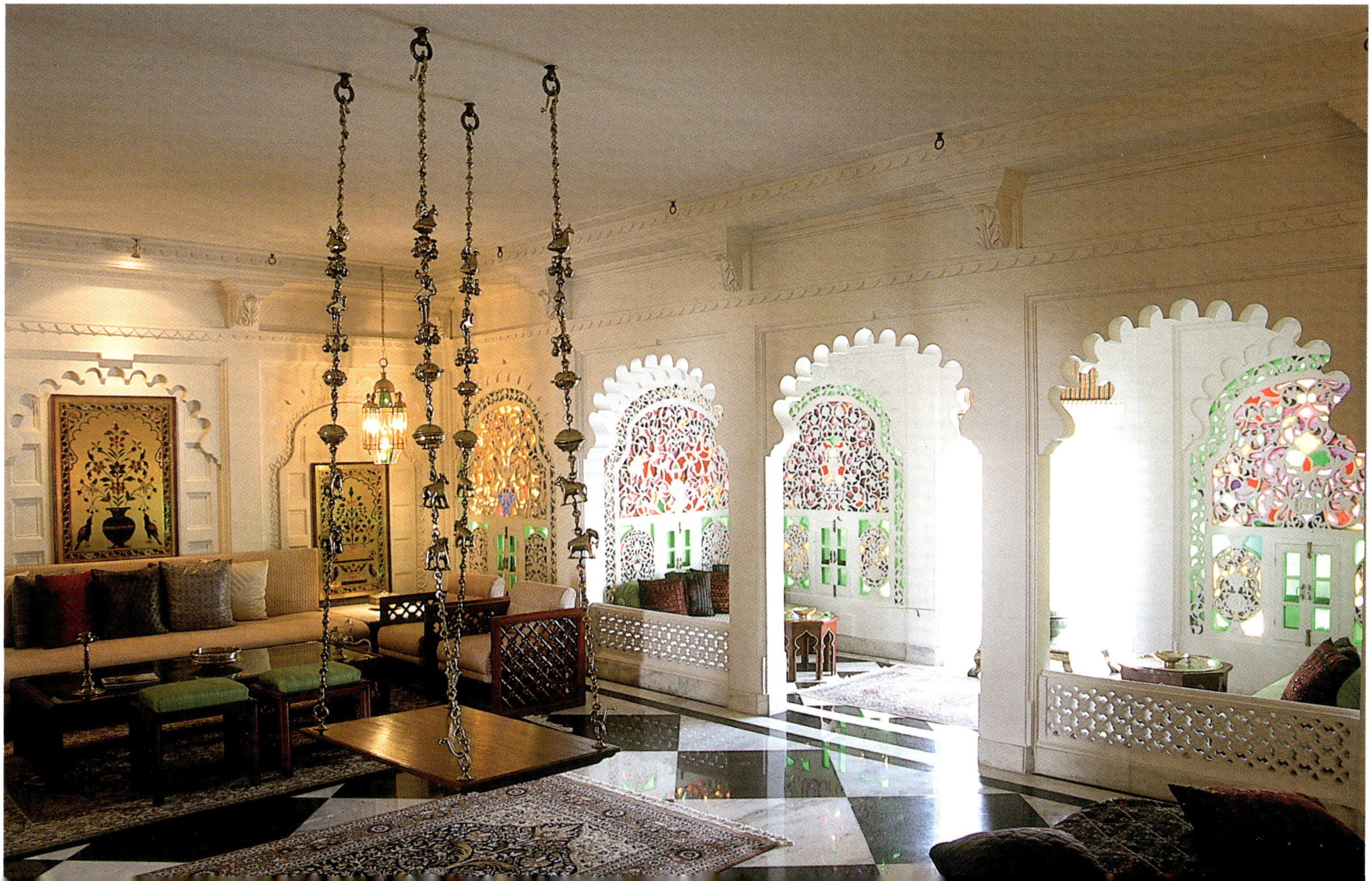

The Most Beautiful Palace-hotel in the World!

Elegance, sense of hospitality, seductive smiles of regulars… Arriving at the Lake Palace is always delightful. Its terraces overlook a superb view onto the royal palace of Udaipur.

The other islet, Jag Niwas, is entirely occupied by a fabulous white marble palace well known by the name Lake Palace, which is described by a long list of visitors' superlatives: the most idyllic, the most romantic… At the time when a Marquise de Pompadour, favourite of Louis XV, gathered artists and philosophers in her Parisian salon, the crown prince of the maharajah of Udaipur thought up (in 1746) this exquisite jewel entirely devoted to pleasure.

Converted into a hotel, some claim the Lake Palace is the most fabulous palace-hotel in the world today. Even if renovation somewhat altered its magic, spending two or three days here is a must for a trip to Rajasthan. The ideal spot for the last evening of an unforgettable visit. Surrounded by elegant multifoil arches, lounging in the soft couches of the Khush Mahal Suite, caressed by the sun filtering through the lacy jali and the colourful glass windows, and rocked by the smell of incense, the most fortunate of travellers need but open the memoirs of Louis Rousselet, the French geographer who visited India from 1863 to 1869. His evocation of the preparations for a party on the island will inspire a sweet reverie: "The servants of the ranah go to and fro, landing supplies, readying everything for our short stay. The apartments are soon furnished: wall hangings or blinds close the arcades; pillows and rugs cover the marble floors. At the tip of the isle an entire building is reserved for us; there are beds, chairs, bathrooms; in a nearby courtyard, the cooks are at work and banghcouli are arriving with so many loads of champagne and still hock that I fear the ranah wants us dead. The fountains cast their spray on every side amidst the copses and a thousand streams cascade between the flowerbeds. Nothing has been neglected; in a pavilion by the water, I chance upon a bevy of laughing young girls, their costumes are spangled with jewellery: they are the Court nautchnis, whom the ranah sent to entertain us with their songs and dances…"

Outside, the languorous full moon shines in the night, a slight breeze gently inebriates Lake Pichola, and the Royal Palace is ablaze with myriads of lights. A last look at Rajasthan…

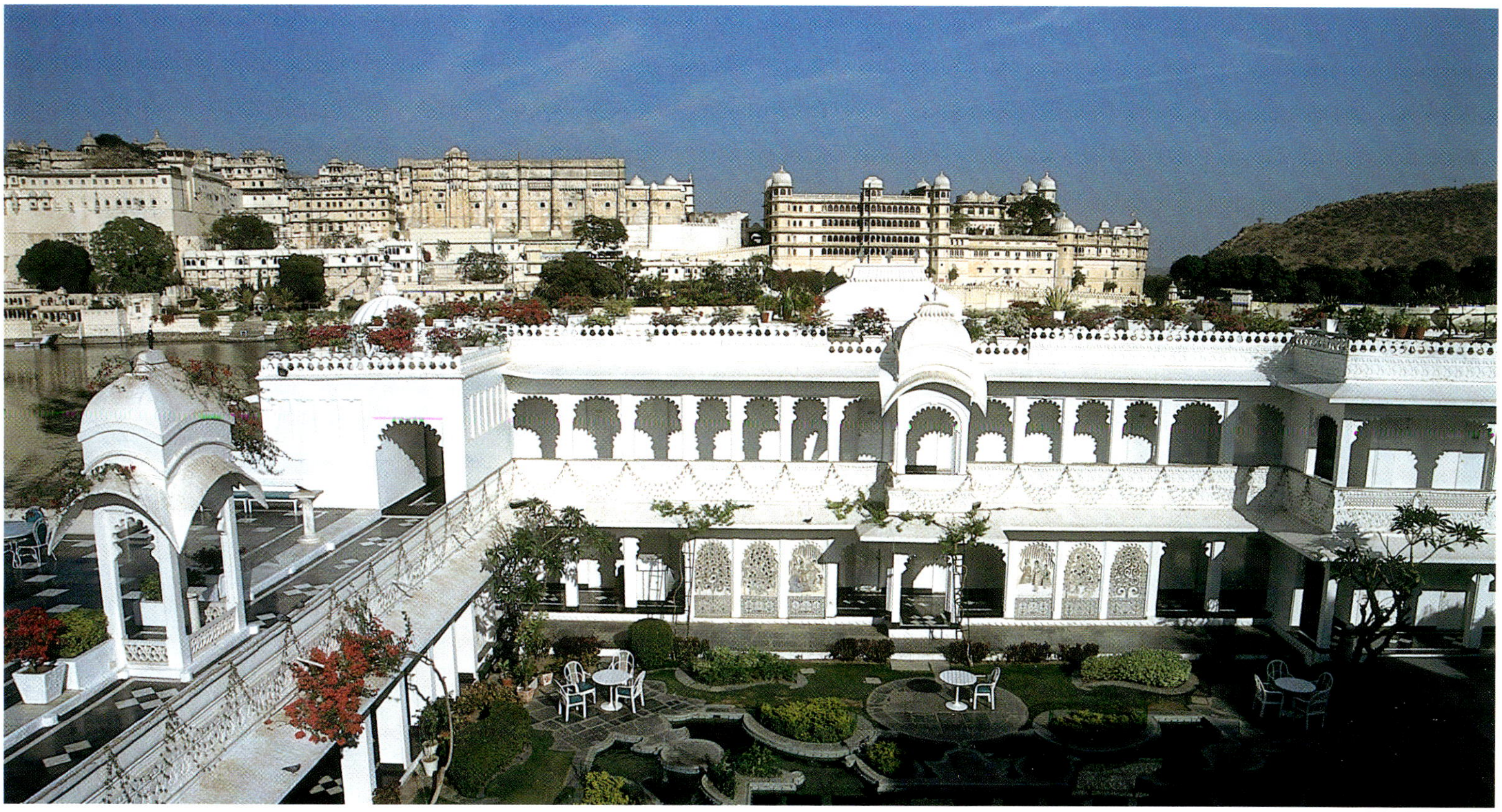

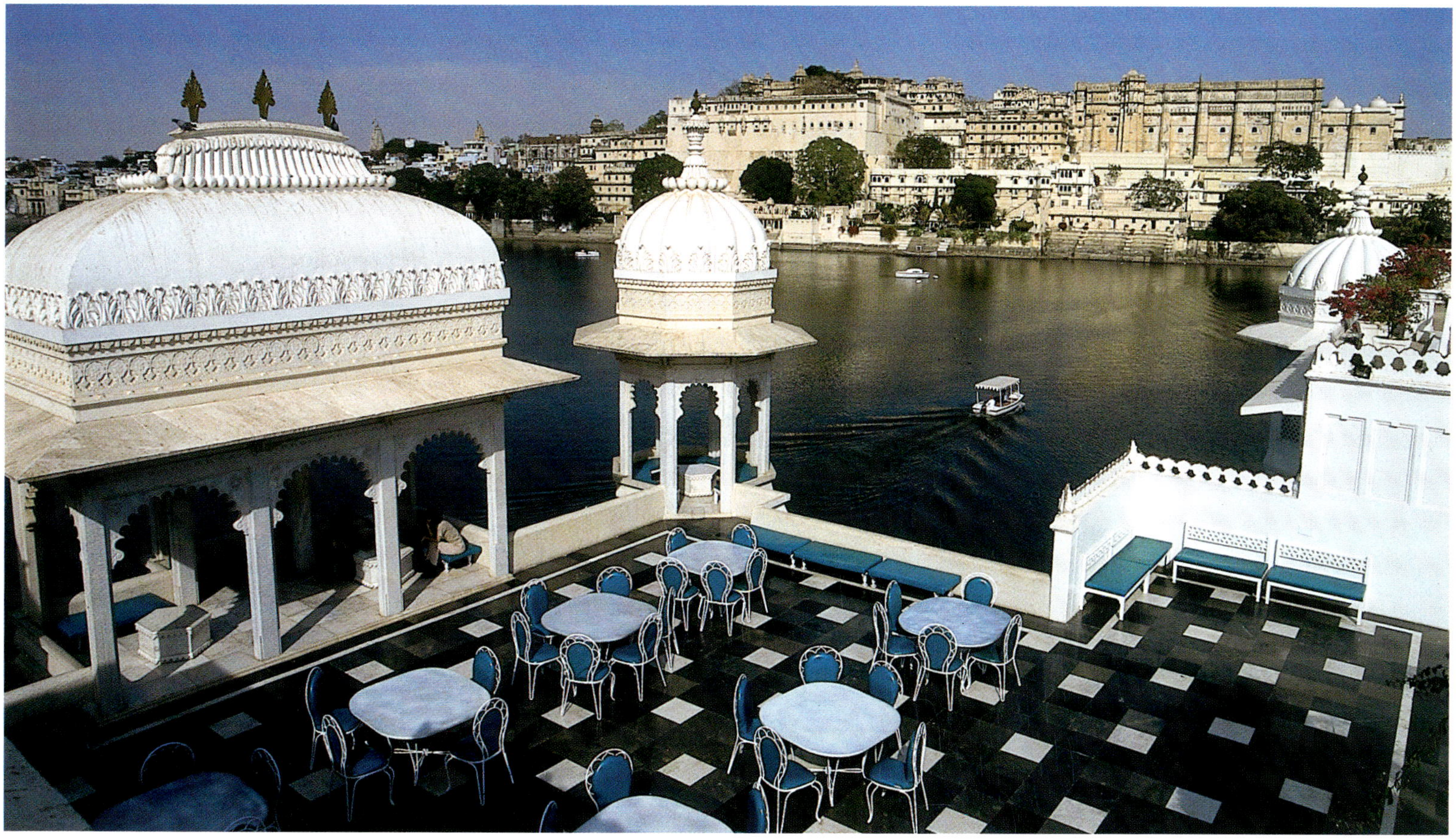

ACKNOWLEDGMENTS

Our thanks to all the Indians, Christian, Hindu, Jain, Muslim and Parsee we met in the course of our travels.
For their patience and their sense of hospitality, we especially thank:
the maharajah of Jaipur Sawai Bhawani Singh;
the maharajah of Jodhpur Gaj Singh II, the maharani, the prince Yuvraj Shivraj Singh and Shoba Kanwar;
the maharana of Udaipur Arvind Singh Mewar;
the princess of Bikaner Rajyashree Kumari;
Sunil Rampuria at Bikaner and his family;
the thakur Sunder Singg, his wife Chanda and their son Vicku;
the rawal of Samode Raghavendra Singh and his brother Yadavendra Singh;
the thakur Gaj Singh of Alsisar at Jaipur;
the thakur Khuman Singh;
Sabina Bailey, Nadine Le Prince, the Poddar family, the thakur Dalip Singh, Dinesh Dhabhai,
as well as Jehangir J. Ghadiali, worthy representative of the Parsee community born in Persia.